POPES

THROUGH THE AGES

Nihil Obstat

Reverend MILTON T. WALSH

Imprimatur

Most Reverend JOHN R. QUINN
Archbishop of San Francisco

Imprimatur

His Eminence TERENCE CARDINAL COOKE
Archbishop of New York

POPES
THROUGH THE AGES

by

JOSEPH S. BRUSHER, S.J.

PHOTOGRAPHS COLLECTED AND EDITED
BY EMANUEL BORDEN

THIRD EDITION

NEFF-KANE
SAN RAFAEL, CALIFORNIA

Third Revised Edition published by Neff-Kane, San Rafael, California

Library of Congress Cataloging in Publication Data
Brusher, Joseph Stanislaus, 1906-
Popes through the ages.

Includes index.
1. Popes—Biography. I. Title.
BX955.2.B78   1980   282'.092'2 [B]   80-19450
ISBN 0-89141-110-0

FOREWORD, 1964

This splendid work is addressed to the reader and student who has not the opportunity, nor perhaps the time, to engage in the study of extensive, more expansive and scientific works of great research. The author, however, has drawn upon the best sources to present a brief but adequate picture of the enormous impact upon human history of the See of Peter. The vast drama of God's Kingdom is, in its contact with the ever-changing face of human events in this relatively brief work, vividly highlighted.

The author has endeavored to present a completely objective account, seemingly realizing that the simple factual narrative is the greatest apologia for the spiritual, moral and cultural influence exerted by the successors of Saint Peter in the shaping not only of Western civilization, but in the most remote mission lands.

The splendid illustrations, featuring all the traditional or actual pictures of the popes gives the work a unique and modern interest and value.

JAMES FRANCIS CARDINAL McINTYRE
Archbishop of Los Angeles
June 25, 1886-July 16, 1979

FOREWORD, 1980

The Papacy has been central to the whole spiritual development of Western civilization and today its influence is felt on every continent. The Neff-Kane Publishing Company does its readers a fine service in reprinting this book that offers so much information on the Popes and the times in which they lived. It is important because public perception of the work of the Papacy varies over the years.

The death of Pope Pius IX, in 1878, the year before St. Patrick's Cathedral in New York City was opened, received little attention from the press and public in America. There were some who believed Pope Pius was the last of his line.

No one who followed the extensive coverage that the press and broadcast media gave to the election of Pope John Paul II in October, 1978, or his visits to Mexico and Poland in 1979, could have any such thoughts today. The resurgence of the Papacy in the last century is only a single small part of the wonderful story this volume tells. It is full of ups and downs, human successes and failures, as it takes us from Peter of Galilee who established the papal chair in Rome to John Paul II who came to it from Poland.

I commend the publishers for providing a new edition of this useful book. It is good to have available to readers a single volume that contains a sketch of each of the Roman Pontiffs and to have that accompanied by the illustrations that have been gathered here with such care.

TERENCE CARDINAL COOKE
Archbishop of New York

The publisher wishes to express his gratitude to Monsignor Florence D. Cohalan, M.A., of the New York Archdiocese, for the skill and scholarship evident in the last three biographies which bring the volume up to date. The publisher likewise acknowledges with gratitude the aid so graciously given by Monsignor Eugene V. Clark, also of the Archdiocese of New York. His tireless efforts to facilitate the production of this edition deserve the thanks of all of us.

PREFACE

History has few subjects so interesting and so important as the long and august line of Roman Pontiffs. Catholics revere the popes as successors of St. Peter and Vicars of Christ ruling His Mystical Body, the Church. Historians, whatever their faith or lack of faith, regard the popes as highly significant factors in man's story. Thomas Babington Macaulay has described this attitude in a passage which has become famous.

"There is not, and there never was on this earth, a work of human policy so well deserving of examination as the Roman Catholic Church. The history of that Church joins together the two great ages of human civilization. No other institution is left standing which carries the mind back to the times when the smoke of sacrifice rose from the Pantheon, and when camelopards and tigers bounded in the Flavian amphitheatre. The proudest royal houses are but of yesterday, when compared with the line of the Supreme Pontiffs. That line we trace back in an unbroken series from the Pope who crowned Napoleon in the nineteenth century to the Pope who crowned Pepin in the eighth; and far beyond the time of Pepin the august dynasty extends, till it is lost in the twilight of fable. The republic of Venice came next in antiquity. But the republic of Venice was modern when compared with the Papacy; and the republic of Venice is gone, and the Papacy remains. The Papacy remains, not in decay, not a mere antique, but full of life and useful vigor. The Catholic Church is still sending forth to the farthest ends of the world missionaries as zealous as those who landed in Kent with Augustin, and still confronting hostile kings with the same spirit with which she confronted Attila. The number of her children is greater than in any former age. Her acquisitions in the New World have more than compensated for what she has lost in the Old. Her spiritual ascendency extends over the vast countries which lie between the plains of the Missouri and Cape Horn, countries which a century hence, may not improbably contain a population as large as that which now inhabits Europe. The members of her communion are certainly not fewer than a hundred and fifty millions; and it will be difficult to show that all other Christian sects united amount to a hundred and twenty millions. Nor do we see any sign which indicates that the term of her long dominion is approaching. She saw the commencement of all the governments and of all the ecclesiastical establishments that now exist in the world; and we feel no assurance that she is not destined to see the end of them all. She was great and respected before the Saxon had set foot on Britain, before the Frank had passed the Rhine, when Grecian eloquence still flourished in Antioch, when idols were still worshipped in the temple of Mecca. And she may still exist in undiminished vigor when some traveller from New Zealand shall, in the midst of a vast solitude, take his stand on a broken arch of London Bridge to sketch the ruins of St. Paul's."

After completing this survey of the popes, the author has been left with a feeling of awe at the high level of character and sanctity displayed by this long series of bishops. The overall impact of the whole series has been inspirational. It is true that there have been popes anything but worthy of their high office. It is true that there have been times when the papal court did not exude the odor of sanctity. And in this book the readers will find those popes and those times quite frankly described. But the lurid and murky flame of a few popes' scandals pales before the strong sunlight of edification given to the world by pontiff after pontiff in the long progress of Popes Through the Ages.

When acknowledgments are to be made, one must first of all pay tribute to the man who conceived the idea of the book, the man whose dream-child the book is, Mr. Emanuel Borden. Some years ago Emanuel Borden approached me and told me of his dream. He dreamed of a book which in one volume would contain a short biography and a picture of every Pope. The picture, as far as possible, would be a reproduction of some work of art. He had already chosen the name, *Popes Through the Ages.* He asked me to write the biographies; he undertook to collect the pictures. This was a difficult task, requiring great patience and labor. It seems proper, now that the book is published, to give this special acknowledgment to Mr. Emanuel Borden.

Our sincere thanks go to the many people who have helped in the preparation of *Popes Through the Ages.* It would be impossible for lack of space to thank them all by name but special acknowledgments must be made to:

His Eminence James Francis Cardinal McIntyre, for his inspiring foreword, The Reverend Charles S. Casassa, S.J., President of Loyola University of Los Angeles, for giving the writer a lighter teaching load to enable him to complete the book, The Reverend William Monahan, S.J., and the other members of the staff of the Gleeson Library of the University of San Francisco for their generous cooperation, especially for the use of the Duchesne edition of the *Liber Pontificalis.* Mrs. Berge, Mrs. Agnes Stephens, Mrs. Elsa Tyler, and Mrs. Ellen Rody, hard-working secretaries, for helping to type the manuscript.

Moreover, Mr. Emanuel Borden wishes to express his appreciation to Mrs. Lillian Borden Kane of San Diego for her assistance in the early inception of the work, the late Harry G. Fairman of Los Angeles for his permission to use his collection of rare postal cards of the popes in research, Mrs. Joyce Sumid for her untiring efforts in drawing the coats-of-arms, Messrs. W. Heffer & Sons of Cambridge, England, for allowing the Eastman Kodak Co., Ltd., of London, to microfilm their rare book *Papal Heraldry* by Galbreath for us to use in our research, D. Anderson of Rome, F. Alinari of Florence, Crea Color Photo Studio of New York, and the late Renato Sansaini and his successor Salvatore Sansaini of Rome, for their help in securing photographs. Most grateful acknowledgment is especially due to Professor Maggi, Director of the Vatican Museums and Galleries; and last but not least to a very dear friend, Simon Carfagno of Alhambra, California, he owes a debt of gratitude for constant inspiration and faith that the work would become a reality and for patient assistance in translating much Italian correspondence.

JOSEPH S. BRUSHER, S.J.

CONTENTS

[xi]

[xii]

[xiii]

POPES

THROUGH THE AGES

ST. PETER

THE FIRST POPE WAS A GALILEAN FISHERMAN named Simon. He was from Bethsaida on the lake of Genesareth. He and his brother Andrew had been attracted by St. John the Baptist. When the Baptist directed them to Christ, Jesus saw in Simon a man of destiny. He saw in the rough fisherman the rock on which He would build His Church, and so He called Simon "Peter," which means rock. Later, Jesus in a scene of historic importance solemnly commissioned Peter.

"And Jesus came into the quarters of Caesarea Philippi: and he asked his disciples, saying: Whom do men say that the Son of man is?

"But they said: Some John the Baptist, and other some Elias, and others Jeremias, or one of the prophets.

"Jesus saith to them: But whom do you say that I am?

"Simon Peter answered and said: Thou art Christ, the Son of the living God.

"And Jesus answering said to him: Blessed art thou, Simon Bar-Jona: because flesh and blood hath not revealed it to thee, but My Father who is in heaven.

"And I say to thee: That thou art Peter; and upon this rock I will build my church, and the gates of hell shall not prevail against it.

"And I will give to thee the keys of the kingdom of heaven. And whatsoever thou shalt bind upon earth, it shall be bound also in heaven: and whatsoever thou shalt loose on earth, it shall be loosed also in heaven." (*Matthew* 16:13-19.)

Peter had made a great act of faith and had been given a great responsibility. He was to be the Vicar of Christ on earth, the first Pope.

Yet Peter fell: in a moment of weakness he denied Jesus; but he was quick to repent. With bitter sorrow he mourned his shameful sin; and Jesus forgave him utterly as only God can forgive. He favored Peter with a special apparition in the glory of the first Easter. He ratified and confirmed the appointment of Peter as first Pope when He gave Peter the charge to feed His flock, lambs and sheep alike.

After the Holy Ghost descended on the apostles that great day of Pentecost, Peter worked hard and worked well for Jesus. He presided over the council which chose Matthias to replace Judas, he supported the newly converted Paul, he threw open the gates of the Church to the Gentiles. He suffered imprisonment only to be released by an angel because he was destined for further labor. He worked in Jerusalem, in Antioch, and in great Rome itself, the imperial metropolis of the Western world. Peter proved by his devotion, a devotion faithful unto death, that Jesus had indeed seen something He could build on in the rough, untried Galilean fisherman.

When Nero struck the Christian flock, the shepherd was not spared. They crucified Peter head down, tradition tells us, because he did not feel worthy to die like his Lord, Jesus. It was on a hill they crucified Peter. The name of that hill was the Vatican.

El Greco. Mildred Anna Williams Collection,
California Palace of the Legion of Honor,
San Francisco.

ST. LINUS

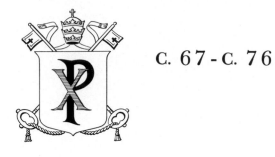

C. 67 - C. 76

ABOUT ST. PETER A GREAT DEAL IS KNOWN; ABOUT his successors, considerably less. For the early popes the main written source is the *Liber Pontificalis*. This account of the lives of the popes was begun probably early in the sixth century while the Ostrogoths ruled Italy. The author had access to earlier written sources, but he was not rigidly critical. Since there are a number of mistakes which historians have checked, the *Liber Pontificalis*, though valuable, is scarcely to be considered infallible. It is, however, the best written source extant for many of the early popes.

St. Linus, according to the *Liber Pontificalis*, was an Italian from Tuscany. His father's name was Herculanus. He died a martyr and was buried on the Vatican near St. Peter.

It is probable that St. Paul refers to him when he writes from Rome to Timothy, "Eubulus and Pudens and Linus and Claudia and all the brethren salute thee" (2 *Tim.*, 4:21).

Little as is known of St. Linus, churchgoers can be reminded of him every time they see a woman in church wearing a hat or kerchief, for it is said that it was this second pope who decreed that women should enter church only with heads covered.

The feast of St. Linus is celebrated on September 23.

Chronologia Summorum Pontificum.

[4]

ST. CLETUS

C. 76 - C. 91

ST. CLETUS HAS GIVEN EARLIER HISTORIANS SOME trouble because of his name. Two of the early lists of the popes, the so-called Liberian Catalogue and the *Poem Against Marcion* list an Anacletus as well as a Cletus. Most ancient lists, however, give the papal succession as Peter, Linus, Cletus, Clement; and modern scholars agree that this is the correct listing. Anacletus is a variant of Cletus, and this seems to have caused the difficulty.

St. Cletus was a Roman. His father's name was Emilianus. Cletus ruled the Church from some time in the reign of the Emperor Vespasian to some time in the reign of Domitian. He was martyred and buried near St. Peter on the Vatican. St. Cletus' feast is celebrated along with that of St. Marcellinus on the twenty-sixth of April.

Ghirlandajo. Sistine Chapel, the Vatican.

ST. CLEMENT I

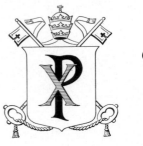

C. 91 - C. 100

ST. CLEMENT, ACCORDING TO TRADITION, WAS ORdained by Peter himself. Some early writers, indeed, thought that Clement was Peter's immediate successor, but modern scholars agree that he is Peter's third successor.

St. Clement has been identified with the Clement mentioned by St. Paul in his *Epistle to the Philippians;* but that Clement seems to have been a Philippian. For a time there were some who identified St. Clement with T. Flavius Clemens, a cousin of the Emperors Titus and Domitian. This is especially appealing because it is highly probable that the noble Roman was a martyr in the persecution of his cousin Domitian. Against this romantic theory is the prosaic fact that the early writers make no mention at all of this. Surely if the fourth pope had been a cousin of the Emperor, it would have been widely heralded. Modern scholars think that St. Clement was a freedman or the son of a freedman of the imperial household. It is doubtful whether he was of Jewish or Gentile origin. Some would argue for Jewish descent because his famous epistle is so steeped in the Old Testament.

St. Clement was a Roman; he was martyred—at some place away from Rome. This is about all that is known for certain of Clement's death. The Greek *Acts of the Martyrs* (written in the fourth century)

gives many and interesting details. St. Clement was exiled by the Emperor Trajan to the Chersonese, modern Crimea. There the holy Pope worked with such zeal among the prisoners laboring in the mines that he was condemned to death. He was thrown into the sea with an anchor tied around his neck. This is probable enough, but the story goes on to say that the sea flowed back a mile or so to reveal the body of the saint resting in a beautiful marble shrine.

In the ninth century, St. Cyril, the Apostle of the Slavs, discovered some bones and an anchor in a Crimean mound. He translated these bones to Rome, where Pope Hadrian II placed them in the altar of St. Clement's Basilica.

Whether or not these bones are authentic, St. Clement left us a real relic of the highest value in his famous letter to the Corinthians. This epistle, which modern scholars agree is authentic, rebukes the Corinthians for a schism which had broken out in their church. Written while one of the apostles was still alive, this letter of Clement is the first great non-inspired Christian document. It is interesting indeed that it shows the fourth pope interfering to put another apostolic church in order.

The feast of St. Clement is celebrated on November 23.

Tuscan School. Sistine Chapel, the Vatican.

ST. EVARISTUS

C. 100 - C. 105

ST. EVARISTUS WAS, ACCORDING TO THE *Liber Pontificalis,* a Greek from Antioch whose father, Juda, was a Jew from the birthplace of Jesus, Bethlehem. He ruled the Church while Domitian, Nerva, and Trajan were emperors. His pontificate saw the end of Domitian's tyranny and the start of the Antonine dynasty.

According to the *Liber Pontificalis* this pope divided Rome into parishes. This, however, is generally believed by modern scholars to be a later organization. He also appointed seven deacons to check the preaching of a bishop for possible slips which might have dogmatic implications. This might refer to the prefaces of the mass where sometimes a sermon was added to the prayer recalling the feast. Evaristus is said to have ordained fifteen bishops, seven priests, and two deacons.

Of his death nothing is known except that according to tradition he was a martyr. St. Evaristus is buried near St. Peter on the Vatican. His feast is celebrated on October 26.

Botticelli. Sistine Chapel, the Vatican.

ST. ALEXANDER I

C. 105 - C. 115

THE NEXT POPE WAS, ACCORDING TO THE *Liber Pontificalis,* a Roman named, like his father before him, Alexander.

St. Alexander is said to have introduced into the Mass the prayer just before the Consecration which recalls the memory of Christ's passion. He is also credited with the order that houses should be blessed with water to which salt had been added.

St. Alexander's death has caused confusion among scholars because an account of the death of another St. Alexander, who was not a bishop, tallies somewhat closely with the account of the Pope's martyrdom in the *Liber Pontificalis.* Duchesne, the learned editor of the *Liber Pontificalis,* concludes that there can be no certainty in the matter.

The traditional account of St. Alexander's martyrdom is that he was beheaded on the Via Nomentana within seven miles of the city of Rome, along with Eventius, a priest, and Theodulus, a deacon. St. Alexander was buried on the Via Nomentana near the spot where he suffered.

His feast, together with that of Sts. Eventius and Theodulus, is celebrated on May 3.

Frà Diamante (?). Sistine Chapel, the Vatican.

[12]

ST. SIXTUS I

C. 115 - C. 125

ACCORDING TO THE *Liber Pontificalis* ST. SIXTUS was a Roman, the son of Pastor. He ruled the Church in the time of Emperor Hadrian. Pope Sixtus I decreed that the sacred vessels should not be touched except by the clergy. This is one of several ordinances attributed to the early popes regarding the sacredness of the ceremonial vessels. Sixtus also decreed that a bishop who had been summoned to Rome should not be received by his people when he returned until he presented the letter of greeting from the Apostolic See. Another very interesting ordinance attributed to Pope Sixtus I is the one which orders the priest after the preface to sing the *Sanctus* with the people. This is truly a beautiful prayer, "Holy, Holy, Holy Lord God of Hosts. The heavens and earth are filled with Thy glory, Hosanna in the highest. Blessed is He Who cometh in the name of the Lord. Hosanna in the highest." Since it is found in all the early liturgies, Duchesne concludes that it quite probably dates back to the time of Sixtus I and even earlier.

Pope St. Sixtus I was martyred, but there are no available details of his death. He was buried on the Vatican near St. Peter. Pope Clement X gave some relics of St. Sixtus I to the well-known seventeenth-century French Cardinal de Retz. He put them in the Abbey of St. Michael in Lorraine.

The feast of Pope St. Sixtus I is kept on April 6.

School of Botticelli. Sistine Chapel, the Vatican.

[14]

ST. TELESPHORUS

C. 125-C. 138

ST. TELESPHORUS WAS A GREEK WHO HAD BEEN AN anchorite. He ruled the Church in the time of Emperor Antoninus Pius. To St. Telesphorus are attributed some church practices which endure down to this day. According to the *Liber Pontificalis* St. Telesphorus ordered a fast for seven weeks before Easter. That the Lenten fast goes back even before the time of Telesphorus, St. Irenaeus gives testimony. But the length of the fast varied considerably in those early days. It is probable enough that Pope St. Telesphorus did make some regulation as to the length of the Lenten fast.

A custom much loved even today is also attributed to St. Telesphorus. He is said to have ordered that although Mass was not celebrated before the hour of tierce (i.e., 9 to 12 o'clock in the morning) at Christmas time Mass should be celebrated at night. This is the first mention of the beloved midnight Mass. However, scholars doubt whether this decree actually does go back to the time of St. Telesphorus.

St. Telesphorus is said also to have decreed that the *Gloria in excelsis* should be sung at the Christmas Mass and only at the Christmas Mass. This magnificent hymn of praise is not said at all Masses even today. As late as the eleventh century, though the Pope could say it oftener, priests were not allowed to say it except at Easter.

St. Telesphorus died a martyr as is known not only from the *Liber Pontificalis* but also from the earlier testimony of St. Irenaeus. He was buried near St. Peter on the Vatican. His feast is kept on January 5 in the Roman liturgy and February 22 in the Greek.

Frà Diamante. Sistine Chapel, the Vatican.

ST. HYGINUS

C. 138-140

ST. HYGINUS WAS A GREEK. ACCORDING TO THE *Liber Pontificalis* he had been a philosopher, but modern scholars are inclined to think that he is confused with a Latin author of the same name.

During the pontificate of St. Hyginus the heretics Valentinus and Cerdo came to Rome. Cerdo, as Eusebius tells us in his *Ecclesiastical History,* was in and out of the Church a number of times. He would teach error, repent, and then fall back into error again.

Since this is the first mention of heresy in these lives, it might be helpful to explain just what is meant by heresy and heretic. Heresy is a diluted or perverted Christianity. The English word comes from the Greek word which means a choosing. A heretic is one who chooses what he will believe of Christ's teaching.

The particular heresy taught by Valentinus and Cerdo was Gnosticism. Valentinus, indeed, was an outstanding teacher of Gnosticism. He taught that Jesus is a higher being who, though not God, is gradually being purified, and will lead the elect with Him into the *pleroma* or "fullness." Gnosticism seems to have been a hodgepodge of lofty philosophic speculation about God and nature, a Manichean fear of matter, and in its later phases, some downright crude superstitions.

St. Hyginus did some organizing of the clergy.

According to tradition he died a martyr, but the ancient writers are silent on this point. His feast is kept on January 11.

Ghirlandajo. Sistine Chapel, the Vatican.

ST. PIUS I

C. 140 - C. 154

ST. PIUS I, ACCORDING TO THE *Liber Pontificalis,* was an Italian from Aquileia. His father's name was Rufinus. He was a brother of the famous Hermas, the author of *The Shepherd,* a precious early Christian document. Hermas in this work says that he was a slave and then a freedman. This, however, is quite possibly a fictional device of the author. If it is true, it would indicate that St. Pius was of a low social origin.

St. Pius had to cope with the Gnostic heretics who were active at Rome during his reign. The Pope excommunicated a Gnostic leader named Marcion, who thereupon set up his own church. But if heretics afflicted the soul of St. Pius, he must have been consoled by the visit of St. Justin, the great defender of Christianity. Justin was a convert from paganism. He had a restless desire for truth which had led him through the Stoic, Pla-tonic, and Pythagorean schools of philosophy to the Bible and Christianity. Not content with securing peace of soul through Christ, Justin wrote much to defend Christ's doctrines, and finally died a martyr.

According to the *Liber Pontificalis,* Pope St. Pius ordered that a heretic coming from the Jews should be received and baptized. This is somewhat obscure, and it is not certain whether he meant a heretic in the modern sense, i.e., some Judaeo-Christian, or a real Jew.

Later legend credits St. Pius with establishing the two Roman churches of St. Pudens and St. Praxedes, but this lacks historical justification.

St. Pius is honored as a martyr by the Church. He was buried near St. Peter on the Vatican. His feast is kept on July 11.

Ghirlandajo. Sistine Chapel, the Vatican.

ST. ANICETUS

C. 155 - C. 166

ST. ANICETUS WAS A SYRIAN FROM EMESA. HIS father's name was John. His pontificate is interesting because during it the controversy over the date for celebrating Easter appears for the first (but by no means the last) time. At this period the Eastern Christians, following the tradition of St. John and St. Philip, celebrated the feast of the Lord's resurrection on the fourteenth day of the Jewish month Nisan, the day on which Jesus ate the Paschal Supper. The Western Christians, on the other hand, celebrated the feast of the resurrection on the Sunday following the fourteenth Nisan. This seemed proper because although it would not always be the actual date of the Lord's resurrection, it would be the day. And this is the reason that Sunday was already holy in Christian tradition. Against the authority of St. John and St. Philip, the West urged the tradition of St. Peter and St. Paul.

Now one of the most venerated figures in the mid-second century church was St. Polycarp, the bishop of Smyrna. This old man, at the time in his eighties, was a disciple of the apostle St. John. (By the fifties of the second century he must have been one of the last.) St. Polycarp, naturally devoted to the practices he had learned from the apostle, wished to have the whole church celebrate Easter on the fourteenth Nisan. Accordingly, he came to Rome to confer with the Pope. Pope Anicetus was not convinced, but in turn he failed to convince Polycarp of the value of the Western date. Since this was not a question of doctrine but only of discipline, the Pope graciously allowed the venerable old saint to return to Smyrna and go on celebrating Easter on the date he had learned from St. John.

Another distinguished visitor to Rome in the time of St. Anicetus was Hegesippus, perhaps the earliest Church historian outside the sacred authors.

An interesting disciplinary decree is attributed to St. Anicetus by the *Liber Pontificalis*. He forbade the clergy to grow long hair after the precept of St. Paul (I *Cor.* 11:14):

St. Anicetus died a martyr and was buried on the Vatican. His feast is kept April 17.

Tuscan School. Sistine Chapel, the Vatican.

ST. SOTER

C. 167 - C. 175

ST. SOTER WAS A CAMPANIAN FROM FUNDI, THE modern Fondi. His father's name was Concordius. He decreed that no monk should touch the consecrated altar cloth or offer incense in church. Some manuscripts read "nun" instead of "monk" in the above prohibition.

These meager details, given for what they are worth, are from the sixth-century *Liber Pontificalis,* but for St. Soter there is a very interesting reference in the early fourth-century *Ecclesiastical History* of Eusebius. Eusebius speaking of St. Dionysius, bishop of Corinth, says (IV, xxiii, 9-15):

"There is moreover, extant a letter of Dionysius to the Romans addressed to Soter who was then bishop, and there is nothing better than to quote the words in which he welcomes the custom of the Romans which was observed down to the persecution in our own times. 'This has been your custom from the beginning, to do good in manifold ways to all Christians, and to send contributions to the many churches in every city, in some places relieving the poverty of the needy and ministering to the Christians in the mines, by the contribution which you have sent from the beginning, preserving the ancestral custom of the Romans, true Ro-

mans as you are. Your blessed bishop Soter has not only carried on the habit but has even increased it, by administering the bounty distributed to the saints and by exhorting with his blessed words the brethren who come to Rome, as a loving father would his children.' "

In this same letter he also quotes the letter of Clement to the Corinthians, showing that from the beginning it had been the custom to read it in the church. "Today we observed the holy day of the Lord, and read out your letter, which we shall continue to read from time to time for our admonition, as we do that formerly sent us by Clement."

This letter shows that Pope St. Soter was very charitable. It also indicates the high respect that the Corinthians had for the letter of Pope St. Clement and the letter of Soter. The "persecution in our own times" mentioned by Eusebius was the persecution of Diocletian. The words of Eusebius are a testimony that the Roman See was as preeminent in charity as it was in dignity.

St. Soter was buried in the cemetery of Calixtus. He is honored by the Church as a martyr. His feast, together with that of St. Caius, is celebrated on April 22.

Botticelli. Sistine Chapel, the Vatican.

ST. ELEUTHERIUS

C. 174 - C. 189

According to the *Liber Pontificalis*, ST. ELEUtherius was a Greek from Nicopolis in Epirus. His father's name was Habundius. He ordered that no food which was fit for a human being should be despised by Christians. This decree, if authentic, probably was aimed at the Montanists, a fanatical puritanical sect, or the Manicheans, who despised meat.

St. Irenaeus, the famous father of the Church, was sent by St. Pothinus and the clergy of Lyons to confer with Pope Eleutherius about Montanism. Unfortunately Eusebius, who narrates the fact, did not preserve the details of this interesting mission. Montanism was a peculiar exaggeration or parody of Christianity started by a Phrygian ex-priest of Cybele, Montanus. This man taught that inspiration and ecstasy rather than the hierarchy should guide the faithful, that martyrdom should be rashly sought, that marriage was wrong, and that Montanus was, if not the Holy Ghost himself, the authentic herald of the Holy Ghost. In a modified form this heresy infiltrated into the West. Since its most common manifestation was an exaggerated strictness and since at first in the West it did not seek to break away from the Church, it is not surprising that it took a little time before it was discovered for the heresy it was. It is not clear whether Pope St. Eleutherius condemned Montanism at this time.

A very interesting item in the *Liber Pontificalis* concerns the reception by Pope Eleutherius of a letter from Lucius, the king of Britain, asking for instruction in the Christian faith: very interesting but almost certainly untrue. Britain at this time was a Roman province. It is true that some highland chief from beyond the wall might call himself king, but it is quite unlikely that such a remote redshanks should have written to Rome. The early British historian Gildas makes not the slightest mention of such an incident. Most modern scholars agree that the story is apocryphal. An interesting theory advanced by some modern scholars is that the author of the *Liber Pontificalis* or a copyist confused Lucius, king of Britain, with Lucius, king of Britium in Mesopotamia.

St. Eleutherius was buried near St. Peter in the Vatican. He is honored by the Church as a martyr. His feast is kept on May 6.

Frà Diamante (?). Sistine Chapel, the Vatican.

ST. VICTOR I

C. 189-199

ST. VICTOR'S REIGN IS NOTED FOR A LULL IN THE persecution and a crisis in the Easter controversy.

According to the *Liber Pontificalis*, Victor was an African, the son of Felix. He decreed that after an emergency baptism, whether in river, spring, sea, or marsh, the neophyte should be treated as a Christian in full standing.

The lull in the persecution was due to a woman named Marcia, who seems to have been a sort of morganatic wife of the Emperor Commodus. Marcia had great influence on Commodus. Friendly to Christianity, she used this influence to soften the lot of the hard-pressed Christians. She asked Pope Victor for a list of the Christians condemned to work in the mines of Sardinia and secured the release of these poor victims.

At this time the controversy over the day for celebrating Easter came to a head. In Rome, where there lived many Asiatics, it must have been disconcerting to see one group of Christians observing the fast of lent and commemorating Christ's passion while other Christians were joyously celebrating the feast of the resurrection. Pope Victor determined to put a stop to this and ordered Polycrates, bishop of Ephesus, to hold a council of Asiatic bishops and get them to follow the Western custom of celebrating Easter on Sunday. Polycrates did indeed assemble the bishops, but informed the Pope that neither he nor the Asiatic bishops could abandon the tradition of St. John and St. Philip. Pope Victor put his foot down and ordered the Church to celebrate Easter on Sunday. All but the bishops of Asia Minor obeyed. Thereupon Victor excommunicated them. St. Irenaeus, now bishop of Lyons, pleaded with the Pope that after all, it was only a matter of discipline and that the Pope's illustrious predecessors had allowed the diversity of dates. Furthermore, St. Irenaeus argued, it was a sad thing for the glorious see of Ephesus to be cut off from Catholic unity. Pope Victor, convinced, seems to have relented. At any rate after this time the practice of celebrating Easter on Sunday spread throughout the East.

Right at Rome a certain Blastus refused to obey the Pope and started a little church of his own. The Pope also had to excommunicate Theodotus, a leather seller who had come from Byzantium to Rome. This tanner denied the divinity of Christ and also set up a little church of his own. The Gnostics too gave trouble to Victor.

Pope St. Victor wrote several treatises including (probably) one on dice throwers. St. Jerome calls him the first Latin writer in the Church.

According to the *Liber Pontificalis*, St. Victor died a martyr and was buried on the Vatican near St. Peter. His feast is kept on July 28.

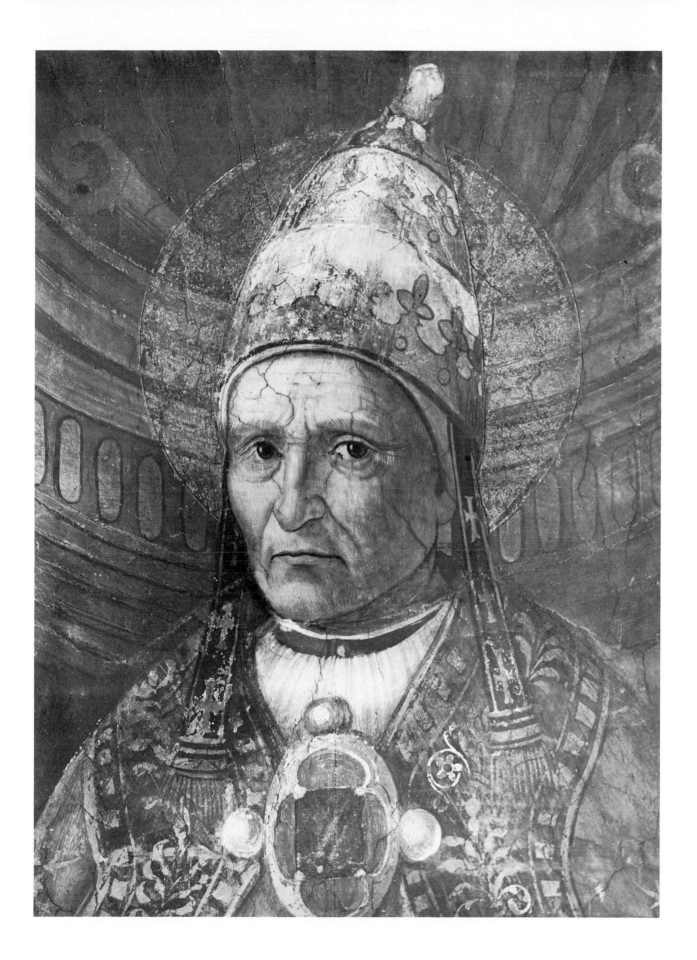

ST. ZEPHYRINUS

C. 199 - C. 217

THE PONTIFICATE OF THIS FIRST THIRD-CENTURY pope was to see a storm of heresy rage around the pontiff, who had to keep a firm hand on the tiller of Peter's bark.

According to the *Liber Pontificalis,* Zephyrinus was a Roman, the son of Habundius. He ordered that all ordinations, whether of priests, deacons, or simple clerics, should take place before the assembled clergy and laity.

The storm which agitated Christian thought in the time of Pope Zephyrinus was due to a double heresy. On the one hand, Theodotus the Tanner, though excommunicated by Pope St. Victor, was still teaching that Christ was not the true Son of God. On the other hand, a certain Praxeas came to Rome to tell Pope Zephyrinus that the old idea of the Trinity was all wrong, that really there were not three Persons in one Divine Nature, but only three modes of one substance.

Pope Zephyrinus, who was no philosopher, clung firmly to the traditional doctrine handed down from the Apostles. In the midst of these metaphysical storms, he also had a good strong adviser in Calixtus, who succeeded him as Pope.

Eusebius in his *Ecclesiastical History* has an interesting story about the heretics in the pontificate of Pope Zephyrinus. Theodotus the Tanner, far from being silenced by Pope Victor's excommunication, had set up his own church. He had found backers in another Theodotus (a banker) and Asclepediotus. The heretics found a man of some prestige to be bishop for them. This was Natalius, who had been a confessor of the faith and had suffered tortures for it. They paid him a yearly stipend—150 denarii, about $25 in prewar money. But as Eusebius tells the story, Jesus, not wishing that one who had suffered for him should go out of the church, sent angels in visions to bring Natalius to a better frame of mind. Natalius, blinded by the pinchbeck glory of being a heretical bishop, at first paid the visions little attention. But one night the angels gave the stubborn fellow a sound whipping. This brought him to his senses. He put on sackcloth, covered himself with ashes and hastened to throw himself before Pope Zephyrinus and plead for pardon.

Besides heresy, Pope Zephyrinus had to cope with renewed persecution. Septimius Severus, friendly at the start of his reign, became decidedly hostile. During the pontificate of Zephyrinus the Emperor issued his famous decree forbidding anyone to become a Christian.

St. Zephyrinus is honored as a martyr by the Church. He was buried in his own cemetery on August 25. His feast is kept on August 26.

Frà Diamante. Sistine Chapel, the Vatican.

[30]

ST. CALIXTUS I

C. 217 - C. 222

ST. CALIXTUS (OR CALLISTUS) WAS A ROMAN from the Trastevere district. His father's name was Domitius. He decreed a fast from corn, wine, and oil three times a year. These fasts together with the lenten fast make up the fasts of the four seasons which the Ember days prescribe even to today. Pope Calixtus is said to have built a basilica across the Tiber in his native Trastevere district. He constructed a cemetery on the Appian Way which is one of the most famous of Christian cemeteries. In it are buried many popes and martyrs.

The *Liber Pontificalis* gives the above information, but Calixtus is chiefly known from the writings of his enemies. Hippolytus accused him of being too friendly to the Monarchian heretics in spite of the fact that Calixtus condemned Sabellius, the leader of that heresy. Both Hippolytus and Tertullian were deeply outraged by an act of the Pope which would endear him to most and shows him to be a true disciple of the merciful Christ. In the early Church there was a strong tendency to rigorism. Some bishops had refused to receive back into communion apostates, adulterers, and murderers. Such sinners, no matter how deeply they might repent, would remain excommunicated until death. By the time of Calixtus this practice had become general in the Church. How painful for repentant sinners this must have been can easily be imagined. Calixtus decreed that all sinners who truly repented could be absolved and received back into the Church after suitable penance.

The grim Tertullian, infected with Montanist puritanism, was furious. Hippolytus went so far as to set himself up as antipope. Both wrote bitterly against the mercy of Pope Calixtus.

St. Calixtus died a martyr. He was buried in the Cemetery of Calipodius on the Aurelian Way. His feast is kept on October 14.

Tuscan School. Sistine Chapel, the Vatican.

ST. URBAN I

C. 222 - C. 230

ST. URBAN'S NAME IS FAMILIAR TO MANY BE-cause of his supposed connection with the beautiful life of St. Cecilia.

According to the *Liber Pontificalis,* he was a Roman, the son of Pontius. He had all the sacred vessels made of silver, and presented to the Church twenty-five silver patens. It seems that in the early Church glass as well as silver was a favorite material for the sacred vessels. He converted many and among them Valerian, the husband of St. Cecilia.

Actually, it is pretty clear that this Urban did not have any dealings with St. Cecilia. The *Liber Pontificalis* seems to have relied on the fifth-century *Passion of St. Cecilia.* This is an account of St. Cecilia's martyrdom which is embroidered with legend. That St. Cecilia was a noble Roman lady who was martyred is certain, but her martyrdom goes back to an earlier time than the reign of Pope Urban.

As a matter of fact, Pope Urban lived in times of comparative peace for the Church. The Emperor Alexander Severus, a mild man, even had a statue of Jesus in his collection of gods. Nor was his prefect, the great lawyer Ulpian, a persecutor. Alexander was influenced by his mother Julia Mammaea, who was a friend of the great Christian writer Origen. He even decided a lawsuit in favor of the Christians. The Christians were disputing the title to some land with a tavern keeper. The Emperor decided in favor of the Christians, saying that it was better to have God worshipped on the land in question than a tavern set up.

Urban was buried in the Cemetery of Calixtus. He is honored by the Church as a martyr. His feast is kept on May 25.

Giulio Romano. The Raphael Rooms, the Vatican.

VRBANVS I

ST. PONTIAN

230-235

ST. PONTIAN WAS A ROMAN, THE SON OF CALPURnius. He had to face a flare-up of persecution. Alexander Severus was assassinated in 235. His successor, Maximinus, an ex-wrestler, had no great preoccupation with matters of religion, but he hated Alexander Severus, and since Alexander had favored the Christians, Maximinus hastened to persecute them. He ordered that the leaders of the Church should alone be struck. And so St. Pontian found himself hustled off to the mines of Sardinia.

In the mines he had as companion none other than the antipope Hippolytus. This priest, it may be remembered, had been so disgusted with Pope Calixtus and his edict of mercy that he had revolted and set himself up as antipope. Now in the mines of Sardinia he came to a better frame of mind. Not only did he become reconciled with St. Pontian, but he ordered all his followers to return to the Church. He made a good end, dying a confessor of Christ, and it is touching that down to this day, the Church celebrates the feast of St. Pontian, the Pope, and St. Hippolytus, once antipope, on the same day, November 19.

St. Pontian seems to have abdicated when sent to the mines and to have been succeeded at Rome by Anterus. At any rate, in November 235 he was brutally beaten to death, a martyr for Christ. Pope Fabian brought his body back to Rome and buried him in the Cemetery of Calixtus.

School of Botticelli. The Vatican.

ST. ANTERUS

235-236

ST. ANTERUS WAS ELECTED POPE EVEN BEFORE the death of St. Pontian. Pontian, evidently considering that he could not rule the Church efficiently from a Sardinian mine, abdicated.

Anterus, according to the *Liber Pontificalis*, was a Greek, the son of Romulus. He ruled the Church for a very short time, about forty days. He ordained a bishop for Fundi in Campania. The memory of Anterus should be dear to historians, for he ordered that the acts of the martyrs should be collected from notaries and kept in the church.

St. Anterus probably died a martyr. At any rate the Church celebrates his feast as that of a martyr on January 3. He was buried in the Cemetery of Calixtus. A stone with the inscription "Antherus Epi[scopus]" written in Greek letters has been discovered in this cemetery.

Frà Diamante (?). Sistine Chapel, the Vatican.

ST. FABIAN

236-250

A PRETTY STORY OF FABIAN'S ELECTION TO THE papacy is told by Eusebius in his *Ecclesiastical History* (VI, xxix):

"It is said that Fabian, after the death of Anteros, came from the country along with others and stayed at Rome, where he came to the office in a most miraculous manner, thanks to the divine and heavenly grace. For when the brethren were all assembled for the purpose of appointing him who should succeed to the episcopate, and very many notable and distinguished persons were in the thoughts of many, Fabian, who was there, came into nobody's mind. But all of a sudden, they relate, a dove flew down from above and settled on his head as clear imitation of the descent of the Holy Ghost in the form of a dove upon the Saviour; whereupon the whole people, as if moved by one divine inspiration, with all eagerness and with one soul cried out "worthy," and without more ado took him and placed him on the episcopal throne."

According to the prosaic *Liber Pontificalis,* Fabian was a Roman, the son of Fabius. He appointed seven deacons to the seven districts of Rome. He ordered subdeacons to cooperate with the notaries in gathering the acts of the martyrs. He brought back the body of St. Pontian from Sardinia and buried it in the Cemetery of Calixtus. This cemetery was enlarged and beautified. Vaults were adorned with paintings. A church rose above the cemetery. Later writers attributed all kinds of regulations to the busy time of Pope Fabian. Gregory of Tours, the famous historian of the Franks, even credits Fabian with starting the evangelization of Gaul. This is manifestly false because the Church existed in Gaul before the time of Fabian, but it is probable enough that he did something for the Gallic Church.

All this activity was made possible by the peace which the Church enjoyed at this time. The first half of the third century was in general a period of peace. Septimius Severus, at the beginning of the century, and Maximinus, just before Fabian's reign, had been persecutors, but they were exceptions. After the death of the ex-wrestler Maximinus, his successors Papienus, Balbinus, and Gordianus had let the Christians pretty much alone. And Philip who murdered and succeeded Gordian was himself a Christian—of sorts. Philip, though he presided at pagan games, was quite friendly to the Christians, and during his reign Christianity flourished. Fabian's activity has been noted; and at the same time Gregory, the wonder-worker, bishop of Neo-Caesarea, Cyprian, bishop of Carthage, the great Origen, and others were writing to create a Christian literature. It looked as if the Church were going to burst out of the catacombs to flourish in the light of day.

But the pagans were angry. Even before the death of Emperor Philip in 249 there had been isolated outbreaks against the Christians. The pagans bitterly resented Christian growth, and when Decius succeeded Philip as emperor, that resentment mounted the throne. Decius was on principle a determined and ruthless enemy of the Christian name. Septimius Severus had tried to stop conversions; Maximinus had gone after the leaders. Decius issued an edict ordering all Christians to deny Christ by some tangible sign such as offering incense to idols. The storm hit a church softened by peace. On all sides many hastened to deny Christ, but there were many too who stood up and faced the worst tortures and death for Him. Among these was St. Fabian. The details of his martyrdom are lacking, but it is historically certain. He is buried in the Cemetery of Calixtus. His feast is kept on January 20.

As restored. Sistine Chapel, the Vatican.

ST. CORNELIUS

251-253

ECIUS IS REPORTED TO HAVE SAID THAT HE would prefer to have a rival emperor rather than a bishop in Rome. As long as such an emperor was in full career, it was impossible for the Christians to elect a new pope. But after over a year the Emperor was distracted by rebels, the persecution slackened, and the Christians were able to elect a new pope. Cornelius, their choice, was a Roman, a man of strong mind and strong character. He was to need both.

The winds of persecution had ceased to blow, but they left the bark of Peter tossing in the swells. The persecution had been too much for many Christians. Many had weakly denied Christ. Some had actually sacrificed to idols. Others had bribed officials to say that they had. Now that peace was restored, these poor weaklings came from all corners to try to get back into the Church. The Pope had to face the double challenge of laxism which too easily passed over the grievous offense and rigorism which repulsed the poor people.

At first the laxists had to be checked. Many confessors, that is, those who had confessed Christ before a heathen judge, took it upon themselves to give the repentant apostates certificates entitling the holder to restoration to communion. This degenerated into a regular traffic, and when St. Cyprian, the bishop of Carthage, tried to stop it, a certain Novatus set up a dupe of his named Felicissimus as antibishop and went off to Rome to get the Pope's support. Cornelius, however, was not deceived. He condemned the schism and the laxist practices. The repentant apostates might indeed return to communion but only after due penance.

This moderate regulation provoked the rigorists, and a man named Novatian came to Rome and set himself up as antipope. He accused Cornelius of having bribed an official to say that he had denied Christ. No wonder Cornelius wrote bitterly about Novatian in a letter to Bishop Fabius of Antioch. St. Cyprian loyally backed the Pope. At this time he wrote the classical treatise, *On the Unity of the Church.*

Novatian the rigorist, oddly enough, joined hands with Novatus the laxist. The movement they started spread into the East. It absorbed many of the old Montanists. These people called themselves Cathari (Puritans).

The persecution once more flared up when a plague set the fanatical populace to demanding death for the Christians. Emperor Trebonianus Gallus yielded to the demand. This time the Christians were better prepared and the shocking wave of apostasy which had marked the Decian persecution was not repeated. Pope Cornelius kept his Romans in high morale. He was exiled to Centum Cellae, the modern Civita Vecchia, and was martyred there in 253. He was buried in the Cemetery of Calixtus. The feast of St. Cornelius, together with that of his friend St. Cyprian, is kept on September 16.

Botticelli. Sistine Chapel, the Vatican.

ST. LUCIUS

253-254

ST. LUCIUS, ACCORDING TO THE *Liber Pontificalis,* was a Roman, the son of Porphyrius. When he succeeded St. Cornelius, the persecution of Trebonianus Gallus was still raging, and the new Pope was exiled. Soon, however, the persecution died away and Lucius was able to return to Rome. There is extant a letter from St. Cyprian congratulating the Pope on his return from exile and praising him for his confession of Christ.

St. Lucius continued the policy of Cornelius in admitting repentant apostates to communion after due penance. St. Cyprian praises him for this.

The *Liber Pontificalis* attributes to Pope Lucius a decree ordering that two priests and three deacons should live with a bishop that they might be witnesses for him. Duchesne, however, considers this decree apocryphal.

According to the *Liber Pontificalis,* Pope Lucius was beheaded in the persecution of Valerian. This is almost certainly inaccurate, for Lucius died before the persecution of Valerian broke out. At any rate, St. Lucius died some time in the beginning of March 254, and was buried in the Cemetery of Calixtus. His tombstone has been discovered. The feast of St. Lucius is kept on March 4.

Botticelli. Sistine Chapel, the Vatican.

ST. STEPHEN I

254-257

ST. STEPHEN'S PONTIFICATE, THOUGH SHORT, WAS to see the Church troubled by a vexatious controversy within and attacked by a bitter persecution from without.

St. Stephen was a Roman, the son of Jobius. He ordered the clergy not to use their consecrated vestments for daily purposes.

The key figure in the vexing dispute over rebaptism was the bishop of Carthage, the great writer St. Cyprian. Cyprian, a man of vigor, called upon Pope Stephen to depose the bishops of Merida and León in Spain because during the persecution they had secured certificates saying that they had sacrificed to idols. Pope Stephen agreed with Cyprian and did depose the weak pair. Cyprian, who certainly kept an eye on things, once more called on the Pope—this time to depose Marcian, bishop of Arles in Gaul, because he had fallen into the Novatian heresy. Once more Pope Stephen consented. But a third time Cyprian found that Stephen could not agree with him, and that was in the thorny question of heretical baptism.

There were a number of converts coming into the Church from heresy. Now if these were lapsed Catholics, they were absolved and given penance. But what if they were pagans who had been baptized by heretics? St. Cyprian firmly believed that they must be rebaptized and, being Cyprian, loudly proclaimed it. For, said Cyprian, outside the Church baptism is simply not valid. Cyprian held a council of African bishops in 255 and this council approved Cyprian's view. He sent the decisions of the council on to Pope Stephen.

The Pope refused to approve. In his answer to Cyprian, Stephen took the stand that tradition was sacred. In often quoted words Stephen said, "Let there be no innovation beyond what has been handed down." In other words, as supreme guardian of Christian tradition, Stephen refused to recognize Cyprian's theory and practice as truly Christian.

St. Cyprian had definitely acknowledged the supremacy of the Pope, but he did not seem to feel that the matter of rebaptism fell within the limits of papal jurisdiction. To bolster his position he held another council in 256, and once more the African bishops backed him up. Although there was no talk of the Pope's decision, it was a defiant act. Stephen began to threaten excommunication. Thereupon St. Firmilian, bishop of Caesarea in Cappadocia, wrote a strong letter attacking such a course. St. Stephen, a patient man, seems to have let matters ride. Soon the persecution of Valerian ended the lives of both principals. As usual the Roman doctrine finally prevailed. By the end of the century all Africa was in accord with Rome in this matter, and the dissident dioceses of Asia followed somewhat later.

The persecution, in which St. Cyprian gloriously atoned for what fault there was in his well-meaning but misguided stubbornness, was roused by Emperor Valerian. Valerian, an honest soldier, was at first favorable to the Christians, but influenced by his right-hand man Macrianus, he turned to magic and soon issued two edicts of persecution. These aimed at the leaders of the Church and the corporate life of the Church.

St. Stephen fell a victim to this persecution. The details of his martyrdom are not clear. It may be that he died an exile. He was buried in the Cemetery of Calixtus. His feast is kept on August 2.

Botticelli. Sistine Chapel, the Vatican.

ST. SIXTUS II

257-258

THE AUTHOR OF THE *Liber Pontificalis* CALLS ST. Sixtus a Greek and a philosopher, but modern scholars think that Pope Sixtus is confused with another Sixtus, a Pythagorean philosopher. Whether a philosopher or not, Pope Sixtus II was a glorious martyr.

St. Stephen had caused a good deal of excitement by his threat to excommunicate those bishops who did not conform in the matter of heretical baptism. St. Firmilian of Antioch had written a bitter letter to Stephen. St. Dionysius of Alexandria had written a mild letter pleading for mercy and forbearance. To St. Sixtus II, Dionysius addressed a similar appeal. His words were heeded. Pope Sixtus II, though he upheld the traditional Roman doctrine, did not break off relations with those African and Asiatic churches which followed St. Cyprian.

Sixtus felt the full force of Valerian's persecution. That emperor had issued his second more drastic edict of persecution in 258. Soon blood was flowing. Since the Cemetery of Calixtus was too well known to government officials for safety, Pope Sixtus held services across the Appian Way in the Cemetery of Praetextatus. This cemetery seems to have been private rather than Church property. The precaution, however, was in vain. One day when Pope Sixtus was giving a talk to the faithful, the police broke in, arrested Sixtus and his chief clerics, and carried them off to the prefect. On this occasion they do not seem to have bothered about the lay people. According to tradition, the touching scene between St. Sixtus and his chief deacon, St. Lawrence, occurred at this time. Lawrence was absent when the police made their swoop. On hearing the news, he hastened to meet the Pope and asked him, "Where are you going, father, without your son? Where are you going, O priest, without your deacon?" Pope Sixtus replied, "My son, you I am not abandoning. Greater strife awaits you. Stop weeping; you will follow me in three days" (Paul Allard, *Les dernières persécutions du troisième siècle*, p. 91). And so it happened. The police pounced on St. Lawrence and put pressure on him to deliver up the treasures of the Church. St. Lawrence agreed to lead the prefect to the treasures, and since the reserve money of the Church had been distributed to the poor, Lawrence, even as Cornelia pointed to her children as her jewels, pointed to the poor as the Church treasure. The prefect was disappointed. Lawrence met death like a hero.

Pope St. Sixtus II was put to death on August 6 in the cemetery where he had been holding services. He was buried, however, in the Cemetery of Calixtus. His feast is kept on August 6, the anniversary day of his martyrdom.

Frà Angelico. "Sixtus II Delivers the Church's Treasury to St. Lawrence." Chapel of St. Nicholas, the Vatican.

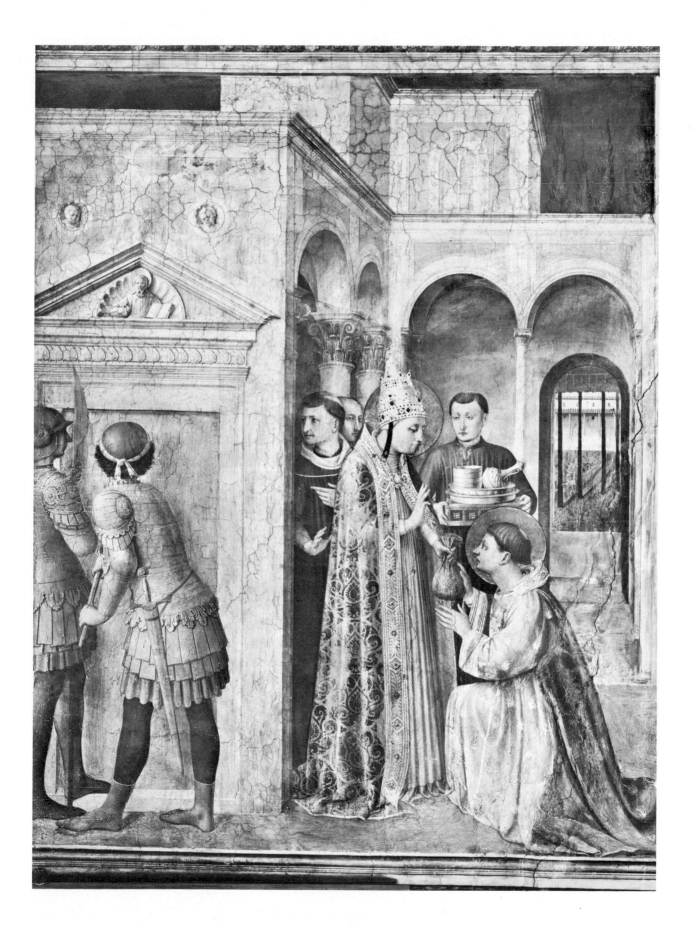

ST. DIONYSIUS

259-268

THE STORM OF PERSECUTION WHICH HAD SLAIN St. Sixtus and St. Lawrence blew throughout Rome with such violence that for some time the Christians could not elect a new pope. But by July of 259 Emperor Valerian was too busy worrying about Persians to pay much attention to Christians. On July 22, 259, the priest Dionysius was elected pope.

St. Dionysius was to have a peaceful pontificate. In 260 Valerian was defeated by Sapor the Persian. He was made prisoner and then skinned. His son and successor, Gallienus, though an incapable ruler, was well-disposed to the Christians. Salonina, his wife, may well have been a Christian herself. Gallienus issued a decree of toleration which not only gave the Christians a breathing spell but even restored confiscated Church property. It is interesting to note that the decree dealt directly with the heads of the churches.

While there was peace at Rome, there was trouble in the East. The Persians had ravaged Cappadocia, and the Christians had shared in the general agony. Pope Dionysius sent the sufferers a letter of consolation and a large sum of money to redeem such of the faithful as had been captured and enslaved.

The Pope was on guard to defend the purity of Christian doctrine. His namesake, Dionysius, bishop of Alexandria, had gone astray in his speculations on the Trinity. The Pope, alarmed, held a synod at Rome, then sent a letter condemning the doctrinal vagaries of the good Alexandrian. This letter is important for its dogmatic content. It is a prelude to Nicaea. In it the Pope defends the true doctrine of the Three Persons in one divine nature. Dionysius of Alexandria was less than exact in his phraseology, but he was no heretic. The good old man died at peace with the Church.

A real heretic, however, was troubling the Church in Asia at this time. Paul of Samosata, who incongruously combined the offices of bishop of Antioch and treasurer of the civil government, taught that Jesus was not true God. To meet this threat, the Asiatic bishops held a council at Antioch in 264 and condemned Paul's teaching. This council sent a circular letter addressed to Dionysius and Maximus, bishop of Alexandria, to inform the Christian world of its doings.

Pope Dionysius also seems to have done some organizing of new parishes around Rome.

Dionysius died in December 268 and was buried in the Cemetery of Calixtus. His feast is kept on December 26.

Frà Diamante. Sistine Chapel, the Vatican.

ST. FELIX I

269-274

ST. FELIX WAS A ROMAN, THE SON OF CONSTANTIUS. He was elected pope in 269. A letter to Bishop Maximus of Alexandria was once thought to be his, but later scholars have decided that it was a forgery.

During the pontificate of St. Felix, the capable organizer and clever general Aurelian became emperor. Aurelian has a very interesting connection with the Pope. The pontificate of St. Dionysius had been troubled by the heresy of Paul of Samosata. A council held at Antioch had deposed Paul as bishop of Antioch, but the wily heretic hung on to the Church property and refused to give it up to his successor, Demetrianus. Emperor Aurelian, passing through Antioch, was called upon to settle the matter. The Emperor decided that he was truly the bishop who was in communion with the bishops of Rome and Italy. And so the orthodox Demetrianus was able to take over from the heretical Paul of Samosata.

St. Felix is credited with ordering the celebration of Masses over the sepulchers of the martyrs.

Pope St. Felix is called a martyr by the *Liber Pontificalis*, which also says that he built a basilica on the Aurelian Way in which he was buried. Modern scholars, however, do not consider this to be true. Duchesne thinks that it is a confusion of Pope Felix with another Felix who was a martyr and was buried on the Aurelian Way. At any rate, Pope St. Felix died in 274 and was most probably buried in the Cemetery of Calixtus. His feast is kept on May 30.

Ghirlandajo. Sistine Chapel, the Vatican.

ST. EUTYCHIAN

275 - 283

EXCEPT FOR THE INFORMATION GIVEN BY THE *Liber Pontificalis* little is known about Pope St. Eutychian, and the accuracy of the *Liber Pontificalis* entry on Pope Eutychian is rather suspect. There is even confusion about the length of his reign between the *Liber Pontificalis,* which says that Pope Eutychian ruled the Church eight years and eleven months, and Eusebius, who gives him a reign of only ten months.

Pope Eutychian made a regulation allowing fruit—but only grapes and beans—to be blessed on the altar.

He is said to have buried 324 martyrs with his own hands. He made the regulation that martyrs should be buried in a dalmatic (a purple tunic) and he wished that all burials of martyrs should be reported to him.

Pope St. Eutychian is called a martyr, but that he died a violent death is considered unlikely. He was buried in the Cemetery of Calixtus. And at least the fact that he was buried in this cemetery is certain, for his tombstone has been discovered there. His feast is kept on December 8.

Ghirlandajo. Sistine Chapel, the Vatican.

ST. CAIUS

283-296

IF AN ACCOUNT OF THE MARTYRDOM OF ST. Susanna were correct, there would be a very interesting fact about Pope St. Caius—that he was a relative of the terrible persecutor, Diocletian. But scholars give small credit to the account of the martyrdom of St. Susanna. It is true that the *Liber Pontificalis* confirms this relationship of Caius with Diocletian, but the *Liber Pontificalis* pretty clearly leaned on the unhistorical account of St. Susanna for its information.

There is little information available on Pope St. Caius except that given by the *Liber Pontificalis*. The accounts of popes and acts of the martyrs were quite probably destroyed when Diocletian made a determined effort to do away with all Christian writings.

St. Caius was a Dalmatian, the son of Caius. He decreed that before a man could be bishop, he must first be porter, reader, exorcist, acolyte, sub-deacon, deacon, and priest. He also divided the districts of Rome among the deacons.

When the persecution of Diocletian began to rage, so we are told, St. Caius took refuge in the catacombs and died there a confessor. But actually the persecution of Diocletian did not even begin until six or seven years after the death of St. Caius. It is true that during the pontificate of Caius, Diocletian ascended the imperial throne, but at first the great organizer was anything but hostile to the Christians.

At this period, however, work on the catacombs was pushed vigorously. New galleries were excavated and small churches built over them.

St. Caius died in 296 and was buried in the Cemetery of Calixtus. His tombstone has been pieced together. The feast of St. Caius together with that of Pope St. Soter is celebrated on April 22.

Chronologia Summorum Pontificum.

ST. MARCELLINUS

296-304

THE NEXT POPE WAS TO SEE THE END OF THE LONG period of peace and the start of a most violent persecution, the persecution of Diocletian.

St. Marcellinus was a Roman, the son of Projectus. When he first became pope, Diocletian was already on the throne, but he had not yet drawn the sword against the Christians. Indeed, at first under the influence of his wife, Prisca, and his daughter, Valeria, the despot left the Christians fairly free. The peace, however, had caused Christianity to grow and grow. This provoked a fierce reaction among the pagans, and they had a leader in no less a dignitary than the Caesar Galerius.

According to Lactantius, the historian of the persecution, Diocletian was first angered by the Christians when the augurs or soothsayers told him that they could not prophesy because Christians made the sign of the cross. The Emperor promptly ordered all Christians to apostatize or get out of the army. This was in 302. The next year at a conference in Nicomedia, Galerius urged the Emperor to extend himself against the Christians. Diocletian asked the opinion of the oracle of Apollo at Miletus. Naturally, the oracle saw eye to eye with Galerius. But Diocletian started easily. At first he ordered the confiscation of Church property and the destruction of Christian books. When a rash Christian actually tore down the imperial edict right un-

der the imperial nose at Nicomedia and two very convenient fires broke out in the imperial palace, Diocletian, enraged, took off the gloves. It was apostatize or die, and soon blood was streaming.

The persecution hit Rome with disastrous results for the historians. The papal archives were seized and destroyed. The famous Cemetery of Calixtus was saved by the Christians, who blocked up the entrance.

Pope St. Marcellinus was accused by Donatist heretics of having handed over the sacred books. Some went so far as to accuse him of having sacrificed to idols. The *Liber Pontificalis* repeats this, but adds that St. Marcellinus repented and died a martyr. Actually it is not certain either that St. Marcellinus weakened or that he was a martyr. St. Augustine denies openly that the Pope had weakened, and there is no conclusive evidence of his having been killed.

At any rate, St. Marcellinus did die a confessor of Christ in 304. According to the *Liber Pontificalis*, after his head was cut off, his body, along with those of other martyrs, was left lying on the street for twenty-six days to terrify the Christians. Then a priest buried the Pope in the Cemetery of Priscilla. His feast is kept on April 26.

Botticelli. Sistine Chapel, the Vatican.

ST. MARCELLUS I

308-309

Diocletian's persecution had so badly disorganized the Church in Rome that not until 308 was a successor to Pope Marcellinus chosen. The new pope was Marcellus, a Roman from the Via Lata district.

By this time the persecution had died down in the West, but the new pope faced enormous difficulties. His first task was to reorganize the badly shaken Church, and this task Marcellus seems to have accomplished. His second task, however, was more difficult. It will be remembered that after the short but very severe persecution of Decius the Church had been troubled by the problem of what to do with the numerous weaker brethren who had fallen under the stress of persecution. Now this same problem once more arose, but this time the trouble came from a different source. In the aftermath of the old persecution the chief trouble had come from harsh rigorists, and it had been necessary for Pope St. Cornelius to insist that the poor weak ones should be readmitted to communion

with the Church after due penance. Now Pope St. Marcellus found that the weaker brethren wished indeed to be readmitted to the Church, but that they had small stomach for penance. The Pope's attempts to enforce this Church discipline were fiercely resented. Under the leadership of one who had denied Christ, even in time of peace, the malcontents raised so much trouble that fights broke out and blood was shed. The Emperor Maxentius seems to have believed that Pope Marcellus was at the bottom of these broils, and sent him into exile.

There is a story, not well authenticated, that the Pope was forced to work in the stables of the imperial post. But at any rate it is certain that after a short time Pope Marcellus died in exile. He is honored as a martyr and a saint. His feast is kept on January 16. The exile of Pope Marcellus is one of the first examples of the secular government interfering with the Church apart from outright persecution.

As restored. Sistine Chapel, the Vatican.

ST. EUSEBIUS

309 or 310

THE MAN CHOSEN TO SUCCEED ST. MARCELLUS was a Greek priest named Eusebius. Except that he was the son of a doctor, nothing is known of his early life. There is some confusion about the date of his reign. He seems to have ruled the Church for only four months from April to August, but whether it was in the year 309 or 310 is uncertain.

It was a troubled community that Eusebius was called upon to rule. The same situation which led to the exile of Pope Marcellus still prevailed. The fight over readmission of fallen Christians to the fold still raged on. Under the circumstances it is not surprising that the election of a new pope was bitterly contested. Pope Eusebius determined to follow the same sane policy of Pope Marcellus. He would readmit the fallen brethren, but only after due penance. The storm increased. The malcontents went so far as to choose an antipope, a man named Heraclius. Once more matters came to the point of open strife. Once more Emperor Maxentius intervened. But this time he exiled pope and antipope alike.

Eusebius was sent to Sicily where he died shortly after. Like Marcellus he is honored as a saint and a martyr. His feast is kept on September 26.

Attributed to G. Finelli. Chapel of the
Treasure, the Duomo, Naples.

ST. MILTIADES

311-314

THE STORM WHICH HAD EXILED POPES MARCEL-lus and Eusebius seems to have prevented an early election of a successor, but finally in 311 Miltiades, an African, was chosen. (His name is also recorded in the forms Milziadus and Melchiadus.) The new pope was to guide the bark of Peter into calmer waters. Actually the Church in the West was already enjoying relief from persecution. But though Maxentius in the West was easy on the Christians, his colleague Galerius continued to scourge the Christians of the East pitilessly. In 311, struck down by disease, Galerius decided to call a halt to his war on Christ. He issued a decree of toleration which had its effect even in Rome. Maxentius turned over to Pope Miltiades several churches which had been confiscated.

Pope Miltiades worked hard to get the Church back in shape after the severe storm. He also brought back the remains of Pope St. Eusebius and buried them with due honor in the Cemetery of Calixtus.

Though St. Miltiades ruled the Church for only three years, he was to witness one of history's turning points—the coming of Constantine and the end of an era, the era of persecution. Constantine had been proclaimed emperor in Gaul, and now in 312 he marched on Rome to overthrow the tyrant Maxentius. Constantine, although not a Christian, had seen the cross in a vision and had learned that "by this sign shalt thou conquer." And for the first time in history the cross of peace appeared on the standards of an army. Under the banner of the cross the legions of Constantine met and routed the army of Maxentius at the Milvian Bridge. This dramatic victory ushered in a new era, an era of peace for the Church. The very next year, 313, at Milan, Constantine and his colleague Licinius issued the famous decree of toleration which really set the Christians free, free to come out of the catacombs.

A new era meant a new position for the Church and new problems. Both position and problems were quickly given emphasis by a gathering of bishops held by Pope Miltiades in the Lateran Palace. This palace, so long revered in Christian memory, had belonged to the Laterani family. Nero had confiscated it, and now Constantine's wife, Fausta, give it to the Pope. Here in this stately palace overlooking the forum with its proud pagan monuments, the Pope presided over a gathering of fifteen Italian and three Gallic bishops to settle an African difficulty. In Africa a schism had broken out headed by an intriguer named Donatus. These Donatists disputed the rule of Carthage with the true bishop, Caecilian. Constantine, troubled by the resulting disturbances, had asked the Pope to do something about the matter, and this synod in the Lateran answered by condemning Donatus.

St. Miltiades died shortly after. He was called by St. Augustine an excellent pontiff. He had given the Church good leadership in a difficult time of transition. St. Miltiades was buried in the Cemetery of Calixtus. It is significant that he was the last pope to be buried in a catacomb.

The National Museum, Florence

ST. SYLVESTER I

314-335

IF LEGEND WERE HISTORY, THE LIFE OF ST. SYLVES-
ter would indeed be interesting. It would be
pleasant to recount how St. Sylvester baptized
the great Constantine and how Constantine was
cured of leprosy by the baptismal waters. But
this is a legend which, along with others, grew up
around the papal contemporary of the colorful emperor.

Sylvester was a Roman, the son of Rufinus. He
was ordained a priest by Marcellinus. Chosen Pope
in 314, he continued the work of organizing the
peacetime Church so well begun by St. Miltiades.
Sylvester saw the building of famous churches, notably the Basilica of St. Peter and the Basilica of
St. John Lateran, built near the former imperial
palace of that name. It is quite probable too that
the first martyrology or list of Roman martyrs was
drawn up in his reign.

Towering over all other events of his pontificate,
however, was the first ecumenical or general council of the Church. An ecumenical council repre-
sents the entire teaching Church as opposed to a
diocesan synod or a metropolitan or a national
council. The ecumenical council, like the pope, is
infallible in matters of faith and morals because it
is the voice of the teaching Church.

A heresy had arisen in Alexandria and at that
time was making great headway throughout the
East, the heresy of Arius, a priest of Alexandria.
Arius taught that Jesus Christ was not truly divine,
that His nature was not the same as that of the
Father but only similar. It was to study this question and to pronounce the true teaching of the
Church that bishops from all parts of the empire
made their way to Nicaea in 325. The Emperor
Constantine, still a catechumen, had at first made
light of the matter, but when his eyes were opened
to the danger of Arian doctrine by Hosius of Cordova, he became so interested that he went to
Nicaea himself.

Pope Sylvester sent two legates to represent him,
Vitus and Vincentius, and it seems that it was the
Pope who suggested the term consubstantial to de-
scribe the relation of Christ's nature to the Father.
The Council condemned Arius and drew up the
famous Nicene Creed. This creed, said in all the
Catholic Churches throughout the world, pro-
claims that Jesus is true God of true God consubstantial with the Father.

St. Sylvester died in 335. He was buried in a
church which he himself had built over the Catacomb of Priscilla on the Via Salaria. His feast is
kept on December 31.

Giulio Romano. The Raphael Rooms,
the Vatican.

SILVESTER · I ·

FIDES   RELIGIO

ST. MARK

336

ST. MARK, A ROMAN, THE SON OF PRISCUS, SUC-ceeded St. Sylvester as pope on January 18, 336. If an epitaph composed by Pope St. Damasus refers to Pope Mark, as the archeologist De Rossi believes, St. Mark was a man who "filled with the love of God, despised the world . . . the guardian of justice, a true friend of Christ."

Emperor Constantine continued to show his generosity to the Church, for he gave to St. Mark two basilicas and the estates necessary to maintain them. One of these, the Church of St. Mark, still exists, though its present structure does not go back to the fourth century. The other was a cemetery church in the Catacomb of Balbina, a cemetery which lies between the Appian and Ardeatine roads.

St. Mark is said to have decreed that a new pope should be consecrated by the bishop of Ostia. This is quite probable, for this custom is very ancient. He is also said to have decreed that the bishop of Ostia should receive the pallium. The pallium is a vestment of white wool which a pope wears as a symbol of the fullness of his apostolic power and an archbishop wears as a symbol of his participation in that power. An archbishop may not exercise any metropolitan prerogative until he has received the pallium from the pope.

St. Mark died on October 7, 336, after a pontificate of less than a year. He is buried in the cemetery of Balbina, a place he seems to have chosen for himself. His feast is kept on October 7.

Chronologia Summorum Pontificum.

ST. JULIUS I

337-352

WITH POPE ST. JULIUS THE PAPACY FINDS AT its doorstep the vexing problem of the Eastern Arians. It is true that the Council of Nicaea had condemned Arianism, but in spite of that Arians had been growing in strength and had even gained the ear of Constantine, and what was more crucial, that of his son Constantius who succeeded him in the East.

The man who was compelled to face the problem was Julius, a Roman who had been chosen to succeed Mark after an unexplained interval of four months. He soon received delegates from Alexandria asking him to acknowledge a certain Pistus as bishop of Alexandria in place of Athanasius, the mighty fighter for orthodoxy. The delegates tried to prove that Athanasius, who actually had been the victim of Arian intrigue, had been validly deposed. Athanasius on his part also sent envoys and later came to Rome in person to plead his case before the Pope. The Arians asked Julius to hold a synod to decide the case, but when in 341 Julius actually did convene it, they refused to attend. The Pope held it without them and over fifty bishops decreed that Athanasius had been unjustly condemned. Julius informed the Arians at Alexandria of this decision and let them know that he was displeased at their uncooperative attitude.

The Emperor Constans, who ruled in the West, was favorable to the orthodox Christians while his brother Constantius, who ruled the East, was pro-Arian. At this time both Emperors agreed to hold a big general council to see if religious unity could be achieved. Pope Julius approved of the plan and sent legates to Sardica, the modern Sofia, where the council gathered. The council did not achieve religious unity because the Arians, when they found themselves outnumbered, walked out. The council once again vindicated Athanasius and once more repeated the solemn Nicene Creed. It also left an interesting set of regulations on the manner in which appeals to the pope should be made.

In spite of the repeated vindications of Athanasius, that good man was unable to return to his see. Emperor Constans supported the Arian George until the usurper died. Then and only then was the long-suffering Athanasius allowed to go home. Pope Julius, delighted, wrote a letter to the people of Alexandria, congratulating them on the return of their true bishop.

At Rome the number of Christians continued to grow during the pontificate of Julius. He built two new basilicas and three cemetery churches. The stay of St. Athanasius at Rome helped to popularize Egyptian monasticism and gave an impetus to religious life there.

Pope St. Julius died April 12, 352. He was buried in the Cemetery of Calepodius. His feast is kept on April 12.

LIBERIUS

352-366

THE SCENE IS A COUNCIL AT MILAN IN 355. Emperor Constantius demands that Athanasius, bishop of Alexandria, be condemned. The bishops cry out that to do so would be against the canon of the Church. Emperor Constantius, a bandy-legged fellow, roars: "My will is the canon." Five words which clearly and brutally define caesaropapism: The Emperor's will is the rule of the Church. From now on the popes will be troubled again and again by imperial interference, and of this Pope Liberius is an outstanding example.

Liberius was a Roman who succeeded St. Julius as pope in the May of 352. He was soon to face despotic meddling. Constans, emperor in the West, had been killed in a rebellion; and though his brother Constantius mastered the rebels to become sole emperor, this spelled trouble. Constantius, under the influence of Arians, had long vexed the Eastern Church. Now he began to make matters unpleasant for the West. Pope Liberius appealed to him to hold a council. Constantius did so, but bullied the assembled bishops and the papal legates into abandoning Athanasius. Liberius, naturally, was displeased. Another council was held at Milan in 335. Emperor Constantius bluntly told the bishops to obey him or face exile. A few brave souls refused and were promptly banished. Pope Liberius wrote to the victims, hailing them as martyrs.

Constantius realized that his pet project of uniting the Christians by a semi-Arian formula would not succeed as long as the Pope defended orthodoxy. He sent his confidential eunuch to Rome laden with gifts and loud with threats. But when Liberius spurned gifts and threats alike, he was hustled off to the imperial court to be browbeaten by Caesar in person. Constantius angrily asked the Pope who he was to stand out for Athanasius against the world. He then exiled Liberius to Thrace and isolated him from friends and counselors. To rule the Church the Emperor set up an antipope, Felix, but the disgusted Romans refused to cooperate with the imperial whim.

Liberius returned to Rome but what price did he pay? Scholars still dispute the matter. There is evidence that Liberius abandoned Athanasius and signed some vaguely worded compromise formula. In any case, the question is historical not theological, for papal infallibility is not involved.

Whether or not Liberius had a moment of weakness in exile, he continued to fight on for orthodoxy after his return. He deplored the weakness of those bishops who signed a compromise formula at Rimini in 359. He had the satisfaction of seeing the Arians first split into factions, then decline rapidly. Their great power at this period depended on imperial backing; when imperial policy changed they had little to fall back on. And change it did. Julian the Apostate succeeded Constantius in 361. Since Julian despised all Christians, orthodox or Arian, the Church was freed from the smothering embrace of Caesar. Liberius had the joy of receiving back into the Church a large number of moderate Arians.

Liberius died April 12, 366. He is not honored as a saint.

Gentile da Fabriano. "St. Liberius Traces the Foundation of the Church of Santa Maria Maggiore in Rome" (detail). The National Museum, Naples.

ST. DAMASUS I

366-384

After Julian the apostate was cut off in full career by a Persian arrow, the Church in the West enjoyed peace. That brave and capable soldier, Valentinian, was not only a Christian but a Catholic. It was a time for growth and development, and in St. Damasus the Church had a leader suited to the time. Damasus was born in Rome of Spanish descent. He was elected pope by a large majority, but a minority refused to accept the election and set up Ursinus as antipope. Rome rang with tumult until finally Valentinian exiled Ursinus.

Damasus was a capable administrator, a writer, and a holy bishop. He repeatedly condemned heresy yet was so merciful to repentant heretics that the dour old Arian-fighter, Lucifer of Cagliari, actually left the Church in disgust to start a rigorist schism. While Arians still troubled the Church, new heresies added to the difficulties of Damasus. Macedonius was teaching that the Holy Ghost was not divine. Apollinaris was holding that Christ did not have a rational human soul. Both heresies were condemned by Damasus.

In the East the Arians were enjoying a final fling. Valentinian's less capable and less orthodox brother, Valens, was under Arian influence. He made it hot for the orthodox, but in 378 Valens was ridden down by the hard-charging Goths at Adrianople. His successor, Emperor Theodosius, threw his support to the orthodox and asked that a council of the Church in the Eastern Empire be held to settle the matter. This council met at Constantinople in 381. Since it was an Eastern council, Pope Dama-sus does not seem to have had any direct connection with it, but the council adopted the Pope's teaching, recondemned Arianism and made a strong declaration of the divinity of the Holy Ghost against the Macedonians. Damasus approved the doctrinal decrees of the council and it became ranked as an ecumenical council.

Damasus published a canon of Holy Scripture, that is, a list of the books of the Old and New Testaments which are to be considered the inspired word of God. To spread the knowledge of Holy Scripture, the Pope urged his friend the great St. Jerome to translate the Bible. St. Jerome did so and produced that Vulgate edition which has served the Church so long and so usefully.

Damasus was noted, too, for his clear statement on the hierarchy in the Church. Quoting the words of Christ to Peter, "Thou art Peter and upon this rock I will build My church," Damasus says that the Roman Church is above all others. Next in importance comes Alexandria, founded by St. Mark at St. Peter's command, and Antioch, where St. Peter ruled before going to Rome.

Now that the persecutions were over, Damasus worked hard to foster devotion to the martyrs. He encouraged pilgrimages to the catacombs. He built stairways and light wells in the sacred vaults. On the martyrs' tombs he placed inscriptions. Indeed, the Pope himself wrote many of these in excellent verse. He diligently searched the records for accounts of martyrdoms. Historians and archeologists as well as lovers of Holy Writ owe much to this intelligent and pious pope.

Giulio Romano. The Raphael Rooms,
the Vatican.

ST. SIRICIUS

384-399

SIRICIUS WAS A ROMAN, THE SON OF TIBURTIUS. He entered the service of the Church as a youth and served as a deacon from the time of Pope Liberius. He was unanimously elected to succeed Pope Damasus in December of 384.

St. Siricius is noted for being the author of the first papal decretal which has survived. There were earlier ones, but this is the first that has come down to modern times. A decretal contains an authoritative decision on questions of discipline. The occasion of this decretal was a letter from Himerius, bishop of Tarragona in Spain, who wrote to Pope Damasus asking for his decision in several matters of discipline. Siricius answered on February 10, 385, and ordered that his reply should be communicated to the neighboring bishops. Among other things the Pope declared that converted Arians did not have to be rebaptized and that priests should be celibate.

On January 6, 386, Pope Siricius held a synod at Rome, attended by eighty bishops, at which a number of disciplinary decisions were made. The Pope sent these decisions to the bishops of North Africa. He also sent out a letter to various churches urging the election of worthy bishops and priests. But around 388, Siricius was to have something to worry about at home. A monk named Jovinian, who had enjoyed a reputation for a strict life, came to Rome and began to teach that after all a strict life was useless. Vows, virginity, fasting, and good works were of small avail. Jovinian, quite consistently, gave up his strict life and not content with taking it easy himself began to persuade a number of monks and nuns to give it all up and get married. Lay people, scandalized at this, urged Siricius to do something. The Pope then held a synod in 390 which condemned the theories of Jovinian and excommunicated him and his chief followers. Siricius then sent three priests to Milan to tell St. Ambrose about the synod. Ambrose himself held a synod which praised the Pope for his watchfulness and repeated the condemnation of Jovinian.

Pope Siricius received an embassy from the East asking him to put an end to the long-drawn-out schism in the see of Antioch. For years two bishops and their successors had disputed the bishopric. Now Pope Siricius granted the plea that he recognize the last survivor, Flavian, as true bishop and readmit him to communion.

The venerable Basilica of St. Paul's-Without-the-Walls, which was destroyed by fire in 1823, was built by Siricius. He dedicated this famous church in 390.

St. Siricius is buried in the Cemetery of Priscilla. His feast is kept on November 26.

Chronologia Summorum Pontificum.

ST. ANASTASIUS I

399-401

ALTHOUGH THE PONTIFICATE OF ST. ANASTASIUS was brief, he had time to show that watchful care for the preservation of pure doctrine which distinguishes the holders of the Roman See. A Roman, the son of Maximus, Anastasius was elected to succeed Siricius in 399.

One of his first problems was an appeal which had been made to Pope Siricius. At this time (and many other times too) the writings of Origen enjoyed a great vogue. This brilliant but erratic third-century writer exercised a charm over men's minds which, in view of his sometimes less than orthodox opinions, could be dangerous. St. Jerome himself, grim watchdog of orthodoxy that he was, had issued an expurgated edition of Origen's *Homilies*. But heretics were now appealing to the authority of Origen and it was imprudent of St. Jerome's old friend Rufinus to choose this moment for a translation of Origen's philosophical study, *Peri Archon*. He explained, however, that since a greater name had already translated Origen's *Homilies* he felt justified. Jerome was furious. Not at all mollified by the reference to one greater, he attacked his old friend with bitterness. Then Rufinus became angry and told his reading public quite bluntly that Jerome was a defamer. The East rang with the shock of this battle of words, and an ap-peal was made to the Pope. Siricius, probably in view of the personalities involved, had been slow to act, but now St. Anastasius felt that the time had come to speak out. He condemned Origen and deprecated the translation of Rufinus. Shortly after the Pope spoke, the imperial government banned the works of Origen.

St. Anastasius also wrote to the bishops of Africa urging them to keep up the good fight against the Donatist heretics. But again, like so many popes, he was merciful to repentant heretics.

Evidently there was some trouble about unauthorized priests drifting in to Rome, for Anastasius ordered that no priest from across the sea should be received unless he had a letter signed by five bishops. He also decreed that priests should stand with heads bowed while the gospel was being read. He built a basilica called the Crescentian.

St. Anastasius was a friend of the great Fathers of the Church, St. Augustine, St. Jerome, and St. Paulinus. St. Paulinus had a pleasant visit with the Pope. St. Anastasius died in December 401 with the empire on the brink of disaster. St. Jerome says that he was a man of apostolic zeal and great poverty, and that Rome did not deserve to possess him long lest the world's head be cut off while ruled by such a bishop. His feast is kept on December 16.

Negges. Portrait Archive of the Austrian National Library, Vienna.

ST. INNOCENT I

401-417

A FRIGHTFUL STORM WAS BLOWING UP OVER Italy as Anastasius died. The man chosen to succeed him and face the storm was Innocent. Innocent was born at Albanum near Rome. He seems·to have been brought up among the Roman clergy. He was unanimously elected pope in December 401.

The great Theodosius had made his sons Honorius and Arcadius emperors in the West and East respectively. They were weak men quite incapable of coping with the barbarian storm. Honorius, however, had at his side the competent general Stilicho who beat off every attempt of Alaric the Visigoth to get down into Italy. But when in 408 Emperor Honorius had Stilicho killed on suspicion of treason, the gates were open and down came Alaric. Honorius, safe in the fortress of Ravenna, defied the Goth and refused to give terms. Alaric rushed on Rome, but Rome's towers and walls were too much for the wild men who marched with Alaric. The Goths blockaded the city and ravaged the neighborhood. At last on the payment of a large ransom Alaric withdrew to Tuscany. But the ambitious Visigoth was determined to have his way. He kept on demanding from Honorius Dalmatia, Venetia, and Noricum, plus tribute. To save Rome from another attack Pope Innocent personally went with an embassy from Rome to the imperial court at Ravenna. Honorius, safe himself, would not budge. Once more Alaric attacked the city; once more he was baffled by Rome's lofty walls. But on a third attempt, traitors opened the Salarian gate and the Goths poured into the helpless city. For five days the barbarians burned and plundered. The world was shocked by the fall of great Rome. Pope Innocent, still at Ravenna, must have been heartbroken. It was to a ravaged city that he returned.

Oddly enough, Pope Innocent found Honorius more cooperative in ecclesiastical than in civil matters. While the Emperor took steps against heretics, the Pope worked hard to maintain discipline. He issued decretals to Bishop Victricius in Gaul and to the Spanish bishops. Innocent began to hear complaints about a new heresy called Pelagianism and to receive decrees from councils in Jerusalem and Africa condemning it. The Pope approved these decrees, and himself condemned the heresy.

From Constantinople came word that the legitimate patriarch, the great St. John Chrysostom, had been driven from his see. Theophilus, a meddling patriarch of Alexandria, had come to Constantinople and intrigued with the weak Emperor Arcadius to have the golden-tongued orator deposed. Pope Innocent wrote a stern rebuke to the Alexandrian meddler and denounced the intruded usurper.

At home a wealthy matron named Vestina gave Innocent the money to build and endow a church dedicated to Sts. Gervase and Protase. This church still exists under the name of San Vitale.

Pope Innocent died in 417. He is buried in a basilica above the Catacomb of Pontian.

ST. ZOSIMUS

417-418

THAT HE WAS A GREEK, THE SON OF ABRAM, IS all that is known of the early life of St. Zosimus. His pontificate, however, though short, is important for a climax in the fight against Pelagianism.

Pelagius (man of the sea) was the nickname by which Morgan, a tall Britisher, was popularly known. This monk had come to Rome some time around 400, and had established a reputation as a spiritual adviser. After a while he moved on to Palestine, and soon his doctrine had the empire in an uproar. Briefly, Pelagianism denied original sin and the necessity of divine grace to perform meritorious acts, indeed even to win heaven itself. A Roman lawyer nàmed Caelestius and a clever thinker, Julian of Eclanum, proved zealous propagators of the Britisher's heresy. But of course this heresy, so fundamentally opposed to basic Christian truths, aroused great opposition. St. Augustine, especially, attacked it with all his learning and genius. Pope Innocent had received decrees from councils in Jerusalem and Africa condemning Pelagianism and had himself approved the decrees.

After Innocent died, Caelestius went to Rome to make a personal appeal against the decisions of the local councils. A fast talker, he loudly proclaimed that he believed whatever the Pope believed. And while Caelestius was edifying all at Rome by his pious demeanor, Pelagius sent a cleverly worded confession of faith to the Pope. No wonder Zosimus was taken in! He wrote to the African bishops that they had acted hastily in condemning Pelagius and Caelestius, since it was not sure that these gentlemen had taught the doctrine for which they had been blamed. But by an interchange of letters the African bishops were able to unmask the real attitude of Pelagius and Caelestius. Once Pope Zosimus was convinced that the pair actually taught heretical doctrine, he spoke out strongly in a famous *Epistola tractoria* or encyclical letter which clearly and forcefully condemned Pelagius and Pelagianism. Of this epistle, worthy to be ranked with the great modern encyclicals, Prosper of Aquitaine said that it put the sword of Peter into the hands of every bishop. St. Augustine was delighted with it and when Julian of Eclanum clamored for a council, the great doctor coolly replied that competent authority had judged the case.

St. Zosimus decreed that clerics should not drink in taverns. He died December 27, 418, and was buried in the cemetery Church of St. Lawrence in Agro Verano.

ST. BONIFACE I

418-422

AFTER THE DEATH OF POPE ZOSIMUS, THE ARCH-deacon Eulalius at the head of a mob of clerics and laymen seized the Lateran Basilica and prevented the rest of the priests from entering and holding the election of the pope according to custom. They then elected Eulalius himself. Meanwhile the majority of the priests set the election for the next day; and since they could not hold it in the Lateran, they agreed to meet in the Church of Theodora. There they elected an old priest, Boniface.

Boniface, a Roman of high character, was consecrated in the Church of St. Marcellus, while Fulalius was consecrated in the Lateran. The rebels succeeded in getting the traditional consecrator of the pope, the bishop of Ostia, to perform the function.

Rome was in a bad way with two men claiming to be the true pope. Both appealed to Emperor Honorius at Ravenna. Honorius, undecided, held a gathering of Italian bishops to discuss the ticklish situation, but no decision was reached. The Emperor then called for a larger council, to which he invited the bishops of Gaul and Africa. The council decided that neither claimant should celebrate Easter in Rome while the case was being decided. Boniface obeyed, but Eulalius entered the city in Passion Week, refused to obey the prefect's order to get out, and finally with a gang of partisans seized the Lateran. The imperial officials had to use force to get him out.

At last a letter from Honorius announced that the council had decided that Boniface was the legitimate pope and that he should be received as such. On April 10, St. Boniface solemnly entered the city amid the cheers of the populace. Even so, a year later when Boniface became sick, the partisans of Eulalius raised their heads; but they were unable to upset the sick Pope.

Boniface continued the fight against the Pelagian heresy on two fronts. While he asked St. Augustine to write a treatise refuting the heretics, he obtained from Emperor Honorius a decree ordering all bishops to subscribe to the condemnation of Pelagius and Caelestius. He used his influence with Honorius also to preserve his jurisdiction as patriarch over Illyricum. Theodosius II, now Emperor of the East, had detached that area from the Western Patriarchate and placed it under the patriarchal jurisdiction of Constantinople. Honorius succeeded in persuading Theodosius to repeal the decree.

St. Boniface I died September 4, 422. His feast is kept on October 25.

Negges. Portrait Archive of the Austrian National Library, Vienna.

ST. CELESTINE I

422-432

TWO ACTS MAKE THE PONTIFICATE OF ST. CELEStine outstanding: the condemnation of the Nestorian heresy and the sending of St. Patrick to Ireland.

A Campanian, Celestine was said to have lived for a while with St. Ambrose at Milan. He was certainly a deacon at Rome in the time of Pope Innocent I. In contrast to the stormy election of Pope Boniface, Celestine's seems to have been quiet and harmonious. Once pope, St. Celestine continued the fight against now dying Pelagianism. He had the satisfaction of seeing it die away in Britain, the native isle of its founder, under the spirited attack of St. Germanus of Auxerre and St. Lupus of Troyes. When the heresy in the diluted form known as Semi-Pelagianism raised its head in Gaul, Celestine wrote against this new danger. A great friend of St. Augustine, he wrote a letter to the bishops of Gaul on the occasion of the mighty father's death, praising him and forbidding all attacks on his memory. The Pope also got the Council of Ephesus to condemn Pelagianism.

But the third great ecumenical council held at Ephesus in 431 was chiefly concerned with still another new heresy. Nestorius, a priest of Antioch, had become patriarch of Constantinople. From the eminence of this lofty position he taught the new doctrine that in Christ there are not only two natures, which is correct, but that there are also two persons, which is incorrect. A logical consequence was that Mary was not the Mother of God but only of the human person of Christ. This aroused horror even in Constantinople itself, while St. Cyril, the patriarch of Alexandria, attacked the new doctrine most vigorously. Both Nestorius and Cyril were soon clamoring to the Pope for a decision. Celestine held a synod at Rome in 430 and condemned Nestorianism. Nestorius was to be deposed and excommunicated if he persisted in teaching false doctrine. Nestorius refused to submit, all the more because Cyril, who had been made the Pope's agent in the matter, demanded more than Celestine had asked. A general council was called to meet at Ephesus in 431. The council condemned Nestorianism, to the great joy of the people.

It is probable, though not certain, that St. Celestine a short time before his death personally commissioned St. Patrick to preach the gospel to the Irish. At any rate, it was at this time that Patrick did begin his marvelous work. St. Prosper of Aquitaine says that Celestine saved the Roman island for the faith and to the "barbarous" island brought the light of Christ.

At Rome Celestine restored the Church of Santa Maria in Trastevere, which had been destroyed by the Goths. He also caused some interesting pictures of the saints to be painted in the Church of St. Sylvester.

St. Celestine died on July 27, 432. His feast is kept on July 27. The Greek Church also honors Celestine because of his part in putting down the Nestorian heresy.

Mosaic in the Basilica of St. Paul-Outside-the-Walls, Rome.

ST. SIXTUS III

432-440

SIXTUS WAS ONE OF THOSE GENTLE SOULS WHO seem to exist for the purpose of binding wounds and healing bruises. A Roman, prominent among the clergy, a friend of St. Augustine, Sixtus was a natural choice for pope. He set himself the task of consolidating the victory over Pelagianism and Nestorianism by kindness and gentleness. Indeed, at one time it appeared as if that clever protagonist of Pelagianism, Julian of Eclanum, was about to pull the wool over the Pope's eyes. But his insincerity was unmasked, and Sixtus refused him readmittance into the Church. At the side of Sixtus in this matter stood a deacon named Leo whose aid was very valuable to the Pope. Of him more shall be heard.

The Pope's kindness had happier results with the Nestorians. In 433, Sixtus held a council at Rome at which he announced that Cyril of Alexandria had informed him that many Nestorian leaders had returned to the Church. Certainly Sixtus made it easy for them to do so.

The condemnation of Nestorianism had been a striking vindication of the honor paid to Mary as Mother of the Person who is God. Indeed, just as the word *consubstantial* was the keyword of orthodoxy against the Arians, so *theotokos* (Mother of God) was the keyword of orthodoxy against the Nestorians. The Council of Ephesus precipitated a spontaneous outburst of devotion to Mary. St. Sixtus celebrated the council by rebuilding the old basilica of Pope Liberius and decorating it with magnificent mosaics picturing the childhood of Jesus and the life of Mary. The church, which was dedicated to the Mother of God, is called St. Mary Major.

Sixtus III did much for the churches in Rome. Not only did he redecorate St. Mary Major but he obtained from Emperor Valentinian III a golden image adorned with jewels on which the twelve apostles were represented. This he placed over the tomb of St. Peter. He did some restoration in the old Lateran Basilica and he erected a silver altar and porphyry columns in the Church of St. Lawrence.

St. Sixtus III died August 19, 440. He was buried in that Church of St. Lawrence he did so much to adorn. His feast is kept on August 19.

ST. LEO I, THE GREAT

440-461

"A BURDEN TO SHUDDER AT"—THUS ST. LEO I spoke of the papal office. Yet few have been so capable of bearing that burden as the clever, energetic, and holy Tuscan who succeeded St. Sixtus III. A deacon in the Church at Rome, Leo was absent in Gaul on an important mission for the Emperor when St. Sixtus III died. He returned to find himself pope.

To rule the mid-fifth-century Church was not easy. The West was filled with the clamor of barbarians wandering through provinces which had lost the nerve to resist. The East was troubled with a new and dangerous heresy. How Leo faced both situations is the story of his pontificate.

Leo acted strongly against all heresies, but the dogmatic crisis of his pontificate arose when the Constantinople monk Eutyches and the patriarch of Alexandria, Dioscorus, began to teach that in Christ there is only one nature. This Monophysite (one-nature) heresy made such progress in the East that St. Flavian, the patriarch of Constantinople, called on the Pope to do something about it. Leo did. In a famous letter to Flavian, the Pope so clearly and forcefully exposed and condemned the Monophysite error that this letter has been venerated as a creed.

The Monophysites, however, gained the ear of the Eastern Emperor, Theodosius II, and succeeded in holding a packed synod at Ephesus. There they so maltreated the saintly Flavian that he died, and they proclaimed the Monophysite error to be true Christian doctrine. Leo came to the rescue. In stinging words he characterized the Ephesus affair as a robbery, and the name has lived. To this day it is known as the robber synod. To counteract Monophysite influence on Theodosius, Leo got Valentinian III, the Western Emperor, to wake up his cousin to the danger of fostering heresy. Though Theodosius died, his successor Marcion heeded the Pope. To settle the matter a great council, the fourth ecumenical, was called to meet at Chalcedon in 451. There the fathers condemned Eutyches and accepted Leo's letter as the symbol of orthodox belief. Though the Monophysite heresy lingered long to trouble the Eastern Church, this great council killed its chance to win the East.

In the West imperial feebleness forced Leo to stand as buffer between his people and barbarian hordes. Attila the Hun, checked at Châlons, had burst over the Alps in 452. Leo went north to meet Attila. On the banks of the Mincio these two giants of the age met, one representing brute might, the other, moral force. And Leo prevailed. Attila agreed to make peace and spare Rome. Three years later when a Vandal fleet sailed up the Tiber, the panic-stricken Romans turned to their bishop. The Pope went outside the walls to meet Genseric, the Vandal king. Genseric agreed to spare the lives and homes of the Romans. Then for fourteen days the Vandals helped themselves to the wealth of imperial Rome, but true to Genseric's promise to the Pope, they set no fires and kept their swords sheathed.

The many-sidedness of Leo is a marvel. Diplomat, statesman, administrator, theologian, orator, and above all a holy man, this pope well deserves the title, Leo the Great.

Giulio Romano. The Raphael Rooms, the Vatican.

ST. HILARY

461-468

To replace a man like Leo was not easy, but the next pope was a man after Leo's heart, the archdeacon Hilary. Hilary was a Sardinian who had joined the Roman clergy and had been sent by St. Leo as one of the papal legates to the council at Ephesus in 449. This council, intended to settle the Monophysite affair, got out of hand. Packed with Monophysites and presided over by Dioscorus, the patriarch of Alexandria, the assembly refused to listen to the protests of the papal legates. Dioscorus steam-rollered through the council a condemnation of the orthodox and saintly Flavian, patriarch of Constantinople, and an approval of the Monophysite leader Eutyches. In vain Hilary protested. He had to fly in fear for his life and hide in a chapel of St. John the Evangelist. It was only with difficulty that he got back to Rome. No wonder St. Leo called this Ephesus council a gathering of robbers!

As pope, Hilary worked hard to foster order in the Gallic hierarchy. When a certain Hermes illegally made himself archbishop of Narbonne, two Gallic delegates came to Rome to appeal to Pope Hilary. He held a council at Rome in 462 to settle the matter. He also upheld the rights of the see of Arles to be the primatial see of Gaul. From Spain also came appeals of a similar nature. To settle these Hilary held a council at Rome in 465. This is the first Council at Rome whose acts have come down to us. According to the *Liber Pontificalis* he sent a letter to the East confirming the ecumenical councils of Nicaea, Ephesus, and Chalcedon, and the famous dogmatic letter of his predecessor St. Leo to Flavian. He also publicly in St. Peter's rebuked the shadow-emperor Anthemius for allowing a favorite of his to foster heresy in Rome.

St. Hilary deserves great credit for his work in building and decorating churches in Rome. Of especial interest is the oratory he built near the Lateran, dedicated to St. John the Evangelist. The Pope attributed his escape from the wild Monophysites at Ephesus to the intercession of the Beloved Disciple, and to show his gratitude he built this beautiful oratory. Over its doors may still be seen the inscription, "To his deliverer, Blessed John the Evangelist, Bishop Hilary, the Servant of Christ." Hilary built two more churches and spent freely in decorating still others. The gold and silver and marble used so lavishly by this Pope in adorning the Roman churches indicate that the wealthy families of Rome must have saved something from the grasping hands of Goths and Vandals.

St. Hilary died on February 29. His feast is kept on February 28.

Mosaic in the Basilica of St. Paul-Outside-the-Walls, Rome.

ST. SIMPLICIUS

468-483

ST. SIMPLICIUS, A NATIVE OF TIVOLI, WAS ELECTED to succeed St. Hilary. His election was peaceful, his pontificate stormy. The empire in the West was dying. After the murder of Valentinian III back in 455, a succession of nine shadow-emperors held the throne. Most of these were tools of barbarian generals, and finally in the time of Pope Simplicius in 476 the Heruli chieftain Odovakar deposed the last of these little monarchs and informed Emperor Zeno at Constantinople that he would rule the West for him. By this time, anyway, the imperial government had ceased to exercise much influence in the West. Visigoths ruled Spain, Franks and other tribes dominated Gaul, Vandals controlled Africa, and Britain had long been abandoned to Picts and Scots, Angles and Saxons.

The Pope was not much troubled by the change. Odovakar, though an Arian, treated the Church well. But Simplicius was very much troubled by affairs in the East.

In 475 a usurper named Basiliscus drove Emperor Zeno from the throne. Basiliscus favored the Monophysites, and now these heretics enjoyed a very resurrection. Timothy the Cat, that old Monophysite who had been deposed from the see of Alexandria by Emperor Marcion, now returned in triumph. Peter the Fuller took over Antioch. The usurper Basiliscus issued an imperial decree known as the *Encyclion* which ordered the dogmatic letter of St. Leo to Flavian and the acts of the Council of Chalcedon to be burned. It looked as if the whole East trembled on the brink of heresy

as five hundred bishops actually subscribed to this audacious bit of imperial dogmatizing. Acacius, the patriarch of Constantinople, still held firm, and to his rescue came Pope Simplicius. He strongly encouraged the monks and clergy of Constantinople to resist the usurper's tyranny. But though Constantinople held firm, Antioch and Alexandria were in heretic hands. When Timothy the Cat died, he was succeeded by his friend the equally ardent Monophysite, Peter the Hoarse.

Just when things looked worst, Emperor Zeno made a comeback and regained the throne. Out went the intruded Monophysite bishops. Back came the Catholics. Pope Simplicius could feel that he had helped the East survive a fierce tempest. The time of peace, however, was very short. When the Catholic patriarch of Alexandria died, the Catholics elected John Talaia to succeed him. The Monophysites once more elected Peter the Hoarse. Now the Emperor Zeno and Patriarch Acacius began to favor the Monophysite, Peter. Strange this! But politics were at work. Zeno, alarmed at the strength of the Monophysites, was thinking of a way to pacify them, and Acacius was hand in glove with the Emperor. In spite of the Pope's protests, Peter the Hoarse was recognized as true patriarch of Alexandria. Then Peter went to Constantinople, where he joined Zeno and Acacius to cook up a compromise known as the *Henoticon.* This was in 482 while Simplicius still lived; but he died before the storm reached its peak.

St. Simplicius built four churches in Rome. He died in 483. His feast is kept on March 2.

Negges. Portrait Archive of the Austrian National Library, Vienna.

ST. FELIX II

483-492

ST. FELIX II HAS THE EXTRAORDINARY DISTINCTION of being not only a pope and saint himself, but the great-grandfather of another pope and saint, Gregory the Great. Felix had been married, but his wife had died before he became a priest. He was a member of an old Roman family of senatorial rank.

No sooner was he elected pope than Felix faced the vexing problem posed by Emperor Zeno's ill-considered attempt to unify the East by compromise. One of the evils which result from politicians meddling in church matters is the tendency to make a deal. And that is just what Zeno did. Alarmed by the hold that the Monophysites had on Egypt and Syria, Zeno issued his famous *Henoticon* (act of union) and ordered all to subscribe to it. This *Henoticon* was a creed drawn up by Acacius, the hitherto orthodox patriarch of Constantinople, and Peter, the Monophysite patriarch of Alexandria. It was orthodox in what it said, but implicitly it condoned the Monophysite heresy by omitting the decision of the Council of Chalcedon and the letter of Pope Leo to Flavian. Like so many compromises it pleased few. The more ardent Monophysites refused to follow their leader, Peter, and Pope Felix denounced it. With true spiritual independence, he warned the Emperor not to interfere in theological matters and "to allow the Catholic Church to govern itself by its own laws."

Pope Felix sent legates to Constantinople to summon Acacius to Rome, but to his dismay the Pope discovered that his legates had approved the election of the Monophysite Peter as patriarch of Alexandria and had communicated with heretics—in short, had sold him out. Felix held a synod at Rome in 484 at which he excommunicated the untrustworthy legates. He also excommunicated Acacius, but the patriarch remained stubborn. Thus started the Acacian schism in which Constantinople was officially separated from the Roman Church over the *Henoticon*. Even after Acacius died, the schism dragged on until the next century.

In the last years of this pontificate Theodoric led his Ostrogoths into Italy to defeat Odovakar and take over the rule of Italy—all in the name of Emperor Zeno. Though an Arian, Theodoric treated the Church well. It was different in Africa, where in the early years of his reign Felix heard anguished cries for help from the hapless Catholics. Hunneric, the Arian Vandal, ruthlessly harried the poor African Catholics. Pope Felix got Emperor Zeno to bring his influence to bear on the fierce Vandal, but this accomplished little. After Hunneric died, the persecution slackened, and the Pope then helped to get the Church in Africa on its feet. He followed the usual papal policy of mildness towards weak brethren who had given way in the storm.

Pope St. Felix died March 1, 492. He is buried in St. Paul's on the Ostian Way.

The National Museum, Florence.

ST. GELASIUS I

492-496

"MORE A SERVANT THAN A SOVEREIGN"—THUS Dionysius Exiguus describes St. Gelasius I. Yet he spoke so beautifully of the majesty of Peter's see that his words have been quoted down the ages. As late as the last ecumenical council, Pope Gelasius was quoted as an authority on papal infallibility.

Gelasius was an African either by birth or descent. A member of the Roman clergy, he worked in close cooperation with St. Felix II, and when he became pope he continued the policy of his predecessor. Gelasius found the Church of Constantinople still in schism. Although the patriarch Euphemius had returned to orthodoxy, he refused to strike the name of Acacius from the diptychs. The diptychs were tablets used in the churches of those days on which were written the names of living and dead dignitaries. Since they were visible signs of the communion of saints, the names of all in heresy or schism or under excommunication were excluded from these diptychs. A number of bishops appealed to Gelasius to relent and readmit Constantinople to communion, but the Pope explained that it was a question not of personality but of principle, that to allow the name of Acacius to remain on the diptychs would be to repudiate his predecessor's actions against the Monophysite compromisers. Gelasius also defended the rights of the ancient patriarchates of Alexandria and Antioch against the encroachments of Constantinople.

Although the Pope had his troubles with Emperor Anastasius over the *Henoticon*, he got along well with the Arian Theodoric. His difficulty at home arose, not from the government, but from a group of superstitious Romans. A plague had afflicted the city and these superstitious citizens, led by the Senator Andromachus, revived the Lupercalia to bring back good luck to the city. The Lupercalia were originally a pagan rite celebrated in mid-February, but it became a good luck superstition. Youths clad in skins ran around the city with whips to chase away bad luck. They struck any woman they met a blow which was supposed to confer fertility. That such rank superstition should be revived was a challenge to the Pope and vigorously he met it. Gelasius forbade all Catholics to have anything to do with the affair, and wrote against it so vigorously that he soon ended the mischievous nonsense.

Gelasius, like his predecessor, spoke firmly to the Emperor on the need of independence for the Church. No history of political theory is complete without a discussion of this pope's masterly exposition of the role of Church and State in a famous letter to Emperor Anastasius. Gelasius defends the position of the Church as a perfect society, and at the same time recognizes the legitimate functions of both Church and State.

Although a great writer, Gelasius made his strongest impression as a man of holiness. Prayerful and austere, he loved the companionship of monks. He was outstanding for his sense of justice and above all for his charity to the poor. "Great even among the saints," Gelasius died November 21, 496.

ANASTASIUS II

496-498

ANASTASIUS II IS A MUCH-MALIGNED POPE. Misunderstood by his contemporaries, he has been abused by medieval historians, and even placed in hell by Dante! Modern historical research, however, has cleared the memory of this pope.

Anastasius II, a Roman, was a man of kindly and peaceable disposition. Distressed at the continued schism of Constantinople, he sent legates to the Emperor and messages of peace to the Patriarch. He did not sacrifice principle. He continued to demand the condemnation of the schismatic, Acacius. But the Romans seem to have misunderstood this, and they began to grumble. Their indignation flamed higher when they learned that Pope Anastasius had received back into communion Archbishop Andrew of Thessalonica, who had been an ardent partisan of the schismatic Acacius. They do not seem to have realized that Archbishop Andrew had repented and had repudiated Acacius and returned to Catholic unity.

The confusion of the Romans was caused perhaps at least partially by the indiscreet remarks of Photinus, Andrew's legate to the Pope. At the same time the pro-Byzantine intrigues of the Senator Festus caused the Romans to be intensely suspicious. All this resulted in a good deal of bitterness on the part of Roman clergy and laity against peace-loving Pope Anastasius.

Anastasius, however, was unable to effect the reunion which he desired and was spared the necessity of pacifying his disturbed Romans by his sudden death in 498.

The *Liber Pontificalis* remarks that he was cut down by divine intervention; but Duchesne regards this as a manifestation of party feeling rather than the recording of cold history. There is no historical justification at all for the horrible death dreamed up for him by the more imaginative chroniclers of the Middle Ages.

While Pope Anastasius was having his troubles, an event full of future significance took place in Gaul. Clovis, the Frankish king, was baptized by St. Remigius.

Chronologia Summorum Pontificum.

ST. SYMMACHUS

498-514

THE DEATH OF ANASTASIUS LEFT ROME TENSE with bitterness and suspicion as two factions struggled for control. The first and larger was the group which, out of misunderstanding, had grumbled at the late Pope's peace policy. The other faction was the pro-Byzantine party led by Senator Festus. This intriguer was anxious to make Rome conform to the imperial wish concerning Zeno's *Henoticon*. The clergy gathered at the Lateran on November 22, 498, and elected Symmachus. Later that same day, the pro-Byzantine minority went to St. Mary Major and elected an antipope, Lawrence. Off to Ravenna went embassies from pope and antipope to Theodoric. Theodoric wisely decided to recognize Symmachus because he had been elected first and by a majority. Lawrence bowed and was made bishop of Nocera.

Symmachus, a Sardinian who had been baptized at Rome and had been a deacon there, took steps to prevent a recurrence of the trouble. He held a synod on March 1, 499, which passed stringent decrees against electioneering for the papacy. The next year he welcomed Theodoric to Rome. The great Ostrogoth received a splendid reception, and in turn promised to respect the privileges of the Romans.

The pro-Byzantine party raised its head again in 501. Led by Festus, they accused the Pope of all kinds of crimes from celebrating Easter on the wrong date to immoral conduct. When Theodoric sent for Symmachus, the Pope boldly refused to be judged by a secular ruler. Theodoric then requested a synod to settle the matter, and sent, as Visitor to Rome, Bishop Peter of Altinum.

The Pope agreed to the synod but refused to accept the Visitor. When, with his approval, the synod met, Symmachus demanded his complete reinstatement before answering any charge. Though the synod agreed to this, Theodoric did not. The Pope then gave in, and set out for the synod, but was attacked by partisans of the pro-Byzantine faction and driven back to St. Peter's.

This outrage ended his complaisance, and he refused to have anything more to do with the synod. Embarrassed, the synod broke up declaring that it had no competence to judge a pope, and that Symmachus should be regarded as free from all crime.

Theodoric, however, refused to accept this, and the pro-Byzantine faction brought back Antipope Lawrence and installed him in the Lateran. For four years this schism dragged on, to the distress of the faithful. The patient Pope was gradually winning back the adherents of Lawrence when Theodoric changed his mind, and by withdrawing his support from the schismatics, put an end to the matter.

In spite of all this trouble, Symmachus kept an eye on the East and rebuked Emperor Anastasius for his support of the Monophysite heresy. As firmly as Gelasius, the Pope maintained the independence of his spiritual power. He found time to do a good deal of building in Rome, including three refuges for the poor. He also sent alms to the persecuted Catholics of Africa. St. Symmachus died July 19, 514. Venerated as a saint, his feast is kept on that day.

Mosaic in the Basilica of St. Paul-Outside-the-Walls, Rome.

ST. HORMISDAS

514-523

GLOOM AND STORM MARKED THE PONTIFICATES of Anastasius II and Symmachus, but on St. Hormisdas the sun of peace and victory shone with cheerful splendor. St. Hormisdas was born at Frosinone in the Roman Campagna. Married before ordination, he had a son, Silverius, who also became pope. As a deacon, Hormisdas had staunchly backed St. Symmachus in his trouble with the antipope Lawrence and the pro-Byzantine faction. Elected with difficulty, St. Hormisdas began his career of peace with victory by receiving back into the Church the last die-hards of the Laurentian schism.

A greater victory was in the making. Ever since 484 the Church of Constantinople had been in schism. First, Patriarch Acacius had supported the *Henoticon* and had died excommunicated and in schism. Then even when the patriarchs had returned to orthodoxy, they could not bring themselves to strike the name of Acacius from the liturgical diptychs or tablets. The fact that Emperor Anastasius, who ruled during most of this time, tended to the Monophysite heresy did not help matters. But more and more the orthodox clergy, monks, and laity of the East longed for an end to this schism which weakened their stand against the Monophysites.

In 514 General Vitalian revolted and forced Anastasius to make overtures towards reunion; but since Anastasius was not serious, nothing came of this attempt. A number of Eastern bishops, however, independently made their submission to Rome. When Anastasius died in 517 hopes rose. His successor, the rugged soldier Justin I was orthodox. Popular opinion, the Emperor, and orthodoxy for once all agreeing, the way to reunion was easy. A synod at Constantinople sent a legate to Pope Hormisdas to seek reunion.

The Pope sent back a legation with a formula of faith, and on Holy Thursday, March 28, 519, the papal legates received the Church of Constantinople back to Catholic unity. The ceremony was hailed with tears of joy, for this union was extremely popular.

The formula of Hormisdas which the Pope sent to be signed on this occasion is a masterpiece of clarity. It repeats the condemnation of the heresies condemned by the ecumenical councils and it formally condemns the memory of Acacius who had started this schism. It so clearly stated the primacy and infallibility of the Roman See that from that day to the time of the Vatican Council, it has been a powerful weapon in the arsenal of Catholic orthodoxy. It was subscribed to by the patriarch of Constantinople, it swept the East and in the end was signed by 2,500 bishops.

Another joyous moment for St. Hormisdas came when word was brought from Africa that after the death of the Vandal king Thrasamund, the hard-pressed African Church enjoyed a little peace.

Hormisdas forbade the use of the expression "one of the Trinity was crucified," not because it could not be understood in a true sense, but because it was used as a Monophysite catchword. He sent letters to the bishops of Gaul and Spain on disciplinary matters.

When St. Hormisdas died in 523 the Church was, on the whole, peaceful, but black clouds were piling up in the West.

Mosaic in the Basilica of St. Paul-Outside-the-Walls, Rome

ST. JOHN I

523-526

JOHN, A TUSCAN, THE ARCHDEACON OF THE Roman clergy, was elected to succeed St. Hormisdas, but he was not to enjoy the same prosperity as his predecessor. Now that the Acacian schism had ended in the East and an orthodox emperor ruled at Constantinople, the hitherto mild Theodoric began to make trouble at home. The Ostrogoth king was growing old and suspicious. He regarded the new friendliness between Rome and Constantinople as a possible danger to his regime. His suspicion rose to fury when he heard that Emperor Justin had taken measures against the Arian heretics in the East and had deprived them of their churches. The angry Goth seems at first to have thought of waging war in favor of his fellow Arians. Then he decided to see what he could accomplish by an embassy. He summoned Pope John to Ravenna and imposed upon him the decidedly disagreeable task of going to Constantinople at the head of this embassy to ask the orthodox emperor to restore the churches to the Arians. John objected, but Theodoric packed him and the embassy on board ship and away they sailed for Constantinople.

The mission was embarrassing but the journey glorious. Wherever they stopped the Pope was hailed with joy, and when they approached Constantinople, Pope John was met at the twelfth milestone by a brilliant procession of clergy carrying crosses and candles.

Emperor Justin received him with the highest honors. On Easter Sunday, April 19, 526, he celebrated Mass in Sancta Sophia. He crowned the Emperor. He received enthusiastic pledges of loyalty from the Eastern bishops. Alexandria alone, now hardening in its Monophysite heresy, remained aloof.

This glorification of Pope John by the devout people of Constantinople was his Thabor. Calvary was before him. Theodoric was waiting for him, now a brutal Theodoric who had just butchered the gentle philosopher Boethius and the senator Symmachus. When the Pope got back to Ravenna Theodoric threw him into prison. Already tired by his journey and worn by new sufferings, Pope John did not last long in a prison cell. He died May 18, 526. He was buried outside the walls of Ravenna, but later his body was brought back to Rome and buried in St. Peter's. St. John is honored by the Church as a martyr; his feast is kept on May 27.

Mosaic in the Basilica of St. Paul-Outside-the-Walls, Rome.

ST. FELIX III

526-530

WHEN THEODORIC LEARNED THAT HIS VICTIM, Pope St. John, had died in prison he took measures to ensure that the next pope would be friendly. He put forward as his candidate Felix of Samnium, a priest of the Roman Church. The King's wishes were respected, and Felix, a man of excellent character anyway, was elected.

In spite of being a royal nominee Felix proved to be a good pope. He used his favor with the Gothic Court to help the Church. Theodoric did not long survive his illustrious victim, Pope John, and died on August 30, 526. He was succeeded by his grandson, Athalaric, a lad of ten. The real power was the Queen Mother, Amalasuntha. This lady, Theodoric's daughter, was quite favorable to the Church, and from her Pope Felix secured a decree, drawn up by the noble old Cassiodorus, which reserved the trial of clerics to the pope. Violations of this law of clerical immunity were to be punished by a heavy fine, and any money thus obtained was to go to the poor. The Pope also received two temples in the Roman forum, that of Romulus, and that of the Sacred City. These he made over into the Church of Sts. Cosmas and Damian. The church still stands and to this day may be seen there mosaics made by order of Pope Felix.

In Gaul there had arisen a mitigated form of Pelagianism. This Semi-Pelagianism had been taught by the ascetic John Cassian and a clever writer, Faustus of Riez. It lingered in Gaul, and St. Caesarius of Arles called on the Pope to help him fight this heresy. Pope Felix backed St. Caesarius by his approval, and by trying to circulate the saint's book against the Semi-Pelagians. He also sent a list of canons which explained the Catholic doctrine on grace against the Semi-Pelagian heresy. These were incorporated in the decrees of the Second Council of Orange, held in 529, which did much to end the Semi-Pelagians.

In 529, too, an event happened of profound importance. St. Benedict founded the Monastery of Monte Cassino, the mother abbey of those hosts of monasteries which did so much for the Church and for civilization. Monasticism was already a powerful force, but St. Benedict is rightly regarded as the patriarch of Western monks. His rule—holy, wise, moderate—has been a ladder to perfection for millions.

By 530 Felix was gravely ill. He worried a good deal about the future, for party feeling was running high in Rome. Pro-Goths clashed with pro-Byzantines as the shadow of the reconquest loomed over the city. In these disturbed circumstances Felix felt justified in taking an extraordinary step. He chose his own successor! He gave his own pallium to the archdeacon Boniface and solemnly proclaimed that he should be the next pope. He died shortly after in 530.

Mosaic in the Basilica of St. Paul-Outside-the-Walls, Rome.

BONIFACE II

530-532

THE CLERGY AND PEOPLE OF ROME HAD YIELDED to the wish of Theodoric and elected Felix, but there was great dissatisfaction with the quite irregular, though well-meant, attempt of Felix to appoint his own successor. When Felix died, the majority of the clergy and people refused to accept his nominee, the archdeacon Boniface, and elected instead the clever diplomat Dioscorus, a Greek from Alexandria. Dioscorus had served the papacy brilliantly on important missions. He was consecrated in the Lateran Basilica while Boniface had to be contented with the Julian Basilica. With two claimants consecrated, it looked as if Rome was in for a bad time; but in less than a month Dioscorus was dead. His followers wisely chose to submit to Boniface. Boniface made them anathematize the memory of Dioscorus and agree that he had the right to appoint his successor.

Boniface, though a Roman himself, was the son of Sigisbald, a fact of some interest because it is the first German name connected with a pope. At first he seemed to proceed with rather a high hand. Not only did he compel the Roman clergy and people to recognize his right to appoint his successor, but he soon summoned a synod in St. Peter's and announced that he had appointed the deacon Vigilius to succeed him and to be the next pope.

The people took it quietly, but soon resentment was sweeping Rome at this highhanded procedure. When Boniface realized that the city was seething with dissatisfaction, he did a big thing. He summoned another synod to St. Peter's and this time he announced that he had been wrong in seeking to appoint his successor. Then in the presence of the clergy he burned the decree appointing Vigilius the next pope.

The old Roman Senate still existed and it is interesting to note that its last decree which has come down to us concerned papal elections. The decree forbade under punishment any bribery in papal elections. This only reinforced Church law, but that the Senate considered it necessary throws light on the disturbed conditions of the time.

Boniface II approved of the decrees of the Second Council of Orange in Gaul, which condemned the Semi-Pelagian error. He helped to reorganize the Church in Africa, now rebuilding after the storm of the Vandal persecution.

Boniface II was a very charitable man. He spent a great deal on the poor, especially when a famine threatened the city. He died in 532 and was buried in St. Peter's.

Negges. Portrait Archive of the Austrian National Library, Vienna.

JOHN II

533-535

IT WAS A GOOD TWO MONTHS AFTER THE DEATH of Boniface II before a successor was chosen, two months which may have been filled with shady electioneering. At last, however, on January 2, 533, the priest Mercurius was elected pope. Mercurius changed his name to John, the first instance of a pope doing this. He had been the priest in charge of St. Clement's Church on the Coelian Hill.

An official complained to the Gothic court at Ravenna that there had been bribery and that even sacred vessels had been offered for sale during the two months' vacancy. King Athalaric then ordered that the decree of the Senate against bribery in papal elections should be carved on marble and set up in the court of St. Peter's. Athalaric added to the decree that henceforth when any disputed papal election should be brought to Ravenna, a sum of money should be paid—the money to go to the poor.

John II got along well with both the government at Ravenna and the imperial government at Constantinople. Emperor Justinian sent him a profession of faith and some rich gifts, including a gold chalice that was richly set with precious stones.

The formula "One of the Trinity was crucified," which had been frowned on by Pope Hormisdas, now began to be used again in the East. Emperor Justinian defended it, while those tireless watch-dogs of orthodoxy the "sleepless" monks opposed it. This time the Pope approved its use. There was no contradiction. Hormisdas had frowned on it, not because it was heretical, but because the Monophysites were using it as a catchword. Now, since it was being used as a catchword of orthodoxy against the Nestorians, Pope John II approved of it.

From Gaul, John received the sad case of Bishop Contumeliosus of Riez. This bishop seems to have fallen into grave sin and to have seized some church property. St. Caesarius of Arles treated the matter in a synod held at Marseilles in 533. He sent the decisions of the synod to the Pope, and John II confirmed them. Contumeliosus was to be confined in a monastery and to make good from his own property what he had taken from the church.

John II died in 535 and was buried in St. Peter's.

Chronologia Summorum Pontificum.

ST. AGAPETUS I

535-536

THE PONTIFICATE OF ST. AGAPETUS I, THOUGH short, is filled with interest. The son of a priest who had been killed in the stormy days of Pope Symmachus, he was archdeacon of the Roman clergy when elected. Agapetus was evidently one of the majority which had backed Dioscorus in the struggle against the appointed pope, Boniface II. At any rate, one of the first things he did was to seek the decree which Boniface had issued anathematizing Disocorus and have it publicly burned.

From Gaul Agapetus received an appeal from Contumeliosus, bishop of Riez, who had been condemned for immorality by a synod headed by St. Caesarius of Arles. Agapetus ordered St. Caesarius to give the accused bishop a new trial. He ratified the decrees of a council held at Cathage. Of interest to lovers of education is the fact that Agapetus cooperated with Cassiodorus in founding his famous monastery at Vivarium.

The main interest of this pontificate, however, lies in the mission to Constantinople which concluded it. King Theodahad, a nephew of Theodoric, asked the Pope to go to Constantinople to plead with Emperor Justinian to call off the threatened invasion of Italy. The Pope agreed to go, all the more readily because he had learned that the Monophysites once more threatened Constantinople. He even pledged the gold and silver vessels of St. Peter's to raise the funds necessary for the journey.

Justinian gave the Pope a warm welcome, but would not hear of peace. Preparations were far too advanced, he told Agapetus, to call off the invasion. The Pope was more successful in his effort to check Monophysite designs on the Church of Constantinople. Justinian, cultured and serious, was an orthodox ruler, but unfortunately he was under the thumb of his wife, the famous Theodora. Theodora, an actress risen to be empress, had the impudence to meddle in theology. Passionately the little comedian backed up the Monophysites, and at this very time she pulled enough wool over Justinian's eyes to get a creature of hers with Monophysite tendencies made patriarch of Constantinople. This man, Anthimus, had been bishop of Trebizond. Without canonical authority he left his see to become patriarch. Once more the Monophysites threatened Constantinople. But Pope Agapetus came to the rescue. Informed of the Monophysite tendencies and irregular position of the Patriarch, the Pope refused to have anything to do with him. Justinian, moved by Theodora's outcries, became annoyed. He went so far as to threaten the Pope, but St. Agapetus replied that he had come to visit the most Christian Emperor only to find a Diocletian. He added that he was not moved by the imperial threats. Justinian, a good man at heart, thought better of it, and allowed justice to take its course. Pope Agapetus then deposed Patriarch Anthimus, and personally consecrated his successor, Mennas. Once more the papacy saved Constantinople from the threat of heresy. And the Greek Church is grateful. Agapetus is celebrated as a saint not only in the Roman but in the Greek calendar.

The old Pope was ailing and before he could return to Rome, he died at Constantinople on April 22, 536.

ST. SILVERIUS

536-537

A SAINT AND THE SON OF THE GREAT POPE ST. Hormisdas, Silverius was to enjoy no such glory as had his father. But if he could not follow him in his brilliant achievements, he could imitate his virtue and devotion. Silverius was the nominee of Gothic King Theodahad. That monarch, quivering with fear at the imminent East Roman invasion, determined to have a loyal pope as the zero hour drew near. He appointed the subdeacon Silverius. Since Silverius was an excellent cleric, the clergy of Rome accepted Theodahad's choice. But while the Goth put his candidate on Peter's throne, Empress Theodora was taking measures to get her pet patriarch back in Constantinople and her pet project of at least a compromise on the Monophysite heresy adopted. She had the power and the tool to make life miserable for Pope Silverius.

Justinian's great general Belisarius, after a triumphant sweep through Sicily, was marching on Rome. Silverius, seeing that resistance was useless, advised surrender and on December 9, 536, the East Roman army filed through the Porta Asinaria to enter Rome in triumph. But the Goths were not finished yet. They deposed the useless Theodahad and made Witiges their new king. He came storming down to Rome with a large army and besieged the city. While this was going on, Belisarius received orders from Theodora to put pressure on Pope Silverius to allow the deposed Anthimus to return as patriarch of Constantinople and to surrender to the one-nature heresy. Belisarius summoned Silverius to his headquarters in the Pincian Palace to answer trumped-up charges of plotting to open a gate to the Goths. He then abruptly demanded that the Pope should surrender to Theodora by recalling Anthimus and giving in on the Monophysite question. Silverius refused and on another visit to the Pincian Palace was seized, stripped of his pallium, and clothed in a monk's habit. It was then announced that Pope Silverius had been deposed. Belisarius summoned the clergy and ordered them to elect another pope. Theodora had her creature ready for the occasion. He was none other than that deacon, Vigilius, who had been chosen by Boniface II as his successor. When Boniface changed his mind about appointing his own successor, Vigilius did not despair. He intrigued with Empress Theodora; indeed, he paid her a large sum of money and promised to carry out her wishes as far as he could. Now he was elected to replace St. Silverius.

St. Silverius was exiled to Patara in Lycia, but the bishop there wrote feelingly to Emperor Justinian that it was a shame to see the "pope who rules the Church through the world . . . a homeless exile." Justinian, troubled, was about to restore the Pope when Theodora once more intervened. Silverius was indeed sent back to Italy, but as a prisoner of his intruded successor. Vigilius sent him to Palmaria, an island in the Tyrrhenian Sea, and very shortly afterward this noble confessor died in exile.

Chronologia Summorum Pontificum.

[116]

VIGILIUS

537-555

H OW VIGILIUS, A ROMAN DEACON AND THE SON of an honorary consul, intrigued to get the papacy has been described in the life of St. Silverius. After Silverius died; Vigilius was generally recognized as legitimate pope. He had schemed to become pope, but he was to reap more trouble than satisfaction from his ambitious sowing. Though he disappointed his patroness, that actress-theologian Theodora, by continuing the orthodox policy of his predecessors, he was not popular at Rome.

Most of the vexations which made life miserable for Vigilius arose from the Monophysite question. Justinian, himself orthodox, had a politician's preoccupation with placating the Monophysites, so numerous in the East. He also had a preoccupation with dogmatic questions as if his great works of reconquest and reorganization of the empire were not enough. It was suggested that a condemnation of three fifth-century ecclesiastics would go far toward placating the Monophysites. Such a condemnation would be orthodox because Theodore of Mopsuestia, Theodoret, and Ibas had manifested Nestorian tendencies. Yet it would please the Monophysites because the one-nature heresy was the opposite of the Nestorian or two-person heresy. Justinian, charmed with the idea, issued the famous Three Chapters or lists of condemnations of Theodore, Theodoret, and Ibas. The Three Chapters, however, aroused some opposition in the East and a great deal more in the West, first because they condemned men who had long ago died at peace with the Church, and then because this condemnation, quite wrongly, was regarded as a slap against the Council of Chalcedon. Then too, the Emperor had no right to meddle in matters of doctrine.

Justinian hauled Pope Vigilius off to Constantinople. Though he received the Pope with the greatest honor, he soon put pressure on him to agree to the Three Chapters. Poor Vigilius! Buffeted between the relentless pressure of the Emperor to agree to the Three Chapters, and the angry determination of the Westerners that he should repudiate them, he did not know which way to turn. It must be remembered that as far as doctrine goes, the Three Chapters were orthodox. At first Vigilius agreed to the Three Chapters. Western bishops defiantly went into schism. The Westerners in his own retinue gave him gloomy looks and loud arguments. Disconcerted, Vigilius took back his agreement. Justinian's answer was to make him an honored prisoner. The Pope escaped out the window down a rope and fled to Chalcedon. The Emperor coaxed him back and proposed a general council. Vigilius at first boycotted it. However, this council held at Constantinople in 553 is regarded as ecumenical because later Vigilius and other popes acknowledged it. While the council was approving the Three Chapters, the Pope delighted the Westerners by condemning them. But at last he changed his mind again and agreed to the Three Chapters and the council. Justinian had his way. Quite pleased with the Pope now, Justinian sent him back to Rome and gave him that famous Pragmatic Sanction which allows the popes a good share of temporal power in Rome.

Vigilius died at Syracuse on his way back, on June 7, 555. His pontificate was stormy and unhappy. Italy was desolated by the war between Byzantines and Goths. With Milan and Aquilea in schism, Vigilius left a legacy of trouble to his successors.

National Museum, Florence.

PELAGIUS I

556-561

A DRAMATIC SCENE ILLUSTRATES THE DIFFI-
culties faced by Pope Pelagius I. On a
solemn occasion before the great General
Narses and a large gathering of the Roman people,
Pelagius mounted the ambo in St. Peter's and holding above his head a book of Gospels and a cross
swore that he was not guilty of plotting evil against
Vigilius. The career of Pelagius explains the need
for so dramatic a gesture.

Pelagius was a Roman, the son of a high government official. As deacon he had accompanied Pope
Agapetus to Constantinople and had remained
as the Pope's ambassador. There he became very
friendly with Justinian. He returned in 543 and
was in Rome when Totila the Goth besieged the
city. He did much for the suffering people. He
spent lavishly to provide food for them and tried
to get a truce from Totila. Here he failed, but he
did succeed in getting the Goth to promise to spare
the lives of the inhabitants when he finally took the
city in December 546. Totila sent him as ambassador to Constantinople to arrange a peace, but
Justinian refused, saying that Belisarius was his
plenipotentiary for Italy.

Pelagius again went to Constantinople to support Vigilius in the struggle over the Three Chapters. He was a strong influence on the Pope against
the Three Chapters. When Vigilius finally did accept them, Pelagius seems to have lost his head for
a time and to have defied the Pope. Later thoughts
were cooler thoughts, and he came to agree with
Pope Vigilius. This change of mind restored him
to the favor of Justinian. When Vigilius died, the
Emperor strongly urged the candidacy of Pelagius.

Ten months after the death of Vigilius, Pelagius
was consecrated. But his troubles were many. He
had to calm the tempest raised by the Three Chapters, and he had to help his poor flock so distressed
by the Gothic War. To calm the Three Chapters
tempest was not easy, especially since Pelagius had
once attacked them so bitterly. Now he was
stormed at and abused as a traitor. Throughout
the West there was general uneasiness. Milan and
Aquileia refused to return to Catholic unity. Gaul
was troubled. Even at Rome Pelagius felt it necessary to make the dramatic gesture described above.
Pelagius handled a difficult situation with skill. He
used a calm, levelheaded approach. All he asked
of angry dissidents was submission to the Holy See
without mentioning the irritating Three Chapters.
He kept on insisting that neither the Three Chapters nor the Fifth General Council were opposed
to Chalcedon. Though he failed to bring back
Milan and Aquileia, he did much to calm the West
elsewhere. He averted trouble in Gaul by a timely
letter to King Childebert and by appointing as his
vicar there the excellent Sapandus, archbishop of
Arles.

An excellent administrator, Pelagius ran the
papal estates or patrimony of Peter with an efficient hand. He was unsparing in his charity to the
poor. He used freely the authority given the pope
by the Pragmatic Sanction. The city of Rome, so
battered by the war, felt his restoring hand.
Pelagius I died March 4, 561, a much more popular man than he had been at his accession.

*Mosaic in the Basilica of St. Paul-Outside-the-
Walls, Rome.*

JOHN III

561-574

IN SPITE OF THE COMPARATIVE LENGTH OF JOHN'S pontificate, not too much is known about it. This ignorance is probably due to the Lombard invasions which began during John's reign. The reconquest of Italy by the Empire had brought little happiness and less peace to the Italians. Belisarius and Narses had indeed destroyed the Ostrogoth power, but their less capable successors proved unable to protect Italy from barbarians far more destructive than the Goths, the ferocious Lombards. Then too Rome had been badly hurt by the repeated sieges undergone in the Gothic war. With the population scattered and the aqueducts broken, Rome was but the shadow of the bustling city of the Caesars. It is at this time that the ancient Senate disappears from history, while more and more the popes are forced to take up the burden of political responsibility. It is a true transition period from ancient to early medieval times.

John III was a Roman, the son of a nobleman, Anastasius. He was consecrated in mid-July 561. The main features of John's pontificate are his relations with General Narses, his ill advised reinstatement of two Gallic bishops, and his care for the monuments of Christian antiquity.

Narses, the famous eunuch and general who completed the conquest of Italy from the Goths, continued to protect the country in the first years of John's pontificate. He destroyed several armies of assorted barbarians, to the great relief of the threatened Italians. But he was accused before the Emperor Justin II of disloyalty and recalled. The whole matter is quite confused. According to the *Liber Pontificalis* Narses had gone down to Naples when Pope John, realizing how necessary he was for the country's safety, went to Naples and pleaded with him to return. After Narses had asked what mischief he had done to the Romans, Pope John replied that he himself would sooner leave Rome than have Narses abandon the city. The great general returned; but some trouble evidently arose, for Pope John retired from the city to the Church of Sts. Tiburtius and Valerian in the Catacomb of Praetextatus on the Appian Way. Narses was accused of inviting the Lombards into Italy, but this is far from certain. His removal, however, did invite them, for it created a power vacuum which these Northern wild men were quick to fill.

John III does not seem to have been well advised in his handling of an appeal from two Gallic bishops. Salonius of Embrum and Sagittarius of Gap had been deposed by a synod at Lyons on serious charges. With the favor of Guntram, King of Burgundy, they appealed to the Pope. John quashed the decision of the synod and ordered the bishops reinstated. This was a mistake, for later on they had to be deposed again by the second synod of Châlons in 579.

In spite of the troubled times, John finished the Church of Sts. Philip and James, a grand structure in the Byzantine manner, gleaming with mosaics, warm with color. He also did much for the catacombs. It is scarcely an exaggeration to say that by his regulations the catacombs were preserved.

John III died July 13, 574, and was buried in St. Peter's.

Chronologia Summorum Pontificum.

BENEDICT I

575-579

THAT BENEDICT WAS A ROMAN, THE SON OF BONI-face, is all that is known of the early life of this first of a long line of popes to bear the name. Benedict seems to have been called Bonosus by the Greeks. After John III died, there was an interval of over ten months before Benedict was consecrated. By now the emperors were claiming the right to confirm papal elections, and with Lombard bands on the prowl, the difficulty of communicating with Constantinople was great.

Benedict's pontificate was filled with misery. The Lombard problem had landed with a thud on the doorstep of the papacy. After the death of Alboin, the chief who had led them into Italy, the Lombards soon broke up into bands led by dukes. While this lack of unity saved several cities for the empire, it increased the sufferings of the people. Without any central control, Lombard war parties ravaged up and down the peninsula. This ten-year period from 574 to 584, the decade of the dukes, was the most miserable period of the Lombard invasions. Nor was the Eastern Empire able to help. When in 577, the Patrician Pamphronius brought from Rome to Constantinople three hundred pounds of gold to persuade the Emperor to send help, he was told that the armed forces of the empire had their hands full fighting Persians. The best use he could make of the money was to offer it as a bribe to the Franks or to the Lombards themselves.

Famine too threatened Rome, but Benedict had the satisfaction of seeing an imperial grain fleet from Egypt sail up the Tiber to relieve his distressed Romans.

It is quite probable that Benedict was the pope who received the famous cross donated by Emperor Justin II to the shrine of the Apostles. At any rate, in an inscription on the cross, Emperor Justin piously hopes that in consideration of his gift, Heaven will send help to the city.

This cross, over a foot high, is covered with silver gilt and adorned with jewels. It still may be seen in St. Peter's.

Benedict I died July 30, 579, as the Lombards were besieging Rome. He was buried in St. Peter's.

Mosaic in the Basilica of St. Paul-Outside-the-Walls, Rome.

PELAGIUS II

579-590

PELAGIUS II WAS A ROMAN, BUT HIS FATHER HAD a German name, Winigild. When Pelagius was elected pope, the Lombards were blockading Rome, making it impossible to send for the imperial confirmation of the election. After an interval of four months Pelagius was consecrated without the imperial confirmation. Once pope, Pelagius succeeded in getting the Lombards to raise the siege. He then sent an embassy to Constantinople to inform the Emperor of his election and to get help. As usual, the plea brought back little but words from the palace on the Golden Horn. Later the Emperor Maurice sent a new official with the title of exarch to handle both military and civil government for the Emperor.

Disappointed with Constantinople, Pope Pelagius turned to the Franks. He wrote to Aunacharius, bishop of Auxerre, pleading with him to use his influence with the Frankish kings to come down and help poor Italy. The emperor added his pleas to those of the Pope, and the Franks did move an army down into the peninsula. But Lombard gold soon turned back the brave Franks and nothing was accomplished.

While his ambassador, the great Gregory, continued to bombard the Emperor with appeals. Pelagius himself asked Decius the exarch to protect Rome. Decius pathetically replied that it was all he could do to protect Ravenna. But at last the exarch did manage to get a truce with the wild men, and for a short spell Italy was at peace.

Pelagius took advantage of this breathing spell to try to bring the Three Chapters schism to an end. Back in the time of Pope Vigilius Northern Italy had revolted from the Holy See over the Three Chapters. Milan and Genoa had returned to Catholic unity but Northeastern Italy, led by the archbishop of Grado, remained stubborn. Actually this schism had begun at Aquileia, but the Lombards had sent Bishop and people scurrying to the island of Grado for safety. To these people Pelagius wrote letter after letter pleading with them to return to Catholic unity. It was no use. Poorly educated, they could ill understand the Pope's arguments, and they remained stubborn in their schism.

The exarch Smaragdus now put pressure on them. At the Pope's request he ordered them at least to attend a council at Ravenna. When nothing came of this, the exarch bluntly ordered Archbishop Severus to enter into communion with the orthodox archbishop of Ravenna. Though Severus obeyed, once out of the exarch's clutches he quickly went back into schism. The schism dragged on, despite the efforts of Pope Pelagius II.

Pelagius worked zealously to foster celibacy among the Western clergy. He adorned St. Peter's and rebuilt St. Lawrence's. A charitable soul, he turned his own house into a hospital. His charity was needed, for at this time Rome was devastated by a great flood.

Pelagius II died, the victim of a plague, February 7, 590.

ST. GREGORY I, THE GREAT

590-604

GREGORY THE GREAT WAS BORN IN ROME AT some time around 540. His father, Gordianus, was a wealthy patrician with a fine town house on the Coelian Hill and large estates in Sicily. More important than noble blood and great wealth, this family had a strong Christian spirit. Gregory's mother, Sylvia, was honored as a saint as were his father's two sisters, and John the Deacon can speak of Gregory's education as that of a saint among saints.

Gregory, with his wealth and family influence, soon became prefect of the city. While in this high position he decided to give up a career in the world for the life of a monk. Never halfhearted, Gregory used his six Sicilian estates to found monasteries and turned his Coelian Hill residence into another, dedicated to St. Andrew. Here he lived the simple, prayerful life of a monk. His retirement was interrupted. Pope Pelagius II sent Gregory as ambassador to the imperial court in Constantinople. After six years at the capital Gregory was allowed to return to his beloved monastery, of which he became abbot.

Probably at this period of his life Gregory saw the Saxon slaves who so stirred his zeal. He tried to go to England, indeed actually received the Pope's blessing and was on his way. But the Romans, who loved the abbot of St. Andrew's, raised so loud a protest that Gregory was recalled.

In 590 when Pope Pelagius died, Gregory was unanimously chosen to succeed him. Reluctantly he had to exchange the quiet life of a monk for the ceaseless activity of the pope. But always eager to do God's will, Gregory plunged manfully into his new work and filled fourteen years with great achievements.

As an administrator Gregory kept a watchful eye on the vast estates which formed the patrimony of Peter. But the money that efficient management brought into the treasury the Vicar of Christ's great charity caused to flow out just as rapidly.

Faced with the frightful menace of the Lombards, Gregory worked hard and intelligently to save Rome from devastation. Although the pope was not at that time the highest civil authority in Italy, the weakness and incompetence of the imperial officials threw a heavy burden on Gregory's broad shoulders. In spite of Lombard ferocity and Byzantine fecklessness, Gregory managed to bring a measure of peace to bleeding Italy.

Gregory made several improvements in the liturgy, and his name is immortalized in the Gregorian chant.

Once pope, Gregory did not forget the English. He sent St. Augustine on his historic mission in 597 and thus accomplished by another what he had longed to do himself. He worked hard with St. Leander to convert the still Arian Spanish Visigoths, and also paved the way for the conversion of the Lombards.

Gregory was a popular preacher and a writer whose works lived. His style, while not that of Cicero or Augustine, was suited to the rougher and simpler taste of his day and of darker days to come. Gregory's *Homilies, Dialogues,* and *Pastoral Care* did much to form the minds of the men of the early middle ages.

Gregory protected the Jews at a time when other rulers were giving the poor people a bad time.

The great Pope died in 604 with Italy at peace, the conversion of Spain accomplished, and that of England under way. He deserves to be called Gregory the Great, but the title which suits the noble old Roman best was that given to him in an early epitaph—God's Consul.

Justus van Ghent. The Barberini Palace, Rome.

SABINIAN

604-606

VERY LITTLE IS KNOWN OF SABINIAN'S EARLY LIFE except that he was born in the town of Blera not far from Viterbo in Tuscany, and that his father's name was Bonus.

In 593 Sabinian was in the Pope's service, for in that year Gregory the Great sent him as an apocrisarius (ambassador) to the imperial court. In Constantinople Sabinian had to deal with the ambition of the patriarch with the Lenten name, John the Faster. John may have fasted from food, but he had a taste for titles. He liked to call himself "Ecumenical Bishop," i.e., universal bishop. Since this high-sounding title seemed to imply a claim to universal jurisdiction in the Church, Pope Gregory, of course, could not allow it, and there was some spirited correspondence between Rome and Constantinople. Sabinian seems to have had trouble handling John the Faster and probably welcomed being recalled in 597. The next thing known about him is his election to succeed Gregory as Pope in 604.

Sabinian's pontificate was as difficult as it was short. The Lombards once more took the warpath, though fortunately the exarch Smaragdus was able to buy them off before too much damage was done. But what the Lombards spared, the forces of nature destroyed. The winter of 604-605 was extremely severe. Frost devastated the Italian vineyards, and following the frost came swarms of mice, and following the voracious rodents came a disease called rust which played havoc with the corn crop. Sabinian had his hands full trying to play Joseph's role by collecting wheat, first to provide against the menace of a Lombard siege, then to sell to the famine-stricken people.

Sabinian consecrated twenty-six bishops and gave gifts to St. Peter's. Outside of this we know nothing for certain except that he died in February 606 and was buried on the Vatican.

Mosaic in the Basilica of St. Paul-Outside-the-Walls, Rome.

BONIFACE III

607

BONIFACE, THE SON OF JOHN CATAADIOCE, WAS A Roman who, like his predecessors, served as a papal official. He was, according to Gregory the Great, "of tried faith and character." Gregory sent him as ambassador to Constantinople, where he seems to have done very well.

As ambassador his chief task was the usual one of pleading with the Emperor not to leave his Italian subjects defenceless before the ever-present threat of the Lombard. Boniface had a peculiarly thorny problem, however, in the case of a refugee bishop who had fled from the menace of raiding Slavs and Avars. It seems that John, bishop of Euria in Epirus, had fled along with his clergy to the comparative safety of Cassiope on the island of Corcyra. Not content, however, with securing safety, Bishop John began to usurp episcopal authority in his hospitable refuge. Naturally the local bishop, Alcison, objected to this—to say the least—uncanonical behavior. But somehow the refugee bishop had won the favor of the Emperor Phocas, perhaps because he, too, was a usurper. Bishop Alcison appealed to the Pope, and Gregory the Great instructed his ambassador at Constantinople to settle the difficulty. It is a tribute to his diplomacy that Boniface was able to bring the affair to a satisfactory conclusion and at the same time to secure the esteem of the Emperor Phocas.

The date of Boniface's return from Constantinople is not certain, but the interregnum of almost a year (Sabinian was buried February 22, 606, and Boniface III consecrated February 19, 607) might be explained by the fact that Boniface was elected while still serving as ambassador at Constantinople. The circumstances of this election are not known, but it is also possible that the long delay was due to difficulties over the election, for Boniface was most insistent on free elections. He held a council at Rome which was attended by seventy-two bishops and the Roman clergy, at which Boniface showed a wise preoccupation with freedom of papal and episcopal elections. He forbade anyone to start working on an election of a new pope or bishop until three days after the late incumbent's burial. He went so far as to forbid anyone under pain of excommunication even to speak of a pope's successor during his lifetime.

The trouble over the title of "Universal Bishop" assumed by the patriarch of Constantinople, John the Faster, flared up again, for John's successor, Cyriacus, also insisted on using this title. Boniface thereupon secured from Emperor Phocas a decree acknowledging that "the See of Blessed Peter the Apostle should be the head of all the Churches" and that the title of "Universal Bishop" should be reserved exclusively for the bishop of Rome. This, of course, was no new departure in imperial policy. Long ago the great lawgiver, Justinian, had legally recognized the primacy of the Roman pontiff. But at this time the repetition was considered necessary to curb the titular pretensions of the Patriarch.

Boniface died in 607, the same year in which he was consecrated. He was buried in St. Peter's, November 12.

National Museum, Florence.

ST. BONIFACE IV

608-615

BONIFACE IV WAS BORN IN THE PROVINCE OF Valeria. His father was a doctor named John. Like St. Gregory the Great, Boniface turned his house into a monastery. Like Gregory, too, he entered the papal service, but unlike Gregory, Sabinian, and Boniface III, he does not seem to have served as ambassador to Constantinople. He became *dispensator,* that is, a high official in the administration of the patrimony of St. Peter; and evidently he gave satisfaction, for Gregory the Great speaks of him as "my most beloved son Boniface the deacon."

Boniface was consecrated pope on either August 25 or September 15, 608. The day is disputed. As pope, Boniface did something which has endeared him to those who love classical antiquity. He turned the Pantheon into a Christian church. The Pantheon was a temple dedicated to Jupiter, Mars, and Venus. Built about 25 B.C. by Marcus Vipsanius Agrippa, the great friend and general of Augustus, it was rebuilt in its present circular form by Hadrian early in the second century. It is an outstanding example of ancient Roman architecture, famed for its large dome and elaborate brickwork. If today this masterpiece of classical antiquity can be admired much as it stood in the days of the Caesars, it is due to Pope Boniface IV. He consecrated the one-time temple of the gods to the one true God under the title of Our Lady and the Mar-

tyrs. Had he not done so, in all probability this architectural gem would have been seized by some turbulent little baron, and its beauty would have vanished under the repeated batterings of feudal brawls.

Boniface took an interest in the newly fledged church in England. He had an interview with Mellitus, the first bishop of Saxon London, and sent letters to Lawrence, the archbishop of Canterbury, and to King Ethelbert.

He also had dealings with that remarkable Irish monk and missionary, the impetuous, restless, lovable St. Columban. St. Columban, a splendid example of Irish missionary zeal, had already preached the gospel in Gaul and Switzerland. Now he was working among the Lombards of North Italy. He became involved in the struggle against heresy, and with more zeal than theological science, Columban sent Pope Boniface a letter in which he mingled expressions of the greatest respect with free reprehensions for the Pope's attitude in a theological quarrel about which the impulsive monk candidly confessed he knew little!

Boniface, if his epitaph may be trusted, took Gregory the Great for his model. He seems to have succeeded in following his holy predecessor, for like Gregory, Boniface is honored as a saint. He died in 615 and was buried in St. Peter's. His feast is kept on May 25.

Chronologia Summorum Pontificum.

ST. DEUSDEDIT

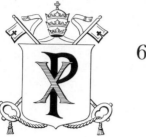

615-618

DEUSDEDIT, A ROMAN, THE SON OF STEPHEN, WAS consecrated pope on October 19, 615. He is also known as Adeodatus I.

His pontificate was filled with troubles, civil commotions, and natural disasters. Rebels flouted the imperial authority both at Ravenna and Naples. Up north at Ravenna the exarch John, along with other imperial officials, had been murdered. Down south at Naples a certain John of Compsa had risen in revolt, taken over the town, and proclaimed his independence of the Emperor Heraclius. Heraclius, who had succeeded the weak Phocas in 610, was not the man to allow his empire to fall to pieces. He sent his able chamberlain, the Patrician Eleutherius to set matters to rights in his Italian dominions. Eleutherius acted with vigor. First he restored order in Ravenna. Then he marched south along the Flaminian Way. After pausing in Rome to receive a warm welcome from the loyal Pope, he marched on Naples, stormed the city, and put the rebel John to death. Instead of letting well enough alone, however, Eleutherius turned on the Lombards and rekindled a war which soon he was forced to end by once more buying off those tough barbarians.

Pope Deusdedit had his hands full taking care of his Roman flock, for disaster struck hard at the city on the Tiber. In August 618, Rome was rocked by an earthquake and soon after devasted by plague. A true vicar of Christ, Deusdedit worked hard to help his people in their troubles.

Pope Deusdedit was especially fond of his secular clergy and seems to have leaned on them rather than on monks for support. His love for his secular clergy was manifested even after death, for in his will he left a sum of money to be distributed among them.

Tradition has it that Deusdedit was the first pope to use the leaden seal for pontifical documents which has given them the name of bull. The Latin *bulla* means seal. At any rate there still exists such a leaden *bulla* or seal dating from this pope's reign.

Deusdedit died in November 618 and was buried in St. Peter's. Like his predecessor, Deusdedit is honored as a saint. His feast is kept on November 8, the day of his burial.

Chronologia Summorum Pontificum.

B O N I F A C E V

619-625

ONIFACE V WAS A NEOPOLITAN, THE SON OF John. He was very probably one of the capable clerical staff of Pope Gregory the Great. His character is indicated by the fact that he was called "the mildest of men."

Boniface was consecrated pope on December 23, 619. Almost immediately he faced an embarrassing situation. The Patrician Eleutherius, who had so vigorously put down all rebels in the time of Pope Deusdedit, now decided to play the rebel himself. First he took over Ravenna. Then he proclaimed that he wished to assume the imperial crown in Rome "where the seat of empire had its permanent place." This was to place Pope Boniface in a delicate situation. Loyalty to the far-off Emperor Heraclius would forbid any such coronation. The presence of the armed cohorts of Eleutherius would be a cogent argument in its favor. But the rebel army spared Pope Boniface the trouble of making the delicate decision. Before Eleutherius could reach Rome, his own soldiers slew him and sent his would-be crowned head to Emperor Heraclius in Constantinople.

The acolytes seem to have been a pushful group in those days, for Boniface twice had to issue decrees restraining their activity, once to prevent them from taking part in the distribution or trans-lating of relics, and again from taking the place of deacons in the ceremony of baptism.

Boniface took a great interest in the infant church in England. He wrote letters encouraging the missionaries there. He also insisted that Pope Gregory had established Canterbury as the metropolitan see and forbade anyone to go against this. Canterbury was under the special guardianship of Rome. Meanwhile, the missionary Paulinus had been hard at work trying to convert the great northern kingdom of Northumbria. Pope Boniface came to his aid by writing letters to the royal family. He also sent gifts—an embroidered tunic and cloak for King Edwin and a silver mirror and an inlaid ivory comb for Queen Ethelberga. Doubtless these latter would console the Christian Kentish lady in her Northumbrian exile.

Pope Boniface's reign saw the rise of great troubles in the East. The Persians under King Chosroes had fought their way to Jerusalem, and to the great grief of the Christians, had carried off the true cross. Meanwhile in 622 a camel-driver with dreams, driven out of Mecca, had been forced to fly to friendly Medina. History was in the making.

Boniface finished the construction of the Cemetery of St. Nocomedes on the Via Nomentana, but when he died in 625, he was buried like his predecessors in St. Peter's.

Mosaic in the Basilica of St. Paul-Outside-the-Walls, Rome.

HONORIUS I

625-638

A POPE CONDEMNED BY A COUNCIL OF THE CHURCH! Such was Honorius I. The Sixth Ecumenical Council held at Constantinople in 680 condemned this pope's slackness in detecting error. Pope Leo II in approving the decrees of the Council stated that Pope Honorius was condemned because "he permitted the immaculate faith to be stained."

Such an introduction to the life of Pope Honorius I is spectacular and suits well the position of this pope in church history, but it does little justice to his achievements as an administrator, highly regarded by his contemporaries.

Honorius was born in Campania, the son of Petronius, a consul. He was consecrated pope in November 625. As pope, he devoted himself to keeping up the churches of Rome. He adorned the principal gate of St. Peter's with 975 pounds of silver. He built a new, lavishly ornamented church in honor of St. Agnes. Honorius was noted for his efficient management of the estate of the patrimony of St. Peter. He also took care of several matters concerning ritual. Indeed, as a practical administrator, Honorius proved to be pre-eminent.

Yet he is remembered today as the pope who was condemned by a Council! A key to understanding this pope's trouble is to remember that he was a practical administrator without being a deep theologian. He was a true father who wished to bring all his children together. And he did have a certain amount of success. He brought to a temporary end the schism of Aquileia. He succeeded—a touchy matter—in bringing the Southern Irish to abandon their traditional date for Easter. St. Patrick had, of course, brought over the date then celebrated at Rome; but since 432 the date had been corrected, and the difference between the corrected Roman date and the Patrician date had been a source of strife and contention.

Now perhaps the most troublesome heresy was still the Monophysite, which though condemned by Pope St. Leo I and the Council of Chalcedon back in 451 still afflicted whole provinces of the East. It is easy to imagine the joy of the Pontiff when Sergius, the patriarch of Constantinople, wrote him that Cyrus, patriarch of Alexandria, had reconciled Monophysite Egypt to the true faith! It is also easy to see how Honorius should have tried to soothe any quarrel which might endanger this great reconciliation. And Sergius informed him that a monk named Sophronius was threatening to upset all this fine work with his stubborn opposition to the use of the term, "one operation," i.e., of the God-Man, Christ.

Actually Sophronius was right, because under the compromise formula the Egyptians still held the basic Monophysite principle; but the eager Honorius wrote a letter to Sergius in which, while he teaches the orthodox doctrine of one person and two natures in Christ, he expressed his opinion that neither the term "one operation" nor the term "two operations" should be used. This is what the Sixth Ecumenical Council and Leo II rightly censured, for Honorius should have been more on his guard, and should have spoken more clearly and forcibly when appealed to as head of the Church.

All this storm rose after the death of Honorius. He was held in high esteem when he died in October 638. He was buried in St. Peter's.

Mosaic in the Church of St. Agnes, Rome.

SEVERINUS

640

Honorius had died in October 658. severinus, a Roman, had been elected almost at once, but the Emperor Heraclius refused to confirm the election. Instead of a confirmation he sent Severinus a formula of faith—a heretical formula of faith. Heraclius, like so many other Byzantine emperors, had taken to dogmatizing. And an emperor amidst dogmas is like the bull in the china shop or at the very least, Saul among the prophets. Since the Monophysite heresy had been a source of great weakness to the Eastern Empire, Heraclius grasped eagerly at any chance to put an end to it. Now the compromise formula of one will in Christ had appealed forcibly to practical men who longed for reunion. Even Pope Honorius had been less than careful in this matter. Consequently when Sergius, the patriarch of Constantinople drew up a compromise formula called the *Ecthisis*, Heraclius adopted it and ordered all to subscribe. Now this *Ecthisis*—the Greek word means exposition (of the faith)—was downright heretical. It held that there is only one will in Christ. This doctrine is called *monothelite* from the Greek words meaning one will. It is open to the same objections as the Monophysite heresy itself. If Christ had no human will, He would not be true man.

The imperial officials in Italy put pressure on the pope-elect to sign this heretical formula. The exarch Isaac sent a representative to Rome who plundered the Lateran Palace. But Pope Severinus meekly waited out the storm. He had sent ambassadors to Constantinople to win the imperial confirmation from Heraclius. The task was difficult, for the emperor was determined to force his pet formula on the Pope, and of course, Severinus could not possibly sign it. At last the Emperor gave way before the firmness and tact of the ambassadors. After over a year and a half, Severinus was consecrated, probably on May 28, 640.

Once consecrated, Severinus promptly and roundly condemned the heretical formula. He also built the apse of St. Peter's. It was all he had time to do, for, an old man when elected, he died on August 2, 640.

JOHN IV

640-642

JOHN, A NATIVE OF DALMATIA AND THE SON OF A lawyer, was chosen to succeed Severinus. John had been archdeacon of Rome and as such had played a prominent part in ruling the see. He was consecrated on Christmas Eve 640.

Pope John IV proved to be a vigorous foe of the Monothelite or One Will heresy. He promptly held a synod at Rome and condemned both the heresy itself and the compromise formula called the *Ecthisis*. This firm stand produced good results, for Emperor Heraclius now dropped the *Ecthisis* and returned to Catholic orthodoxy. And when Heraclius died in 641 the Pope encouraged his successors to remain constant in the faith.

John also defended the memory of Pope Honorius and rebuked those who tried to make him a friend of the Monothelites. In a letter to the sons of the Emperor Heraclius, John explained the real meaning of the Honorius letter.

Pope Honorius had succeeded in bringing Southern Ireland—Mogh's half of Ireland as it was called by the ancient Gaels—into line with the current corrected date for celebrating Easter. John IV tried to do the same for the Northern Irish and the frontier Gaels in Scotland—in vain. It took another lifetime to convince the stubborn men of Conn's half of Ireland that there had been an improvement in the reckoning of Easter since 432 when good St. Patrick landed.

Pope John did not forget his native Dalmatia. This land badly needed a little friendly aid, for it was being harried by the still untamed Serbs and Croats. To the distressed country the Pope sent an abbot named Martin with an ample supply of money to see what he could do about redeeming poor Dalmatians who had been carried off by the barbarians.

Through this abbot the Pope also secured the translation of relics of the saints from the troubled churches of Dalmatia to the haven of Rome. To receive these relics the Pope built a church which still stands.

Pope John IV died in October 642. He was buried in St. Peter's.

Mosaic in the Basilica of St. Paul-Outside-the-Walls, Rome.

[144]

THEODORE I

642-649

THEODORE, A GREEK FROM JERUSALEM, WAS elected to succeed John IV. He was consecrated on November 24, 642. He proved to be a father to the poor and a zealous caretaker of the churches in Rome.

Once more the story of a pope's life is taken up with the One Will heresy. Once more a supreme pontiff has to cope with an imperial meddler. Theodore did not shirk the difficulties he faced. He fought continually to bring back all to Christian unity. And he was kept busy. Letters poured in from Cyprus and from Africa to ask the Pope's protection against heresy. At Constantinople the patriarch Pyrrhus had been deposed and replaced by Paul. The Pope insisted that Pyrrhus should have a fair trial.

A great consolation was afforded Pope Theodore when the Abbot Maximus, a hard-working champion of the Catholic faith, brought to Rome none other than the deposed patriarch of Constantinople, Pyrrhus. In 645 Pyrrhus recanted his errors before the Pope, but later he seems to have relapsed.

Meanwhile a new storm had been gathering in the palaces of Constantinople. The patriarch Paul, though enraged at Pope Theodore's insistence on a fair trial for Pyrrhus, was no fanatical Monothelite. Like many Byzantine statesmen of the period, he wanted to restore a sense of union and solidarity in the shaken empire. Together with the energetic but unfeeling Emperor Constans II the Patriarch concocted a new formula, the *Type of Constans*. This *Type* pretended to teach no doctrine, whether orthodox or heretical; it merely forbade any more discussion on the whole matter of the will of Christ. Christian teachers could not allow the Emperor to stop their mouths on a question of faith, and so the stage was set for a tragedy in which Constans played the villain and the pope the hero, but it was not to be Pope Theodore. Theodore's reply to the *Type* was to declare the patriarch Paul deposed, an act which caused violent repercussions in Constantinople. Theodore died in May 649. His successor was to feel the full force of the imperial wrath.

Chronologia Summorum Pontificum.

ST. MARTIN I

649-654

THE MAN CHOSEN TO FACE THE STORM RAISED by the Emperor Constans was Martin from Todi, of noble birth, learned, experienced, and above all a man of solid virtue. He had served as ambassador to Constantinople and had had dealings with the Byzantine bureaucracy over the question of the deposition of Pyrrhus. He was to need all his experience and all his virtue to face the imperial fury.

Scarcely had Martin been consecrated on July 5, 649, when he was bombarded with appeals to make a downright condemnation of Monothelism and a ringing declaration of the true doctrine that in Christ there are two wills. Martin held a council in the Lateran attended by 105 bishops. The Fathers strongly condemned the notion that there is but one will in Christ. They further condemned the Emperor's *Type* for daring to silence the teaching of truth. Prudently the council gave credit to Constans for good intentions, but that did not appease the furious Emperor.

Constans decided on strong measures. Olympius, his new exarch, was ordered to force all Italians from the Pope down to accept the *Type*. But Olympius found himself at a loss. He tried to persuade the Pope, with no success. He tried to prevent a schism. In vain. At last he decided to have the strong and popular Pope assassinated. But what seemed a miraculous intervention caused Olympius to repent, wash his hands of the affair, and go off to Sicily to fight Moslem raiders.

Constans was furious. He sent another exarch, Theodore Calliopas to bring Pope Martin back to Constantinople. Calliopas entered Rome with his armed cohorts and carried off the unresisting Pope. This terrible voyage took over a year. The Pope already sick, was reduced to utter misery by the time the ship landed. He was so weak he could not stand unsupported.

Martin was accused before the imperial court of crimes ranging from intrigue against the Emperor to lack of faith in regard to the Mother of God! Weak as he was and in dire peril, Martin could only laugh at the absurd accusations.

And indeed the witnesses brought against him were so contradictory that the kindly Pope pleaded that they be excused from testifying on oath lest they add perjury to false witness.

Constans, determined to break the Pope, had him condemned to death in a public square with a large crowd to witness his degradation. The crowd, however, showed by silence its disapproval of the shameful goings on. After eighty-five days in a Byzantine prison, Pope Martin was exiled to Cherson in what is now the Crimea. There in that frontier outpost he suffered until death released him on September 6, 655.

In life Martin was disgraced, loaded with chains and exiled, but after death, miracles were worked at his tomb. He was hailed as a saint. And to this day the gallant Pope is regarded as a martyr for the faith not only by the Roman Church but also by the Greek and the Russian.

ST. EUGENE I

654-657

ONCE MARTIN HAD BEEN TORN AWAY FROM Rome, the exarch Theodore Calliopas tried to get the Romans to elect another pope. At first they refused, and the Apostolic See was administered by the archpriest, the archdeacon, and the chief notary, as was the custom during a vacancy. What happened next is obscure, but it is known that a Roman named Eugene was consecrated pope on August 10, 654, at a time when St. Martin was still living. Either Eugene was an antipope forced on the reluctant Romans by the Emperor, or he was chosen freely on the presumed consent of St. Martin to keep the Emperor from forcibly planting a docile tool on the throne of St. Peter. Two facts indicate that the latter was the case. First, Eugene was a noble character who refused to yield to imperial pressure. Second, Pope St. Martin seems to have recognized Eugene as legitimate Pope.

Eugene was a Roman from the Aventine, a gentle and holy man who had been a cleric from his youth. He was a man of great charity to the poor. However, like his predecessors, he had to face the troublesome problem of the One Will heresy.

Eugene promptly sent legates to Constantinople to inform Constans of his election. These legates, with more simplicity than shrewdness, received the patriarch of Constantinople into communion with the Holy See in spite of the fact that the patriarch remained ambiguous on the question whether Christ had one will or two wills. Pope Eugene disavowed this action. The legates, he claimed, had authority to deal with the Emperor alone. The legates brought back from Constantinople a synodical letter of the Patriarch which was also obscure. When it was read in the Church of St. Mary Major, the people raised such an uproar that the Pope could not go on with his Mass until he had assured them that the objectionable letter would not be accepted.

To cross the Emperor was dangerous business, and the firmness of St. Eugene might well have been punished as had that of St. Martin. Indeed when the imperial officials were exiling that sturdy defender of the faith, the abbot Maximus, they told him bluntly that when they had a little rest from the Moslems, they would roast him and the present Pope just as they had roasted Pope Martin. But the Moslems did not give them the little rest. Constans had his hands full fighting the men of Islam, who were hammering relentlessly on the empire's bastions.

And so Eugene was able to end his brief pontificate in peace. He died in 657. He is considered a saint and is commemorated in the Roman martyrology on June 2, the day of his burial in St. Peter's.

Chronologia Summorum Pontificum.

ST. VITALIAN

657-672

EXCEPT THAT HE WAS A NATIVE OF SEGNI IN THE Campagna and that his father's name was Anastasius, nothing is known of this saintly pope's early life. Enthroned on July 30, 657, Vitalian at once held out olive branches to the estranged East. He sent letters to the Emperor Constans II and to Peter, patriarch of Constantinople. The Emperor replied graciously and sent the Pope a copy of the Gospels with a gold cover adorned with jewels. At this time Constans seems to have abandoned his policy of persecution. The patriarch also replied in a friendly manner. In answer to Vitalian's exhortation to return to Catholic unity and orthodoxy, Peter replied that he believed like the Pope. Vitalian's name was inserted in the Constantinople diptychs. Vitalian has been accused of being too conciliatory towards heresy, but the charge is, to say the least, not proven. Actually his name was removed from the Constantinople diptychs later by a more actively Monothelite patriarch.

In 662 Emperor Constans decided to go west and establish himself in Italy. Not too popular at Constantinople, he sought new prestige in the West. When he approached Rome he was met at the sixth milestone by Pope Vitalian and the clergy. His stay in the Holy City was harmonious, and peacefully he visited Rome's famous shrines. His parting gesture, however, gave the city little cause to remember his visit with pleasure. Constans seized all the bronze he could lay hands on, taking even the bronze tiles from the famous Pantheon, now St. Mary of the Martyrs. Unable to cope with the Lombards, Constans withdrew to Sicily. Here in the midst of a reign of terror, the despot was knifed in his bath. With the accession of his son Constantine IV, better times dawned.

Pope Vitalian had trouble with Ravenna and Crete. The archbishop of Ravenna wished to get more independence from Rome, and had successfully appealed to Emperor Constans II. This trouble lasted until the pontificate of Leo II. From Crete came an appeal from John, bishop of Lappa. Bishop John had been deposed by a synod under the direction of the metropolitan of Crete, John. The Pope held a synod at Rome, decided that John had been unjustly condemned, and ordered the metropolitan to reinstate him in his see.

Vitalian had the satisfaction of learning that in the great synod of Whitby, England definitely adopted the Roman date of Easter. To England he sent one of Canterbury's greatest archbishops, the learned and pious monk, Theodore of Tarsus.

Vitalian was considered a firm ruler of the Church, one who preserved discipline. He died January 27, 672. Venerated as a saint, his feast is kept on that date.

The British Museum, London.

[152]

ADEODATUS

672-676

ADEODATUS, A KINDLY MONK, WAS ELECTED TO succeed St. Vitalian in 672. Adeodatus was a Roman, the son of Jovinian. He was a monk in the monastery of St. Erasmus on the Coelian Hill. This monastery had been established in the mansion of the Valeri, one of the great patrician families of old Rome.

Consecrated April 11, 672, Adeodatus from the first seems to have made a great impression with his kindness and liberality. He was accessible to all and did what he could to send all away satisfied. He also increased the allowance which the popes of this period granted to the clergy.

Liberal to all, Adeodatus was most generous to his own old monastery. He granted to St. Erasmus the revenues from many estates. He also restored the Church of St. Peter which is situated some miles out of the city on the Via Portuensis.

During his pontificate the Saracens made a destructive foray into Sicily.

There are extant two letters of this Pope which deal with exemptions of monasteries from the control of the local bishop. In a letter to the bishops of Gaul, Adeodatus remarks that since Crotopert, bishop of Tours, had himself exempted the monastery of St. Martin, he would confirm this exemption, but that it was not the custom of the Holy See to do so.

Adeodatus, also known as Adeodatus II, died in 676 and was buried in St. Peter's.

Mosaic in the Basilica of St. Paul-Outside-the-Walls, Rome.

DONUS

676-678

THERE WAS AN INTERVAL OF 138 DAYS BETWEEN the death of Adeodatus and the consecration of Donus his successor, an interval filled with remarkably bad weather. Lightning killed men and beasts, and storms so raged that the people prayed in daily litanies that the necessary farm work might go on.

Donus was a Roman, the son of Maurice. He had the satisfaction of receiving the submission of Reparatus, archbishop of Ravenna, who had revolted from papal control. At Constantinople, however, the Patriarch Theodore showed a disqui-eting tendency towards the One Will heresy. Right at home, the Pope found a colony of Syrian monks, in a monastery called Boethius, who were Nestorians. Donus broke up the heretical community, dispersing the monks throughout Italy. The Boethius monastery he staffed with Romans.

Donus paved the courtyard of St. Peter's with large marble blocks. He also restored the Church of St. Euphemia on the Appian Way and another on the Ostian way the identity of which is obscure.

Donus died in 678 and was buried in St. Peter's, April 11.

Chronologia Summorum Pontificum.

ST. AGATHO

678-681

ST. AGATHO RANKS WITH ST. LEO THE GREAT AND St. Hormisdas for his outstanding contribution to orthodoxy in the East. Agatho was a Sicilian, probably from Palermo. It is possible that he is the Agatho referred to by St. Gregory the Great in a letter to the abbot of St. Hermes in Palermo. The abbot, wrote Gregory, could receive Agatho into his monastery if Agatho's wife was willing to enter a convent. There are reasons to believe that Pope Agatho is this monk, but on the other hand it would make him a very old man indeed. Monk or not, Agatho was a man of amiable disposition who got along well with people. Probably he was efficient in business matters too, for contrary to custom, he kept the treasurer's office in his own hand after becoming pope.

The great event of this pontificate was the Sixth General Council, the Third of Constantinople, which extinguished the Monothelite heresy and reunited Constantinople to Rome. It started when Emperor Constantine IV, the Bearded, having pacified the empire politically, desired to pacify it religiously. This capable ruler had defeated the Saracens and held back the Avars. Now he deplored the schism which separated the East from Rome. He wrote to Pope Donus suggesting a conference on the matter. Donus was dead by the time the letter arrived, but Agatho was quick to seize the olive branch proffered by the Emperor. He ordered councils held throughout the West so that legates could present the universal tradition of the Western Church. Then he sent a large delegation to meet the Easterners at Constantinople.

The projected conference developed into a general council. The legates, patriarchs, and fathers gathered in the domed hall of the imperial palace on November 7, 680. The Monothelites or One Will heretics presented their case. Then the letter of Pope Agatho was read which explained the traditional belief of the Church that in Christ there are two wills, divine and human. The council agreed that Peter spoke through Agatho. Patriarch George of Constantinople accepted Agatho's letter, as did most of the bishops present. The council proclaimed the existence of the two wills in Christ and condemned the old Monothelites Sergius and Cyrus. Pope Honorius was included in the condemnation. When the council ended in September of 681 the decrees were sent to the Pope, but Agatho had died in January. The Sixth General Council not only ended the Monothelite heresy but it healed the schism between Constantinople and Rome.

Pope Agatho also had to judge an appeal made from England by Wilfrid, bishop of York. Wilfrid arrived in Rome in 679 to protest against the action of Theodore, archbishop of Canterbury. Theodore had carved up Wilfrid's diocese, appointing three bishops to govern the new sees. Wilfrid appealed to the Pope against this rather arbitrary proceeding. Pope Agatho held a council to discuss the matter, and the wise decision was that Wilfrid's diocese should indeed be divided, but that Wilfrid himself should name the bishops.

Agatho is venerated as a saint by both Latins and Greeks.

Umbrian School. From a vaulting in the Holy Crypt, Monastery of St. Benedict, Subiaco.

[158]

ST. LEO II

682-683

LIKE HIS PREDECESSOR ST. AGATHO, LEO II WAS A Sicilian. Elected shortly after the death of Agatho, Leo was not consecrated for over a year and a half. The reason for this odd delay is not evident, but it may have been due to negotiations regarding imperial control of papal elections. Pope Agatho had been engaged in these negotiations and Constantine the Bearded had already promised to abolish or at least reduce the tax which for some time now popes had been compelled to pay to the imperial government at their consecration.

Leo II was a man learned for his time who knew Greek and was an orator of some polish. Virtuous too, he was a lover of poverty and very good to the poor. Highly esteemed by his contemporaries, he is considered a saint by the Church.

Though his pontificate was quite short, Leo did accomplish something. Since St. Agatho had died while the Sixth Ecumenical Council was still in progress, it was Leo who received the decrees of this council. He confirmed them with pleasure. He accepted the inclusion of Pope Honorius among those condemned for the Monothelite heresy, but made it clear that Honorius was condemned not for teaching heresy, but for allowing it to spread by his negligence. Leo wrote to the bishops of the West publishing the decrees of the council, and explaining the condemnation of Pope Honorius. Since the Monothelite heresy had never been popular in the West, there was no difficulty in getting the West to accept these decrees.

At this time Leo put a period to the attempt of the Ravenna archbishops to get away from the control of the Bishop of Rome as primate. The friendly Constantine the Bearded revoked the decree of his father Constans in favor of Ravenna. The kind Pope sweetened the matter for the Ravenna bishops by abolishing the tax it had been customary for them to pay when they received the pallium and by other concessions.

Probably because of Lombard raids, Leo transferred the relics of a number of martyrs from the catacombs to churches inside the walls of the city. He also dedicated two churches, St. Paul's and Sts. Sebastian and George.

St. Leo II died June 28, 683, and was buried in St. Peter's. His feast is kept on June 28.

Mosaic in the Basilica of St. Paul-Outside-the-Walls, Rome.

ST. BENEDICT II

684-685

ONCE AGAIN THERE WAS A LONG INTERVAL BE-tween the election and the consecration of a pope, but this time something was done about it. Benedict, a Roman, the son of John, was elected to succeed St. Leo II; but he was not consecrated until June 26, 684. Churchmen were weary of these long delays which were due to the necessity of waiting for imperial confirmation of the papal election. Benedict obtained from Emperor Constantine the Bearded a change in regulations which permitted the exarch of Ravenna to make the confirmation. This shortened considerably the interval between election and confirmation.

Benedict II was a man richly endowed with noble qualities. He had been in the service of the Church from his youth. Humble, patient, and generous, he was well-schooled in the Scriptures and sacred music. His pontificate, however, was too short to allow him much accomplishment.

Following his predecessors' example, Benedict wrote to Spain to hurry the bishops along in sending in their adhesion to the Sixth General Council. King Ervig then held a council at Toledo in November 684 to discuss the matter. The council condemned the Monothelite heresy, and St. Julian, archbishop of Toledo, drew up a profession of faith which he sent to the Pope. Benedict, though pleased, was not quite satisfied with some of the expressions used in this profession and sent it back with a request for some changes in terminology.

Like all the contemporary popes of this efficient emperor, Benedict got along well with Constantine the Bearded. Indeed Constantine asked the Pope to adopt his two sons, Justinian and Heraclius. As a token of this adoption he sent Pope Benedict locks of the princes' hair.

The charity and kindness of St. Benedict II appears in the effort he made to convert Macarius, ex-patriarch of Antioch. Macarius had been condemned as a Monothelite and deposed by the Sixth General Council.

The Pope took the occasion of his orthodox successor's death to send Macarius one of his special advisers to attempt to win him back. It was no use; Macarius died a heretic.

Since Benedict was very good to his clergy, it was fitting that his last big ceremony was the distribution of gifts and favors on Easter Sunday, March 26, 685. At once after this ceremony the saintly Pope fell sick and soon died. He was buried in St. Peter's on May 8. Benedict is venerated as a saint; his feast is kept on May 7.

National Museum, Florence.

JOHN V

685-686

MEDIEVAL ROME WAS SCARCELY A HEALTH RE-sort, but even so the extreme shortness of so many seventh-century pontificates does seem to indicate that venerable old age was one of the things the electors looked for in a pope. John V was another example of this; he ruled the Church for just over a year.

John V was a Syrian from the neighborhood of Antioch. By 680 he must have been well established in the Roman clergy, for Pope St. Agatho sent him as legate to the Sixth Ecumenical Council. From Constantinople he brought back the account of the proceedings of the council and also some imperial decrees. John was elected in a return to the ancient manner by the generality, that is, by the clergy and laity of Rome in the Lateran basilica. He was consecrated at once in July 685. It is not clear just what the author of John's biography in the *Liber Pontificalis* means by the return to the ancient manner. Popes before and after John V were elected by the generality in the Lateran basilica. Duchesne supposes that the expression refers to the new imperial regulations of Constantine the Bearded. These regulations, whether they merely permitted the exarch of Ravenna to confirm the election or allowed complete freedom, certainly marked a change. They did away with excessive intervals between election and consecration which had been due to the necessity of sending all the way to Constantinople for imperial confirmation.

This Syrian Pope was a man of energy and learning, but his health was not equal to the strain. Not long after his election he fell ill, and though he lingered on for a time, he could not get much accomplished. He had the misfortune to lose the best friend the papacy had had on the imperial throne for some time. Constantine IV, the Bearded, died in 685. While still legate, John had secured from this friendly emperor a decree lowering the taxes the popes paid on their estates of the patrimony of Peter. Constantine had left the empire more united religiously and stronger politically than he had received it from his father Constans II. Under his clever and vigorous leadership, Constantinople had returned to Catholic unity and orthodoxy. The Sixth Ecumenical Council had condemned the Monothelites. The fierce onslaught of the Saracens had been checked before the walls of Constantinople, and if Egypt and Syria were gone, the remaining provinces were protected by a better organization.

John V settled a jurisdictional squabble over Sardinia. Citonatus, archbishop of Cagliari, had presumed to consecrate Novellus bishop of Torres without so much as a by-your-leave of the Pope. John V held a council at Rome and decided to place Torres under his direct supervision.

John V died in the summer of 686 and was buried in St. Peter's on August 2.

Mosaic in the Basilica of St. Paul-Outside-the-Walls, Rome.

CONON

686-687

AFTER JOHN'S DEATH TROUBLE BREWED IN Rome. The army pushed forward, as their candidate for the papacy, Peter the archpriest, while the clergy favored the priest Theodore. Matters looked bad for a while. The army held the gates of the Lateran Basilica, and there was danger of a double election. Fortunately, however, after some negotiations, clergy and army agreed on a compromise candidate, the excellent priest Conon. A strikingly venerable old gentleman, Conon was just the man to pacify the spirit of faction. He was very old, he was kind, he enjoyed an excellent reputation.

Conon was the son of a soldier. He had been educated in Sicily but had come to Rome and had been ordained priest there. He enjoyed excellent relations with the new Emperor Justinian II. There was no indication of the trouble this unworthy son of a great father was to give. Conon received a letter from the Emperor which informed the Pope that the original acts of the Sixth Ecumenical Council had been recovered and that the Emperor, after making all high ecclesiastical, civil, and military officials sign them, had taken measures for their preservation. The Emperor also showed his good will toward the papacy by lowering some of the taxes on the patrimony.

Pope Conon seems to have been influenced by schemers, for he appointed as manager of the Si-cilian estates of the patrimony a character named Constantine. Apparently this was against the advice of the Roman counselors of the pope. It would have been well had Conon taken his counselors' advice. Constantine by his extortions soon had the Sicilian papal estates in an uproar. The governor had to intervene and clap Constantine into prison.

More consoling were the Pope's dealings with the great Irish missionary St. Killian. Ireland at this time was at the peak of its prestige as a country of saints and scholars. Irish monks swarmed over Europe, bringing Christ to thousands. A group of these pilgrims for Christ led by Sts. Killian and Colman had visited Würzburg on the Main River in Franconia. Much taken by the beauty of the countryside and the fine character of the Germans, St. Killian determined to go to Rome to see Pope John and secure from him an apostolic commission to preach the gospel to the Germans. When the zealous Gaels reached Rome, John was dead; but Conon received them most kindly. He ordained Killian bishop and sent him to preach Christ to his beloved Germans.

Conon, very old when elected, was soon so sick he could hardly go through with the usual ordinations. He died in September 687 and was buried in St. Peter's.

Mosaic in the Basilica of St. Paul-Outside-the-Walls, Rome.

ST. SERGIUS

687-701

SERGIUS WAS A COMPROMISE CHOICE FOR THE papacy, an excellent one. The archdeacon Paschal had bribed John, the exarch of Ravenna. The exarch obligingly ordered his minions at Rome to put Paschal in as pope, but a large party supported the archpriest Theodore. Once more, just when things looked bad, the common sense of the majority led to a compromise. Sergius was elected. Theodore at once submitted. Paschal was forced to do so, but he sent to the exarch at Ravenna, promising him a hundred pounds of gold if he would come to Rome and make him pope. The greedy exarch came swiftly, but he was realistic enough to see the folly of overriding the majority. He coolly dropped Paschal and agreed to the choice of Sergius, but he insisted on the payment of the huge sum Paschal had promised. In vain did Sergius and the Romans protest against this outrageous demand. Not until the money was paid did the rapacious exarch allow the consecration of Sergius to take place. Sergius was a Syrian from Antioch. Probably his family had fled from the Moslem invasion, for he was educated at Palermo. He went to Rome, joined the school for sacred music, was ordained priest, and was placed in charge of the Church of St. Susanna. Noted for his devotion to the martyrs, he often said Mass in the catacombs.

Sergius received much consolation from the West. In 688 Caedwalla, the mighty king of the West Saxons, came a pilgrim to Rome seeking baptism from the Pope. St. Willibrord, an Anglo-Saxon monk, came to seek the Pope's blessing on a mission to the Frisians. Sergius consecrated him bishop and sent him off to fruitful labor among the barbarians. Then too, the old Three Chapters schism finally ended with the submission of the bishop and clergy of Aquileia-Grado.

From the East came trouble. At Constantinople, Emperor Justinian II decided that since the last two general councils, the fifth and sixth, had issued no disciplinary decrees, he would hold one to supply the deficiency. Justinian's council is, therefore, called the Quinisext (fifth-sixth). It is also called the Trullan Council because it was held in the same domed hall, the Trullus, in which the Sixth Ecumenical Council had been held. The Westerners called it the erratic synod, and with reason. For this gathering of Eastern bishops presumed to issue 102 canons, some of which were quite objectionable, notably the one which stated that Constantinople had the same rights in the Church as Rome. When Pope Sergius refused to confirm these decrees, Justinian acted to force him. He sent Zacharias, captain of the bodyguard, to bring back the decrees signed or the Pope a prisoner. It was to be Constans II and St. Martin over again. But times had changed. The imperial forces in Italy, now more Italian home guards than regulars from the East, refused to cooperate. Indeed, the army from Ravenna marched on Rome to attack not Sergius but Zacharias. Zacharias pleaded with Sergius to save him and when the army of Ravenna approached, the bold captain went to cover under the Pope's bed! Sergius calmed the soldiers, who spared the captain's life but drove him from the city. Since Justinian himself was driven into exile by a rebellion at home, there was nothing he could do about it.

It was this pious and firm Pope who ordered the beautiful prayer *Agnus Dei* to be added to the Mass.

St. Sergius died, and was buried in St. Peter's on September 8, 701. His feast is kept on September 9.

Chronologia Summorum Pontificum.

JOHN VI

701-705

SINCE THERE IS NO MENTION OF DISCORD AT THE election of John VI, it may be presumed that it went off peacefully. He was consecrated on October 30, 701. That John was a Greek is about all that is known of his early life.

Coming events cast their shadow before, and two incidents in John's pontificate form a large shadow of the approaching temporal power of the papacy. Shortly after John's accession, a new exarch of Ravenna, the Patrician Theophylact, entered Rome. The reason for the exarch's visit to Rome remains somewhat obscure, but whatever it was, his arrival excited the Italians. Marching on Rome, the Italian home guards threatened the exarch, but Pope John, like Pope Sergius, protected the Emperor's representative. He sent priests to the angry soldiers and succeeded in quieting them. They spared the exarch, but did punish some of his minions and informers.

Once more the Lombards took the warpath. This time it was Duke Gisulf of Benevento who sent his warriors swarming over Campania. The smoke of burning towns and the wailing of captives marked the progress of these wild men. The imperial authorities could not stop them, but the Pope did what he could. John VI sent a number of priests on an embassy to Gisulf to persuade him to release his captives and go home. The Pope's emissaries succeeded, but at the cost of a large ransom. In these two incidents—the Pope saving the exarch from the Italians and the Pope saving the Italians from the Lombards—may be seen an indication of the future temporal power of the papacy. Not as a glittering honor but as a burdensome duty did temporal power come to the popes.

Over twenty years before, St. Wilfrid of York had come to Rome to seek and find justice at the hands of Pope St. Agatho. Now once more enmeshed in a network of troubles and annoyances, Northumbria's great bishop came to John VI. John held a synod, which after listening to Wilfrid and his accusers, cleared Wilfrid. The Pope gave Wilfrid letters to King Aldfrid of Northumbria and King Ethelred of Mercia. After a little more trouble, Wilfrid was able to close his stormy life in peace.

John VI died in January 705, and was buried in St. Peter's on January 11.

National Museum, Florence.

JOHN VII

705-707

JOHN VII WAS A GREEK OF ILLUSTRIOUS FAMILY. His father, Plato, was a curator of the imperial palace. He had done much to restore the decaying palace of the Caesars on the Palatine Hill. John became rector of the estates of the patrimony of Peter on the Appian Way. He was learned, eloquent and very devoted to Mary, the Mother of God. He seems, however, to have been somewhat timid, and timidity was not the quality most desirable in a pope who had to face the restored Justinian II.

Justinian had been overthrown and, with his nose sliced off, exiled to Cherson. Now in 705, with the help of the Bulgarians he stole into Constantinople through an aqueduct and reestablished himself on the throne. Blood flowed in torrents. The slit-nosed one, as he is termed, was not gentle. He put out the eyes of Patriarch Callinicus and sent him to Rome. No doubt the city was filled with horror stories of this Grand Guignol emperor.

Once his enemies were disposed of, the tenacious Justinian turned his attention to reviving his pet project—getting the Pope to confirm the decrees of the Quinisext or Trullan Council. It will be remembered that only the violent reaction of the Italian soldiers had saved Pope Sergius from being carried off to Constantinople because he had refused to confirm these decrees, some of which were highly objectionable. Now Justinian sent Pope John VII copies of the decrees and a letter in which he urged the Pope to hold a synod and decide which decrees he could confirm and which he would reject. This sounds quite reasonable, but Pope John was evidently too much afraid of Justinian to take the slit-nosed one at his word. He sent the decrees back unsigned and without comment. And shortly afterwards in 707, he died.

For a wonder, John had more pleasant relations with the Lombards. Aripert II, king of the Lombards, restored to the Pope the estates of the patrimony in the Cottian Alps area which had been confiscated years ago in the time of King Rothari. To confirm this restitution, Aripert sent the Pope a deed written in golden letters.

It is interesting to note that the English clergy of that day were not sticklers for propriety in dress. Pope John VII had to rebuke them for their love of the gay clothes of laymen. John seems to have inherited from his father, the curator of the palace, an interest in restoring buildings. He restored the Lateran Basilica and had frescoes painted in St. Mary Antiqua.

Mosaic in the Holy Crypt, the Vatican.

SISINNIUS

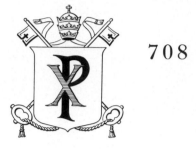

708

Sisinnius is remarkable for the shortness of his pontificate, which lasted about twenty days, and for the fact that he was so tormented by gout that he could not even feed himself. Except that Sisinnius was a Syrian, the son of John, nothing is known of his early life. It remains obscure just why a man in his ailing condition should have been elected pope. His biographer in the *Liber Pontificalis* says that he was a steady man who was solicitous for the welfare of the citizens of Rome. Perhaps it was this reputation which caused the Romans to take a chance on his health.

That Sisinnius was a man of foresight is proved by one of his first acts. He ordered that lime should be prepared so that the walls of Rome could be strengthened. The papal limekilns were ordered into full production, but, of course, Sisinnius died before much could be done. This anxiety about Rome's walls proves that Sisinnius was a man of vision. The Lombards were always a threat, and now the crescent of Islam was beginning to swell toward the full moon.

Sisinnius had time to ordain a bishop for Corsica and for nothing more. He was dead and buried in St. Peter's by February 4, 708.

Mosaic in the Basilica of St. Paul-Outside-the-Walls, Rome.

CONSTANTINE

708-715

CONSTANTINE, LIKE SISINNIUS, WAS A SYRIAN. He was a mild, amiable man.

Felix, archbishop of Ravenna, refused to sign the customary act of submission to the Pope. Terrible punishment followed swiftly, not from the good-natured Pope, but from the grim Justinian. The Emperor ordered Ravenna to be sacked because some of its citizens had taken part in the rebellion of 695. Archbishop Felix had his eyes torn out, and he was driven into exile. After the murder of Justinian in 711, Felix was allowed to return. He then submitted to the Pope.

Consolation came from England when Coenred, king of Mercia, abdicated and entered a Roman monastery. Even more impressive was it when Offa, the beautiful young prince of Essex, left throne and wealth to serve Christ in the monastic habit.

Constantine received an invitation from Justinian II to visit him at Constantinople to settle the question of the Quinisext or Trullan Council decrees. The Pope, with visions of eyeless bishops and tortured victims, might well have trembled at this invitation, but if he did fear, he was most agreeably surprised. The Emperor received him with the highest honor. The people of Constantinople joyously greeted the Pope at the seventh milestone. Justinian received Holy Communion from the Pope and promised to renew all the privileges of the Church. Then Constantine and the Emperor went into consultation on the vexed problem of Justinian's pet project, the Quinisext Council. Constantine seems to have done what John VII feared to do, to have approved whatsoever in the canons of this council did not oppose, faith, morals, or the decrees of the Roman Church. Justinian appears to have been satisfied with this. At any rate, Pope Constantine returned safely, complete with eyes, on October 24, 711.

The Pope soon learned that Justinian had been murdered. He had reason to regret the loss of the slit-nosed one, for the next emperor, Philippicus, was a Monothelite. He decided to wipe out the Sixth Ecumenical Council and make the One-Will heresy the official religion of the empire. A council of Eastern bishops obediently went into heresy at the imperial nod. They repudiated the Sixth Ecumenical Council and adopted the Monothelite heresy. The Pope's answer was to have a series of pictures painted in the portico of St. Peter's showing the six ecumenical councils. The Romans refused to place the heretic Emperor's name or image on their coins. Imperial troops carried the answer of Philippicus and blood flowed. The Pope, however, quieted the struggle and his patience was rewarded. It was the usurper's turn to be deposed and have his eyes put out. Anastasius II who took the throne was orthodox, and the Monothelite heresy at last sinks into a memory.

Constantine died and was buried in St. Peter's on April 9, 715.

Mosaic in the Basilica of St. Paul-Outside-the-Walls, Rome.

ST. GREGORY II

715-731

ST. GREGORY II WAS A ROMAN OF NOBLE FAMILY. From his youth a cleric, Gregory was made treasurer by St. Sergius, and papal librarian. As a deacon he accompanied Constantine on his visit to Justinian II and is credited with the skillful answers which at once satisfied the half-mad monarch and safeguarded Catholic doctrine and practice. Gregory was consecrated on May 19, 715. A man of virtue and eloquence, he was well versed in Holy Scripture. Above all, he was prudent and firm.

Gregory II showed great interest in the vital work of conversion going on in lands beyond the old empire's far-flung borders. He encouraged St. Corbinian to keep on sacrificing his desire for solitude and continue his work among the Bavarians. In 718 Pope Gregory received Winfred, a zealous young English monk who sought his blessing on a mission to the Germans. The Pope gave him not only a blessing but a name glorious in the annals of Christianity—Boniface. He recalled St. Boniface to Rome in 722, questioned him about his faith, and thoroughly satisfied, consecrated him bishop and sent him back to his Germans.

Gregory was fond of monks. He turned his ancestral mansion into a monastery and rebuilt Monte Cassino. This mother abbey of the Benedictines, destroyed by the Lombards around 580, had been a desolate ruin.

On the Lombards, Gregory had a good influence. He helped them with their laws. But when these still untamed barbarians began raiding imperial territory in Italy, Gregory tried to stop them. Loyalty to the Emperor, however, was becoming difficult.

Leo III, a tough soldier from the Isaurian uplands, had saved the empire from the Saracens by his spirited defense of Constantinople in 717. Leo was a very demanding taxgatherer. His impositions caused discontent especially in Italy, where the small protection afforded by imperial forces made high taxes seem a bad investment. Discontent flamed higher when in 726 the Emperor touched not only his subjects' purses but their devotion. Leo, rough soldier that he was, decided to play the theologian. His pet idea was to forbid the use of sacred images. Iconoclasm, the Greek word for image breaking, is a Jewish-Moslem idea, quite alien to Christian tradition. The imperial decree, issued in 726, provoked riot and rebellion in the East. More constructively, it occasioned the masterful writings of the great Eastern doctor of the Church, St. John Damascene.

The imperial decree forbidding images reached Italy in 727. Pope Gregory held a synod at Rome which stated the traditional teaching of the Church. He then wrote to Leo reproving him for his meddling and teaching him the traditional doctrine of the Church. He quite bluntly warned the Emperor against enforcing his decree in the West. The Pope also supported the deposed patriarch of Constantinople and threatened his intruded successor. Leo sent a fleet to seize the Pope, but a storm destroyed it. He did seize the estates of Peter's patrimony in Sicily and Calabria. His officials in Italy were prevented by the aroused Italians and the Lombards from taking measures against the Pope. The Italians wished to set up a rival emperor, but Gregory dissuaded them. The extraordinary circumstances forced Gregory to assume more temporal power in Rome.

This great Pope died in February 731. His feast is kept on February 13.

By the Master of the Liesborn School of Westphalia. National Gallery, London.

ST. GREGORY III

731-741

As the funeral procession of st. gregory ii moved slowly along, there was a sudden outcry. The clergy and people shouted that Gregory, a Syrian who was walking with the Pope's bier, should be the next pope. And they hurried him off without further ado, and elected him. The man who could arouse such unusual and universal enthusiasm must have been a striking personality. And indeed the biographer of Gregory paints him in glowing colors. He was an educated man who knew both Latin and Greek, polished in style, learned in Holy Scripture, pious, zealous for the faith, and a lover of the poor.

Consecrated on March 18, 731, Gregory III at once turned his attention to the image-breaking controversy. To recall Leo the Isaurian to an orthodox state of mind, he sent him the priest George with letters of warning and instruction. When George returned from the East, the Pope was surprised to find that the timid legate had been afraid even to deliver the letters to the fierce Isaurian. Not unnaturally angry, Gregory was going to degrade George from the priesthood, but the clergy of a synod held to consider the situation, persuaded the Pope to let George off with a penance. However, Gregory sent him back to the Emperor. This time the imperial officials in Sicily seized George and exiled him.

Gregory held another synod, this time with ninety-three bishops and the clergy and people of Rome. The council decreed that anyone who should destroy or dishonor holy images should be excommunicated. But the Emperor would not allow the envoys even to reach him. His answer was to send a fleet to carry out the imperial decrees. The fleet was shipwrecked, but Leo punished the Italians by raising their taxes and the Pope by confiscating the estates of the patrimony in Sicily and Calabria.

The Emperor also transferred the Church in Calabria, Sicily, and Illyricum from the jurisdiction of the bishop of Rome as patriarch to the jurisdiction of the patriarch of Constantinople. This arbitrary act was a remote cause of the unhappy Eastern Schism. It made the patriarchate of Constantinople practically coterminous with the Eastern Empire. And in spite of the fact that it had been thus arbitrarily given to them by a heretical emperor, the patriarchs of Constantinople clung to their increased jurisdiction.

St. Boniface visited Pope Gregory III in 737 to receive consolation from him. Gregory asked Boniface's cousin, the holy monk Willibald, to help in the conversion of the Germans. The Pope granted the request of Egbert of York that he should be made archbishop, thus restoring to England the two metropolitan sees planned by Gregory the Great.

Once more a pope was troubled by the Lombards. Liutprand, King of the Lombards, strove to break the Lombard Dukes of Spoleto and Benevento and to overrun all Italy. He ravaged the exarchate of Ravenna and marched south. The Dukes allied themselves with Pope Gregory, but nothing could stop Liutprand. Once more the Lombards ravaged Roman territory. The Pope, at a loss, appealed to Charles Martel, the Frankish "hammer." Charles sent an embassy to Rome, but no help. Actually he could do little, for his health was broken.

In the middle of all this trouble, late in 741, St. Gregory III died. His feast is kept on November 28.

Chronologia Summorum Pontificum.

ST. ZACHARY

741-752

ZACHARY, A GREEK FROM CALABRIA, WAS NOT only saintly and capable, but one of those happy people with a gift for making friends. This personal charm was manifested in the first problem he faced, the recovery of four cities from the Lombards. Though Liutprand, king of the Lombards, after much dealing and negotiating, had promised to restore the cities, he did not. Pope Zachary then went directly to the king with astounding results. Not only did Liutprand give back the four cities, but he restored the Sabine estate of the patrimony, and gave the Pope outright some other cities. Pope and king had dinner together to celebrate, and Liutprand declared that he had never had so glorious a dinner. The power of Zachary's charm was even more strikingly revealed when Liutprand began to invade Ravenna. The exarch, left without adequate help by the Emperor, cried out for help to the Pope. Zachary sent an embassy which accomplished nothing. He then went north to see Liutprand personally. The Pope was received with grateful joy at Ravenna, but Liutprand, firmly set on taking over the exarchate, tried to stop him from coming to court. When Zachary refused to be stopped, Liutprand received him graciously. This time it took argument, but again Zachary won. Liutprand ended by not only stopping the invasion of Ravenna but actually restoring territory he had already taken!

St. Boniface continued his great work under Zachary. Christianity was now so far advanced in Germany that a synod could be held. Not content with his mighty missionary activity, Boniface, helped by Pippin the Short, worked hard to reform the Frankish church. Zachary helped him by wise words of cheer and received with good-humored kindness complaints that Boniface made about certain matters in Rome.

In the East, Constantine V Copronymus had succeeded his father Leo, but Constantine was even more devoted to smashing images than Leo. Vainly did Zachary urge him to return to Catholic orthodoxy.

More successful with the Lombards, Zachary once again checked an invasion. King Ratchis was dissuaded from carrying fire and sword into Roman territory. Ratchis soon after abdicated and came to Rome to receive the monastic habit from Zachary. Another distinguished prince, Pippin's brother Carloman, had already done the same thing.

In 751 Zachary received a momentous case of conscience from Pippin, the Frankish mayor of the palace. For years these mayors of the palace had ruled the Franks while the Merovingian kings vegetated. Now Pippin determined to dethrone Childeric II, the last of these shadow monarchs, and mount the throne himself. Before so grave a step, he and the nobles sent to Pope Zachary for advice. Zachary's famous answer was that he who did the work of king should be king.

It is no surprise that this genial Pope should be very kind to the poor and the sick. He was generous to the clergy and did much to restore the Roman churches. St. Zachary died in March 752. His feast is kept on March 15.

Chronologia Summorum Pontificum.

STEPHEN II

752

Two things are noteworthy about Pope Stephen II. He had the shortest pontificate in the whole history of the papacy and he caused annoyance to historians because of the dispute as to whether or not he should be included in the list of popes.

Stephen was a priest of the Roman clergy. After the death of the great St. Zachary, Stephen was elected unanimously. He accepted and was sitting down doing business in the Lateran Palace the third day after his election when apoplexy struck him. He died the day after.

Many historians did not include him in the list of popes, and as a result in some books the numeral after later popes named Stephen is placed thus: Stephen (II) III. This is confusing and quite unnecessary. Everything points to the conclusion that the short-lived Stephen should be included in the list of popes. He was duly elected. He accepted. He actually was governing the Church when he was struck down. According to tradition, he should be included in the list of popes, and indeed his picture has its place in the famous medallions of the popes in the basilica of St. Paul-Outside-the-Walls. Last, but not least, Stephen is included in the list of popes given in the *Annuario Pontificio*. For these reasons, even though he was never consecrated, Stephen has his place in this book, and his successor will be called Stephen III without any parenthesis.

Chronologia Summorum Pontificum.

STEPHEN III

752-757

THE BIOGRAPHIES OF PRECEDING POPES REVEAL how gradual was the growth of the temporal power of the papacy. More and more the rude pressure of circumstance compelled popes to play the civil ruler. Now by mid-eighth century, the emperors had left Italy derelict and the popes were forced to choose between letting the hated Lombards overrun his people or taking power themselves. Stephen III had to make this decision.

Stephen III was a Roman deacon brought up by the popes after the death of his father. Since he was formed by men like St. Gregory III and St. Zachary, it is no surprise that Stephen was devoted to ecclesiastical tradition, a lover of the poor, and a firm defender of the people.

The East still groaned under the fury of the image-breaking Emperor Constantine. There was not much Stephen could do but try to recall the Emperor to his duty. He wrote to Constantine, but it did no good.

The Lombards, under fierce King Aistulf, having overrun the exarchate of Ravenna, had their eyes on Rome. The Pope, alarmed for the city's safety, made a peace treaty for which he paid handsomely. But Aistulf cared little for treaties. The Emperor, his hands full with Bulgarians and Saracens, was devoting his spare time to smashing images. The best he could do for Italy was to send an ambassador with an order for the Pope to persuade Aistulf to give back Ravenna. Stephen did go to Pavia, but when he could get nothing out of Aistulf, he passed the Alps and made a personal appeal to Pippin.

The Pope solemnly anointed Pippin and his sons Charles and Carloman as kings. Then Pippin, after Aistulf repulsed three embassies, led a Frankish army into Italy and brought the tough Lombard to terms. He was to give up Ravenna and keep peace. But once the Franks disappeared over the Alps, Aistulf called for an all-out war to overrun Italy. Burning and ravaging, the Lombards marched on Rome and blockaded the city. Frantically the Pope multiplied appeals to Pippin, the last being written in the name of St. Peter himself. After three months the situation looked black, but the Lombards raised the siege and went north. Pippin was on his way at last.

Another embassy appeared from Constantinople. When they heard about Pippin, the envoys hurried to meet him and offered him presents if he would restore the exarchate to the Emperor. Pippin replied that it was only for Blessed Peter that he had taken arms, and it was to Blessed Peter he would restore the territory.

Pippin defeated the Lombards again, and this time saw to it that peace was kept. Stephen III was put in control of the exarchate of Ravenna and now in 756 may be considered the first of the papal monarchs.

Stephen died in 757. Though known to history as the first pope-king, he was better known to the Roman poor for his great charity.

Mosaic in the Basilica of St. Paul-Outside-the-Walls, Rome.

ST. PAUL I

757-767

PAUL WAS THE BROTHER OF POPE STEPHEN III, and like him was educated under the tutelage of the popes. Paul served his brother on many diplomatic missions. The two brothers seem to have been quite close, and when Stephen fell ill in 757 Paul devotedly nursed him. Even while Stephen was dying, a party began an intrigue to seat the archdeacon Theophylact on the papal throne. But when Stephen was buried, the great majority chose Paul to succeed his brother. He was consecrated on May 29, 757.

Naturally Paul continued the policy of his brother. He maintained close relations with Pippin and relied on his aid to hold the Papal States against Lombard and Greek. The greatest danger was from the Lombards. Aistulf had died shortly after his final defeat and he was succeeded by Desiderius, duke of Istria. But the new king met a sudden and strange challenge, ex-king Ratchis, who had abdicated in 768 to become a monk, now left his monastery to dispute the iron crown with Desiderius. Desiderius promised peace to the Pope if he would help him, and Stephen had sent an embassy including Paul which had persuaded Ratchis to return to his duties in the cloister.

Desiderius, forgetful of this act of friendliness, had designs on the Papal States. He even made an alliance, strange enough, with the Eastern Empire. Pope Paul pleaded with Pippin for help, but the Frankish king was so involved in wars with the dukes of Aquitaine and Bavaria, that he could help the Pope only by diplomacy. Actually Paul succeeded in holding on to his kingdom without any major war. Toward the end of his pontificate he even asked Pippin to get Desiderius to help him against the Greeks!

The threat from the Greeks was not too serious. The Emperor, with no army to spare for Italy, relied on diplomacy. He tried to pervert Pippin to his iconoclast heresy, but his pleas were resisted by the stout-hearted Frank. The Pope, of course, was not idle. He wrote to Pippin and encouraged him to remain loyal and orthodox. The Pope's care was rewarded. The Frankish bishops assembled in a synod at Gentilly in 767 and reaffirmed their belief in traditional Catholic doctrines, especially in the correct veneration of holy images.

Paul also wrote to Emperors Constantine and Leo to win them back from their heresy, but again in vain.

Paul was a man of noble character, outstanding even among the popes for his charity to the poor. During the night he would often visit prisons and perform acts of mercy. His only defect was, perhaps, a poor choice of officials; but if he discovered any injustice, he hastened to make up for it. He died outside the city on June 28, 767. Paul I is venerated as a saint. His feast is kept on June 28.

Mosaic in the Basilica of St. Paul-Outside-the-Walls, Rome.

[188]

STEPHEN IV

768-772

THAT THE POPE SHOULD BE KING HAD NUMEROUS advantages, but one grave disadvantage was the intense stimulus royal power gave to the ambition of the little lords who infested the area around Rome. One of these, Toto, duke of Nepi, led an armed gang into Rome, held his private election, and declared his brother Constantine pope. That Constantine was a layman did not trouble the duke. But Christopher and his son Sergius, two high officials of the late Pope Paul, managed to get out of the city and fly to the Lombards. They got a Lombard army to come down and throw out the intruder. After a fight in which Toto was killed, the way was open for an honest election; but before Christopher could get back to the city, Waldipert, a Lombard priest, staged his private election, and proclaimed Philip, a monk, the next pope. Christopher demanded the removal of this intruder and finally held an open and honest election, from which the priest Stephen emerged pope.

Stephen had come to Rome from Sicily at an early age and had entered the Benedictine monastery of St. Chrysogonus. St. Zachary ordained him priest and used him in the papal service. Stephen remained with the dying Pope Paul while Toto was beginning his intrigues. His early career of goodness and service fits the character given him by his biographer in the *Liber Pontificalis,* but horrible cruelties took place in his reign. Probably he was not able to control his subordinates. Even before he was consecrated on August 7, 768, the terror began. Antipope Constantine, his brother Passious, his official Theodore, the Lombard priest Waldipert —all had their eyes torn out.

In 769 Pope Stephen held a synod at the Lateran at which the eyeless Constantine was ordered to be beaten and cast out of the Church. More constructively, the synod decreed very wise regulations for future papal elections. The pope must be chosen from the cardinals, that is, the more important of the Roman clergy. The clergy are to elect, and only after the election are the Roman army and the people to acclaim the elected pope. Nobles outside the city are to have nothing to do with the election. The synod also upheld the veneration of holy images and condemned Emperor Constantine's image-breaking council of 754.

Christopher, the primicerius, had been the hero of Stephen's election; and he remained the Pope's right-hand man. He tried to get back the territory which Desiderius had promised to restore. And when Desiderius forgot his promises, Christopher had tried to get Charlemagne to intervene. Naturally Desiderius hated Christopher. He paid the Pope's chamberlain, Paul Afiarta, to blacken the character of Christopher and his son Sergius. Then in the Lent of either 770 or 771, he came down to Rome with an army to pray! Christopher manned the walls and refused to let this strange pilgrim inside. But after some obscure intrigues, Christopher and his son Sergius went out to St. Peter's (then outside the walls) to Pope Stephen who had been talking to the Lombards. The Pope went back to the city and Paul Afiarta came out, seized Christopher and Sergius, and put out their eyes.

Pope Stephen died in February 772. His last years like his first were troubled by cruelty. Paul Afiarta, now in power, wreaked vengeance on his enemies.

Stephen is venerated as a saint in certain districts of Sicily but not by the universal church.

Chronologia Summorum Pontificum.

HADRIAN I

772-795

THE STORMY PONTIFICATE OF STEPHEN IV HAD been not the beginning but only the forerunner of a time of troubles for the papacy. On Stephen's death, there was a speedy quiet, unanimous election of the holy priest Hadrian. Hadrian, a Roman of noble family, had been known for his austere piety even before he became a cleric. Now as pope his first act was one of justice to recall the exiled victims of Paul Afiarta.

The Lombard menace still loomed over Rome. Desiderius, after a deal of ravaging, marched on Rome as a pilgrim—he said. Hadrian, not at all reassured by the Lombard's pilgrim staff, mobilized his army and forbade Desiderius to enter Rome under pain of excommunication. Though the Lombard turned back, his continued depredations forced Hadrian to appeal to Charlemagne. Charlemagne, after a vain try at diplomacy, marched into Italy, defeated Desiderius, and blockaded him in Pavia. While the siege was in progress, Charlemagne hurried to Rome to pay the Pope a visit. Hadrian, at first a little suspicious, was delighted to find in his powerful protector a true friend. Charlemagne confirmed Pippin's donation. Then having captured Pavia, he put Desiderius in a monastery and made himself king of the Lombards.

Hadrian found a new version of an old heresy arising in Spain. Elipandus, bishop of Toledo, and Felix, bishop of Urgel, taught that the Second Person of the Trinity did not really become Man but only adopted human nature in such a way that Jesus Christ the Man is only an adopted Son of God. The Pope wrote to the Spanish bishops to condemn this Neo-Nestorianism, and Charlemagne had a council at Ratisbon in 785 and another at Frankfort in 794 echo the Pope's condemnation.

Ever since the iconoclast or image-breaking heresy had separated Constantinople from Catholic unity, the popes had not ceased to urge the emperors to repent. Now at last a ruler arose who would listen. When Leo IV died in 780, he left a beautiful wife, Irene, who ruled for her little son Constantine VI. Empress Irene at once allowed the veneration of images, and soon she listened to the Pope's plea for a general council. The Seventh Ecumenical Council, held at Nicaea in 787 under the legates of Pope Hadrian, reaffirmed Catholic belief in the proper veneration of images. Both Empress Irene and Patriarch Tarasius accepted the decrees and ended the iconoclast schism. Once more Constantinople returned to Catholic unity and orthodoxy.

Hadrian was delighted, but he was annoyed because the imperial government refused to return the estates of the patrimony confiscated by Leo the Isaurian, and refused also to return to the Western patriarchate jurisdiction over Illyricum.

The Pope was embarrassed to find the Franks attacking the Seventh Ecumenical Council. The Caroline Books were a bitter and stupid attack on the council, and the Council of Frankfort had the boldness to censure the Seventh Ecumenical Council. This Frankish furore seems to have been caused by a misunderstanding and perhaps a mistranslation of the acts of the Nicaea council. Hadrian was patient. He contented himself with gently reminding Charlemagne that after all it was to St. Peter and his successors that Christ left the government of the Church. He explained the true meaning of the decrees of Nicaea.

Hadrian was a great builder, who did much for Rome. Above all, he was a true father to his people. Not content with giving help to the needy and distressed, he visited them personally.

Hadrian died on Christmas Day 795. He had been a great leader for the Church.

Mosaic in the Basilica of St. Paul-Outside-the-Walls, Rome.

ST. LEO III

795-816

ON THE VERY DAY OF HADRIAN'S FUNERAL, DEcember 26, 795, the pious priest Leo was unanimously elected to succeed him. Leo, from a family of ordinary folks, had been a cleric from his youth. He had risen to be cardinal-priest of Santa Susanna and a high papal official. He was a kind, charitable, and devoted ecclesiastic.

The new Pope lost no time showing Charlemagne that he intended to maintain friendly relations. It was well that he did so, for kind and amiable as he was, Leo was to be attacked in body and reputation. In 799 a conspiracy was hatched by Paschal the primicerius, a nephew of the late pope. While Leo was walking in the procession of the Greater Litanies on April 25, armed men scattered the procession and fell on the Pope. They threw the Pope down, hurriedly stabbed at his eyes and tore at his tongue. Then after leaving Leo lying all bloody in the street, they came back, dragged him into St. Sylvester's Church and had another go at blinding him. Then they placed him in the monastery of St. Erasmus. Quite surprisingly, Leo recovered the use of eyes and tongue. His friends got him out of the monastery and Winichis, duke of Spoleto, took him under his protection. Leo went to Paderborn to get Charlemagne's aid. The great Frank received the Pope with honor and sympathy. He sent Leo back with officials to settle the matter. The Pope's entry into Rome was a triumph, for the conspiracy was not popular. Charlemagne himself came down to Rome in 800 and held a great assembly in St. Peter's. He wished to clear the Pope of serious accusations which the frantic conspirators brought against their victim. The bishops, of course, refused to try the Pope, but Leo willingly mounted the ambo in St. Peter's and solemnly swore that he was innocent of the charges. Charlemagne ordered the conspirators to be executed, but at the Pope's kind plea, commuted their sentence to exile.

Two days later at the Christmas Mass, the Pope placed a jeweled crown on Charlemagne's head while St. Peter's rang with the glad shout. "To Charles, the most pious Augustus, crowned by God, to our great and peace-loving emperor, life and victory!" The empire in the West was restored. Leo hoped to see the new Emperor of the West marry Irene, the Eastern Empress, but the deposition of Irene in 802 ended the project.

Leo got along well with Charlemagne, but after the Emperor died in 814, new troubles broke out in Rome. A fresh conspiracy was organized, but this time the Pope got wind of it in time and had the ringleaders seized and executed. Then the little lords of the Campagna banded together to march on Rome, but the duke of Spoleto dispersed them.

Leo helped the monks of Constantinople who, led by St. Theodore Studites, had been exiled for opposing imperial tyranny. From Charlemagne the Pope had received a large share of the treasure the Frank had captured from the Avars. Leo used his money as a just steward, to help the poor and to beautify churches. This busy Pope worked to build or restore 160 churches. Under Hadrian and Leo III the decay of Rome was checked.

St. Leo III died in June 816. His feast is kept on June 12.

Chronologia Summorum Pontificum.

STEPHEN V

816-817

THE FIRST ELECTION OF A POPE UNDER THE RE-stored empire of the West shows the independence the papacy intended to have in the new regime. The Byzantine emperors' claim to confirm the election of a pope had caused some difficulties. Now since the time of Zachary confirmation of an election was no longer sought, even from the Exarch of Ravenna. The Roman clergy did not give the new Western emperor, Louis the Pious, any chance to interfere. Speedily they elected the deacon Stephen, and speedily was he consecrated.

Stephen was a Roman of noble family, a family that was to give to the papacy not only himself, but two other ninth-century popes, Sergius II and Hadrian II. Stephen had been trained by Pope Hadrian I and had gained an excellent reputation as a young man of virtue and ability. Ordained a deacon by Leo III, he was a zealous worker in the Lord's vineyard. He was an amiable man who loved peace.

Such a pope was bound to do nothing to provoke the Emperor. Once the independence of the papacy was safeguarded, Stephen showed the greatest good will. He had the Romans swear allegiance to the Emperor as protector. He sent a legation to Louis the Pious to notify the Emperor of his election and to arrange for an interview.

Pope Stephen crossed the Alps in August and met Emperor Louis the Pious at Rheims. The Emperor received the Pope with joy and profound respect. Stephen crowned Louis and his wife, Irmengard as emperor and empress. To Theodulf, bishop of Orleans, one of the Emperor's principal advisers, the Pope granted the pallium. Louis gave the Pope many presents including an estate in France. The meeting at Rheims was most harmonious.

On the way back to Rome, Stephen visited Ravenna whose archbishop, Martin, had given Leo III some trouble. But now all was sweetness, and the Pope celebrated Mass in the cathedral and exhibited a relic, very precious, if authentic—the sandals of Christ. Stephen entered Rome in November. With him came a number of prisoners from the time of Leo III to whom the kind Pope gave pardon.

Stephen died on January 25, 817, and was buried in St. Peter's.

Chronologia Summorum Pontificum.

ST. PASCHAL I

817-824

BECAUSE ST. PASCHAL I, LIKE HADRIAN I AND ST. Leo III, was devoted to beautifying churches, something is known of this Pope's personal appearance. Contemporary mosaics picture him as a tall man with large eyes and without a beard. Paschal was a Roman who was brought up in the Lateran seminary. Ordained priest, he so impressed St. Leo III by his piety that he was made superior of St. Stephen's monastery. There he took care of the pilgrims who came to visit the Apostles' shrine. He was a kind man, who quietly supplied whatever the poorer pilgrims might need.

Paschal was elected unanimously to succeed Stephen V. He was consecrated without any reference to the Emperor. But though firm in his stand for independence, he enjoyed good relations with Louis. Indeed in 817 he received from Louis a document confirming the donations of Pippin and Charlemagne and recognizing the independence of papal elections. In 823 Lothair, the Emperor's oldest son and King of Italy, came to Rome to be crowned by the Pope.

A faction arose headed by no less a personage than Theodore, the primicerius, or chief minister, which favored imperial control of Rome. After Lothair's departure, a group of papal supporters entered the Lateran, seized Theodore and Leo his son-in-law, blinded them, and cut their heads off. Their followers, furious and frightened, complained hotly to Emperor Louis. When Louis sent envoys to investigate the killing, Paschal adopted the Frankish custom of compurgation to clear himself. He and a number of bishops solemnly swore that he was innocent of the bloody deed. But at the same time, the Pope refused to punish the killers because after all the victims had been guilty of high treason.

Paschal was pained to learn that image-breaking was once more rampant in the Eastern Empire. Leo V, the Armenian, replaced the Orthodox Patriarch Nicephorus with a layman, called a synod which repudiated the Seventh Ecumenical Council, and persecuted the Orthodox. The Pope wrote to Emperor Leo instructing him in true Catholic doctrine, but it was no use. He wrote letters of consolation to the great St. Theodore Studites and the persecuted clergy and religious of the East. He welcomed those who fled to Italy.

Paschal encouraged missionary activity in the North. He commissioned Abbo, archbishop of Rheims, and Bishop Halitgar to preach the gospel to the Danes.

His great kindness makes Paschal a likable saint. As superior of St. Stephen's, he had been very good to poor pilgrims. As Pope he not only helped refugees from iconoclast persecution, but he spent freely and widely to ransom poor prisoners taken by the Saracens, who at that time were making life on the Mediterranean coasts miserable for Christian folk.

St. Paschal died in 824. His feast is kept on May 14.

Mosaic detail of vault. Church of St. Praxed,
Rome.

EUGENE II

824-827

WHEN ST. PASCHAL DIED, FACTIONAL FEELING, which had flared up in the killing of Theodore and Leo, embittered the election. The nobles, who stood against Paschal's independent policy, prevailed and secured the election of the archpriest Eugene. Abbot Wala, a great minister of Charlemagne and Louis, who was present in Rome at the time, threw his weight to Eugene. Eugene, a spiritual man, may have been the candidate of a faction, but he was no tool. As archpriest he had been in charge of Santa Sabina Church and had an excellent reputation for learning and goodness.

Emperor Louis naturally was pleased at the election, and quick to seize the favorable moment, sent his son Lothair to Rome to put imperial relations with the papacy on a more favorable footing. The imperialist nobles were now reinstated. Some were brought back from exile; others recovered confiscated property. Lothair then arranged with the Pope a Roman Constitution which definitely recognized the Emperor as overlord of Rome while it conceded immediate temporal power to the Pope. Papal elections were to be held correctly, but the newly elected pope could not be consecrated until in the presence of imperial envoys he had taken an oath of loyalty to this Constitution. The increasing weakness of the Carolingian empire, however, doomed this Constitution to an early death.

The Eastern Emperor, Leo V, had been assassinated in 820. His successor, Michael II, the Stammerer, though an image-breaker, at first showed an inclination to compromise; but when he found out that the Orthodox had no wish for compromise with heretics he resumed the persecution. St. Theodore Studites had written to him urging the Emperor to consult the Pope as head of the Church. Michael did write to Pope Eugene and to Emperor Louis the Pious, but nothing came of the matter. Louis had some Frankish bishops study the matter, and they, still misunderstanding the acts of the Seventh Ecumenical Council, wrote an attack on the straw men their imaginative ignorance had constructed. Naturally this was no help in clarifying ideas for Michael!

In 826 Pope Eugene held a council at Rome which passed thirty-eight canons, most of them concerning reform. Simony was strictly forbidden; churches destroyed by war were to be rebuilt; schools were to be opened in all parishes.

Archbishop Abbo had given up the work of converting the Danes, but the great St. Ansgar stepped into his place. Pope Eugene encouraged the Apostle of the Scandinavians and commended him to all Catholics.

Eugene died in August, 827.

Chronologia Summorum Pontificum.

VALENTINE

827

VALENTINE WAS A ROMAN OF AN UPPER-CLASS family living in the area of the Via Lata, then the aristocratic section of the city. His parents, who were as good as they were noble, brought Valentine up in a truly Christian manner, and he grew up to be a serious young man devoted to prayer and his studies. He became a cleric and caught the eye of Pope St. Paschal I, who placed him in charge of the Lateran Palace. Paschal grew to be very fond of this promising cleric and made him archdeacon of the Roman Church. Pope Eugene II also appreciated Valentine's excellent qualities and, like Paschal, relied upon his help in governing the Church.

After Eugene's death, the Roman clergy and nobles gathered in the Lateran to elect a new pope. This time there was no contest at all. Clergy and nobles alike raised the cry: "Valentine, the most holy archdeacon, is worthy of the Apostolic See; Valentine must be made pope!" Then they streamed out of the Lateran and hurried to the Church of St. Mary Major where they found Valentine at prayer. In spite of his earnest protests that he was not worthy, they insisted on Valentine's election.

Valentine seems to have been an ideal choice. He certainly did enjoy a wonderful reputation. But he was to have little chance to prove his worth as pope. Within about forty days of his election, Valentine was dead.

The nobles had triumphed in the election of Eugene II. In Valentine's election there had been no contest, but it is noted that the nobles like the clergy, took part in the affair. So far the nobles' influence had not been bad. Eugene was a good pope; Valentine promised to be an excellent one. But as their power grows and the imperial grip on Rome relaxes, the little lords will prove to be unworthy of the responsibility of sharing in a papal election. Their participation in these elections foreshadows a dark and stormy time for the papacy.

Mosaic in the Basilica of St. Paul-Outside-the-Walls, Rome.

GREGORY IV

827-844

BLESSED ARE THE PEACEMAKERS FOR THEY SHALL be called children of God. But sometimes their efforts are not appreciated by the children of men. So it was with Gregory IV.

Gregory IV was a Roman of noble family, ordained priest by St. Paschal. He became cardinal-priest of St. Mark. He was a handsome man with an excellent reputation. Gregory was elected without difficulty, but the imperial envoys insisted that his consecration should be held up until the Emperor confirmed the election. This took some time, and it was not until March 828 that Gregory was consecrated.

Europe at this time is entering a period of darkness and agony. The long ships of the Norsemen scoured the coasts and stabbed up the rivers. Saracen galleys made the Mediterranean coasts horrid with cries of grief and pain. The Saracens were tearing Sicily from feeble Byzantines and getting a foothold in Southern Italy. The Avars were raiding the Eastern Marches. And all the while the descendants of Great Charles were earnestly ruining the empire with their bitter and bloody family fights.

Pope Gregory did what he could to defend Christendom from these evils. He was persuaded by Lothair, the Emperor's oldest son, to cross the Alps to mediate between the sons and the father. When Gregory reached Alsace, he was welcomed by an angry protest from bishops favorable to Emperor Louis. Gregory told the malcontents plainly that they should not forget that "the government of souls, which belongs to the supreme pontiff, is greater than the imperial power which is temporal." But Gregory failed in his attempt at mediation and must have felt frustrated on that "field of lies."

Later on, after the death of Emperor Louis, Gregory tried to bring peace to the quarreling sons. But the brothers smashed each other on the disastrous field of Fontenay in 841, and the empire was divided by the famous treaty of Verdun in 843.

From the East Gregory received more consolation. The iconoclast persecutor Theophilus was dead, and his widow, the Empress Theodora replaced the iconoclast Patriarch John with the Orthodox Methodius. A synod was held in 842 which restored the veneration of holy images.

St. Ansgar visited Rome and Gregory gave him the pallium and made him papal legate to the countries of the North. Gregory also extended the feast of All Saints on November 1 to France and Germany.

Peace-loving though he was, Gregory had to take military measures to protect the Papal States against the Saracens. He built a fort at Ostia near the mouth of the Tiber to defend Rome from these bold marauders.

Gregory IV died in January 844.

Mosaic in the Basilica of St. Paul-Outside-the-Walls, Rome.

SERGIUS II

844-847

SERGIUS II PRESENTS A PUZZLE TO THE HISTORIAN. His early career so successful, his actions in many cases so wise and prudent, conflict violently with the character given him by one manuscript of the *Liber Pontificalis*. This manuscript, after describing the Pope most favorably in the usual way of an official biographer, suddenly changes tone completely. Sergius was an irritable old man tormented with gout who left all business to his brother, Benedict. And Benedict carried matters with a high hand. Simony (the buying and selling of sacred things) became the order of the day, and extortion was practiced on a wide scale. At any rate, there must have been some grounds for so severe an indictment. But since there are no other sources to confirm or deny the guilt of Pope Sergius, the historian must be cautious.

Sergius was a Roman of the same noble family as Stephen V. Orphaned at twelve, Sergius was placed by Leo III in the School for Sacred Music. Here he did well, and when he became Pope he remembered his happy school days and rebuilt the school on a grander scale. The talented young man was favored by all the popes from Leo III to Gregory IV. Made cardinal priest of Sts. Silvester and Mark by Paschal, he was made archpriest by Gregory IV.

When Gregory died, Sergius was put forward as the candidate of the nobility. At first it looked as if he would be elected easily, but suddenly a mob proclaimed the deacon John pope and by force took over the Lateran Palace. The nobility, furious, rallied and drove the mob out. It would have gone hard with John had not Sergius interceded for him.

Sergius was consecrated without waiting for imperial confirmation. When Emperor Lothair heard of this, he sent an army led by his son Louis to teach the Romans manners. Though the army approached Rome burning and ravaging, Pope Sergius went out to meet Louis and succeeded in calming him. The Pope would not allow Louis to enter St. Peter's until he had given assurance of his good will. And even then, he firmly refused to allow the destructive army inside the walls.

Pope Sergius crowned Louis King of Italy, but he refused to allow the Romans to swear allegiance to him. Only to the Emperor Lothair would Pope and Romans swear allegiance.

Warnings had been coming in that the Saracens might strike at Rome. In 846 a Saracen fleet sailed up the Tiber, took Ostia and Portus, and defeated all relief forces. The city itself was saved by its old walls, but St. Peter's was outside the walls, and to the horror of Christendom the Moslems pillaged the venerable basilica which housed the Apostles' body. It is estimated that they carried off from the basilicas of St. Peter and St. Paul-Outside-the-Walls three tons of gold and thirty of silver.

Christendom rose up in horror, and the next year the Saracens were driven from Italy for the time being.

Sergius died suddenly on January 27, 847.

Mosaic in the Basilica of St. Paul-Outside-the-Walls, Rome.

ST. LEO IV

847-855

WITH ST. PETER'S STANDING FORLORN AND desolate, the Romans, terrified at the Saracen peril, hastened to elect the holy priest Leo. After two months' delay, they decided to go ahead with his consecration without waiting for imperial confirmation. But they sent to Emperor Lothair to assure him that they did not mean to lessen his prerogative.

Though Leo was a Roman, his father's name Radoald might possibly be an indication of Teutonic descent. Educated in the monastery of St. Martin, Leo made such a reputation for holiness that Gregory IV took him for the papal service. Sergius II made him cardinal-priest of the Four Crowned Martyrs' Church.

Leo, though a spiritual man, had to devote a great deal of time to temporal matters. Determined that the sack of St. Peter's should not be repeated, Leo started to build a wall around the Vatican Hill and district. It was a great undertaking for those rude times, but the energy of the Pope was unflagging. He got money from the Emperor and workers from the agricultural estates of the patrimony. But while the walls were rising, news came that near Sardinia a great Saracen fleet was being readied to sail against Rome. This time, however, the Italians took measures to defend the Eternal City. A fleet from the Southern seaports of Naples, Amalfi and Gaeta, sailed into the Tiber. Since these cities were nominally under the Eastern Emperor, the Romans wondered whether the fleet had come to help them or attack them. When Admiral Caesarius reassured the Pope, Leo led a Roman army to Ostia to join the fleet. He celebrated Mass and gave Holy Communion to all hands. Thus fortified spiritually and ready with their arms, the Christians met the Saracens. After some indecisive fighting, a strong wind blew up, separated the fleets, and completely wrecked the Saracen fleet; Rome was saved.

Leo did not remain idle. He kept the walls rising, and finally in 852, they were ready. The new enclosed area, justly called the Leonine City, was dedicated by the Pope with a solemn procession around the walls and a Mass. Leo also built a fortified town at Portus near the mouth of the Tiber and settled Corsican refugees there to man the walls. He rebuilt Centumcellae, sacked by the Saracens back in 813, in a better location. He also did what he could to restore St. Peter's and adorn other churches.

Leo held a synod in 853 which renewed the reform canons of Eugene's synod in 826. He gave added solemnity to the feast of Mary's Assumption by giving it an octave. He protected his subjects from rapacious underlings.

Two monarchs were crowned by Leo. Louis, Lothair's son, was crowned emperor in 850. In 853 a far more interesting coronation took place. Ethelwulf, king of the West Saxons, sent his young son Alfred to be crowned by Pope Leo. The Pope made Alfred his spiritual son.

St. Leo died July 17, 855, with a great reputation for sanctity. Indeed he was credited with working miracles. His feast is kept on July 17.

Raphael. "The Battle Near Ostia" (fresco detail). The Vatican.

BENEDICT III

855-858

IT IS BETWEEN ST. LEO IV AND BENEDICT III THAT the medieval gossips put the marvelous and fabulous Pope Joan. For this odd story of a woman pope there is not the slightest historical justification. Dark as was the age, there is enough light on the election of Benedict III to show that there is no room for any pope or popess between Benedict and Leo. And there was enough excitement and scandal too in the daring attempt of the excommunicated priest Anastasius to steal the papacy without the old wives' tale of Pope Joan.

After Leo's death, Benedict, a Roman, the cardinal-priest of St. Calixtus, was elected pope. Legates were sent to the Emperor with notice of the election. Then came trouble. Arsenius, bishop of Horta, an ambitious man, got hold of the legates and persuaded them somehow to betray Benedict and get the Emperor to put in his son Anastasius instead. That Anastasius had been excommunicated under St. Leo IV seemed not to have bothered him at all.

When the legates returned to Rome with the imperial envoys, they brought Anastasius to Rome in triumph. He smashed the notices of his excommunication and took over the Lateran Palace. Benedict was stripped of his vestments and kept a prisoner. But the Frankish envoys and the Roman plotters did not reckon with public opinion. At a new election the crowd boldly cried that Anastasius was excommunicated. The Frankish envoys,

impressed by the determination of the Romans to have Benedict, gave in. Out went Anastasius and Benedict returned in triumph to the Lateran. He used his victory mercifully, even restoring Anastasius to lay communion and making him an abbot.

Benedict was a man who as a young student had soaked up knowledge like a sponge. Under St. Leo IV he had become cardinal-priest of St. Calixtus. Though he was a mild man, Benedict could take vigorous action when it was necessary in the interest of good morals. He was horrified by the distressing state of affairs in the Frankish realms. Under Charlemagne's incapable descendants anarchy grew and disorders multiplied. Benedict wrote to the bishops of France rebuking them for not speaking out against the mushrooming evils. He also rebuked Emperor Lothair II for sheltering Ingeltrude, the runaway wife of the Italian, Count Boso. This Ingeltrude was an international scandal, and the Pope had her excommunicated.

A more consoling event was the visit of King Ethelwulf of the West Saxons with his young son Alfred. He brought the Pope many presents from England.

Benedict made a regulation that the pope and all the clergy must attend the funeral of a priest. He worked to repair the damage done by the Saracens to St. Peter's and St. Paul's, but his time was short. He died on April 17, 858.

The British Museum, London.

ST. NICHOLAS I, THE GREAT

858-867

THERE HAVE BEEN MANY GREAT POPES, BUT TO three only has posterity awarded the title of the Great: St. Leo I, St. Gregory I, and St. Nicholas I. Nicholas, a man of handsome appearance, was noted for two virtues, charity and justice. He took loving care of his poor, and for the oppressed or wronged he was a mighty protector. Add great strength of soul and dynamic energy, and it is easy to see why this man made so strong an impression on his age.

Nicholas was a Roman, the son of an official in the papal service. Educated at the Lateran, he joined the clergy, was highly favored by Popes St. Leo IV and Benedict II, and after Benedict's death was easily elected his successor.

His passion for justice led him to oppose Lothair, king of Lorraine, when that unworthy monarch wished to exchange his wife for his mistress. Lothair had the subservient Frankish bishops at his beck, but when the injured wife appealed to the Pope, it was a different story. Nicholas not only quashed the unjust verdicts but deposed the influential archbishops of Cologne and Trier. Angrily they appealed to Emperor Louis II. Louis marched on Rome to teach the Pope a new canon law by force of arms. He blockaded Nicholas and had the indomitable Pope reduced almost to starvation, when a fever brought the Emperor to think better of his brutal conduct. The Franks marched away, Lothair remained married, the archbishops remained deposed. It was a striking stand for the independence of the spiritual and the maintenance of moral standards.

As for an injured wife, so did the Pope act for a deposed bishop. Rothad of Soissons, deposed by the famous Archbishop Hincmar of Rheims, appealed to Nicholas. The Pope, after studying the case, ordered Rothad reinstated. As for a bishop, so did the Pope act for oppressed people. Archbishop John of Ravenna had caused great complaints by his oppression. Nicholas, after several unsuccessful attempts to get justice, went personally to Ravenna and saw to it that property was restored to rightful owners.

The Bulgarians at this time were becoming Christians. In contact with both the Eastern and the Western rite, they hesitated between the two. Nicholas sent them legates and wrote a regular treatise to answer their questions.

Constantinople resented the efforts of the Pope to attach the Bulgarians to the Western Patriarchate. But it was an internal conflict which caused a schism to break out. St. Ignatius, the patriarch, was deposed. Photius, the most brilliant Greek of the age, replaced him. According to Dvornik, whose studies have undermined the traditional view of this Photian business, St. Ignatius actually resigned and Photius was legitimate patriarch. When Photius and Emperor Michael III appealed to the Pope, Nicholas sent legates to a synod held at Constantinople to judge the affair. But even though the legates favored Photius, Nicholas still refused to recognize him. It seems that bitter opponents of Photius had fled to Rome to give the Pope their side of the picture. Then Photius lost his temper. He held a synod in 867 which denounced certain Western practices and declared Nicholas deposed. But it was Photius who was deposed. His protector Michael III was overthrown by Basil the Macedonian. Basil promptly replaced Photius with St. Ignatius.

Nicholas encouraged St. Ansgar and his successor Rembert in their activity among the Scandinavians. He also tried hard to bring peace to Europe, but to keep the descendants of Charlemagne from fighting was too much even for Nicholas.

Nicholas the Great died November 13, 867. His feast is kept on that day.

Raphael. National Gallery, London.

HADRIAN II

867-872

ADRIAN WAS A MOST RELUCTANT CANDIDATE for the papacy. After the death of St. Leo IV and again after the death of Benedict III the Romans had turned to him as their first choice only to meet with a firm refusal. A third time, however, Hadrian gave in. Hadrian was a Roman of the same family as Popes Stephen V and Sergius II. His father Talarus became a bishop, and Hadrian himself had married and had a daughter before he became a priest. As cardinal-priest of St. Mark's he made so vivid an impression on the Romans by his prodigal charity to the poor that a story is preserved that once he miraculously multiplied some money he was distributing until every man in a huge crowd got three pennies.

When the people heard that Hadrian had at last accepted the papacy, nothing would do them but that he should be consecrated at once, and it was only with difficulty that the nobles persuaded them to await the Emperor's confirmation. Louis gave it quickly, and Hadrian was consecrated December 14, 867.

It is not easy to follow a strong pope like St. Nicholas. Party feeling ran high. Enemies of St. Nicholas urged Hadrian to change policies, while the numerous admirers of the late Pope watched jealously to see that he changed nothing. The nobles were becoming more insolent. The Duke of Spoleto entered the city and practically sacked it. Arsenius, bishop of Orta, was still an important man in Rome. His son Anastasius, the former antipope, was papal librarian. Another son, Eleutherius, decided to marry the Pope's daughter. That the lady was already engaged bothered him not at all. The rascal kidnapped the girl and her mother, and when imperial officials closed in on him, he brutally slew both mother and daughter.

In the East Hadrian had the satisfaction of ending the Photian schism. When Emperor Basil asked the Pope to settle the matter, Hadrian held a synod at Rome, and then sent legates to Constantinople. There at the Eighth Ecumenical Council, held in 869-870, the deposition of Photius and the reinstatement of St. Ignatius as patriarch were confirmed.

Hadrian followed Nicholas in refusing to grant the request of Boris, king of the Bulgarians, that Formosus, bishop of Porto, should be archbishop for the new Christians. Boris then turned to Constantinople and joined the Eastern Patriarchate and the Greek rite.

Those great apostles, Sts. Cyril and Methodius, visited Pope Hadrian in 867. The Pope treated them with all honor, encouraged their grand work among the Slavs, and permitted them to use the Slavonic language in the liturgy.

Like his predecessors, Hadrian tried and failed to keep peace among the Carolingian kings. He encouraged Emperor Louis II in his efforts to clear the Saracens out of Southern Italy.

An old man when elected, Hadrian died in November or December 872.

Mosaic in the Basilica of St. Paul-Outside-the-Walls, Rome.

[214]

JOHN VIII

872-882

I N A SAD PERIOD OF ANARCHY THE CHURCH RE-ceived a strong leader when John, archdeacon of the Roman clergy, was elected to succeed Hadrian II. Although probably old and in failing health when elected, John's strong will rose above age and ailments to make him a very active pope.

From Constantinople John received messages asking him to acknowledge Photius as patriarch. After the death of St. Ignatius, Photius once more had been made patriarch. The Pope sent legates to a synod held in 879-880. Although Photius did tamper with papal letters, he explained the matter to Pope John's satisfaction, and John not only ac-knowledged Photius but approved the acts of this synod which wiped out the synod of 869-870, the so-called Eighth Ecumenical Council. The Greeks acknowledged the Pope's primacy. Even more, they restored Bulgaria to the Western Patriarchate. Emperor Basil cooperated with Pope John in his efforts against the Saracens.

Toward the Western Slavs John also acted wisely. Germans with ambitions for political and religious domination over Moravia resented the work of St. Methodius. When they actually made him a prisoner, Pope John ordered that he be re-leased. At the same time he forbade the use of the Slavonic liturgy. After German complaints about the disloyalty of St. Methodius kept coming in, John called Methodius to Rome. Convinced of the loyalty and sanctity of the great apostle, the Pope sent him back with honor and with permission to use the Slavonic liturgy again.

John tried desperately to keep the sinking West-ern Empire afloat. After the death of Louis II, he decided that of all the claimants, Charles the Bald of France would make the best emperor. He crowned Charles in 875 and encouraged the French emperor's attempt to put new life into the empire. Charles in turn granted the Pope freedom of papal elections and other favors. But Charles died in 877. After a period of anxious searching, the Pope had to be content with a shadow em-peror, Charles the Fat.

John struggled manfully against the Saracens. He strained every nerve to unite the Italians against the common foe, but sadly he had to re-buke some for even allying themselves with the Moslem. He extended the fortifications of Rome. He built a fleet and defeated the Saracens in a sea fight at Circe.

Nor was Pope John less active against enemies at home. German resentment at his coronation of Charles the Bald had led the duke of Spoleto to chase him from Rome. But he came back deter-mined to do his duty. He struck a blow for de-cency by cleansing the city of a nest of corrupt offi-cials and evil nobles. Oddly enough, associated with the rascals was the austere Formosus. Formo-sus, a focus of discontent, was banished.

John died December 16, 882. A gruesome story is told of his death. According to one German an-nalist, a relative of Pope John gave him poison, but sick and old though the Pope was, the poison worked slowly. Impatient, the villain seized a hammer and beat the Pope to death. But this story is not at all certain.

Chronologia Summorum Principum.

MARINUS I

882-884

MARINUS WAS A NATIVE OF GALLESE, A LITTLE town on the Rome-Ravenna road. His father Palumbo was a priest, and he himself started out in the service of the Church at the early age of twelve. The capable young man rose steadily. He was ordained subdeacon by St. Leo IV, and as subdeacon he assisted at the reception of the imperial embassy for Michael III in 860. In 866, after being made a deacon, Marinus was sent on a legation to Constantinople, but imperial officials refused to allow the legates to cross the Bulgarian-imperial frontier. He reached Constantinople in 869 as the third of the papal legates to preside over the Eighth Ecumenical Council. His firm conduct so irritated Emperor Basil that the bold legate was actually imprisoned for a time. Even after being made bishop of Caere, Marinus continued to be employed by the Pope. As late as 882 he was sent on a diplomatic mission to Athanasius, bishop of Naples.

Though it was quite against custom to elect a bishop to be pope, Marinus was chosen to succeed John VIII. His long record of service probably led the clergy to break the custom. It was no easy task the new pope faced. John had been a strong ruler, and now Italy tossed restlessly. The Emperor, Charles the Fat, was no help. The Pope met him at the monastery of Nonantula in 883 to discuss the sad state of affairs. But Charles the Fat's policy of taking away fiefs from nobles increased the confusion. The nobles, led by Guido of Spoleto, defied the Emperor successfully.

At home Marinus reversed the policy of John VIII by recalling Formosus, bishop of Porto. John had not only banished Formosus but had made him swear never to come back to Rome. Marinus absolved him from the promise and recalled him. Formosus, austere man that he was, kept strange company. He was a focus for party feeling and remained a stormy petrel in Roman politics even as a corpse.

It is said that Marinus condemned Photius again, but Dvornik denies this. It is certain that out of regard for the great King Alfred, Marinus exempted the district of the Anglo-Saxons from taxation.

Marinus I died around the middle of May 884.

Mosaic in the Basilica of St. Paul-Outside-the-Walls, Rome.

ST. HADRIAN III

884-885

EXCEPT THAT HE WAS A ROMAN, THE SON OF Benedict, and that he was elected pope probably on May 17, 884, practically nothing is known about Hadrian before he became pope.

As pope, Hadrian had his troubles with the gang of evildoers broken up by Pope John VIII. After that strong pontiff died, they had drifted back to Rome. One of them, George of the Aventine, had a life which would make headline material for the yellow press. He had poisoned his brother for the sake of his mistress. He had solidified his position by marrying the niece of Pope Benedict III; but later on, wishing to marry the daughter of Gregory, a high official, he killed his wife almost in public. George had escaped punishment by his influence with the imperial officials and his father-in-law, Gregory. But now, for reasons that remain obscure, justice caught up with him. Pope Hadrian III had his eyes put out. Criminals often have little significance for the historian, but when, like George, they are part of the ruling class of Rome, the nobles who are coming to influence papal elections, then they have a sad significance.

Hadrian sent a friendly letter to Photius. He took under his protection the Monastery of St. Giles in France and the Monastery of St. Sixtus in Piacenza.

According to the medieval chronicler Martinus Polonus, the Italian nobility, seeing that the Carolingians could do little but fight among themselves, asked Pope Hadrian to do something for Italy. Hadrian then issued two decrees. The first proclaimed that the pope-elect should be consecrated without waiting for any imperial confirmation. The second stated that if Emperor Charles the Fat died without heirs male the nobles of Italy should select one of their number to be Emperor and King of Italy. Since the only source for these decrees is an uncritical thirteenth-century chronicler, it is doubtful whether Hadrian actually did issue these decrees.

Emperor Charles the Fat invited Pope Hadrian to a diet at Worms at which the question of the imperial succession would be discussed. Hadrian, after appointing John, bishop of Pavia, to rule Rome in his absence, left for Germany. But he did not get out of Italy. Sickness struck him down, and he died near Nonantula probably in September 885. He was buried in the Church of the Monastery of St. Silvester. Except for the exiled Pope St. Martin I, Hadrian III is the first pope since Gregory the Great not to be buried in St. Peter's.

Mosaic in the Basilica of St. Paul-Outside-the-Walls, Rome.

STEPHEN VI

885-891

WHEN HADRIAN III DIED ON HIS WAY TO Worms, Rome was suffering from famine and drought. The people, hoping God would bless them under a holy pope, cried out for Stephen, cardinal-priest of the Four-Crowned Martyrs. All agreed on Stephen, and he was consecrated the next Sunday without waiting for any imperial confirmation. Emperor Charles the Fat was angry when he heard of this, but when he discovered how universal was the desire for Stephen, he let the matter rest.

Stephen was the son of Hadrian, a noble, living in the upper-class Via Lata district. Hadrian, a man of good life, had his son educated by Zachary, bishop of Anagni and papal librarian. Then he entered the Lateran and was made cardinal-priest of the Four-Crowned Martyrs by Marinus I.

Stephen deserved the reputation he enjoyed for holiness. But he was also a practical man. He took the people around the papal treasury and showed them how empty it was. Then he helped them as best he could. To fight the plague of locusts which was then desolating Rome, he offered a reward for every pint of locusts brought in. When this failed to make an appreciable dent in the millions of insects, Stephen, after prayer, blessed holy water and gave it to the people to sprinkle on their fields. The plague ended.

Stephen did what he could to adorn the churches, but above all he was interested in souls. He preached frequently. He denounced magical and superstitious practices; above all, he was good

to the poor. A lover of justice, he personally consecrated Teutbold, bishop of Langres when his metropolitan tried to override the people's will. He checked the impudence of Frothar who had usurped the see of Poitiers, and rebuked the archbishop of Ravenna for uncanonical conduct. When Photius was removed from the patriarchate of Constantinople to make way for Emperor Leo's brother Stephen, the Pope refused to acknowledge Stephen until he had been assured that Photius had resigned. At the beginning of his pontificate he had found a letter addressed to Hadrian from Emperor Basil which denounced the Roman Church for allowing Marinus, already a bishop, to become pope. Stephen defended the act of the Roman See in a dignified and skillful manner.

The sad condition of the Western Empire presented the Pope with a vexing problem. Charles the Fat, deposed in 887, had died the following year. The old empire of Charlemagne was now broken up into five or six pieces. Shadowy as was the imperial title, there was heated competition for it. Stephen crowned Guido, duke of Spoleto, emperor on February 21, 891. The turbulent dukes of Spoleto had been thorns in papal sides, but Stephen seems to have got along well with Guido. However, the title did not mean much because Guido could not control Italy, much less the territories beyond the Alps.

In the midst of gathering gloom, in September 891, the saintly Stephen died.

Mosaic in the Basilica of St. Paul-Outside-the-Walls, Rome.

FORMOSUS

891-896

FORMOSUS IS ONE OF THE MOST PUZZLING OF THE popes. His friends described him in glowing terms—his chastity, his austerity, his prayer, and his kindness to the poor; and if his friends' testimony might be suspected, there remains the fact that he was given high honors and great responsibilities by the great St. Nicholas, that he was used on important missions by several popes, and that Boris, king of the Bulgarians, admired him so much that he insisted on having Formosus as archbishop of the Bulgarians and was very much put out when his pleas were not granted. On the other hand, John VIII deposed him from his see, excommunicated him, and made him swear not to return to Rome. And the same praise and blame followed him even after death. It may be that, as happens often enough to good men, Formosus was taken advantage of by rascals. It is certain that he was a storm center in Roman politics.

St. Nicholas made Formosus cardinal-Bishop of Porto in 864, and in 866 sent him to convert the Bulgarians. He made such an impression on King Boris that he demanded Formosus for his archbishop, but neither Nicholas nor Hadrian II would listen to the Bulgarian's plea. Formosus served on several important legations, and his career was brilliant until John VIII made his famous purge. When John swept away the nest of evildoers, headed by men like Gregory and George of the Aventine, Formosus fled. John then had him deposed and excommunicated. It still remains obscure just what the trouble was. Formosus was accused of ambition and of conspiracy. Pope Marinus I recalled Formosus to Rome and restored him to his position as cardinal-bishop of Porto.

At the death of Stephen VI, Formosus was the popular choice for pope. If his friends may be believed, he showed no ambition, even clinging to the altar of his Church at Porto when they came to bring him to Rome.

Formosus lived up to his high character by his efforts to rule the Church wisely. He held a council at Rome and ordered or encouraged councils at Châlons, Tribur, and Vienne. He was deeply concerned with the growing interference of laymen in church affairs. He made some regulation about the ordinations of Photius. He decided that Bremen should remain under the archdiocese of Hamburg.

In high politics, Formosus was, perhaps, not so wise. In the welter of anarchy which followed the deposition of Charles the Fat, Stephen VI had crowned Guido, duke of Spoleto, emperor. Formosus had followed the same policy, even crowning Guido's little son Lambert as emperor; but since order and peace were not to be expected from the turbulent Spoletans, Formosus invited Arnulf of Carinthia, King of Germany and the ablest of Charlemagne's descendants, to come down to Italy and rescue the Holy See from the stifling grasp of the house of Spoleto. Arnulf defeated Guido, who died at that time, and then marched on Rome to expel the empress mother Ageltruda. Formosus welcomed Arnulf and crowned him emperor in 896. Arnulf marched on Spoleto, but was struck down by paralysis. Ageltruda was now safe, but she did not forget what she considered was the double-dealing of Pope Formosus.

Formosus died April 4, 896, but even dead he remained a storm center.

Mosaic in the Basilica of St. Paul-Outside-the-Walls, Rome.

BONIFACE VI

896

AFTER THE DEATH OF FORMOSUS, ANARCHY touches even the papal throne. This period is well termed by Cardinal Baronius the Iron Age. Magyars now were to add their savage raids to the misery caused by the fury of Norsemen and Saracens. And over the corpse of Charlemagne's empire little lords fought brutally. There was little room for learning, little time for culture in the midst of raids and burnings. Sanctity itself, while present, was not overconspicuous. The tide of ancient culture had gone out, leaving malodorous and muddy flats. The tide of the great medieval culture was not yet beginning to flow. Even the papacy felt the impact of this gloomy age. The Italian nobles, free from imperial interference, felt themselves masters of Rome. They dominated papal elections, they thrust relatives onto Peter's throne, they proved themselves unworthy of power and responsibility. Yes, it was the Iron Age of the tenth century that was dawning for the papacy too.

Boniface VI was a Roman, the son of Adrian. His career, like those of many popes of this period is obscure. Boniface had been degraded from both the subdiaconate and the priesthood. Now a popular faction made him pope. The third canon of a council held at Rome in 898 by Pope John IX declared this election of Boniface was invalid because, as a degraded priest, he was ineligible.

Boniface lasted as pope only fifteen days. Some say that he was deposed by the Spoleto gang to clear the road for their man, Stephen. Others say that he was carried off by gout on May 22, 886.

Horace Mann, the historian of the popes, doubts whether the third canon of Pope John's council actually refers to a pope. He claims that Boniface was acknowledged as pope, both at the time and by later popes. Most historians, however, agree that the Boniface mentioned in the council is Boniface VI. In favor of Mann's theory is the fact that Boniface VI has maintained his place in the list of true popes even in the last revision published in the *Annuario Pontificio* in 1948.

Mosaic in the Basilica of St. Paul-Outside-the-Walls, Rome.

STEPHEN VII

896-897

THE YEAR 897 OPENED WITH THE LOSS OF A grand relic of early times. The venerable old Lateran Basilica crashed in ruins. It was a fit beginning for a black year.

Stephen VII was a Roman, the son of John, who himself became a priest. Stephen had been consecrated bishop of Anagni by Pope Formosus. The circumstances of his election to the papacy are obscure.

Stephen's correspondence with Fulk, archbishop of Rheims, shows that he was interested in synods and that he planned to hold one in September 896, but for some unknown reason he was unable to do so. He did hold a local synod in the early part of 897, the strangest synod ever held and the most gruesome.

Although he had been consecrated bishop by Pope Formosus, Stephen seems to have belonged to the opposite faction. But probably the moving spirit in this horrid business was the house of Spoleto. It will be remembered that Formosus, after crowning young Lambert, had called in Arnulf to become emperor and put down the Spoletans. Driven out of Rome by Arnulf and threatened in Spoleto itself, Lambert was saved by Arnulf's sudden sickness. Then he cleared out Arnulf's officials and took over central Italy. In January 897 Lambert and his mother, the fiery Ageltruda, entered Rome in triumph. But Formosus was beyond vengeance. He was dead and buried with honor as pope. This last fact could still be canceled.

Stephen VII herded together some of the Roman clergy into a synod. Terrified and aghast, they watched a grisly scene unfold. The decaying corpse of Pope Formosus was carried into the hall. Clad in pontifical vestments it was seated in a chair. A quaking deacon stood by the corpse as defense attorney while a series of charges against the late pope were read. The synod then condemned Formosus because he had exercised his functions after having been deposed and because he had left the see of Porto for that of Rome. His ordinations were declared invalid. Then the three fingers used by a Pope in blessing were cut off and the pontifical vestments were torn from the poor corpse. Underneath the ceremonial splendor was found a hair shirt. The body was then buried in a pilgrims' cemetery, but a gang dug it up and threw it into the Tiber.

Stephen, by declaring the ordinations of Formosus invalid, defended himself against those who blamed him for leaving the see of Anagni for that of Rome. Since he had been consecrated by Formosus, he had not really been a bishop. He ordered all those ordained by Formosus to turn over to him written resignations of their offices. It looked like a purge of all friends of Formosus.

Stephen VII did not survive the shocking synod very long. When Lambert had to leave to fight the marquis of Tuscany, the Romans rose against Stephen. Then he was seized and himself stripped of the pontifical robes. Clad in a monk's habit, he was thrown into a dungeon, and in August, 897, Stephen VII was strangled.

Mosaic in the Basilica of St. Paul-Outside-the-Walls, Rome.

ROMANUS

897

THE CIRCUMSTANCES OF THIS PONTIFF'S ELECtion and death are obscure. Indeed probability is the best that can be had except for some routine actions. Romanus was a native of Gallese, which was also the birthplace of Pope Marinus I, the friend of Formosus. His father's name was Constantine. Romanus was cardinal-priest of St. Peter-in-Chains when he was elected pope. He was elected pope in the summer of 897, probably in August.

Since Stephen VII had been overthrown and killed by an uprising, it is probable that Romanus was not one of Stephen's faction. Indeed a fifteenth-century edition of a papal catalogue mentions that Romanus took measures against Stephen. But all that is certain about the pontificate of Romanus is the following administrative facts. He granted the pallium to Vitalis, patriarch of Grado, and gave a privilege to the church of Grado. When the Spanish bishops of Elna and Germa came to Rome to seek papal confirmation of the goods of their dioceses, Romanus granted it. He also coined money. He had time to do little else, for he was dead in November.

It is possible, though not highly probable, that Romanus was deposed. One manuscript, and one only, mentions that Romanus was made a monk. To make a pope assume the monastic habit was a way to depose him. But in this case it is more probable that the lonely manuscript confused Romanus with Stephen VII. At any rate, nothing is known of Romanus' death.

Chronologia Summorum Pontificum.

THEODORE II

897

THE HOLY PRIEST THEODORE WAS ELECTED TO succeed Romanus. Theodore was a Roman, the son of Photius. It is interesting to note that his brother Theotius was also a bishop. Theodore had been ordained a priest by Pope Stephen VI.

If Flodoard, canon of Rheims, can be trusted, Theodore II was a man of excellent character. Moderate, chaste, a lover of the poor and the clergy, and a peacemaker, Theodore seemed to be just the man for the troublous times. And what is known of Theodore confirms this good opinion. But Theodore was to be pope for less than three weeks.

At once the new Pope ordered a synod to be held. At this synod the clergymen who had been ordained by Formosus and deposed by Stephen VII were restored. Theodore ordered the written resignations which Stephen VII had collected from them to be burned. And now at last the poor battered body of Formosus found rest. After it had been thrown into the Tiber the corpse had washed ashore near the Church of St. Acontius in Porto. According to one story, Formosus then appeared to a monk and asked him to bury the body. The monk did so, but secretly for fear of the late pope's enemies. According to another account, fishermen found the body. At any rate when Pope Theodore II learned of the discovery of the body, he had it brought back to Rome in solemn procession. Once more clothed in the pontifical vestments, the body was placed before the Confession of St. Peter. Then in the presence of Pope Theodore, a Mass was said for the soul of Formosus, and his poor battered body was restored to its own tomb. One chronicler remarks that he heard from the Romans that when the body entered St. Peter's, certain images of the saints bowed their heads to it.

Theodore had time for little else. He granted a privilege to the church of Grado and had a coin struck. Twenty days after his election he was dead.

Mosaic in the Basilica of St. Paul-Outside-the-Walls, Rome.

JOHN IX

898-900

ALTHOUGH JOHN IX RULED THE CHURCH FOR only two years, he did much to bring order out of confusion. Had he lived longer perhaps the papacy might have been spared some of the misery it suffered in the dark tenth century.

John IX was born in Tivoli, the son of Rampoald. He became a Benedictine monk and a priest. After the death of Theodore II, the majority which favored that pontiff's actions in favor of Formosus rallied around John. The other faction tried to elect Sergius, but John prevailed. Sergius, excommunicated, had to leave Rome.

John at once displayed his power of organization. He held a synod at Rome which confirmed the acts of Theodore's synod and repealed those of the ghastly corpse-synod of Stephen VII. These were burned. Those who had been ordained by Formosus were restored to their positions. Reordinations were forbidden. Yet John in a spirit of moderation did not punish those who had taken part in the corpse-synod. He accepted the excuse that they had done so under compulsion. In the field of politics, the synod recognized as valid the anointing of Lambert of Spoleto as emperor, and rejected that of Berenger of North Italy.

John then went to Ravenna where he held another synod in the presence of Emperor Lambert. He had been horrified at the miserable disorder of the country through which he passed, and he earnestly besought Lambert to keep order in Italy.

This synod echoed a decree of the Roman synod to insure order in papal elections. The elections were to be made by the clergy with the consent of the people and in the presence of the imperial envoys. At this wild time imperial protection seemed desirable even at the risk of imperial interference. But the decree was to mean nothing. No emperor had much power; and the very next year Emperor Lambert was killed in a hunting accident. Poor Arnulf, also a crowned emperor, was paralyzed and died shortly after. With no emperor, the door of control of papal elections swung open to the unbridled ambition of the nobles.

John was not so lost in political dealings that he forgot the spiritual. He pleaded with the bishops assembled at Ravenna to give the good example so desperately needed, and to bring down God's blessing by prayer and fasting.

In spite of scolding letters from German bishops, Pope John IX protected the Slavs from German domination. He appointed a metropolitan and three bishops for Moravia.

In the East John IX had the great satisfaction of seeing unity and harmony prevail at Constantinople. Whether or not there had been a second Photian schism, it was certainly over now.

John's accomplishments are amazing in view not only of the great difficulties of the time, but of the shortness of his pontificate. Some time in the year 900 this wise and energetic pope died.

Chronologia Summorum Pontificum.

[234]

BENEDICT IV

900-903

To succeed John IX another excellent man was chosen—the priest, Benedict. Benedict was a Roman, the son of Mammalus. He had been ordained priest by Formosus and had a high regard for that storm-tossed pope. Nothing is known of his election, but it may be presumed that the party which favored the memory of Pope Formosus still had the upper hand. The date of his election is not certain, but it was some time in the first half of the year 900. Benedict seems to have been a man of noble character. Both the author of his epitaph and the historian Flodoard agree that he was worthy of his name.

Pope Benedict was grieved to learn that Winedmar, a henchman of Count Baldwin of Flanders, had murdered Fulk, the excellent archbishop of Rheims. Benedict ordered the bishops of France to publish the excommunication of the sacrilegious murderer.

The Eastern Empire under the weak rule of Leo VI, the Philosopher, was staggering under Saracen blows. Since the Moslems had captured Amasia in Pontus, its bishop, Malacenus, came to Rome to seek help from the Pope. Benedict received him with great kindness and gave him a letter to all bishops and counts, urging them to treat the poor refugee bishop with all consideration.

The political situation in Italy after the death of Emperor Lambert was more chaotic than ever. The North Italian prince, Berenger, tried to get the imperial title and power over all Italy. To oppose him Adelbert II, marquis of Tuscany, called for a more distant king, Louis of Provence. Louis came down into Italy, defeated Berenger, and reached Rome in 901. Pope Benedict crowned him emperor. The Pope and the new emperor got along well together. They discussed various problems of church and state at a great meeting in a hall near St. Peter's. But Louis was unable to make good his claim to Italy. The next year, 902, defeated by Berenger, Louis was forced to swear never to return to Italy. In 905 he broke his word, invaded Italy, and was again captured by Berenger. This time Louis was sent back over the Alps without his eyes. Hence, he is known to history as Louis the Blind.

Benedict IV held a synod in the Lateran Palace. He died sometime in the summer of 903.

Mosaic in the Basilica of St. Paul-Outside-the-Walls, Rome.

LEO V

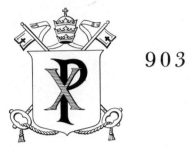

903

THE BRETONS HAVE AN OLD LEGEND THAT ST. Tugdual, the patron of Treguier, went to Rome on a pilgrimage and while in the Holy City was elected pope. He chose to be called "Leo Britigena" as is narrated in the Roman Catalogue. This much can be said for the legend: The Roman Catalogues that come down to us do make Leo V a priest from outside Rome. But they also say that he was from Priapi in the Ardeatine district of Italy.

Leo V is spoken of as a praiseworthy and holy man, but practically nothing is known of his early life or of his election. Whatever his qualifications, his pontificate was so short that he had no time to do more than grant the canons of Bologna the pleasant privilege of exemption from taxes.

After a few weeks, Christopher, the cardinal-priest of St. Damasus, led an uprising against Leo, overthrew him, and put him in prison. Christopher then usurped the papal throne. But he was not popular, and Sergius, who had been excommunicated and driven into exile by Pope John IX, plotted with the Romans against him. With French help and Roman fifth-column activity, Sergius overthrew Christopher and put him in prison. Since Sergius then was elected pope, it is highly probable that Leo was already dead. One lone author, however, states that Sergius, out of pity, had both Leo and Christopher executed. This is not probable, and it is not mentioned by any other author of the period. At any rate, whatever the manner of his death, Leo V disappeared from history at this time.

Mosaic in the Basilica of St. Paul-Outside-the-Walls, Rome.

SERGIUS III

904-911

POOR FORMOSUS WAS NOW BURIED IN PEACE, BUT his grave must have trembled when Sergius marched into Rome to complete the overthrow of the usurping Christopher and take over the papacy, for Sergius was a bitter enemy of Formosus. It is said that Formosus had consecrated Sergius bishop of Caere to prevent him from becoming pope. Whether this was true or not, Sergius certainly hated the memory of Formosus. Though Sergius indulged in no resurrection-man tactics himself, he heartily approved of Stephen VII's corpse-synod. He had an epitaph placed on Stephen's tomb which honored that pontiff and insulted Formosus.

Not content with assailing the memory of his hated predecessor, Sergius now reversed the policy of Theodore II and John IX. He held a synod and declared that the ordinations performed by Formosus were invalid. This caused a tempest in the holy-water fonts throughout Italy. Bishops and priests, who were given the choice of submitting to reordination or losing their positions, protested angrily. Sergius threatened to imprison any stubborn followers of Formosus. He was a thoroughgoing party man, whose narrow policy inspired intense bitterness.

Sergius was a Roman of noble family. He had tried for the papacy in the election which had produced John IX and had been excommunicated and exiled by that vigorous pontiff. He had returned in triumph, at the request of the Romans, and had succeeded the antipope Christopher. He associated himself closely with the most powerful noble in Rome, the Duke, Commander of the Army, and Master of the Wardrobe, Theophylactus. The family of this man will control the papacy for decades. Sergius is even accused of having a son by Marozia, the daughter of Theophylactus, a son who became Pope John XI.

On the other hand, there are glowing accounts of Sergius which make such shameful goings on quite improbable. With the manuscripts available, the just historian can scarcely convict Sergius of such misconduct. But neither can he acquit him.

Sergius seems to have been a hard-working pope, and except for his unfortunate policy against the party of Formosus, a fairly wise one. He showed great solicitude for the welfare of the Church by getting a number of synods held. He defended the doctrine that the Holy Ghost proceeds from the Father and the Son. He brought peace to Constantinople by declaring valid Emperor Leo's fourth marriage. The other three wives were dead, but some Greeks refused to consider a fourth marriage valid no matter how free the prospective bridegroom.

In a material way he took steps to get help for John, archbishop of Ravenna, against the depredations of the Count of Istria. He rebuilt the Lateran Basilica which had crashed in ruins in 896.

Sergius III died either in April or June, 911.

Mosaic in the Basilica of St. Paul-Outside-the-Walls, Rome.

ANASTASIUS III

911-913

Not much is known of Anastasius III. He was a Roman, the son of Lucian, and he was elected pope either in April or June, 911. He seems to have been an excellent man and a good pope.

One interesting fact about the pontificate of Anastasius III was the visit of Howel the Good, king of Wales. Howel was engaged in drawing up a code of laws for his hill-country Celts. Determined to see that the laws were well drawn up, he made the difficult journey to Rome to see Pope Anastasius and ask him to confirm the new Welsh laws.

Outside of the fact that he granted the pallium to Ragenbert, bishop of Vercelli, and various privileges to the bishop of Pavia, and confirmed the privileges of the church of Grado, nothing else is known of the acts of Pope Anastasius III.

In Germany, however, an event of some significance took place. Louis the Child, whose reign was disaster to the strife-torn country, was replaced by Conrad the Franconian. Louis was the last of Charlemagne's line to rule in Germany.

Anastasius III died some time in the summer of 913. He was buried in St. Peter's. His epitaph pithily remarks that the tomb holds the bones but could not contain the merits of this Pope who ruled the Church well.

The Vatican Library.

LANDUS

913-914

L ANDUS WAS A NATIVE OF SABINA WHOSE FA-
ther's name was Taino. He granted a privilege to the Church of the Holy Savior in
Forum Novum in his native district of Sabina. He
was a man of good character and ruled the Church
for about six months. Elected in July or August
913, he died in February or March 914, and this is
all that is known of Pope Landus.

The characters of Anastasius III and Landus
prove that if Theophylactus was controlling the
papal elections at this time, he was seeing to it that
good men were chosen. Since the house of Theophylactus will pretty much dominate the papacy
for the next half century, it is useful to understand
the position of this interesting family in history.
Theophylactus was a Roman noble who became a
high official in the papal service. Sparked by his
ambitious wife Theodora and their vigorous
daughters, Theodora and Marozia, this family secured so dominant a position in Roman politics
that they reduced the temporal power of the pope
to a shadow. Even worse, they placed in the papal
throne men tragically unfit for the high office. Naturally such power aroused a good deal of opposition, and unfortunately for their memory much of
what is known of this dark period comes down
from their enemies. If these may be believed, the
family of Theophylactus was a nest of horrible corruption. Older historians, Catholic and non-Catho-
lic alike, have accepted the charges against the
house of Theophylactus. Cardinal Baronius, the
great counterreformation church historian, de-
nounces this family and some of their popes in un-
measured terms. But modern historians, more critical, are a bit dubious about accepting the invec-
tives of party foes as gospel. Still, when all allowance for partisan feeling is made, the story of the
house of Theophylactus and its influence on the
papacy is black enough.

National Museum, Florence.

JOHN X

914-928

As a diplomat, warrior, and ecclesiastical administrator, John X stands out among the popes of this period. John was born at Tossignano in Romagna. He entered the ranks of the clergy and in 905 was elected Archbishop of Ravenna. On the death of Landus, the dominant faction among the Roman nobles, probably led by Theodora, invited John to come to Rome and be elected pope. Although by this time several popes had been bishops before they became popes, the tradition against exchanging dioceses died hard, and there were not wanting those who called John X an intruder.

A vigorous and able man, John at once decided to put an end to the frightful devastation caused by the Saracens. A group of Moslems had fortified themselves on a hill overlooking the Garigliano River in Southern Italy, and from this stronghold they brutally harried the poor Italians. John X worked feverishly to form an alliance and for a marvel he succeeded. Northern, central, and southern Italians were for once united. Helped by Greek naval units from the Eastern Empire, they moved against the Saracens. Pope John in person led the Roman contingent. The allied army defeated the Saracens and drove them back into their stronghold. Then when the starving Moslems tried to break through the iron ring, they were cut to pieces. A wave of rejoicing swept through Italian homes. Pope John X, on his return to Rome, was given a triumphant reception. He deserved it.

John X tried to unite the South Slavs more closely to Rome. He discouraged the Slavonic liturgy, and succeeded in having his views adopted by a national synod of Spalato in 926. He also worked on the Bulgarians and enjoyed some passing success in bringing Bulgaria under his jurisdiction. In Germany Pope John encouraged the clergy to support the hard-pressed King Conrad in his efforts to bring law and order to that distressed country. He sent a legate to preside at a synod held at Altheim in 916, which not only enacted decrees to better church discipline but threatened rebels with excommunication. In France too the Pope tried to protect a distressed king from treacherous nobles. When Heribert, Count of Vermandois, seized King Charles the Simple in 923, Pope John threatened him with excommunication. He did, however, make an odd concession to this Heribert; he confirmed the election of his son Hugh to the great diocese of Rheims. Hugh was all of five years old! Of course the Pope provided for the spiritual rule of the diocese, but such a confirmation shows the unholy power of the nobility.

In Italy, John crowned Berenger Emperor in 915, but a faction invited Rudolf of Burgundy to compete with Berenger. When Berenger was assassinated in 924, the Pope seems to have called on Hugh, the successor of Louis the Blind, of Provence, to come down and be King of Italy. He met Hugh at Mantua, but Hugh was either unable or unwilling to help the poor Pope in his home troubles.

It seems that John X was getting too independent for Marozia, now the dominant figure of the Theophylactus clan. In 928 she had the Pope's brother Peter killed and the Pope himself thrown into prison. Whether he was smothered with a pillow or died of anxiety, John X did not long survive his imprisonment.

Mosaic in the Basilica of St. Paul-Outside-the-Walls, Rome.

LEO VI

928-929

AGAIN, HERE IS A POPE ABOUT WHOM LITTLE IS known. Leo was a Roman. His father, Christopher, had been primicerius, i.e., a high official in the papal service in the time of John VIII. He seems to have supported that pontiff in his vigorous purge of disorderly elements in Rome. Leo entered the ranks of the clergy and at the time of his election was attached to the Church of Santa Susanna. It would be very interesting to know the circumstances of his election. Since Marozia had overthrown Pope John X, it is highly probable that she had something to do with putting in Leo VI, but no documentary evidence describes the election.

The only act of Leo VI which has come down to posterity is his approval of the decrees of the national synod held at Spalato in 926. He granted the pallium to the archbishop of Spalato and decreed that he was to have metropolitan jurisdiction over all Dalmatia.

Leo VI seems to have been a good man. Certainly no historian has anything to say against him. The thirteenth century writer Ptolemy of Lucca says "he exercised no tyranny and died in peace, and . . . according to most writers he was buried in St. Peter's."

Leo's pontificate extended probably from June 928 to February 929.

Mosaic in the Basilica of St. Paul-Outside-the-Walls, Rome.

STEPHEN VIII

929-931

A GREEK WRITER OF THE TWELFTH CENTURY AT a time when Constantinople was in schism, brought a remarkable accusation against Pope Stephen VIII, an accusation which, if true, makes this pontiff a pioneer in clerical appearances. According to this hirsute Greek, Pope Stephen VIII was "the first pope who was shameless enough to shave himself and to order the rest of Italy to do likewise."

Stephen VIII was a Roman, the son of Teudemund. He was cardinal-priest of St. Anastasia. Nothing is known of the circumstances of his election, and not much more about his brief papal career. His memory survives in the privileges he granted to several monasteries in Italy and France.

Although it was in 910 in the pontificate of Sergius III that it was founded, and it was from Pope John X that it received papal protection, it can be mentioned here that by now the great monastery of Cluny was quietly at prayer and work. In 910 William the Pious, duke of Aquitaine, founded this abbey for the good of the souls of his late King Eudes, of his parents and his servants. At the time of Stephen VIII, St. Odo was abbot. This Benedictine monastery, Cluny, was to reorganize Benedictine monasticism and from Cluny would come spiritual leaders who would do much to start the great renaissance in the eleventh century.

Stephen VIII seems to have been a virtuous man whose pontificate passed peacefully. He died sometime in the early part of 931.

Mosaic in the Basilica of St. Paul-Outside-the-Walls, Rome.

JOHN XI

931-936

JOHN XI IS CALLED THE SON OF POPE SERGIUS III by the *Liber Pontificalis;* but as has been mentioned in the biography of Sergius III, this is not at all certain. Whoever his father was, John's mother was certainly the famous daughter of Theophylactus, Mary, known to history as Marozia. (Marozia means "little Mary".)

John entered the ranks of the clergy and became cardinal-priest of Santa Maria in Trastevere. His mother Marozia now dominated the political scene in Rome, and when Stephen VIII died, it was small wonder that her son John should be chosen pope. John seems to have been a good young priest. Only in his twenties, he was probably pretty much under his powerful mother's influence.

John granted privileges to the great monastery of Cluny. It is interesting to note that at St. Odo's request, John granted privileges not only to Cluny, but to dependent monasteries. Cluny was more than a strict and pious abbey, it was the mother house of a congregation of monasteries. Since in the primitive Benedictine system, the abbot of each monastery was supreme, the dependence of a whole chain of monasteries on a mother abbey is a new departure. It proved very useful in the stormy days of the tenth century when a monastery, left to itself, could easily fall into decay.

Whatever John's gifts as a ruler, he had little opportunity to exercise them. His mother Marozia naturally had strong influence over her young son. Marozia, widowed twice, had married Hugh, King of Provence. Hugh was at first well received by the Romans, but soon it became clear that Marozia's son Alberic II was not happy. Rome was too small for Hugh and Alberic. Alberic struck first. Raising a mob, he rushed in on his mother's headquarters, the Castle of St. Angelo, with such force that Hugh fled. Alberic put his mother in prison. He also made his brother Pope John XI a prisoner. And after this revolution, which took place either in late 932 or early 933, Alberic ruled Rome like a dictator. He called himself Senator, Patrician, and Prince of the Romans. He usurped the temporal power completely and allowed his brother, the Pope, only the exercise of his spiritual duties. Indeed even in spiritual matters he interfered. It was at Alberic's insistence that John granted the pallium to Theophylactus, patriarch of Constantinople, and Artaud, archbishop of Rheims.

John XI died either in December 935 or January 936. His pontificate marks the complete supremacy in Rome of the house of Theophylactus.

Mosaic in the Basilica of St. Paul-Outside-the-Walls, Rome.

LEO VII

936-939

ALBERIC II, NOW HOLDING SUPREME TEMPORAL power in Rome, had no intention of seeing an independent pope arise who might try to get back the papacy's temporal power. Accordingly, Alberic saw to it that the clergy always chose his man. This much must be said for Alberic: usually his man was a good man.

After the death of his brother, John XI, Alberic secured the election of Leo VII. Leo was a Roman, the priest of St. Sixtus. He was probably a Benedictine monk. He was certainly a pious and spiritual man. Learned and gracious, Leo was not interested in becoming pope, and it took a little pressure to gain his consent. His lack of ambition probably commended him highly to Prince Alberic.

Leo VII granted privileges to various monasteries, especially to Cluny. He sent for St. Odo, the abbot of Cluny, to help bring peace to war-torn Italy. Hugh of Provence, though driven from Rome by his stepson Alberic, was still king of Italy, and actually had some power in the North. Not the man to accept defeat easily, Hugh continually attacked Alberic and on three occasions laid siege to Rome itself. It was on one of these occasions that Pope Leo VII asked St. Odo to come down from France and mediate between Hugh and Alberic. The great abbot worked hard and produced a patched-up peace. Alberic agreed to marry Alda, Hugh's daughter, and Hugh agreed to take his army home. Alberic and Pope Leo saw eye to eye in their attitude toward monks and monasteries. Alberic persuaded St. Odo to take over the supervision of all the monasteries around Rome. He also gave his old home where he had been born to be a monastery in honor of Our Lady. To this day the monastery of Our Lady on the Aventine survives as a memorial to the piety of Prince Alberic II.

Pope Leo VII cooperated in the grand work of restoration being done in Germany by Henry the Fowler and his son Otto. He appointed Frederick, archbishop of Mainz, to be his legate for all Germany so that he could reform the clergy. He refused to allow the overzealous German to baptize Jews by force, but he was enough the child of his age to permit Frederick to drive the Jews out of the cities if they would not accept baptism.

Leo VII died in July, 936.

STEPHEN IX

939-942

STEPHEN WAS A ROMAN. HE ENTERED THE RANKS of the clergy and became cardinal-priest of Sts. Silvester and Martin. He was elected pope on July 14, 939.

A protégé of Prince Alberic, Stephen had little to do with ruling the Papal States, but he did make his influence felt in France. It is interesting to note that at a time when their temporal power was reduced to nothing, the popes could still exercise so much influence for peace.

What happened was this. Louis, the young son of Charles the Simple, was called back to France from England by the great lords. This not unworthy descendant of Charlemagne, however, actually tried to rule France. When the lords saw this, they plotted, intrigued, and rebelled against Louis. And soon they were pressing him hard. Pope Stephen now intervened. He sent a legate named Damasus on a peacemaking mission. The result was that the French bishops, assembled in synod, tried to persuade Hugh, duke of Francia, to submit peacefully to his monarch. In vain. Hugh continued to make life miserable for young Louis. Then Stephen took two measures, one conciliatory, the other threatening. He granted the pallium to Hugh's nephew, the boy archbishop of Rheims. He told the nobles that if by Christmas 942 they had not sent him envoys to assure him of their submission to their lawful king, they would be excommunicated. This threat bore fruit; the feudal opposition died down a little and some of the pressure was lifted off King Louis.

The same year, 942, Rome itself was again besieged by Hugh of Provence, and again St. Odo, abbot of Cluny, intervened to bring peace.

Stephen IX died toward the end of October, 942.

Mosaic in the Basilica of St. Paul-Outside-the-Walls, Rome.

MARINUS II

942-946

MARINUS II WAS ANOTHER ONE OF PRINCE AL-beric's candidates for the papacy and an-other good man. Marinus was a Roman. At the time of his election to the papacy he was the priest of the Church of St. Ciriacus. He was elected Pope in October, 942.

Like all of Alberic's popes, Marinus got along well with the dictator, and seemingly allowed him to run the Papal States without any attempt at in-terference. In spiritual matters, Marinus worked to promote good order and discipline among the clergy and granted privileges to monasteries. He continued the legation of Frederick, archbishop of Mainz, in Germany. Frederick had been ap-pointed by Pope Leo VII as papal vicar for all Ger-many with full power to root out abuses among the clergy.

In Italy Pope Marinus protected the Benedictine monks from a greedy bishop. Sicus, bishop of Capua, took from the monks a church which an earlier bishop of Capua had given them. Sicus then gave the church as a benefice to a deacon who seems to have been a boon companion of the bishop. When Marinus got word of this, he not only ordered Bishop Sicus to restore the church to the monks, but he forbade him to associate any longer with the deacon.

Though not too much is known about Marinus II, what is known indicates that he was a spiritual man, a man with a strong sense of responsibility for the Church, and a lover of the poor.

It is said that St. Ulric, famous archbishop of Augsburg, came to Rome at this time and had a visit with Pope Marinus II.

Marinus II died in the spring of 946.

Chronologia Summorum Pontificum.

AGAPETUS II

946-955

AGAPETUS II WAS A ROMAN AND AN EXCELLENT man. And that is about all that is known of him before he became pope. He was consecrated pope on May 10, 946.

Agapetus II finally settled the vexed dispute between Artaud and Hugh for the see of Rheims by deciding in favor of Artaud. This settlement was in line with the papal policy of supporting the house of Charlemagne. Louis IV wished to see Artaud archbishop of Rheims because he did not want that influential see to fall into enemy hands. Hugh was the nephew of Hugh the Great, duke of Francia, and trouble-maker-in-chief to the King.

Agapetus II worked well for reform and spreading the gospel. He cooperated with German efforts to christianize the Scandinavians. He confirmed the privileges of Hamburg as metropolitan see for the nascent church in Denmark. From Jutland he received an embassy asking for missionaries. He worked well, too, for reform of the monks and clergy. He granted many privileges to monasteries. One religious house which received a privilege from Pope Agapetus II was Gandersheim, famous for its talented nun Hroswitha. Hroswitha was a poet and a dramatist. Agapetus also protected monks from greedy princes.

The pontificate of Agapetus II is marked by the entry on the Italian scene of a great man and a great precedent. The man was Otto I, king of Germany. The precedent was the interference of German kings in Italian politics. North Italy was again in turmoil. Hugh of Provence abdicated as King of Italy and went back to Provence to die. His son Lothair died in 950 and Berenger, marquis of Ivrea, was recognized as king. But Berenger proved worthless. He stirred up enemies on all sides and he treated Adelaide, the beautiful young widow of Lothair, with harshness. Adelaide escaped from his clutches and appealed to Otto. The great German promptly marched into Italy, overthrew Berenger, married Adelaide, and was crowned King of Italy. But when he wished to come to Rome to be crowned emperor, Prince Alberic said no. He had no wish to see the powerful German in his preserves. Pope Agapetus was probably willing enough to crown Otto, but in Rome Alberic was still the real temporal ruler.

Agapetus II died in December 955. He is buried in the Lateran.

The British Museum, London.

JOHN XII

955-963

JOHN XII MIGHT BE CALLED A POOR LITTLE RICH boy. His father Prince Alberic had secured the election of good, if not overaggressive, popes. He had even favored monastic reform. But he left a miserable legacy to the Church—his son. Alberic had made the clergy promise to elect his son Octavian as successor to Agapetus II. Brought up free and easy with plenty of money, Octavian was a young man more fitted to adorn the ranks of café society than the Chair of Peter. On his father's death he had succeeded to his titles and power. On the death of Agapetus, he became pope. The first pope since John II to change his name, he took the name John XII.

John XII has a bad reputation, but it is only fair to remember that many of the stories told about him come from political enemies, especially that evil-tongued old gossip, Liutprand of Cremona. But even after allowing a generous discount for prejudice, enough remains against John XII to rank him as one of the few bad popes.

Though John enjoyed temporal power as well as spiritual, he was not long to enjoy this double power. Berenger, king of Italy, had made himself so unpopular that Pope John voiced the sentiments of the Italian people when he called on King Otto I of Germany to free Italy from Berenger's tyranny. Otto chased Berenger into the mountains, then entered Rome to be welcomed by the Pope. Otto guaranteed the privileges and territory of the Pope and John agreed to support Otto. Once more the Roman Empire came alive as on Candlemas Day, 962, the Pope crowned Otto emperor.

But after Otto went north to complete the liquidation of Berenger, John, realizing that Otto meant to supervise matters in Rome, plotted against him with Berenger and his son Adalbert. At first Otto laughed it off, but the imperialist faction at Rome, not amused, urged the Emperor to come back. When he approached the city in November 963, Pope John fled. Otto made the Romans swear henceforth never to elect a pope without his approval. A synod summoned John to come back and stand trial for his misdeeds. John answered by threatening to excommunicate anyone who should attempt to set up an antipope. The council did just that. After a month it declared John deposed and elected Leo, a layman. But Leo's power lasted only until Otto left the city. Then back came John in triumph. He made good his threat of excommunication and made life miserable for the imperialists. Otto, on hearing of all this, was preparing to return when he learned that on May 14, 964, John XII had died.

John, if Liutprand can be believed, died an evil death; struck down while in the act of adultery, he lingered eight days and died without Holy Viaticum.

Mosaic in the Basilica of St. Paul-Outside-the-Walls, Rome.

BENEDICT V

964

THE DEATH OF JOHN XII GAVE THE ROMANS A chance to make peace with Emperor Otto by accepting his pope, Leo VIII. But the Romans did nothing of the kind. At once they elected the cardinal-deacon Benedict. Benedict was a Roman, a notary from the region of Marcellus. He enjoyed a reputation for learning. He had taken part in the council which had deposed John XII and elected Leo VIII. Now, however, he repudiated Leo and accepted the election.

Though the Romans elected Benedict in defiance of the Emperor, they did send an embassy to tell him about their proceedings. The embassy met with a cold reception. Otto refused to hear of another pope. Leo was his pope and he proclaimed that he would as soon give up his sword as give up Leo. These words from a German warrior boded ill for Benedict. But Benedict, undaunted, first made the Romans swear to support him, then calmly proceeded with his consecration. When Otto heard of this he was furious. And now, completely victorious over Berenger, he had his hands free to attend to the Romans. Soon a large imperial army stood before the walls of Rome and soon the Romans felt the pinch of hunger. Benedict showed plenty of fight. He did not spare himself in encouraging the Romans to fight on for liberty and the papacy. But though the old walls resisted the battering of Otto's clumsy engines, famine entered the city and compelled the Romans to surrender.

All the fight seems to have oozed out of Benedict. If Liutprand can be trusted, Benedict asked for pardon. Though he was true pope, Benedict's position was weakened by the fact that he had taken part in the election of his rival Leo VIII, a fact the imperialists were quick to point out. They asked the unfortunate Benedict how he dared to have assumed the pontifical robes while Leo yet lived. Benedict, according to Liutprand, caved in. He admitted he had been wrong and agreed to his deposition.

Otto brought the deposed pope back to Germany and entrusted him to Adaldag, archbishop of Hamburg. Adaldag seems to have treated the unfortunate Benedict with kindness. Benedict edified all by bearing his misfortunes with patience. This was not easy, for though Adaldag was considerate, other Germans regarded Benedict as an insolent fellow who dared to defy their Emperor.

Benedict died a happy death on July 4, 965, at Hamburg. Some years later his body was brought back to Rome.

Mosaic in the Basilica of St. Paul-Outside-the-Walls, Rome.

[264]

LEO VIII

963-965

WAS LEO VIII TRUE POPE OR ANTIPOPE? FOR A long time he was considered by many historians as only antipope. But the latest revision of the list of popes in the *Annuario Pontificio* includes Leo VIII. This might seem to indicate that the more or less official opinion is that Benedict actually did agree to his deposition and that Leo's position was regularized by the consent of the Roman clergy.

Leo was a Roman of well-known family. A lay official of the papal court, he had taken part in the council which had deposed John XII. He was then chosen to succeed John. This was highly irregular, not only because the council had no right to depose the pope, but because Leo was a layman. The bishop of Ostia hurried through the necessary ordinations without the customary intervals. Elected as a layman on December 4, Leo was consecrated bishop on December 6.

Leo was quite unpopular with the Romans, who regarded him as an imperial tool. Shortly after his consecration Otto sent a part of his army north. At once the Romans revolted. Otto's remaining warriors sallied into the streets and wrought havoc on the poor Romans. Realizing how much his hold on Rome depended on brute strength, Otto took a hundred hostages from Roman families. Leo, with more good nature than shrewdness, urged Otto to release them. The result was that when Otto went north the Romans soon sent Leo packing and welcomed John XII back to the Lateran.

After John's death in 964 the Romans still refused to accept Leo, but when Otto's army forced them to surrender, Leo's moment of triumph arrived. Entering the city in the train of the victorious Otto, Leo was able to summon a council and have Benedict V brought before him. Liutprand had described the scene. Assembled in the Lateran Basilica were the Pope, the Emperor, and a number of bishops. Benedict, clad in the pontifical robes, stood before them. After admitting his fault, Benedict took off the pallium and handed it to Leo. Leo then removed the chasuble and stole from Benedict and declared that he was reduced to the rank of deacon. Since Benedict seems to have consented to his deposition, Leo may be regarded as true pope from July 964.

Leo was said to have repaid his imperial maker by giving him extraordinary privileges and indeed by surrendering to the Emperor the lands donated by Pippin and Charlemagne. But these concessions and gifts were only forgeries cooked up in the bitter days of the lay-investiture struggle.

Leo VIII died in March 965.

The Vatican Library.

JOHN XIII

965-972

JOHN XIII, LIKE JOHN XII, WAS A MEMBER OF THE house of Theophylactus. But except for name and family he had little in common with his kinsman. John XII might have been called John the Bad; John XIII was called John the Good. John's father, also named John, had married the younger Theodora, the sister of the famous Marozia. Later he became a bishop. John himself, quite unlike John XII, was brought up strictly and educated at the Lateran with the young clerics. He served in the papal chancery, took part in the condemnation of his relative, John XII, and then in his restoration. With a reputation for learning and virtue he became papal librarian, then bishop of Narni. One homely little detail, all too rare in these early biographies, comes down to us. John was nicknamed "white hen" on account of his fair hair.

John was not the first choice of the Romans. When Leo VIII died the Romans sent to the Emperor, asking him to give them back Benedict V; but before this request could be acted on, Benedict died. Otto sent representatives to Rome to see that his choice was made pope, and the Emperor's choice was John, bishop of Narni, who was duly elected. Otto probably thought that in choosing John he was not only getting a good and reliable pope, but one that would be pleasing to the Romans. After all, John was of the family of Theophylactus, and Otto hoped that this would help to reconcile the sensitive Romans to the imperial yoke. But because he was Otto's choice, the Romans turned against John.

A faction led by Rofred, a Campagna count, and Peter, the city prefect, raised the cry: "Out with the foreigners!" They seized John and threw him into the Castle of St. Angelo. Later when he was removed to a castle in the country, John escaped. He fled to Pandulf of Capua, and after an exile of almost a year made his way back to Rome. The Romans, learning that Otto was coming, gave the Pope a grand reception. But Otto was angry, and when he entered the city in August 966, rough German hands administered bloody justice to the Romans. This brought peace, and for the rest of his pontificate John had little trouble with the Romans. He got along well with Otto. On Christmas Day, 967, the Pope crowned his young son Otto II as co-emperor. John assisted Otto in the marriage negotiations which brought to young Otto the hand of the beautiful and remarkably able Theophano, young daughter of the Eastern Emperor Romanus II.

John XIII cooperated with the Emperor in forwarding missionary activity on the frontiers. He confirmed the erection of Magdeburg as a metropolitan see. The famous diocese of Posen was established for the Poles in 966. John also backed St. Dunstan in his efforts to reform the Church in England.

John XIII died peacefully at Rome, September 6, 972. Though noticeably under Otto's influence, he was a good pope.

Chronologia Summorum Pontificum.

BENEDICT VI

972-974

LITTLE AS IS KNOWN OF THE ACHIEVEMENTS OF Pope Benedict VI, the somber circumstances of his death throw a baleful light on conditions in tenth-century Rome. Benedict VI was a Roman from the Forum district. His father's name was Hildebrand. At the time of his election, Benedict was cardinal-deacon of the Church of St. Theodore at the foot of the Palatine Hill. Though elected shortly after the death of John III in September 972, Benedict was not consecrated until January 19, 973. This delay was doubtless due to the wait for Emperor Otto's approval of the election.

Except for a few privileges granted by Benedict, nothing is known of his rather short pontificate until the events leading to his death.

Otto I died May 7, 973, leaving the throne to his son Otto II, then eighteen years old. The next year young Otto had to fight a civil war with Henry the Wrangler, duke of Bavaria. While the young emperor had his hands full in Germany, some Romans planned a revolution. In 974 Crescentius, a brother of the late Pope John XIII, and a scheming deacon Boniface Franco, seized control of the city. Crescentius made himself Patrician; Boniface took over the papacy. He called himself Boniface VII. Benedict VI was shut up in the Castle of St. Angelo.

When Otto II heard of this outrageous attempt, he sent Count Sicco to restore order. Sicco demanded the release of Pope Benedict, but the antipope hastened to have the Pope killed. Before Count Sicco could overthrow the usurpers, a priest named Stephen strangled poor Pope Benedict.

Benedict VI seems to have been a good pope. He was certainly an unfortunate one.

Mosaic in the Basilica of St. Paul-Outside-the-Walls, Rome.

BENEDICT VII

974-983

T HE CRUELTY OF THE ANTIPOPE BONIFACE DID not do him much good. So great was the indignation against the murderer that Count Sicco, the imperial agent, was able to overthrow Boniface and the Patrician, Crescentius. This cleared the way for a new election. Emperor Otto II and his mother, St. Adelaide, wished Maieul, abbot of Cluny, to take the papal throne. But Maieul firmly refused. He felt that it was his duty as it was his preference to continue to rule the monastic flock entrusted to his care. Otto then chose Benedict, the bishop of Sutri. Thus Benedict, like his predecessor and namesake, was a Roman. He was elected pope in October 974.

One of the new pope's first acts was to hold a synod to condemn the antipope Boniface. Though Boniface fled to Constantinople, he had a party at Rome which gave Benedict some trouble. Benedict was able to maintain himself for six years without much help from the Emperor, who was very busy in Germany. But it was not easy, and in 980 Pope Benedict was relieved to hear that Otto had crossed the Alps. The Emperor celebrated the Easter of 981 in Rome and so overawed the factions that Benedict was able to finish his pontificate in peace.

The Pope held a great council in the presence of Otto, which legislated against simony. Benedict then addressed an encyclical letter to the Church throughout the world, publishing the decree against simony. (Simony is the buying or selling of sacred things.) The Pope added that if any bishop-elect could not get consecrated without paying money to his metropolitan, he could come to Rome and be consecrated there.

Besides the Emperor, another visitor to Benedict VII was Hugh Capet, founder of France's great third dynasty. He secured from the Pope an exemption for a French monastery. Indeed, Benedict was very generous in the matter of privileges. Many were the German bishops and abbots who obtained various privileges from this gracious Pope.

It is interesting to note that Benedict consecrated a bishop for Carthage, a city which had long been under Moslem domination. He also gave the tonsure to Dunwallon, a Southern Welsh king, and was kind to Sergius, archbishop of Damascus, a refugee from the Saracens.

Benedict died probably on July 10, 983. According to his epitaph he was very good to widows and orphans. Though epitaphs are not the most critical sources, it is not difficult to believe that Benedict VII was a very charitable pope.

Mosaic in the Basilica of St. Paul-Outside-the-Walls, Rome.

JOHN XIV

983-984

BENEDICT VII HAD DIED IN PEACE, AND SINCE Otto II was still in Italy the new pontificate got off to a smooth start. It was to have a rough ending.

To succeed Benedict VII, Otto secured the election of Peter, bishop of Pavia. A native of Pavia, Peter Canepanova rose to be not only bishop of Pavia, but chancellor of the Kingdom of Italy. He also served as imperial agent in Rome. While chancellor he had had a disagreement with the famous scholar Gerbert, then abbot of Bobbio. Later, however, they became quite friendly. When he was elected pope, Peter took the name John XIV.

With a good churchman and a close friend of the Emperor on the papal throne, much could be expected from such a harmonious pope-emperor relationship. But Otto, only twenty-eight years old, fell a victim to his doctors. Four drachms of aloes proved too much for the young Emperor's constitution, and assisted by Pope John, he died a most edifying death. He was buried in St. Peter's.

Otto's premature death was a calamity for the empire; it was stark disaster for the Pope. With the Emperor's strong hand removed, the party of the antipope Boniface raised its head. At Easter 984 a revolt broke out. Back came the cruel antipope from Constantinople. Well supplied with gold, Boniface spent money lavishly to secure the triumph of his party. With the help of the Patrician Crescentius he seized Pope John, declared him deposed, and thrust him into the Castle of St. Angelo. While Boniface lorded it at the Lateran, the Pope languished in his cell, and by August 20 he was dead. There was a report that he had died a violent death, but this is not at all certain. It is certain that John XIV died in prison on August 20, 984.

The antipope Boniface did not long survive his victim. He died quite suddenly in July 985. His body was seized by a gang of his own party, who resented the antipope's strong hand. These rascals skinned the corpse and dragged it to the statue of Marcus Aurelius in front of the Lateran. Some clerics removed it and gave it a decent burial.

The British Museum, London.

[274]

JOHN XV

985-996

JOHN XV WAS A ROMAN, THE SON OF A PRIEST named Leo. At the time of his election John was cardinal-priest of St. Vitalis. The only authentic fact about his election is that it took place in August 985.

John XV was a learned man and a writer. He has been accused of rank nepotism and grasping avarice, but the accusations are far from proved. Indeed the poor man had little to say about civil government in Rome. A kinsman of Prince Alberic II now repeated Alberic's seizure of civil power in Rome. Crescentius of the Marble Horse, as he was called, was the son of that Crescentius who had led the revolt against Benedict VI. Shortly after John's election, Crescentius established himself as practically dictator in Rome. A smooth politician, he even got along with the Empress Theophano when she visited Rome in 989.

Though John XV was limited in temporal power at Rome, he made his influence felt in distant lands. His mediation was sought in a quarrel between Ethelred the Unready, king of England, and Richard, duke of Normandy. Through his legate Leo, the Pope succeeded in bringing about a peaceful settlement. The most interesting case of Pope John's pontificate was the fight over the archbishopric of Rheims in France. Hugh Capet, helped by Archbishop Adalberon of Rheims and the monk, Gerbert, had finally supplanted the Carolingian dynasty on the throne of France. The Carolingian Charles, duke of Lorraine, invaded France in an attempt to dethrone Hugh. He captured Rheims and its archbishop Arnulf. Now Arnulf was himself a Carolingian, and Hugh suspected that Arnulf had sold out his king for his family. Hugh therefore asked Pope John to depose Archbishop Arnulf. Before the Pope could answer, the tide of war swung in favor of Hugh, and he drove Lorraine's forces out of Rheims and seized Arnulf. The King then had a synod depose Arnulf and elect his friend and backer, the monk Gerbert. Pope John did not allow this highhanded action to go without rebuke. He ordered the French bishops to hold a free synod, which quashed the deposition of Arnulf. The affair caused an outbreak of antipapal sentiments among Gerbert's supporters. But in the end Gerbert had to go.

John V canonized Ulrich, the holy bishop of Augsburg on January 31, 993. He also granted numerous privileges to various churches and monasteries.

In 995 the tyranny of the Patrician Crescentius so irked the Pope that he fled to Tuscany and appealed to Emperor Otto III to put an end to the Patrician's usurpation. Crescentius, ever more the diplomat than the fighter, pleaded with the Pope to come back to Rome, and before the Emperor arrived, John was once more back in the Lateran. While all eyes were turned on the approaching Emperor, John XV was carried off by a fever in March or April, 996.

Chronologia Summorum Pontificum.

GREGORY V

996-999

THE APPROACH OF THE EMPEROR'S ARMY IN-
spired the Romans with such respect for Otto
that they sent to ask him to name his choice
for pope. Otto promptly designated his chaplain
and cousin, Bruno. Bruno was thereupon elected
and consecrated. He took the name Gregory V.
The first German pope was a young man in his
twenties. He was learned and could preach not
only in Latin and German, but in the budding
Italian. He was a bit quick-tempered, but on the
whole an excellent priest and a good pope.

On May 21, 996, Gregory crowned Otto emperor. Naturally enough, he and Otto got along
well together. But he could show his independence too, as when he condemned the monk Gerbert for the attempt to take over the see of Rheims;
Gerbert was a friend of Otto's. When Gerbert submitted, however, he was made archbishop of Ravenna.

Emperor Otto had started for Rome at the request of the late Pope John XV to check the
tyranny of the Patrician Crescentius. The Emperor
intended to punish the usurper, but papal good
nature prevailed and Gregory begged the rascal
off. It was a mistake. Scarcely had Otto left Rome
when Crescentius began to plot against the Pope.
Alarmed, Gregory begged Otto to return, but the
Emperor was unable to do so. Within a few
months Crescentius drove the Pope out of Rome
and set up as antipope the Calabrian Greek, John
Philagathus.

Gregory went to Pavia and held a synod. The
synod condemned all those who supported the
antipope and excommunicated Crescentius. This
synod also condemned King Robert of France for
attempting matrimony with his kinswoman Bertha.

The next year, 998, after all attempts to bring
Crescentius and his antipope John XVI to their
senses had failed, Otto marched on Rome. Crescentius holed up in the Castle of St. Angelo; the
antipope fled to a castle in the country. Without
waiting upon the angry Emperor's arrival, a Roman faction seized the antipope, tore out his eyes
and tongue, cut off his ears and nose, and confined
him in a monastery. The Pope and Emperor made
a triumphant entry in February 998. Gregory held
a Council which deposed John from his rank as a
priest. The mutilated wretch was then insulted by
the mob and finally kept in a monastery for the
rest of his life. Crescentius held out stubbornly in
St. Angelo, but at last the Germans battered their
way into the Castle. Crescentius was beheaded on
the battlements and his body tossed into the moat.

In spite of these political ups and downs, Pope
Gregory found time to do much for monasteries.
The great religious reform of the coming century
was to be powered by monks, and Gregory V did
his part in preparing for it by favoring these spiritual champions against bishops, all too often
mixed up in worldly and political matters.

Gregory V died on February 4, 999.

*Francesco de Mura. Church of Sts. Severino
and Sossio, Naples.*

SYLVESTER II

999-1003

CREDULOUS FOLK BELIEVED THAT GERBERT, THE learned monk who became Pope Sylvester II, was a magician, and around this interesting personality grew an aura of occult legend. But the cold facts of Sylvester's career are too interesting to need any seasoning from fervid imaginations.

Gerbert was born of lowly origin in Auvergne. Educated by the Benedictines and by the bishop of Vich in Spain, Gerbert became the leading Western scholar of his day. Brought to Rome by Borel, count of Barcelona, the learned monk so impressed Pope John XIII that he sent Gerbert to Otto the Great. Otto made him tutor to his son, and Gerbert always was close to the imperial family. After Otto's death Gerbert went to Rheims to teach in the cathedral school there. He interested himself in literature, music, philosophy, theology, mathematics, and the natural sciences. His inspirational teaching made Rheims an intellectual center. As a collector of books Gerbert resembles some of the more avid Renaissance humanists. Not contented with speculation, this practical man constructed globes, observation tubes, and a complicated abacus. He is credited by some with having introduced Arabic numerals to the west and with the invention of the pendulum clock.

Otto II made him Abbot of St. Columban's monastery at Bobbio, but he had to fight so much to preserve his abbey's temporalities from greedy hands that in disgust he soon withdrew to Rheims. There he became a bosom friend of the political-minded Archbishop Adalberon and threw himself into the maze of intrigue which ended the Carolingian dynasty in France. After this intrigue was successfully climaxed by the coronation of Hugh Capet in 987, Gerbert might reasonably have expected to become archbishop of Rheims on Adalberon's death. But Hugh passed him over for Arnulf. Arnulf, however, sided with his kinsman Charles of Lorraine when that duke invaded France in an effort to dethrone Hugh. Hugh captured Arnulf and had a council depose him and elect Gerbert in his place. Gerbert, who believed devoutly with St. Paul that "if a man desireth the work of a bishop he desireth a good work," was delighted. Not so Pope John XV, who frowned on such arbitrary depositions and elections. When the Pope ordered another and more free council to study the matter, Gerbert grew rebellious. He gained nothing by it. Suspended, he left France for the court of Otto III. Though his ambition caused him to be less than obedient he had too much virtue and good sense not to submit at last. He was rewarded, for if Otto was unable to get him reinstated at Rheims, he did have him made archbishop of Ravenna. Soon afterwards Gregory V died and Otto had Gerbert elected Pope.

The combination of the learned Sylvester II, as Gerbert was now known, and the idealistic Otto promised much for Christendom but the promise was not fulfilled. The Romans drove both Emperor and Pope out of Rome in 1001, and though Sylvester managed to return after Otto's early death in 1002, he was overshadowed by Crescentius III.

Though this short pontificate was something of an anticlimax to a colorful career, Sylvester did accomplish something. He called attention to needs of the Holy Land, he created the see of Gnesen for the Poles and that of Gran for the Hungarians. He sent a royal crown to St. Stephen of Hungary.

Sylvester II died May 12, 1003.

Chronologia Summorum Pontificum.

JOHN XVII

1003

THE LAST POPE NAMED JOHN WAS JOHN XV. There had indeed been a man who called himself John XVI, but he was John Phila-gathus the unfortunate antipope set up by Cres-centius II against Pope Gregory V. John XVII, therefore, should have been called John XVI. The reason why John Sicco, who became Pope Sylves-ter's successor, was called John XVII is not hard to guess. Crescentius III was now Patrician and the real power in Rome; and Crescentius III was the son of Crescentius II who had set up antipope John XVI. Consequently, Crescentius III would naturally insist that the pope whose election he had secured should assume the style of John XVII. Thus his father would be saved from being publicly branded as the supporter of an antipope.

Crescentius III dominated the papacy during this period and carried matters with so high a hand that by one chronicle he is called "the destroyer of the apostolic see." This however, was probably be-cause he usurped the popes' temporal power. As far as can be known, Crescentius III seems to have secured the election of worthy men as popes.

John XVII was a Roman named John Sicco. Be-fore he became a priest he had been married and had had three children, all of whom entered the ecclesiastical state. All that is known of his brief pontificate is that he was consecrated on June 13, 1003, and that he died on November 6 of that same year.

John XVII was buried in the Lateran Basilica.

Mosaic in the Basilica of St. Paul-Outside-the-Walls, Rome.

JOHN XVIII

1003-1009

ON THE DEATH OF JOHN XVII, CRESCENTIUS III secured the election of another John—John Phasanus. John Phasanus was a Roman of the Metrovian Gate district. His father, Ursus, had become a priest. John himself was cardinal of St. Peter's. It is uncertain whether it was St. Peter's in the Vatican or St. Peter-in-Chains. John seems to have been a man of excellent character. He was consecrated on Christmas Day, 1003, under the title of John XVIII.

Stirring events took place in this pontificate as Ardoin, the last independent medieval King of Italy, strove vainly to hold his kingdom against the attacks of Emperor Henry II. Crescentius seems to have kept the Pope from taking any part in this struggle.

John XVIII, however, did accomplish some things in the ecclesiastical sphere. He seems to have put an end to an obscure Eastern schism. For some reason not known, Constantinople had revolted from Rome in the last years of the tenth century. Now in the pontificate of John XVIII the breach was healed and Constantinople once more returned to Catholic unity.

If John XVIII had been unable to help Henry II in his Italian campaign, he did work closely with the pious Emperor in his German affairs. Henry, like the Ottos, relied on churchmen to balance the power of the turbulent lay lords. He now revived the see of Merseburg which had been suppressed in the reign of Otto II. Henry also wished to establish a new see at Bamberg to serve as a base for missionary activity among the Slavs. In both of these matters Pope John cooperated closely.

In France the Pope came to the rescue of Goslin, abbot of Fleury. The archbishop of Sens and the bishop of Orleans were both trying to make the abbot give up his papal privilege of exemption. The Pope took this seriously. He sent the bishop of Piperno into France to investigate the matter, and he ordered the offending bishops to come to Rome and give an account of themselves.

John also gave the pallium to Meingaudus, archbishop of Trier, and to Alphege, archbishop of Canterbury. In the temporal sphere, he set up salt works near Porto. But John's pontificate was not easy. Plague and famine desolated Rome, and to add to the misery, Saracens operating out of Sardinia ravaged the coasts.

The end of John's pontificate is interesting but obscure. It seems that he abdicated and retired to become a monk in the Monastery of St. Paul-Outside-the-Walls. He died shortly afterwards, probably in the summer of 1009.

Mosaic in the Basilica of St. Paul-Outside-the-Walls, Rome.

SERGIUS IV

1009-1012

SERGIUS IV HAD WHAT WAS PROBABLY THE MOST unusual name of any of the long line of St. Peter's successors. Before his election to the papacy, Sergius was known as Peter Pig's Mouth! Peter Pig's Mouth (Buccaporca) was born of a poor family in the Pina district of Rome. His father, likewise named Peter, was a shoemaker. His humble origin did not prevent Peter from rising in the ranks of the Church. A pious and intelligent young man, he rose to be cardinal-bishop of Albano in 1004 and in 1009 he was elected pope. He was enthroned under the name of Sergius IV.

In 1010 Christendom was deeply moved by the news from the East that the fanatical caliph of Egypt, El Hakim, had destroyed the Church of the Holy Sepulcher in Jerusalem. This vandalism had two effects in the West; one bad and one good. The bad one was that the Jews were attacked because of rumors that they had incited El Hakim to act against the Christians. This was quite probably false for that madman mixed up Jews and Christians in his violent vagaries. The good result was that devotion to the Holy Sepulcher of Christ grew and pilgrimages increased as a reaction to the horrifying news. Pope Sergius, if a bull attributed to him be authentic, called on the kings and princes of the West to drive the Saracens out of the Holy Land. Whether or not the bull is authentic, the crusading idea is beginning to show signs of life.

Sergius continued the policy of his predecessors in exempting monasteries from episcopal control. At Rome he evidently chafed under the yoke of the Patrician Crescentius, for there is evidence that the Pope was working to foster an imperialist party. Indeed an old twelfth-century chronicle of the counts of Anjou has a curious account of how Crescentius met his death. According to this chronicle when the fierce Count Fulk the Black was passing through Rome on pilgrimage to the Holy Land, Pope Sergius IV complained to him about the evil deeds of Crescentius. Thereupon the redoubtable Angevin, without much ado, had the Patrician shot down by his archers. An interesting story, but definitely not true. Crescentius, though he died at this time, did not perish at the hands of Angevin archers. But the story does reflect the tension between Pope and Patrician.

When a famine hit Rome, Sergius showed himself to be a true shepherd of his flock and worked devotedly to help his hungry people.

Sergius IV died on May 12, 1012. He is buried in the Lateran. Though not canonized, Sergius is venerated as a saint by the Benedictines.

Chronologia Summorum Pontificum.

BENEDICT VIII

1012-1024

WITH THE ACCESSION OF BENEDICT VIII, THE house of Tusculum mounts the papal throne. This family, like that of Crescentius, was a branch of the house of Theophylactus which had so frequently dominated Rome in the past century. Now in 1012 the Tusculan branch of the family prevailed over the Crescentian. Theophylactus, one son of Gregory, count of Tusculum, became Pope Benedict VIII; Romanus, another son, was made senator of all the Romans.

The election of Theophylactus was disputed by a certain Gregory. Unable to prevail at Rome, Gregory fled to Henry II for help, but Henry recognized Benedict VIII. Benedict VIII proved to be an excellent ruler both in spiritual and temporal matters. He welcomed Henry to Italy and on February 14, 1014, he crowned Henry emperor. Benedict's relations with the saintly ruler were always cordial.

Benedict quickly showed that he was a strong man who would brook no disobedience from turbulent lords. Crescentius, a cousin of the late Patrician, had seized a castle belonging to the monastery of Farfa. The monks had appealed to Henry and the Emperor asked the Pope to see that justice was done. Crescentius mocked the Pope's invitation to do justice, but when he found Benedict coming after him with an army, he agreed to be reasonable.

In tackling the Saracen menace Pope Benedict showed vigorous and competent leadership. The Saracens had seized Luna in Tuscany and from this base were spreading misery over the land. Benedict attacked them by land and by sea and drove them out of Italy. Furious, the Moslem chief sent the Pope a bag of chestnuts with the threat that he would be back the next summer with a soldier for every chestnut. Benedict, not to be outdone in this war of nerves, sent the Moslem a bag of rice with the warning that he when he came would find a soldier for every grain of rice! The Pope was better than his word. Believing that the best defence is a good offence, Benedict succeeded in getting the Genoese and Pisans to sail against Sardinia, the Moslem base. The combined fleets captured the island. This was a great Christian victory, for the Moslems had held Sardinia for over a century.

Benedict also opposed the aggression of the Eastern Empire in Southern Italy. He made allies of some adventurous Normans, and finally went to Germany to warn Emperor Henry of the danger. While there he consecrated the cathedral of Bamberg and visited the famous monastery of Fulda. Henry gave the Pope a confirmation of the donation of Charlemagne and Otto. Then coming down into Italy, he checked the Greeks.

Though much occupied with temporal matters, Benedict also vigorously acted in spiritual matters. He held a Council at Pavia in 1018 which legislated against the prevailing abuses of simony and clerical marriage. The holy Emperor worked closely with the Pope in his reform efforts. Benedict also encouraged the Truce of God, that interesting attempt to limit the private wars of that turbulent period. He also encouraged the Cluniac reform which was still working quietly toward a better day.

Benedict VIII died on April 7, 1028. The first of the Tusculan popes had been a good one.

Mosaic in the Basilica of St. Paul-Outside-the-Walls, Rome.

JOHN XIX

1024-1032

At benedict's death, his brother romanus, the consul and senator of all the Romans, decided to become pope. Though he was a layman, Romanus was elected. A little influence, a little judicious spending, and the papacy was his. Disgruntled observers remarked that he was senator in the morning and pope in the evening. And indeed there was a hurried conferring of holy orders until sometime in April 1024, Romanus was consecrated pope as John XIX.

Though his accession to the papacy was, to say the least, somewhat irregular, John did not make a bad pope. Unfortunately, however, he was not the man his brother Benedict had been, nor was Conrad II the emperor that St. Henry II had been. During this pontificate the cause of reform suffered a setback. Conrad II, the first of the Salian emperors, came down into Italy in 1026 and the next year proceeded to Rome for coronation. This was an unusually splendid affair, graced as it was by the presence not only of the Pope and Emperor but of King Canute of England and Denmark and King Rudolf of Burgundy. Conrad, an energetic ruler, was too much occupied with consolidating his power to further the cause of reform. Indeed, if anything, he impeded it by his appointments.

A curious incident occurred shortly after John became pope. Envoys from the powerful Eastern Emperor Basil II arrived in Rome and with golden arguments began to press the Pope to grant to the Patriarch of Constantinople the title of Universal or Ecumenical Patriarch and recognize that the Patriarch should have in the East the same jurisdiction the Pope had in the whole world. News of this request spread rapidly, and Western public opinion rose up against the ambition of Constantinople. Pope John, though he may have been inclined to grant the request, finally refused it. The Easterners were furious, and Pope John's name was stricken from their diptychs or liturgical tablets.

Though John was not the fighter against abuses that his brother had been, he did favor the Cluniac monks and grant privileges to monasteries. Then too, he showed good sense in handling appeals. Indeed, in one case he showed more than good sense; he showed true humility. Abbot William of St. Benignus in Dijon wrote to the Pope scolding him for his lack of vigor in carrying on the fight against simony. Pope John thanked him and praised the outspoken monk for his zeal.

John XIX did a little building. He also summoned to Rome Guido of Arezzo, the famous monk who organized the *do-re-mi* scale. The Pope encouraged the great music reformer and urged him to instruct the Roman clergy in music.

John XIX died probably in October 1032. Though his method of becoming pope was not above reproach, he had not done badly.

Medal by Georg Wilhelm Vestner. The American Numismatic Society, New York.

BENEDICT IX

1032-1044

AT THE DEATH OF JOHN XIX, HIS BROTHER ALBERIC decided to keep the papacy in the family by having his young son Theophylactus elected. Theophylactus, a young man probably about twenty years old, was a cleric. That was about his only qualification for the papacy. Unqualified by his youth, his bringing up, his depravity, Benedict IX became one of the very few really disreputable popes.

The story of Benedict's pontificate is as unsatisfactory as his life. The Romans rose against him probably about 1036 and drove him from the city. Benedict proceeded to Cremona, where he met Emperor Conrad II and received a promise of protection. By imperial influence Benedict returned to Rome, only to be driven out again in 1044. This time there was a fight, and Benedict's supporters grimly clung to a foothold in the Trastevere district. Inside the city, John, bishop of Sabina, was set up as Pope Sylvester III; but Benedict was not idle. He had fled for help to his family's base at Tusculum and within two months his tough Tusculans fought their way into the city, sent Sylvester III back to his diocese of Sabina, and restored Benedict IX.

Once restored, Benedict did not feel at ease on the papal throne. For some reason, in 1045 he decided to abdicate. As Desiderius, the abbot of Monte Cassino (later Pope Victor III), put it, "Devoted to pleasure, he preferred to live like Epicurus rather than like a pope." Consequently, he abdicated and handed over the papacy to the worthy archpriest, John Gratian. Benedict did not go empty-handed. Gratian paid a large sum to get rid of this offensive character.

The charms of retirement soon wore thin for Benedict, and a short time after his abdication he was once more claiming to be pope. With Sylvester III and Benedict IX fighting Gregory for the control of Rome, things were in a frightful muddle. This was ended by Henry III, who had succeeded his father Conrad II in 1039. Henry came down into Italy, cooperated with Gregory to get rid of the pretensions of Sylvester and Benedict, and then had a council demand and receive Gregory's abdication. Henry then put in a German pope—Clement II.

Benedict made one more comeback. After the death of Clement II, he once again entered Rome and held sway at the Lateran, but only from November 8, 1047 to July 17, 1048. Henry III insisted on his removal and brusquely ordered Boniface, marquis of Tuscany, to expel Benedict.

What happened to Benedict after this is obscure. According to one report, which it may be hoped is true, Benedict retired to the abbey of Grottaferrata, resigned all claim to the papacy, and spent his last years as a penitent.

Scandalous as Benedict had been, he carried on the routine business of the papacy. And like the few other bad men who were popes, Benedict taught nothing but the pure doctrine of Christ, though by so doing he condemned and did not excuse his own evil life.

Chronologia Summorum Pontificum.

GREGORY VI

1045-1046

GREGORY VI IS NOTED AS THE POPE WHO PURchased the papacy! Yet Gregory VI was a good man, a good priest, and a good pope. What happened was this. When the scandalous Benedict IX began to grow weary of being pope, he went to his godfather, John Gratian, the worthy archpriest of St. John-at-the-Latin-Gate, and asked him if it were legitimate for a pope to abdicate. John joyously assured him that it was and urged Benedict to take a step so profitable for the Church. Benedict, however, demanded compensation, and John gave him a large sum of money he had at hand for some worthy object. He did not think the money could be better spent than in ridding the Church of so scandalous a pastor. The good priest does not seem to have realized that such a proceeding would itself give scandal as an act of simony, especially since simony, the sale or purchase of sacred things, was an abuse of the period.

John Gratian himself was elected to succeed Benedict. According to some he accepted reluctantly. He was consecrated as Gregory VI. His election was hailed with joy, for the venerable priest enjoyed an excellent reputation. The fiery reformer St. Peter Damian wrote from his Camaldolese monastery to congratulate Gregory and urge him to campaign vigorously against abuses. Gregory took that advice. He tried hard to rule the Church well, and he relied for help on his chaplain, a holy and able young monk named Hildebrand. But it was a difficult task. The confusion of the years preceding had caused anarchy in the Papal States. Armed bands roved about. The

Pope's temporal authority was defied. Gregory tried first by gentle means, then by raising an armed force, to restore order. But soon confusion was worse confounded. Sylvester III, the antipope of 1044, came back to Rome to dispute the papacy with Gregory. Worse still, Benedict IX, weary of retirement, once more claimed the papal throne. Since each had his supporters in the city, the turbulent state of affairs can be imagined. At last a faction sent to Henry III and asked him to set things straight. Down into Italy came King Henry, and Gregory went to meet him at Piacenza. He cooperated with Henry and called a council at Sutri which declared that Sylvester's election had been invalid. Benedict was passed over because he had abdicated. Prospects for Gregory looked bright, but when Henry came to Rome for Christmas, another synod was held and it became evident that King Henry intended to oust Gregory. Using the excuse that Gregory had committed the sin of simony, the council demanded his abdication. The good man freely admitted that he had paid money to Benedict, but declared that he considered the transaction justified by extraordinary circumstances. He now acknowledged that he had done wrong and humbly begged pardon. Such humility was exemplary, but it did not satisfy Henry. He wanted the Pope out, and so just before Christmas 1046, Gregory abdicated.

Henry sent the ex-pope to Germany as a state prisoner. With him went his chaplain Hildebrand. Gregory died some time after 1047, but the date and place of his death are unknown.

Chronologia Summorum Pontificum.

CLEMENT II

1046-1047

AFTER HENRY III HAD DISPOSED OF GREGORY VI (and Sylvester III and Benedict IX) the way was open for a new election. When the Romans meekly told Henry to select the new pope, he chose Adalbert, archbishop of Hamburg. Adalbert definitely refused, but he suggested a substitute, Suidger, bishop of Bamberg. Suidger was not particularly anxious to exchange his beloved Bamberg for turbulent Rome; but Henry liked the idea and persuaded Suidger to accept. He was enthroned as Clement II.

Suidger was born in Saxony of noble parents. He entered the ecclesiastical state and became chaplain of Herman, archbishop of Hamburg, canon of Halberstadt, and finally in 1040, bishop of Bamberg. He was a holy man and a kind one.

On Christmas Day 1046, Clement was enthroned. Immediately after the ceremony the new pope crowned Henry and his wife Agnes. Henry not only became emperor but assumed the title of Patrician, and to him the Romans conceded the right of nominating the pope. So general was the disgust at the irresponsible conduct of the Roman nobility that this act, which tended to place the papacy in thraldom to the Emperor, was actually hailed with joy even by reformers. And indeed as long as Henry III lived it worked well enough. But the danger is that not every emperor is a Henry III.

Clement II wasted no time in starting his reform campaign. Early in January 1047 he held a synod in Rome which condemned simony and punished those guilty of this sin by excommunication. Indeed, anyone who knowingly even accepted ordination at the hands of a simoniacal bishop was condemned to do penance for forty days. Clement sought the advice of the great St. Peter Damian. This monk, whose outspokenness in denouncing abuses would make a modern gasp, did much to help Clement.

Clement accompanied Emperor Henry III in a progress through Southern Italy. At the Emperor's wish, the Pope excommunicated the people of Benevento when they refused to open their gates to the imperial party. Clement then accompanied Henry at least to Northern Italy. At Pesaro he was struck down by illness and on October 9, 1047, Clement II died. There was suspicion that ex-Pope Benedict IX had poisoned him, but this suspicion does not seem to be justified.

Clement was an able and holy pope, but his pontificate had been too brief to allow him to do more than make a good start toward reform. He granted a number of privileges especially, of course, one to his beloved see of Bamberg.

DAMASUS II

1048

WHEN AN EMBASSY FROM ROME REPORTED the death of Clement II to Emperor Henry III and asked him to name a new pope, the Emperor did not reply at once. A conscientious man, he asked the advice of Wazo, bishop of Liége. Wazo, after mature deliberation, informed the Emperor that Gregory VI should be sent back to Rome. But Wazo's reflection was a little too mature. Henry had grown impatient, and by the time Wazo's answer reached him, he had already made his choice. The Romans had asked for Halinard, bishop of Lyons, but Halinard would not hear of becoming pope. Henry then named the Bavarian Poppo, bishop of Brixen.

It was one thing for the Emperor in far-off Saxony to name Poppo as the next pope. It was something else to get him seated on the papal throne in St. Peter's. That throne was once more occupied by ex-Pope Benedict IX! After Clement's death, Benedict, by judicious spending, had gained enough supporters in Rome to make a comeback, and he was also backed by Boniface, the powerful marquis of Tuscany. Henry was detained in Germany, but he ordered Marquis Boniface to escort Poppo to Rome and see to it that he was enthroned in St. Peter's. Boniface dared not disobey openly. He simply told Poppo that Benedict now had full control over the city, and that now a poor old man, he did not feel equal to the task of dislodging the ex-pope. Back went Poppo to Henry with this disheartening message. Henry, not unnaturally, was furious. He sent Poppo right back to the reluctant marquis with an order to get Benedict out of Rome and install Poppo or face trouble. This time Boniface's age did not interfere with his obedience. He promptly ousted ex-Pope Benedict and finally on July 17, 1048, Poppo was enthroned as Pope Damasus II.

Damasus had no chance to show what he could do as pope. July is a hot month in Rome and was probably too hot for the Bavarian pope. Though he quickly got out of Rome and retired to rural Palestrina, he was soon a very sick man. By August 9, Damasus II was dead. He was buried in the Church of St. Lawrence-Outside-the-Walls.

Mosaic in the Basilica of St. Paul-Outside-the-Walls, Rome.

ST. LEO IX

1049-1054

ST. LEO IX, THE FIRST OF A NUMBER OF TRULY great reform popes, was born at Egisheim in Alsace, June 21, 1002, of a family connected with the imperial house. Bruno became a cleric quite young, and already in 1017 was a canon at Toul. When his father's cousin Conrad came to the throne, Bruno was sent to serve in the royal chapel. At court as at home he distinguished himself by his goodness. In 1026 Bruno led his bishop's feudal levy into Italy to support Conrad's demonstration. The next year Bruno became bishop of Toul. He worked hard to reform his diocese.

After the death of Damasus II, Henry III named his cousin Bruno to the papacy. Bruno showed a spirit of independence by refusing to accept until the Roman clergy elected him. Already popular with the Romans, Bruno was enthusiastically received, and on February 12, 1049, he was enthroned as Leo IX.

The great objective of the new Pope was reform. He held a Council at Rome in April, 1049, which once more legislated against simony and clerical marriage. Reform decrees already existed, but this time something new was added—a personal determined effort on the Pope's part to get these decrees enforced. Leo took to the road and at Pavia in North Italy, Mainz in Germany, and Rheims in France the energetic Pope filled the bishops with an ardent will to cooperate with the reform.

While Leo's pontificate saw a grand start toward reform in the West, it also witnessed the events leading to the sad Eastern Schism. Michael Caerularius, the ambitious patriarch of Constantinople, launched an anti-Western propaganda campaign to loosen the bonds of union. When he proceeded to close Latin churches in Constantinople and force Latin monks to adopt the Greek rite, Leo protested. The Emperor forced the patriarch to give in, but when Leo sent legates to investigate, they were defied by the patriarch. The legates then on July 16, 1054, excommunicated the patriarch. The patriarch thereupon revolted from Rome, and the sad Eastern Schism had begun. Leo died before this final break occurred.

Leo had been hearing bitter complaints about the brutal conduct of the Normans in South Italy. He went to Germany for help, but though he got little, he decided to lead an army against the Normans anyway. The tough Normans routed the papal army and soon were battering at the gates of Civitella, the papal headquarters. To avert more bloodshed, Leo surrendered himself to the enemy. His dignity accomplished more than his army. The Normans, embarrassed at having the Pope a prisoner, promised to become his allies!

This campaign took a great deal out of Leo. A sick man, he covered the distance back to Rome, but died piously on April 9, 1054.

Among the interesting visitors received by Leo was Shakespeare's famous Macbeth of Scotland. Leo arranged for the appointment of a bishop for far-off Iceland. Not only a great leader and administrator, Leo was a musician of note. He composed music for feasts of St. Gregory and St. Columban. But more than all these, Leo was kind, patient, humble—a true pope, a real saint.

Francesco de Mura. Church of Sts. Severino and Sossio, Naples.

VICTOR II

1055-1057

WHEN ST. LEO IX DIED, EX-POPE BENEDICT IX made a final attempt to get back in the papal throne. The Romans beat him off and then waited for the return of Hildebrand before taking steps to elect a new pope. Hildebrand had been in France working for reform and in Leo's name investigating a heretic named Berengarius. He hurried back to Rome to find that the clergy were anxious to have an independent election and that he was a favored candidate. Though few more clearly realized the need for papal independence than Hildebrand, this monk was no fanatic. He knew that Emperor Henry III would take it very ill if the Romans elected a pope without consulting him; and he realized that Henry, a conscientious man, would pick a good candidate. Therefore, Hildebrand persuaded the Romans to hold up the election and send him to ask Emperor Henry to give the Romans a pope of their choice. Under Hildebrand's guidance they chose Gebhardt, Bishop of Eichstätt, a powerful minister of the Emperor. Henry, though reluctant to lose his trusty councilor, consented. Gebhardt himself was also reluctant, but finally he too consented and went down to Rome, where he was joyously elected and enthroned as Victor II on April 13, 1055.

Gebhardt, count of Calvi, Tollenstein, and Hirschberg, was born in Suabia sometime around 1018. Through the influence of his uncle Gebhardt, bishop of Ratisbon, young Gebhardt, though only twenty-four years old, received the bishopric of Eichstätt. Young though he was, Gebhardt proved to be an excellent bishop and a top-flight administrator. Henry soon drew him into the imperial service and made him one of his most important ministers.

Victor II continued the strong reform policy of St. Leo. And while he was not the man to truckle to the Emperor, he got along very well with him. This close cooperation of Pope and Emperor enabled the work of reform to go forward with dispatch. Victor also secured restitution to papal control of some territory and indeed also the addition of the Duchy of Spoleto to the Papal States. He relied on Hildebrand to keep the papal finances in some kind of order.

In 1056 Victor visited Henry III at Goslar. A clever diplomat, he succeeded in appeasing the Emperor's wrath against the house of Tuscany. Countess Beatrice and her daughter Matilda, who had been state prisoners, were allowed to return to Italy. Matilda would later repay the papacy for Victor's kindness. The Pope helped Henry on his death bed, and after this untimely death Victor did much for the Empress Agnes and her boy Emperor Henry IV, who was only six years old.

By the Lent of 1057 Victor was back in Rome. He used diplomacy to quiet the restless Normans of South Italy. He made Frederick, abbot of Monte Cassino and brother of Godfrey, duke of Lorraine, a cardinal. While he was in Tuscany settling a jurisdictional dispute between the bishops of Arezzo and Siena, he fell sick and on July 28, this fine reform pope died.

Chronologia Summorum Pontificum.

STEPHEN X

1057-1058

THE PONTIFICATE OF STEPHEN X MARKS A STEP forward in the fight for reform. Preceding popes had struck hard at simony and clerical marriage. Now the axe began to swing at the root —lay control of church offices. It is true that the strong hand and good heart of Henry III had rescued the papacy from irresponsible Roman lords. Still imperial control of the papacy was dangerous, and lay control of any church position from pope to abbot was not only an evil, but a root of evils.

At the death of Victor II the situation favored a move toward papal independence. Henry IV was a small boy. His mother, the empress-regent Agnes, was not likely to raise too great a stir if a pope were elected without waiting for her approval. Then too, the Romans acted shrewdly. They elected Cardinal Frederick, abbot of Monte Cassino and brother of Godfrey, duke of Lower Lorraine and Tuscany. If anyone could make an independent election stick, it would be a clergyman with such very powerful connections.

The Romans' choice was good in many ways. Frederick was the son of Gozelon, duke of Lower Lorraine. After studies at St. Lambert's in Liége, Frederick became a canon, and then archdeacon of that Church. St. Leo IX made him chancellor and librarian of the Apostolic See. He became an important aid to the great reforming pope. St. Leo sent him to Constantinople on the mission which ended so sadly in the Eastern Schism. On his return, Frederick was attacked by a robber baron and stripped of all the treasures given to him by Emperor Constantine. Then, learning that Emperor Henry III was angry with him, Frederick retired to Monte Cassino and became a monk. Elected abbot, he was consecrated by Pope Victor II and made cardinal-priest of St. Chrysogonus.

Frederick was consecrated pope as Stephen X because his election took place on August 2, 1057, Pope St. Stephen's feast day. Stephen gathered around him the great reformers of the age. He forced the fiery monk of Fonte Avellano, St. Peter Damian, to become cardinal-bishop of Ostia. He sent Hildebrand to smooth over the free election with Empress-Regent Agnes. And after the capable monk succeeded in this delicate mission, he was sent into France to push on the work of reform.

The condition of the clergy in Milan was so bad that the city might be considered a capital of the antireform party. The Milanese people, however, rose against their unworthy pastors, and though given the contemptuous name of "patari", i.e., ragamuffins, they made matters hot for the abuse-ridden clergy. While Pope Stephen moderated the violence of these eleventh-century vigilantes, he approved of their association.

For some reason, possibly to wage war on the troublesome South Italian Normans, Stephen asked the monks of Monte Cassino to lend him all their gold and silver. But when he saw that the monks were less than delighted with the proposal, the good Pope relented and let them bring their treasures back.

Like his German predecessors, Stephen was soon sick. He died on a trip to Tuscany on March 29, 1058. To the Romans he left a legacy of good advice—not to elect a successor until the return of Hildebrand.

Mosaic in the Basilica of St. Paul-Outside-the-Walls, Rome.

NICHOLAS II

1059-1061

THE ROMANS DID NOT HAVE A CHANCE TO TAKE the late Pope Stephen's advice about waiting for Hildebrand before holding an election. When news of Stephen's death arrived, Gregory, count of Tusculum, and other lords swarmed into the city with their men-at-arms and took over the election. In vain the cardinals protested; in vain St. Peter Damian lifted his voice. In spite of the cardinals, a tumultuous mob proclaimed John, bishop of Velletri, pope. He was enthroned as Benedict X. But the election was not uncontested. Even at Rome in the Trastevere district, a group refused to acknowledge Benedict. St. Peter Damian and the cardinals fled North. And on his way back from France, the man was coming for whose arrival Pope Stephen had wished the Romans to wait, Cardinal Hildebrand.

When Hildebrand learned that the house of Theophylactus was once more trying to get control of the papacy, he acted swiftly. First he secured the support of Duke Godfrey and of the German court. Then he held a meeting with the cardinals at Siena at which Gerard of Burgundy, bishop of Florence, was named pope-elect. Duke Godfrey and Wibert, the imperial chancellor, mobilized at Sutri. Then after Gerard held a council which declared Benedict deposed, the army marched on Rome. A little fighting sent Benedict and his barons flying. Then a great assembly gathered at the Lateran to investigate the election of Benedict. The council declared the election invalid and deposed Benedict. Gerard was elected and enthroned as Nicholas II.

Gerard was born in Burgundy, and like his predecessor he had been a canon at Liége. While bishop of Florence he had made a reputation as a reform prelate. As pope he lived up to this reputation.

The main blow struck for reform by Nicholas was the promulgation of new papal election decrees at a synod held at Rome in 1059. According to these decrees the pope should be elected by the cardinal-bishops. The rest of the clergy and the laity of Rome had the right to acclaim the election. The pope should normally be a member of the Roman clergy, but in case of necessity could come from outside Rome. The election, if possible, was to be held at Rome; but if necessary, it could be held elsewhere. The pope-elect was to wield full authority even if he could not reach Rome. Imperial control was limited to a personal right granted by the pope to confirm papal elections.

These decrees, an important move toward papal independence, were bitterly resented by the German court, and a papal legate, sent to smooth matters over, was turned away. A German synod dared to condemn the decrees and declare Nicholas II deposed. But Nicholas could ignore the angry clamor, for he had two strong supports in Duke Godfrey and the Normans. Nicholas had secured the aid of the Normans at Melfi in 1059. At a meeting there, the Pope agreed to recognize Robert Guiscard as duke of Apulia, and the Normans agreed to supply the strong arms Nicholas needed to seize Benedict and maintain his independence.

In his short pontificate Nicholas did much. He renewed the election decrees in 1061. He condemned Berengarius, a Frenchman who denied transubstantiation. He fostered reform by means of energetic legates; and he made Hildebrand, reform's greatest champion, archdeacon of the Roman church.

Nicholas II died at Florence in July 1061.

Benvenuto di Giovani. National Gallery, London.

ALEXANDER II

1061-1073

THE DEATH OF NICHOLAS II AND THE ANGER which his election decrees had aroused in the German court raised the hopes of the Roman barons. Eager to outflank the cardinals, they sent to the Empress Agnes to ask her to give Rome a pastor. But the cardinals proceeded to elect one of the foremost reformers of Italy, Anselm, bishop of Lucca. Hildebrand persuaded the reluctant Anselm to accept; and he was enthroned as Alexander II on October 1, 1061.

Anselm was born near Milan and studied in the famous monastery of Bec under Lanfranc. As a member of the Milanese clergy he became a leader of the Patari, those embattled folk who made things miserable for evil-living priests. Archbishop Guido got the fiery Anselm out of Milan by having him made bishop of Lucca, but Anselm continued to encourage the Patari and even returned to Milan as papal legate with Hildebrand.

Before this zealous pope could devote himself to reform he had to establish himself on a throne set shaking by intrigue. The antireform party and the Roman nobles had secured the ear of Empress Agnes, and at a council held at Basel in October 1061, the antireform candidate Cadalus, bishop of Pavia, was declared pope by young Henry IV. In spite of St. Peter Damian's fiery expostulation, Cadalus accepted and called himself Honorius II. Alexander, however, had a powerful friend in Godfrey, duke of Tuscany. And soon in a palace revolution Anno, archbishop of Cologne, replaced Empress Agnes as the power behind the young king's throne. Anno held a diet at Augsburg in October 1062 which decided in favor of Alexander.

Safe on his throne, Alexander blasted away at abuses. He held a synod at the Lateran in 1063 which condemned Cadalus and passed a series of reform decrees. One of these reflects the vigilante attitude of the Milanese Patari. It forbade lay folk to hear the Mass of a priest who did not live chastely.

Cadalus advanced on Rome with an army, but Duke Godfrey and the Normans drove him back. To break the antipope's morale a great council was held at Mantua in 1064, and once more Alexander was proclaimed legitimate pope. Though Cadalus continued to claim to be pope, he sank from being a menace to being a minor nuisance.

The Normans also gave trouble to the Pope when they tried to take over Rome in 1066. Godfrey came to the rescue, and after a little fighting, more talking, and the payment of a round sum of money, the Normans went home. In other directions Alexander II encouraged the Normans. He blessed a banner for William, duke of Normandy, and approved of his famous expedition to England. He encouraged the Italian Normans to attack Sicily and begin the reconquest of that island from the Moslems.

Alexander's great work was pushing the reform movement. He not only enacted decrees but strove with all his might to get them carried out. No respecter of persons, he refused to annul the marriage of Henry IV. He deposed simoniacal bishops no matter how influential, and his legates carried the fight into far corners. He boldly excommunicated King Henry's advisers when they practiced simony. When Alexander II died on April 21, 1073, he had prepared the way for Hildebrand, and he had fired the opening gun in the great fight against lay investiture.

*Luca Giordano. "Alexander II Consecrates the
Abbey of Montecassino" (detail).
National Museum, Naples.*

ST. GREGORY VII

1073-1085

HILDEBRAND WAS BORN OF POOR PARENTS AT Soana in Tuscany. Educated at a Roman monastery and the Lateran school, he became a monk. Pious, bursting with energy, and gifted with administrative ability, the little monk was to become a great pope. When his old teacher, John Gratian, became Pope Gregory VI, he took Hildebrand into his service and ordered him to clean up the city, tormented by violence and barefaced robbery, grim heirlooms of Benedict IX's disorderly pontificate. The young monk organized a police force which knocked some order into the Roman lordlings. At Gregory's resignation Hildebrand followed him into Germany. At Gregory's death, he retired to Cluny. Pope Leo IX took Hildebrand back to Rome and henceforth he served as a strong right arm to the reforming popes. After Alexander II died, the demand for Hildebrand was too great to be resisted. He was consecrated as Gregory VII on June 30, 1073.

With St. Gregory VII the fight against abuses reached a new pitch of intensity. This devout, very sincere man faced squarely the sad condition of the Church. No fanatic, he concentrated on the worst abuses. Now the root of abuse was the way kings and lords appointed bishops and abbots by lay investiture. Gregory swung the axe at this root by absolutely banning lay investiture at a Roman synod in 1075. The stage was set for the clash with King Henry IV.

Henry had talked fair, but continued to act evilly. Cencius, a Roman noble friendly to the king, broke in on Gregory's Christmas Mass and carried him a prisoner to his tower. But the Romans swarmed so angrily around his tower that the rascal lord quickly released the outraged Pope.

Gregory then summoned Henry under pain of excommunication to appear before a Roman synod to answer charges. Henry's answer was to hold his own synod at Worms and have his subservient bishops condemn Gregory. The Pope excommunicated Henry and released his subjects from their allegiance. Saxony rose in arms and Henry's throne quaked when the nobles of Germany gathered at Tribur in October 1076. Gregory's legates persuaded the nobles to give Henry a chance to repent before deposing him. A national diet under the Pope's presidency was summoned at Augsburg for 1077.

Henry, knowing his unpopularity with many nobles, had no wish to face this assembly. He hurried over the Alps before Gregory could reach Germany. As a suppliant he appeared before the castle of Canossa where Gregory had retired. Cleverly the King stood shivering in a penitential garb while Countess Matilda, the Pope's hostess, and St. Hugh of Cluny pleaded for mercy. Gregory knew he should await the Augsburg meeting, but he had been jockeyed by Henry into a position where he simply had to absolve the king.

Once absolved, Henry went back to his old ways. He set up an antipope, the abuse-loving Guibert of Ravenna. He defeated the German nobles, captured Rome, and installed his creature in the Lateran as Clement III. Gregory, besieged in the Castle of St. Angelo, was rescued by the Normans. But soon he had to leave Rome. Worn out, the brave old saint died at Salerno in 1085. "I have loved justice and hated iniquity, therefore I die in exile," he said; but he had paved the way for a better future. He was canonized by Benedict XIII in 1728.

Federigo Zuccari. "Pope Gregory VII Absolving the Excommunicated Emperor" (detail). The Vatican.

BLESSED VICTOR III

1086-1087

FEW HAVE BEEN MORE RELUCTANT TO ACCEPT the papacy than the monk who became Victor III. Dauferius was born of the noble family of the princes of Benevento. Though his family planned a marriage for him, Dauferius was determined to be a monk. When his father died fighting the Normans, Dauferius escaped the watch of his relatives and entered a monastery. But the enraged relatives hunted him down, tore off his religious habit and hustled the would-be monk home. Dauferius, however, had a mind of his own, and soon escaped again. This time his relatives agreed to let him remain a monk. As a Benedictine monk, he received the name Desiderius.

In spite of his aversion to honor and power, his sweet disposition and pronounced ability caught the attention of the reforming Popes. St. Leo IX and Victor II took a great liking to the young Benedictine, and Stephen X made him abbot of Monte Cassino. Desiderius proved to be one of the greatest in the long line of Cassinese abbots. Desiderius found the old abbey in a ruinous state and energetically undertook a wide-scale rebuilding program. Under his leadership there rose a chapter house, an abbots' house, a library, a dormitory, and a great church. From far-off Constantinople he procured artists in mosaic and marble to beautify his church. Pope Alexander II consecrated it in 1071.

No mere bricks-and-mortar abbot, Desiderius took great pains to help his monks advance in the spiritual life. Nor was he neglectful of the abbey's intellectual life. He was zealous to secure manuscripts for his library, among them works of Cicero, Ovid, and Virgil.

As abbot of Monte Cassino, Desiderius was a great personage in Southern Italy. This power he used loyally to back the reform popes. Nicholas II made him a cardinal and papal legate. He had great influence with the Normans, and it was he who secured their help for St. Gregory VII in his time of need. It is not surprising that when Gregory VII died, Abbot Desiderius was sought as his successor. But Desiderius simply would not agree to accept the heavy honor. At last on Pentecost Sunday, May 24, 1086, the exasperated Cardinals and clergy carried Desiderius to the Church of St. Lucy, and forcibly clothing him with the papal mantle, called him Victor III. But four days later Victor put off the papal insignia and withdrew to Monte Cassino. It was almost a year before he finally consented to serve as pope. At a great council held at Capua in 1087 Victor at last surrendered. When the Normans drove antipope Guibert out of Rome, Victor was solemnly enthroned in St. Peter's May 9, 1087.

Much could be hoped for from such a pope as Blessed Victor III; but his health was shattered, and his short pontificate was stormy. Unable or unwilling to maintain himself in Rome against Antipope Guibert, Victor held a council at Benevento which once more excommunicated the antipope and once more condemned lay investiture. After this Victor sank rapidly until on September 16, 1087, the gentle Pope died at Monte Cassino. He was buried in his beloved monastery.

E. Le Sueur. "Pope Victor III Confirms the Establishment of the Carthusians." The Louvre, Paris.

BLESSED URBAN II

1088-1099

ODO OF THE KNIGHTLY FAMILY OF LAGERY WAS born around 1042 at Châtillon-sur Marne in Champagne. His parents were pious and Odo followed their example. After studies at Rheims under St. Bruno, the founder of the great Carthusian order, Odo became a canon and archdeacon of Rheims. But he left rank and honor to be a monk at Cluny. There under the great abbot St. Hugh he progressed mightily in the spiritual life and was made prior. When St. Gregory VII asked Hugh for some monks who would make good bishops, Hugh sent Odo to Rome. Made cardinal-bishop of Ostia in 1078, Odo served Gregory with loyalty and skill in the fight against Henry IV, Antipope Guibert, and church abuses. As legate in Germany from 1082 to 1085, Odo did accomplish much for reform by securing the election of worthy bishops. He held a synod in Saxony which passed reform decrees and condemned Antipope Guibert. After the short pontificate of Victor III, Odo was elected pope by acclamation on March 12, 1088. He took the name Urban II.

Urban never knew lasting peace in the bitter fight with Henry IV. He was in and out of Rome a number of times, and at his death the struggle was far from ended. But more important than the monotonous ups and downs in the struggle for reform was the great event which did so much to change the Middle Ages—the crusade.

The East had been swamped by a horde of Seljuk Turks who had swarmed out of Central Asia to threaten the Eastern Empire and make life miserable for Christian pilgrims to the Holy Land. The great St. Gregory VII had planned to organize a crusade in answer to anguished appeals from the shaky Eastern Empire, but the fight over lay investiture had prevented him from doing this. Now Urban II decided to do something about it. Most eager to end the unfortunate Eastern Schism, Urban was anxious to oblige the Emperor. Indeed he absolved Alexius from excommunication. Besides recovering the Holy Sepulcher of Christ, Urban hoped that the expedition would lead to reunion of the Eastern Church with Rome and that given a nobler ideal to fight for, the warriors of the West would rise above petty squabbles. Accordingly, in November 1095 Urban assembled at Clermont in France 13 archbishops, 225 bishops, and 90 abbots. After the council passed reform decrees, Urban addressed the assembly in words which set the West ablaze with ardor. "God wills it!" was the enthusiastic reply, and from the great feudal principalities came hard-fighting knights led by Godfrey of Lorraine, Robert of Nomandy, Hugh of Vermandois, Raymond of Toulouse, and Bohemond of Norman Italy. To control these strong personalities, Urban appointed Adhemar, bishop of Le Puy, as his legate.

Urban worked hard to make the crusade a success. And before his death Jerusalem had fallen to the Christian army; but before he could hear the good news, Urban II died on July 27, 1099. From the time of his death Urban was honored for his sanctity, but it was only in 1881 that he was officially beatified by Leo XIII.

E. Le Sueur. "Urban II Offers the Archbishopric of Reggio to St. Bruno."
The Louvre, Paris.

PASCHAL II

1099-1118

IT IS USUALLY TRAGIC WHEN ONE WHO VIVIDLY realizes his lack of aptitude for a position is forced to accept it. Such was the pathetic situation of the gentle monk Rainerius who became pope in a stormy time.

Rainerius was born in Blera near Faenza in Italy. From his early youth, he was a monk. Sent to Rome by his monastery, he caught the eye of Gregory VII, who made him cardinal-priest of St. Clement's. He also became abbot of St. Lawrence's. Under Urban II he served as legate, and at Urban's death he was chosen to succeed the crusader pope. Aghast at the thought, Rainerius fled, but was discovered and brought back. Practically forced to be pope, he took the name Paschal II.

A mild, peaceable man, Paschal at first seemed to have fallen on happy days. The formidable Henry IV first abdicated, then died. Henry V, his son, had overthrown his father and had promised much to the Church. But once secure on his throne, Henry V was as bad as his father. Paschal condemned lay investiture, but soon Henry V was marching on Rome with two objectives: imperial coronation and permission to practice lay investiture.

Paschal made a revolutionary attempt to end the lay investiture quarrel once and for all by having churchmen give up their feudal possessions. How then could they live? By alms. The solution was beautiful and simple. Too simple. The great German prince-bishops and lord-abbots looked bleakly on the proposal while Henry himself was not enthusiastic. He liked the idea of great church vassals; all he wanted was to control them. The proposal was considered, however, and Henry entered

Rome peacefully on February 12, 111. But when the time came for Henry's coronation, the affair exploded in a stormy scene in St. Peter's. The Germans would not hear of Paschal's plan to extricate the Church from the octopus grasp of feudal ties. Angrily they demanded that Paschal crown Henry at once. When Paschal refused, Henry carried him off a prisoner. The cardinal of Tusculum rallied the Romans and forced Henry to evacuate the city. But he dragged the Pope with him. At last when rescue seemed impossible, and Henry brutally threatened to butcher or mangle the companions of the Pope, the gentle Paschal gave way and agreed to allow Henry to practice lay investiture. Henry then released Paschal, followed him to Rome, and was crowned emperor on April 13, 1111.

Scarcely had the news of Paschal's surrender spread when indignant messages rained in on the poor Pope. He was accused of being weak, which was true; of being heretical, which was false. The tortured Pope put off the papal robes and fled to a desert island. Alarmed, the reform party brought him back. They then prevailed on Paschal to revoke his concession to Henry, since it was granted by force, and once more condemn lay investiture.

For some years Paschal had peace because Henry was busy in Germany, but in 1117 the Emperor once more took Rome. Paschal fled to Benevento, but soon he was able to return to Rome. He died there on January 21, 1118. Though Paschal II had had a tormented pontificate, he did have the satisfaction of seeing the lay investiture question reasonably settled in England by Henry I and St. Anselm.

Chronologia Summorum Pontificum.

GELASIUS II

1118-1119

WHEN CONRAD OF SALZBURG, A GALLANT fighter for reform, heard that John Coniulo had become Pope Gelasius II, he cried out: "Among the cardinals a worse choice could not have been made than John, but there may be some virtue in Gelasius." There was indeed. Few suffered so much in so short a time for ecclesiastical liberty as Gelasius II.

John Coniulo was born of noble parents at Gaeta. He became a monk at Monte Cassino, but Urban II brought him to Rome to serve as chancellor. Urban wished to improve the style of papal documents, and it was for this that he called on John. John did much to improve the style of papal documents. He served Urban and Paschal loyally. Indeed, it was his unswerving loyalty to Paschal II in his time of trial that had aroused the suspicions of the more extreme reformers.

When Paschal died, Rome was torn between papal and imperial factions. The cardinals managed to meet in a monastery, and there they elected John of Coniulo. He accepted and was called Gelasius II. His initiation into the papacy was rude. A nobleman named Cencius Frangipane broke into the monastery, grabbed Gelasius by the throat, threw him to the ground and actually kicked the old man with his spurred feet. Then he dragged him off by the hair and threw him into a dungeon. The Romans, infuriated, went right after the ruffian and soon secured the Pope's release.

This brutal act was seemingly a sideshow to the main struggle with Henry V over lay investiture. Henry, as soon as he learned of the election, hurried to Rome to put pressure on the new pope. Gelasius quickly showed his mettle. He fled and took a ship down river to Porto. The Germans chased the Pope and fired arrows at his ship. Unable to get to sea because of a furious storm, the old Pope left his galley and made his painful way to the castle of Ardea thirty miles distant. There followed a grim game of hide and seek as the Germans scoured the countryside, but Gelasius gave his pursuers the slip, got back safely on his ship and sailed away to Gaeta. There he was ordained priest on March 9, and bishop the next day.

When Henry set up Maurice, archbishop of Braga, as antipope, Gelasius excommunicated Henry and his "idol." The Normans helped Gelasius get back to Rome but could not clear the city of the antipope's forces. Gelasius was chanting vespers in the Church of St. Praxed when the Frangipani burst in. The old Pope managed to get on a horse and fly. He was found by his friends in a field outside the city.

Disgusted with Rome, he left for France. After consecrating the new cathedral at Pisa, he reached France safely and there was treated royally. Gelasius worked hard, but his health was shattered. When he realized that he was dying, he asked to be carried to the monastery of Cluny, and there in that wellspring of reform the gallant Gelasius II died on January 29, 1119.

National Museum, Florence.

CALIXTUS II

1119-1124

BLUE BLOOD OF BLUE BLOODS WAS GUY OF VIENNE who became Calixtus II. Guy was born probably at Quingey in 1060, the son of William, count of Burgundy. By blood or marriage he was related to Emperor Henry V, Henry I of England, Louis VI of France, and Alfonso VII of Castile. Guy became a priest when quite young and soon rose to be archbishop of Vienne. He acted as legate for Paschal II and held a council at Vienne which boldly excommunicated Henry V when that monarch wrested the privilege of lay investiture from poor Paschal. The council urged Paschal to confirm its decrees and hinted that he had better do so—or suffer worse! Since Paschal did so, there was no trouble; but the incident reveals a lack of perfection in Guy's obedience and loyalty. He was, however, a strong reform bishop and a popular one. Elected pope by the cardinals at Cluny, Guy was most reluctant to accept; but finally all objections were overruled and he was enthroned at Vienne on February 9, 1119, as Calixtus II.

The outstanding event of this pontificate was the settlement of the lay investiture quarrel. While Calixtus captured Henry's antipope at Sutri, Henry was meeting much opposition in Germany. And all this time a great tide of public opinion favoring a peaceful settlement was rising swiftly. After some preliminary negotiations, Henry held a great diet at Worms in September 1122 to discuss the matter. After heated discussions, the papal legates and the Emperor drew up a concordat or agreement between Church and State. By this concordat the Emperor renounced the right of investiture by ring and crozier, thus conceding the independence of the spiritual power. The Pope allowed investi-

ture by scepter as a symbol of the temporal fiefs connected with the bishopric or abbey. Thus while the principle of spiritual independence was saved, the legitimate rights of civil rulers to some control over fiefs was safeguarded. The Emperor guaranteed free elections, but the Pope agreed that the Emperor could be present at elections, a concession which could easily make free elections a mockery.

The Concordat of Worms was hailed as a victory for the Church and sent papal prestige skyrocketing. In cold sober fact it left the Church still far too open to secular control. At any rate Henry was released from censures, and men rejoiced in the peace that followed.

In March 1123 Calixtus held the ninth ecumenical council, the First Lateran. This, attended by over 300 bishops and 600 abbots, confirmed the Concordat of Worms. It passed the usual reform decrees and one striking new one. Before this, if a priest married, the marriage, though illicit and sinful, was valid. Now such a marriage was declared null and void; in other words, no marriage.

Calixtus II favored St. Norbert and approved the Premonstratensian order. He also approved the Knights of St. John or Hospitallers, that famous crusading order. An able spiritual ruler, Calixtus proved also a capable king. Heads literally rolled when he stormed the castles of lawless Roman lords. Even in turbulent Rome itself there was a momentary pause in the clash of arms. No wonder an old chronicler calls Calixtus II, "the father of peace."

Calixtus II died on December 13, 1124.

The British Museum, London.

HONORIUS II

1124-1130

IN SHARP CONTRAST TO THE HIGH-BORN BLUE blood Calixtus II, his successor Lambert was born of a poor family. But in the Middle Ages the Church provided a career open to talent, and of talent Lambert had plenty. About his early life little is known except that he was born at Fiagnano near Imola. He must have had a good education, for he had the reputation of being crammed full of literature. He became archdeacon of Bologna and then under Urban II joined the papal court. Paschal II made him cardinal-bishop of Ostia and Calixtus II sent him as legate to the famous Diet of Worms. There his diplomatic skill helped to bring an end to the lay investiture struggle. This success gave Lambert a reputation and made him an outstanding possibility for the papacy. Yet his election was to be most peculiar.

With the strong hand of Calixtus removed, Rome rapidly returned to its customary disorder. The powerful Frangipane family wished to secure the election of Lambert, but the popular choice was Cardinal Saxo. The cardinals, as often happens, chose neither favorite, but a dark horse, Theobald Buccapecu, who was called Celestine II. But while the cardinals, Lambert among them, were singing the Te Deum, the irritated Frangipani began to shout, "Lambert Pope!" and without more ado hustled Lambert off to a throne and proclaimed him Honorius II. A nasty schism was in the making, but Theobald, a good humble man, seeing that most of the cardinals went over to Honorius, resigned. Honorius also had qualms. Calling the cardinals together he too resigned; but though the cardinals accepted the resignation, they immedi-ately re-elected him. His conscience appeased, Honorius accepted.

Although the lay investiture quarrel had been settled at Worms, Honorius might have had trouble with Henry V. That wily monarch was not proving to be overnice in his fulfillment of the Concordat. But Henry died in 1125 and with him ended the Salian dynasty. His successor, Lothair of Supplinburg, loyally carried out the Concordat. Honorius, in turn, loyally backed Lothair against a rebellion raised by Henry's nephew, Frederick of Hohenstaufen.

When Roger of Sicily tried to take over South Italy, Honorius used both spiritual and temporal arms to stop him. Roger defied both, and Honorius gave in and allowed Roger to unite South Italy and Sicily. Honorius had to intervene strongly to restore good order in the great monasteries of Monte Cassino and Cluny. He also tried to settle the quarrel between Latin bishops in Palestine.

A positive achievement was the solemn confirmation of the Premonstratensian Order in 1126. Honorius also approved the order of Knights Templar. These fighting monks along with the Hospitallers were a mighty bastion to the Kingdom of Jerusalem.

In 1130 Honorius felt that he was dying. Since Cardinal Pierleone openly planned to succeed him, Honorius withdrew to a monastery on the Celian. Even there his deathbed was disturbed. A rumor of his death brought Pierleoni swarming around the monastery, and they dispersed only when the sick Pope showed himself at a window. Honorius died on February 14, 1130.

Mosaic in the Basilica of St. Paul-Outside-the-Walls, Rome.

INNOCENT II

1130-1143

IF THE FRANGIPANI HAD FORCIBLY THRUST THEIR candidate into the papal throne in the person of Honorius, their rivals, the Pierleoni, were ready to take over on the death of Honorius. But they had a big difficulty. Their candidate, Peter Pierleone himself, although formerly a monk of Cluny and now a cardinal, was not noted for his ecclesiastical character. And so when his faction openly prepared to put the eager Pierleone on the throne of Peter, the alarmed cardinals made an agreement to entrust the election to a committee of eight. This committee elected Cardinal Gregory Papareschi of St. Angelo, who took the name Innocent II. The Pierleoni refused to give in, and other cardinals of their faction elected Peter, who took the name Anacletus II. The Church was faced by a schism.

Innocent had to fly from Rome to France, but if Rome rejected him, the Church did not. To his support rallied the two most respected and powerful personalities in Europe, St. Bernard and St. Norbert, and in their train came the Emperor and the kings of France and England; Roger of Sicily was the only great ruler to support Anacletus. After the death of Anacletus, the schism fizzled out. Though Roger set up another antipope, he soon submitted.

Innocent II was a man of high character against whom even his enemies had nothing to say. Indeed it was his excellent reputation in contrast to that of Anacletus which had moved St. Bernard to support him so vigorously. A Roman of the Trastevere district, Innocent had become a monk and then abbot and was made cardinal by Blessed Urban II. He had served with distinction at the Council of Worms.

Much could be expected from such a pope, but political difficulties plagued Innocent. His greatest achievement was the general council held at the Lateran in 1139. Here over 500 bishops and abbots passed a series of reform decrees which confirmed those of St. Gregory VII. But the clash of arms distracted the Pope during much of his reign.

Innocent had taken stern measures against Anacletus and his followers. He had even proclaimed a crusading indulgence for those who would fight against that arch supporter of the schism, Roger of Sicily. But Roger had his revenge. The Pope, in a dispute over Capua, advanced with an army against the Normans. The armies clashed on the Garigliano with disastrous results for Innocent. The Pope and his whole court were taken prisoner by the redoubtable Roger! Roger, like Robert Guiscard with St. Leo IX, treated the Pope deferentially, but he made Innocent confirm the royal title which Anacletus had given him. On his part he agreed to hold the Kingdom of Sicily as a fief from the Pope.

Innocent gave Rome good government and beautiful churches. But the Romans proved ungrateful. Because the Pope tried to moderate their vengeance against Tivoli, the Romans revolted and set up a republic. In the midst of all this turmoil, Innocent II died on September 24, 1143.

Chronologia Summorum Pontificum.

C E L E S T I N E   I I

1143-1144

FOLLOWING INNOCENT'S DEATH, ROME ENJOYED the first peaceful papal election for years. While the barons kept their swords sheathed, the cardinals unanimously elected Guido de Castellis, the cardinal-priest of St. Mark. He took the name Celestine II.

Guido was born either at Citta de Castellis on the Tiber or Macerata in the March of Ancona. Authorities differ as to his birthplace, but it is certain that he was a man of excellent character. He had studied under Peter Abelard and greatly admired this powerful thinker and brilliant lecturer. Indeed, the outspoken St. Bernard, who regarded Abelard with high suspicion, warned Guido, then a cardinal, not to carry his love for his old teacher to the point of loving his errors.

Learned and hard-working, Guido rose in the ranks of the Church. He served in the papal court and was created cardinal by Honorius II in 1127. In the stormy times when Innocent II was opposed by Pierleone or Anacletus II, Guido from the first stood by Innocent. Innocent raised him to the rank of cardinal-Priest of St. Mark.

Celestine's election was hailed with high satisfaction. Great hopes were entertained, but Celestine, quite an old man, was soon to die.

His one achievement was the reconciliation of King Louis VII. This settled a painful problem left over from Innocent's reign. Louis had forbidden the canons of Bourges to elect Pierre de la Châtre archbishop, but the chapter defied the king and elected Pierre. Louis thereupon determined that though the canons might elect Pierre, he would see to it that the new archbishop never sat on his episcopal throne. Pierre appealed to Pope Innocent against this highhanded interference, and the Pope bluntly stated that Louis was but a boy and must be educated. He personally consecrated Pierre archbishop, and when the king still refused to let him into Bourges, Innocent put an interdict on every place the king might enter. This meant that such places could have only the most necessary church services and these performed without solemnity.

The count of Champagne, one of France's great feudal lords, gave the exiled archbishop asylum. There was bad blood between king and count, and soon, despite the efforts of St. Bernard, war flamed out in Northern France. In this struggle occurred the horrible affair in which over a thousand people were burned to death in a church at Vitry.

The war still dragged on and the interdict still hung heavy over Louis when Innocent died. St. Bernard, the count of Champagne, and finally King Louis himself, all pleaded with the new pope to bring about peace. This Celestine succeeded in doing. The king allowed Archbishop Pierre to enter his cathedral city, and Celestine removed the interdict.

Celestine was quite determined to choose a foreign policy of his own. Unlike Innocent, he was not satisfied with Stephen's title to rule England. Still less did he like the concessions Innocent had made to Roger of Sicily. Perhaps it was as well for the Pope that he died before trying conclusions with that tough and capable Norman.

Celestine II died on March 8, 1144. He was buried in the Lateran.

Mosaic in the Basilica of St. Paul-Outside-the-Walls, Rome.

LUCIUS II

1144-1145

THIS POPE'S LIFE PRESENTS AN INTERESTING PARadox. Defied and set at naught in his own city by the turbulent Romans, he found his fingers on the pulse of Europe.

Gerard Caccianemici was a native of Bologna. His was the standard successful career in the papal service. Canon of St. John Lateran, papal librarian, chancellor of the Apostolic See, and cardinal, he rose steadily under Popes Honorius II and Innocent II. There are no extant details of his election to the papacy. Gerard was consecrated March 12, 1144. He took the name Lucius II.

Though he ruled less than a year and was forced to fight to control his own city, Pope Lucius yet found time to send legates to and receive embassies from the far corners of Europe. The king of Portugal sent to Lucius to commend Portugal to the Pope as a feudal fief. Historians consider that when Lucius accepted the homage of Alfonso Henriquez the independence of Portugal was assured. The City of Corneto, once papal territory, returned voluntarily to the Pope's lordship in the time of Lucius. Humbert, lord of Pringins, a castle near Lake Geneva, came to Rome to offer feudal homage to the pope.

But what a different picture at home! At first indeed the Romans accepted the Pope. Relations between Celestine and King Roger of Sicily had been badly strained, but Lucius was a personal friend of Roger's—indeed, had stood godfather to one of his children. And so when Pope Lucius and Roger met at a conference at Ceprano, there was good hope for peace. But in spite of the friendship of the principals, peace did not come. The cardinals and the Romans were quite anti-Norman, and through their efforts the conference broke up. Roger, enraged, sent his mail-clad knights against the Pope and soon even the Romans had to agree to a truce.

But if the Normans subsided, the Romans did not. Angry at the Pope's peace policy and filled with delusions of grandeur, they set up the republic. Jordan of the Pierleoni family, a brother of the old antipope Anacletus, was made Patrician. Pope Lucius, in distress, turned to Emperor Conrad, but Conrad was deaf to his appeals even when St. Bernard added his voice to that of the Pope. Finally, Lucius turned to those natural enemies of the Pierleoni, the Frangipani, and soon Rome rang with the clash of steel and the hoarse war cries of barons and burghers. Jordan had fortified the Capitol. The Frangipani operated from the Circus Maximus. According to one chronicle, Pope Lucius, leading an assault on the Capitol, was struck down by enemy stones. The silence of most chronicles leads historians to doubt this, but at any rate Lucius did die on February 15, 1145.

Mosaic in the Basilica of St. Paul-Outside-the-Walls, Rome.

BLESSED EUGENE III

1145-1153

AFTER THE DEATH OF LUCIUS THE CARDINALS withdrew to the Monastery of St. Caesarius where, protected by Frangipani swords, they could elect a pope in peace. The election was speedy and surprising. Quickly the cardinals chose, not one of their own number, but Bernard, the Cistercian abbot of St. Anastasius. He took the name Eugene III.

Bernard Paganelli was born in Pisa. He was a canon of the cathedral there and a high official when he met St. Bernard. This meant a radical change. He resigned his high offices to follow St. Bernard, that spiritual pied piper, into a Cistercian monastery. When Innocent II asked St. Bernard to send Cistercians to Rome, it was Bernard Paganelli who led the monks to St. Anastasius. There he attracted many vocations and the monastery was flourishing when Bernard was elected pope.

Eugene was a man of real holiness, humble, kindly, and cheerful. If he was severe, he was severe on principle as when he deposed the archbishops of Mainz and York. He accomplished much for the church. He might have done more if he had not been so troubled by the perennial Roman problem.

Eugene had to go to Farfa to be consecrated in peace. But soon, tired of the excesses of Jordan, the Patrician, the Romans welcomed the Pope back and agreed to a compromise. The office of Patrician was abolished. The senate was to remain but to acknowledge the lordship of the Pope. This did not work well and soon the disgusted Pope once more left the city.

The fall of Edessa, a bastion of the crusader kingdom, had alarmed Europe. Eugene proclaimed the second crusade. St. Bernard preached it. Louis VII of France and Emperor Conrad III were its leaders. Weak leaders they proved to be. The Germans were cut up in Asia Minor, the French butchered in a mountain defile. Louis and Conrad reached Jerusalem indeed, but rather as pilgrims than war leaders. The crusade which had begun in hope ended in disillusionment. So keenly did Eugene feel this that he left France.

The Pope was active in promoting the spiritual welfare of the church. He received an embassy from the Catholic Armenians and sent those good people a letter of instruction. He arranged discussions with the Greeks. He held a council at Rheims at which the Trinitarian vagaries of Gilbert de la Porrée were condemned. On the other hand the pope approved of the visions of the holy mystic Hildegarde.

Though he had actually been guardian of France during the crusade, Eugene could not control his own city. Arnold of Brescia, whom the pope had once pardoned, was now the idol of the factious Romans. Diplomacy and a show of force enabled Eugene to enter Rome once more in 1149, but he had so hard a time keeping order that he appealed to Conrad to come down and settle matters. The Emperor died before he could do so. His nephew and successor agreed to come into Italy. He was to come many times and the popes would not be pleased. Conrad's successor was Frederick Barbarossa.

Blessed Eugene died at Tivoli July 8, 1153. He was buried in St. Peter's with great marks of veneration.

Portrait Archive of the Austrian National Library, Vienna.

ANASTASIUS IV

1153-1154

THOUGH THE SUCCESSOR OF EUGENE RULED LESS than two years, he earned something of a reputation as an archeologist and an appeaser. On the very day of Eugene's death the cardinals chose the vicar-general of Rome, Conrad, cardinal-bishop of Sabina, as his successor. Conrad took the name Anastasius IV.

Conrad was a Roman by birth, probably the nephew of Pope Honorius II. He had been a staunch supporter of Innocent II in the struggle with antipope Anacletus. He enjoyed great prestige, but at the time of his election was an infirm old man.

Anastasius IV was charitable and kind. He displayed a great interest in archeology. He repaired the Pantheon, made important excavations under the Lateran, and found the bodies of the famous martyrs Saints Cyprian and Justina.

When Pope Anastasius wrote to the holy nun Hildegarde asking to see her writings so he could advance in virtue, the mystic roundly told him that he neglected justice and that he must arouse himself and save his flock! Anastasius is blamed also by the famous historian Otto of Freising for appeasing the Emperor Frederick Barbarossa.

What happened was this: Frederick had, without the Pope's consent, translated Wichmann, bishop of Naumburg, to the see of Magdeburg. Pope Eugene had refused to approve of this. Anastasius sent a legate to confer with Frederick about the matter, but Frederick without much ceremony sent him back to the Pope. The poor legate died on the way and Frederick then sent an embassy of his own. This embassy included Wichmann, the very cause of the trouble! Anastasius not only received the embassy, but he approved of the translation and gave Wichmann the pallium.

This was a resounding victory for the Emperor. It may have had great influence on his future policy. At any rate, Frederick felt that Anastasius was a fine pope from his standpoint and hastened preparations for an expedition to Rome. But Anastasius died before Frederick could arrive, and the pope he was to deal with was the calm, capable Englishman Hadrian IV.

Anastasius died December 3, 1154. He was buried in a porphyry sarcophagus believed to have once sheltered the remains of St. Helena, mother of Constantine.

Chronologia Summorum Pontificum.

HADRIAN IV

1154-1159

HADRIAN'S LIFE IS A CONSOLATION TO THOSE who make a slow start in life. Born near St. Alban's, England, Nicholas Breakspear started slowly indeed. Educated at the famous abbey of St. Albans, Nicholas was refused admission as a monk, probably owing to indolence. After further studies and some drifting in France, he became abbot of the Monastery of St. Rufus near Avignon. But the community grew to dislike him so much that for the sake of peace Pope Eugenius removed him. The Pope, however, showed what he thought of Nicholas by making him bishop of Albano and cardinal.

Cardinal Nicholas was sent on a difficult and delicate mission. Norway and Sweden were becoming restive because their bishops were under the archbishop of Lund in Denmark. Nicholas handled this affair with great wisdom and tact.

Shortly after he returned from his Scandinavian mission, Pope Anastasius died and the cardinals elected Nicholas by acclamation. Unwillingly he accepted. He took the name Hadrian IV.

The cardinals chose well. Hadrian was big. It is pleasant to relate that he showered favors on St. Albans, the monastery which rejected him, and St. Rufus, the monastery which had driven him out.

Hadrian is noteworthy as the only English pope —and also because he gave Ireland to King Henry II of England. He allowed Arnold of Brescia, that stormy petrel of Roman politics, to be executed. He fought the Normans and was beaten by them at Benevento in 1156. But overshadowing all other events of his reign was the start of the papacy-Hohenstaufen fight.

Frederick of Hohenstaufen, the emperor, was filled with absolutist ideas. At first, indeed, he helped Hadrian, but a clash between an emperor consumed with power lust, and a pope determined to be independent was inevitable. At the diet of Besançon the growing strain snapped the cable of understanding with a crash that reverberated around Europe. The Pope had sent legates with a letter reproving the Emperor because he had allowed the murder of the archbishop of Lund by a robber baron to go unpunished. In the letter Hadrian appealed to the Emperor's gratitude because of the benefits he had given him. The Germans took this to mean that the Pope claimed to have given Frederick the empire as a fief! Frederick sent the delegates packing, and although Hadrian explained that by the word *beneficia* he meant not fiefs but benefits, real peace did not come.

In 1158 Frederick captured Milan, and with the Lombard cities overawed, proceeded to hold the famous diet of Roncaglia. There he played the absolutist, and practically destroyed the self-rule of the Lombard cities. Hadrian demanded that he recognize the Pope's independence in Rome. Frederick's answer was to stir up the Romans to drive Hadrian out of the city. Hadrian threw his support to the embattled communes of Lombardy. In the midst of this strife Hadrian died at Anagni, September 11, 1159.

National Museum, Florence.

ALEXANDER III

1159-1181

ROLAND BANDINELLI, WHO SUCCEEDED HADRIAN IV, was a man of great qualities of character and mind. He had taught canon law at Bologna at the very time when Gratian was at work on his monumental decree. Pope Eugene III made him a cardinal and chancellor of the Apostolic See. Much could be expected from such a pope and much was accomplished; but owing to imperial interference, the Pope was not free to devote himself entirely to constructive activity until the last years of his long pontificate.

What happened was this. Hadrian's death had left Rome seething. Most of the cardinals wished to hold the election at Anagni far from the Roman mob, but the Romans quickly stopped that. They refused to allow Hadrian to be buried until all was set for the election. In spite of all the imperialists' efforts, Cardinal Roland Bandinelli was elected by a large majority. Then followed an undignified scene. Cardinal Octavian, the imperialist candidate, tried to tear the papal mantle away from Roland, then produced a mantle of his own, and fighting off the angry cardinals, made his way to the high altar of St. Peter's, where he announced his election as Victor IV. The imperialists acclaimed him with enthusiasm and forced the real pope to retire to a fortress for safety. Alexander III, as the new pope chose to be called, thus began his pontificate in strife.

Emperor Frederick naturally backed Octavian. He called a council at Pavia, and when Alexander refused to have anything to do with it, the council finally proclaimed Octavian or Victor IV true pope. But if the Emperor and his minions backed Octavian, most of Europe rallied to Alexander. Yet for years the fight went on. It was under these circumstances that Henry II of England and St. Thomas of Canterbury fought over the Constitutions of Clarendon, and if Alexander seemed to lack firmness sometimes in dealing with the fierce Plantagenet, his delicate circumstances must be kept in mind.

At last Alexander forged the alliance between pope, Normans of Sicily, and Lombard communes which was to check the haughty Frederick. After many vicissitudes Frederick's German chivalry went down before the Italian burghers at Legnano in 1176, and the next year at Venice a truce was signed between Alexander and Frederick which brought peace.

Once peace gave him the opportunity, Alexander called the tenth general council, the Third Lateran, to meet in 1179. At his council many decrees were passed reforming the Church and remedying outstanding social abuses. Tournaments were strictly forbidden, the truce of God reemphasized, and excommunication hurled at those who robbed poor shipwrecked people.

Alexander was a great defender of the downtrodden. Jews enjoyed his protection and indeed even occupied positions in the papal service. He took many steps to help the poor and was always quick to praise rulers who did something for their poorer subjects.

Even greater was Alexander's contribution to education. He protected masters from undue exactions for the license to teach, he insisted on freedom for those who were competent to teach, he worked to spread free education "so that the poor may rejoice." He has been called Europe's first minister of education.

Alexander III died August 31, 1181, at Civita Castellana. The Romans, once more in a state of turmoil, insulted his body, but the North Italian city states have left him an epitaph and a monument in the city which checked Frederick Barbarossa, the city named after the great Pope—Alessandria.

Spinello Aretino "Alexander III and Frederick Barbarossa" (detail). The Palazzo Pubblico, Siena.

LUCIUS III

1181-1185

UBALDUS ALLUCINGOLUS, WHO SUCCEEDED ALEXander III, was born at Lucca probably in 1097. At any rate he was quite an old man when elected pope. His election, in contrast to Alexander's, was quiet. The cardinals were unanimous for Ubaldus. He took the name Lucius III.

Ubaldus studied canon law at Pisa, took the Cistercian habit from St. Bernard, was made cardinal-priest by Innocent II, and cardinal-bishop by Eugenius III. He served on legations to the emperor at Constantinople and to the Norman court at Palermo. He had been a commissioner at the peace conference of Venice.

Lucius, like so many medieval popes, had great trouble with Romans. The Romans, once more on the war path against Tusculum, had that city in a desperate condition when an appeal to Pope Lucius brought help. The Pope first pleaded with the senate to show reasonableness—in vain. Then Lucius turned to that fighting archbishop, Christian of Mainz. Christian, a powerful Rhenish princebishop, advanced on Rome; but fever, the slayer of Germans, struck him down. To the Pope's consolation he died with the sacraments, sorry for his evil life. To the Pope's dismay, his death gave the Romans the upper hand and they used it brutally. They were especially hard on clerics who supported the Pope. On one raid they captured some clerics, blinded them all but one, and putting paper caps on their heads with the name of a cardinal written on each, they put the poor victims backward on asses and ordered the lone one left with sight to lead the pitiable procession to the Pope! Lucius excommunicated the brutes who had committed the outrage.

Lucius went to Verona in 1184 to discuss outstanding problems with Emperor Frederick. Though the Peace of Constance had confirmed the Truce of Venice, there were two questions on which Pope and Emperor disagreed. One, a disputed episcopal election, was settled later. The other was of great importance. Emperor Frederick had for some time been working to unite the imperial crown with that of Norman Sicily. Now his chance arrived and he succeeded in negotiating a marriage between his son and heir Henry and Constance who, though considerably older than Henry, was the heiress to the rich Norman dominions in Italy and Sicily. Pope Lucius opposed this marriage—as well he might, for in it was the germ of the terrible papacy-Hohenstaufen fight which rocked the thirteenth century, ruined the Hohenstaufens, and did no good to the papacy.

The Pope and Emperor were in agreement on two other matters, repression of heresy and the need for a new crusade. Lucius ordered the bishops to hunt out heretics while Frederick put them under the ban of the Empire. While both agreed that a new crusade was necessary to check the might of Saladin, nothing was done until too late.

Pope Lucius received letters from the Armenians asking him for help against Byzantine persecution. They claimed that they were orthodox and asked for instructions on the Roman discipline. Pope Lucius answered them most affectionately and sent them copies of the Roman liturgical books.

Lucius III died at Verona on November 25, 1185. His death interrupted the conference with the Emperor.

Mosaic in the Basilica of St. Paul-Outside-the-Walls, Rome.

URBAN III

1185-1187

ONCE AGAIN A POPE WAS ELECTED WITHOUT DIS-order. On the very day of Lucius' death, December 25, 1185, the cardinals at Verona unanimously elected Humbert Crivelli, the archbishop of Milan.

Humbert Crivelli was a native of Milan. He is known first as archdeacon of Bourges in France. He became a close friend and admirer of St. Thomas Becket who said of him: "One more loyal to . . . the Church could not possibly be found." At once eloquent and business-like, Humbert rose to be cardinal-priest in 1183, and archbishop of Milan in January 1185. In December of the same year he was chosen pope. He took the name Urban III.

Urban's brief pontificate was much taken up with quarrels with the Emperor Frederick and his son Prince Henry. Indeed, Urban has been accused of being anti-imperialist because his relatives had suffered when Frederick had captured Milan in the old war. But such a supposition is quite unnecessary to explain Urban's policy. If it was somewhat unyielding, it was no different from that of most of the popes of this period.

Urban III, like Lucius, had little desire to see Prince Henry marry Constance, the heiress to the Norman dominions in South Italy and Sicily. But since nothing could be done to prevent it, the Pope sent legates to assist at the ceremony. He did, however, refuse to crown Henry co-emperor. Frederick, without the Pope's consent, proclaimed his son Caesar and had him crowned King of Italy at Aquileia. Urban's answer was to suspend the bishops who had taken part in the coronation.

The Pope, on his part, irritated Frederick considerably by intervening in the disputed Trier episcopal election, to consecrate Volmar the anti-imperialist candidate.

Frederick left Italy to his son Henry, who proceeded to make life miserable for the Pope, even going so far as to cut off the nose of some poor papal official. Meanwhile, Frederick summoned the German bishops to meet at Geilenhausen, and the assembled bishops obligingly sent Urban a letter asking him to come to terms with their imperial master. This annoyed Pope Urban because he felt that in opposing Frederick he was upholding the cause of the German bishops.

The Pope decided to excommunicate Frederick, but the people of Verona pleaded that they belonged to the Emperor and that such a blow launched in their city might bring dire consequences. Urban thereupon left for Venice, but at Ferrara dysentery struck him down. His last days were saddened by fear for the Holy City of Jerusalem. On July 7 the knighthood of the crusading kingdom had been almost wiped out by Saladin, in the dust and heat of the disastrous day at Hattin. Indeed Jerusalem had fallen on October 2, but the bad news had not yet reached Urban when he died October 20, 1187. He is buried in Ferrara Cathedral.

Mosaic in the Basilica of St. Paul-Outside-the-Walls, Rome.

GREGORY VIII

1187

U RBAN'S DEATH IN THE GLOOMY DAYS WHEN
Jerusalem had just fallen left the cardinals anxious to pick a strong leader. They
first wished to choose Henry of Albano, but he
firmly declined and urged them to choose Albert
de Mora, the chancellor of the Apostolic See.
Thereupon the cardinals turned to Albert, who accepted and took the name Gregory VIII.

Albert de Mora was born in Benevento of noble
parents. He was a man of learning, piety, and winning ways. He had been a Premonstratensian, but
was made cardinal deacon by Hadrian IV in 1155.
He served as vice-chancellor when Roland Bandinelli was chancellor, and when Roland became
Pope Alexander III Albert succeeded him as chancellor of the Apostolic See. He was the last head
of the papal chancery to hold the title of chancellor until the twentieth century.

Alexander III made Albert cardinal-priest and
employed him in missions of the highest importance. Albert crowned Alfonso II of Portugal. He
went as legate to Hungary and was sent to England to investigate the famous murder in the cathedral of St. Thomas Becket. He it was who absolved the repentant King Henry.

He was a holy man, severe with himself, but
kind to others, a great foe to superstitious practices. No wonder that when Cardinal Henry of Albano proposed him, the cardinals were quick to
agree.

Gregory soon showed that he grasped the key
problem of the hour—the rescue of fallen Jerusalem. He realized that it was first necessary to have
peace among Christians if war was to be successfully made on the infidel. He soon let it be known
that there was no longer any question of excommunicating Emperor Frederick, and he tacitly ignored the causes of friction between Pope and Emperor. Frederick, now really anxious to go on a
crusade, was delighted and did what he could to
help the Pope have peace. These tactics of appeasement worked well for the time. Frederick did
get ready to lead an army toward Palestine. The
third crusade was under way.

Gregory set out for Pisa to try to put a stop to
the fight between that port and its commercial rival
Genoa. The Christians would need the help of
both. On the way the Pope stopped at Parma
where he held a council filled with the business of
the crusade. It is interesting to note that this pope,
usually so mild and merciful, yet ordered the bones
of Octavian, the antipope Victor IV, to be thrown
out of the church in Parma where they were buried.

To Pisa Gregory called the Genoese leaders and
the cause of peace was making progress when a
fever carried off this likable pope on December 11,
1187. His pontificate though brief was glorious.
He had promoted peace among Christians; he had
set in motion the Third Crusade.

Chronologia Summorum Pontificum.

[342]

CLEMENT III

1187-1191

PAUL SCOLARI, WHO BECAME POPE CLEMENT III, was a native of Rome. A distinguished member of the Roman clergy, he was first archpriest of the Basilica of St. Mary Major, then cardinal-bishop of Palestrina. He had been considered as a possible choice for pope before this, but his poor health had been regarded as an impediment. And indeed Paolo did suffer from heart trouble. Even now at the death of Gregory VIII the first choice of the cardinals was Theobald, cardinal-bishop of Ostia, but Theobald refused and then on December 19, 1157, the cardinals turned to Paolo, weak heart and all. On December 20 Paolo was crowned as Clement III.

The first Roman to be elected pope for some years, Clement was popular with his fellow citizens. A peace was patched up, and soon the Pope was settled in the Lateran. To enjoy peace at Rome, Clement consented to allow the walls of hated Tusculum to be torn down. A charter drawn up in 1188 regulated the rights of Pope and the commune.

Clement's chief interest, however, was to rescue Jerusalem. He continued and developed the policy of his predecessor, Gregory VIII: peace among Christians, war on the Moslem. The Pope did everything possible to favor Emperor Frederick Barbarossa and had the satisfaction of seeing the old hero lead a large army toward the Holy Land. He had less success in his efforts to make peace between Henry II of England and Philip Augustus of France; but after Henry's defeat and death, Richard the Lion-Hearted and Philip finally got started for Palestine. Clement III deserves great credit for his vigorous efforts to support the Third Crusade. By diplomacy, by encouragement, by financial aid, this farsighted Pope did everything possible to win back Jerusalem. The small result of this great effort was not the fault of the Pope, and he died before the crusade had definitely failed.

The death of William II, Norman king of Sicily, presented Clement III and his successors with a thorny problem. The legitimate successor of William was Constance, wife of Henry of Germany. The Sicilians, not liking the idea of German rule, backed Tancred, an illegitimate relative of the Norman family. Clement, who had absolutely no desire to see Hohenstaufens on both sides of him, recognized Tancred as king of Sicily. But Henry VI had no intention of allowing his wife's magnificent inheritance escape him. Soon he was on his way south with a large army.

Clement III did not have to cope with the difficult situation. Before Henry reached Rome, Clement was dead. He died in March 1191. Scotsmen may well revere his memory, for Clement III definitely freed the Church in Scotland from ecclesiastical dependence on the English archbishop of York. This large-hearted Pontiff helped to redeem captives and protected the Jews.

National Museum, Florence.

[344]

CELESTINE III

1191-1198

WITH HENRY OF GERMANY MARCHING ON THE city, the cardinals turned to old Hyacinth Bobo, cardinal-deacon of Santa Maria in Cosmedin. The old veteran refused to accept the burdensome honor, but when the danger of delay was pointed out to him, he gave in. Hyacinth Bobo was a Roman. His brother Ursus is considered the founder of the famous Orsini family. Already a cardinal in 1144, Hyacinth had a long and distinguished career in the papal service. While in France he had become a great admirer of the philosopher Peter Abelard, and had backed him even against the formidable St. Bernard. On three different occasions he went on papal missions to Spain, and as recently as 1187, when he had tried to depose the bishop of Coimbra, he had been bluntly warned by the angry Portuguese monarch to get out before his feet were cut off! Perhaps his most important mission was that given him by Hadrian IV in 1157. The English pope sent him to soothe Frederick Barbarossa after the Emperor had been so irritated by Roland Bandinelli. With a record like this it is easy to see why the cardinals ignored his great age and elected the octogenarian Hyacinth. He was ordained priest on April 13 and consecrated pope on the next day— Easter Sunday—under the name Celestine III.

The new pope welcomed Henry VI, and after receiving pledges of loyalty to the rights of church, he crowned Henry emperor. Henry won the support of the Romans by allowing them to destroy hated Tusculum. Though Henry guaranteed the rights of the Church, he was a dangerous man. His ambitions were as far-reaching as his means to obtain them were ferocious. He enjoyed initial success in his campaign to take over the Norman king-

dom of Naples-Sicily, but disease soon decimated his army and sent him flying north, a sick man. Constance, his wife, was then seized by the Neapolitans and turned over to Tancred. Pope Celestine came to the rescue and by a threat of excommunication forced King Tancred to release the lady.

The Pope was less successful in his attempt to protect Richard the Lion-Hearted from Henry. The mean-spirited Emperor had taken the returning crusader from Leopold of Austria and was holding him for a huge ransom. The Pope should have acted most strenuously against this gross violation of a crusader's rights, and Richard's old mother, the fiery Eleanor of Aquitaine, told the Pope so in spirited if respectful pleas. Celestine did threaten the Emperor, but greedy Henry released Richard only after a king's ransom was exacted.

After the death of Tancred, Henry once more, and this time successfully, invaded South Italy. With the fierce Hohenstaufen on both sides of him, Pope Celestine might have had trouble, but Henry died in 1197, leaving only an infant son.

Celestine acted vigorously to protect the sanctity of the marriage bond when Philip II of France tried to repudiate his Danish wife, Ingeborg. He fostered the Teutonic Knights and the Bridge-building Brothers. He canonized several saints, among them the Irish Malachi. He protected the Jews and victims of shipwreck. Greatly interested in the Holy Land, he did much for the Knights Templar and the Knights of St. John.

Celestine III died after a busy pontificate on January 8, 1198.

Mosaic in the Basilica of St. Paul-Outside-the-Walls, Rome.

INNOCENT III

1198-1216

O N THE VERY DAY CELESTINE III WAS BURIED, the cardinals elected a young intellectual named Lotario de' Conti. They did well, for Lotario became one of the greatest medieval popes, Innocent III. Lotario de' Conti was born at Anagni about 1160. His father Trasimund, count of Segni, was a powerful lord. Lotario was interested in things of the mind and in the full intellectual current of his day. He studied at Rome, Paris, and Bologna. A canon lawyer of distinction, he was created cardinal by his uncle, Clement III. But during the pontificate of Celestine III, Lotario retired from the papal court and wrote two spiritual treatises. It was with reluctance that he mounted the papal throne. He was consecrated on February 22, 1198.

Innocent III was in full accord with the Italian patriotism which sparked risings against the Germans left by the late Henry VI to lord it in Italy. The troubled state of the empire, with Otto of Nordheim and Philip of Swabia battling for the crown, gave Innocent a chance not only to reassert papal independence but even to extend papal influence. Here, however, Innocent was not particularly successful. Otto of Nordheim, whom he crowned as Otto IV, out-Hohenstaufened the Hohenstaufens in trampling on Church rights. And when Otto was finally defeated, Innocent's ward, Frederick II, was ready to take over, and he was to multiply griefs for the Church. Constance, the widow of Henry VI, had left her little orphaned son Frederick to the Pope's guardianship, and Innocent loyally preserved Sicily for his ward.

A great lover of justice and a first-rate judge, Innocent attracted many cases to the papal court. His influence was far-reaching. He became feudal overlord of Aragon and England when Pedro II and John handed over their respective realms as fiefs. John, badgered by rebellious barons, threatened by the French, and excommunicated by a shocked Pope, wriggled out of a bad situation by this shrewd move, which cost him little. Indeed, Innocent later declared the Magna Charta null and void because it was extorted from his vassal by violence!

Innocent acted to clear the Papal States of the Manichean heretics, but did not resort to the death penalty. When the Albigensians, as the Manicheans were called in France, murdered a papal legate, Innocent preached a crusade against them. He also started the Fourth Crusade. But flouted and tricked by the worldly Venetians, the Pope had the mortification of seeing the crusaders attack first the Catholic city of Zara, then the Christian city of Constantinople.

Innocent's real greatness lies in the spiritual sphere. In 1215 he held the famous Fourth Lateran Council. This, the twelfth ecumenical council, condemned the Albigensians and the vagaries of Abbot Joachim. It encouraged learning, took measures against abuses, and made the rule in force to this day that every Catholic must receive Holy Communion at Easter time. It also called for a crusade, and it was while trying to get this crusade going that Innocent III died at Perugia on July 16, 1216.

Innocent III is truly remarkable for the way he retained his keen spiritual sense in the hurly-burly of business. He helped the Armenians and Maronites to return to Catholic unity. He welcomed St. John of Matha and encouraged his order for the redemption of captives. St. Dominic found him sympathetic and won approval for the Friars Preachers. And when that lyric poet of Christian spirituality, Francis of Assisi, came to Rome, he found, not a political-minded bureaucrat, but a priest who could understand the magnificent Franciscan folly of the Cross. If Innocent III did nothing more than enable Dominic and Francis to start their orders, he would deserve to be remembered as one who had done much for the Church and for the world.

Chronologia Summorum Pontificum.

HONORIUS III

1216-1227

Honorius III was elected pope by the method of compromise. This means that the cardinals entrusted the choice of the next pope to a committee. In this case the committee was composed of Ugolino, cardinal-bishop of Ostia, and Guido, cardinal-bishop of Praeneste. The two chose the aged Cencio Savelli.

Cencio Savelli was born in Rome of a powerful family. As a very young man he entered the ranks of the clergy and rose to be canon of St. Mary Major, cardinal-deacon and cardinal-priest. He worked for Cardinal Hyacinth Bobo, and when Hyacinth became Pope Celestine III, Cencio became his chamberlain, or prime minister. While chamberlain, he drew up a tax list which was of great value to the papal government. After Celestine's death Innocent III likewise made use of Cencio's capable services.

Cencio was about sixty-eight years old when chosen pope, and he accepted the honor with reluctance. He was consecrated as Honorius III on July 24, 1216, at Perugia and was crowned at Rome on August 31.

Honorius III was an attractive personality. He combined love of learning, a practical aptitude for affairs, and a charming kindliness. Though old, Honorius threw himself into the work of ruling the Church with plenty of vigor. He was determined to carry out his great predecessor's plan for a new crusade, and he made great efforts to get it under way. In this he was not particularly successful. Emperor Frederick II, who had vowed to go on the crusade and was its natural leader, dillydallied and hemmed and hawed down to the death of Honorius. Meanwhile the ambitious monarch secured the imperial coronation from the hopeful Honorius on November 22, 1220. In 1217 King Andrew of Hungary led a group of knights to the Holy Land, but accomplished little. Even more disastrous was the movement led by John de Brienne in 1218 which is known as the Fifth Crusade. The crusade got off to a grand start when the Christian army captured Damietta, a key port in Egypt. The Sultan El Kamil actually offered to surrender Jerusalem and other holy places in exchange for Damietta, but Honorius guessed wrong. Expecting Frederick to start any time now, he declined the offer. The crusaders advanced on Cairo, were trapped in the Nile Valley, and had to surrender anyway. This fiasco was a cruel blow to Honorius, but to the end of his life the gallant old Pope continued to work for a new crusade.

Honorius worked hard to promote peace among Christian princes. Like Innocent III, he made his influence felt in the far corners of Europe. He urged Louis VIII of France to take over the Albigensian crusade. In England he protected King John's little boy Henry III and took measures to safeguard his throne. He crowned Peter Courtenay as Latin Emperor of Constantinople in 1217. He took a militant interest in spreading the gospel among the Prussians.

Like Innocent III, Honorius favored the great new orders of friars. He approved the Dominicans in 1216 and the Franciscans in 1223. In January 1226 he approved the Carmelites. The Cistercians, too, felt the strong support of the pious Pope. A canonist who contributed much to church law, Honorius took a keen interest in the ardent intellectual life of the universities. He granted privileges to the great universities of Paris and Bologna.

One of this kind pope's last acts was to help the Roman people during a famine. Highly indignant when merchants stored grain and sent prices skyrocketing, Honorius secured grain from Sicily to feed his hungry people.

Honorius III died greatly respected on March 18, 1227.

Giotto. "St. Francis Presents the Rule of the Order to Pope Honorius." Church of the Holy Cross, Florence.

GREGORY IX

1227-1241

UGOLINO DE' CONTI, SON OF THE COUNT OF SEGNI and a grandnephew of Innocent III, was born at Anagni. Educated at Bologna and Paris, Ugolino developed into a first-rate papal diplomat. Made cardinal-bishop of Ostia by Innocent III, he served on the committee which elected Honorius III. Chosen to succeed Honorius on March 19, 1227, Ugolino took the name Gregory IX. Although an old man, he abounded in vigor. His achievements were many and all the more remarkable because so much of his time was taken up fighting Frederick II.

As cardinal, Gregory had given the Cross to Frederick back in 1220. Now as pope, he urged the Emperor to fulfill his crusading vow. Frederick did sail in 1227, but a few days later he returned on a plea of sickness. Suspecting trickery, Gregory excommunicated the reluctant crusader. Frederick answered by stirring up an imperialist revolt in Rome which sent the Pope flying from the city. After vainly seeking release from censure, Frederick went off, an excommunicated emperor, to win a crusade without a fight. While the Emperor was gaining Jerusalem by a treaty with the Sultan, the Pope was vainly trying to replace him on the imperial throne. Finally in 1230 a peace was patched up, but Gregory grew increasingly uneasy as the despotic Frederick strove to enchain Italy. After the Emperor smashed the embattled North Italian burghers at Cortenuova in 1237, Gregory tried to rescue the hard-pressed Lombard communes. Frederick invaded the Papal States, and once more Gregory excommunicated him. Since curses and pleas fell on deaf ears, Gregory called a crusade against Frederick and summoned a council to meet at Rome. Frederick stopped the council by capturing a fleet-load of prelates bound for Rome! Gregory died suddenly on August 22, 1241, with Frederick's army threatening Rome.

Though Gregory must have felt frustrated in his efforts to curb Frederick, he could look back on a record rich in achievement. A personal friend of St. Francis, St. Clare, and St. Anthony, he did much to foster Franciscan growth. His keen legal sense was a great help in the order's early days. He had presided at St. Dominic's funeral and regarded the Friars Preachers with high favor. This intelligent Pope deserves credit for the blooming intellectual life of the age, for he it was who saved Aristotle for the schoolmen when the Philosopher, mistranslated and misinterpreted, was in danger of being driven from Christian classrooms. He gave his alma mater, Paris, the bull *Parens scientiarum*, the Magna Carta of that university. In this medieval Wagner Act, the right of the university to go on strike is fully recognized.

Very much the man of his age, Gregory IX climaxed a century of resentment against the antisocial Albigensians by starting the papal inquisition. A severe man toward heretics, he had approved of Emperor Frederick's law which decreed death by fire for unrepentant heretics.

Gregory's vision was not limited by the West. He strove unsuccessfully to promote reunion with the Greeks. He did succeed in bringing back the Syrian Monophysites to Catholic unity. He planned great missionary enterprises, and he made a collection of canon law so valuable that its influence extends to modern times.

Raphael. "Pope Gregory Delivers the Decretals to a Consistorial Lawyer." The Vatican.

CELESTINE IV

1241

THE DEATH OF GREGORY IX WAS GOOD NEWS TO Emperor Frederick II, and he loudly proclaimed his jubilation to the world. According to Frederick's smug expression, Gregory had flouted the August One, i.e., the Emperor, and therefore had not been allowed to live through avenging August. Frederick expressed the hope that the next pope would be more favorable; and to give some force to his hope, the Emperor remained with his army threatening Rome.

Meanwhile in Rome the senator Matteo Rosso Orsini promptly confined the cardinals in the Septizonium to hurry them on to an election. This appears to be the first conclave in the strict sense of the word, that is, the locking up of the cardinals until they had elected a pope. Though Frederick withdrew his army into Apulia, the cardinals had a hard time coming to a decision. Cardinal Godfrey Castiglioni took an early lead in the balloting but was unable to command the necessary two-thirds majority. When the Romans heard the rumor that the cardinals were going to elect an outsider as a compromise, a mob insulted the conclave. Indeed it is said that the Romans threatened to dig up the corpse of Pope Gregory and put it in with the cardinals if they did not elect one of their number. Through the frightful heat of August and September into October the conclave struggled. At last on October 25, 1241, Godfrey Castiglioni gained the necessary majority. He accepted and chose the name Celestine IV.

Godfrey Castiglioni was born in Milan, the son of John Castiglioni and Cassandra Crivelli, the sister of Urban III. He entered the rank of the clergy and rose to be a canon and chancellor of the church of Milan. In 1187 he resigned his honors to enter the Cistercian monastery of Hautecombe. There he is said to have written a *History of the Kingdom of Scotland*. Forty years later, in 1227, Gregory IX made him cardinal-priest of St. Mark, and twelve years later still, in 1239, Gregory made him cardinal-bishop of Sabina. He must have been a very old man indeed when elected pope.

His advanced age and weak health were probably the chief reasons why the divided cardinals agreed at last on Celestine. He might have made a good pope, for he was an excellent theologian and was charitable to the poor, but he had no time to prove his ability. The sick old man lasted exactly seventeen days as pope. On November 10, 1241, Celestine IV died. His death was the signal for most of the cardinals to hurry out of Rome, because they had no wish to undergo another ordeal like the last conclave. The few cardinals who remained buried Celestine IV in St. Peter's on November 11.

Mosaic in the Basilica of St. Paul-Outside-the-Walls, Rome.

INNOCENT IV

1243-1254

WHEN AFTER A STORMY INTERVAL OF OVER seventeen months, the cardinals managed to hold an election at Anagni in June 1243, they quickly elected Sinibaldo de' Fieschi. He chose to be called Innocent IV. With the Emperor still hostile, Sinibaldo seemed a good choice. He had been friendly with Frederick, yet his character indicated that he would be nobody's puppet. Sinibaldo was born in Genoa, the son of the count of Lavagna. After teaching canon law at his alma mater, Bologna, he joined the papal court and rose to be vice-chancellor of Rome, cardinal and bishop of Albenga.

The first problem facing Innocent was to end, if possible, the struggle with Frederick. Hope rose as the Emperor congratulated the new pope and peace negotiations got under way. Soon Innocent released Frederick from censure and Frederick agreed to evacuate the Papal States and release his clerical prisoners. Peace was restored—and high time, for the Mongols threatened Eastern Europe, and in 1244 the Moslems recaptured Jerusalem.

The peace, however, was momentary. Frederick, slow to keep promises, exasperated Innocent by holding on to his clerical prisoners, and still more by stirring up trouble at Rome. His patience exhausted, Innocent fled to Lyons and called a council to meet there in 1245. This First Council of Lyons, the thirteenth ecumenical, passed some reform decrees, but the outstanding event was the condemnation and deposition of Frederick II.

When Frederick heard of his deposition, he is said to have placed a crown on his head and defied the Pope to knock it off. Innocent tried to do just that. He ordered the German nobles to elect a new king, but neither Henry of Thuringia nor William of Holland was able to do much against Frederick's son Conrad. Innocent preached a crusade against Frederick, but St. Louis of France, the only monarch powerful enough, had no stomach for such a crusade. He did go on a crusade, but it was against the Moslems. Though St. Louis protected the Pope at Lyons against imperialist attack, he would go no farther.

Even Frederick's death in 1250 did not bring peace. His son Conrad IV continued the quarrel. Innocent, as suzerain of Sicily, hawked the Sicilian crown around Europe, but with Conrad's half-brother Manfred holding Sicily in arms, there was no rush of takers. At last at Conrad's death in 1254 hopes rose. Conrad left his baby son to the Pope's guardianship, and Innocent recognized the rights of the little Conrad to Sicily. But Innocent's stormy pontificate was not to end in peace. Manfred revolted and routed a papal army at Foggia. Once more war was kindled. Innocent, gravely ill from pleurisy, died shortly after on December 7, 1254.

This fight of the papacy with the Hohenstaufen might have been necessary to safeguard freedom; it was certainly disastrous. Italy was desolated; papal taxation grew and grew, and with it a loud chorus of complaint. Abuses increased while Innocent was preoccupied with the struggle.

Yet Innocent IV did accomplish something positive. He added significantly to church law. He did a great deal for the rising universities. He sent missionaries to the Mongols, and he defended the Jews from the ridiculous charge of ritual murder.

Mosaic in the Basilica of St. Paul-Outside-the-Walls, Rome.

ALEXANDER IV

1254-1261

THERE WAS CONSTERNATION AMONG THE CARDI- nals at Naples when Innocent IV passed away. The papal army had just been routed, and the cardinals yearned to set distance between themselves and the victorious Manfred. But the podesta of Naples locked up the cardinals and told them bluntly that they would stay locked up until they gave the Church a new pastor. On December 12, 1254, the second day of the conclave, the cardinals elected by compromise Rinaldo de' Conti. He accepted and chose to be called Alexander IV.

Rinaldo was the son of the count of Segni and the third pope of that family to reign in the thirteenth century. He rose swiftly in the ranks of the hierarchy and was made cardinal deacon by his uncle, Gregory IX, in 1227 and cardinal-bishop of Ostia in 1231. He received from his uncle not only honors but also a strong attachment to the Franciscans. When he learned that St. Clare was gravely ill, he went to Assisi to console her and heeded the saint's dying request to obtain from Innocent IV a confirmation of the Poor Clares' privilege of poverty.

As pope, Alexander was not the strong man that Innocent IV had been. It is true that he rejected the peace feelers put out by the victorious Manfred and re-excommunicated Frederick's son, but he was quite unable to make head against him. Down to Alexander's death Manfred maintained himself in Sicily. Alexander also had a hard time in Rome.

The senator Brancaleone of Bologna practically set the Pope's civil authority there at naught. In Germany too Alexander timidly intervened to support Richard of Cornwall against Alfonso of Castile in the futile struggle for the imperial crown. Neither ever became real emperor.

At Paris a great fight was brewing in the university. The secular masters hotly resented the invasion of the friars. Led by the Burgundian William of St. Amour, they furiously denounced both Dominicans and Franciscans. Small chance they had of being listened to with favor by Alexander! He loved the friars and backed them up strongly. Alexander IV did the university a great favor when he confirmed the right of men like Albert the Great and Thomas Aquinas to teach in its lecture halls.

Alexander also repealed a decree of his predecessor which had revoked some of the privileges granted to the friars. He absolved Henry III of England from his oath to observe the famous Provisions of Oxford, because King Henry was his vassal and had no right to take such an oath without his approval, and also because Henry had been forced to take the oath.

Alexander IV showed himself less broadminded than Innocent IV in his dealings with the Greeks.

On the whole, Alexander was a good spiritual man but not at all as gifted with ability to govern as his kinsmen Innocent III and Gregory IX. Alexander IV died at Viterbo on May 25, 1261.

Benozzo Gozzoli. "The Triumph of St. Thomas"
(detail of triptych showing Alexander IV at
the Council of Anagni). The Louvre, Paris.

URBAN IV

1261-1264

AT ALEXANDER'S DEATH THERE WERE ONLY EIGHT cardinals left, and they had a hard time agreeing on the new pope. At last after three months they went outside their number to choose Jacques Pantaléon, the patriarch of Jerusalem. Jacques accepted and took the name Urban IV. Jacques Pantaléon was born at Troyes in Champagne. After studies at the cathedral school of Troyes, he took the doctorate in canon law at Paris. He attracted the attention of Innocent IV at the First Council of Lyons in 1245. Thereafter his rise was rapid. He served as papal legate, became bishop of Verdun and patriarch of Jerusalem. As a papal legate, Jacques enjoyed success in peace negotiations between the Teutonic Knights and the Prussians. He helped the Poles and raised money for Innocent's fight with the Hohenstaufen. As patriarch of Jerusalem, he wrote an account of the Holy Land. It was while back in Italy seeking aid for the troubled crusading kingdom that he was elected pope.

With goodness, energy, ability, and experience on his side, Urban should have accomplished much; but he had only three years, and the miserable Hohenstaufen fight still ate deeply into a pope's time and energy. Manfred, Frederick's son, was still powerful in Sicily, but Urban was determined to root out the Hohenstaufen. First he worked diligently and with intelligence to whip papal finances into order. Then by a mixture of diplomacy and a pretty free use of his spiritual authority, he did much to discomfit Ghibellines and encourage Guelfs throughout Italy. But the key to

the situation was to find some prince willing to accept the throne of Sicily and strong enough to push Manfred off it. Edmund of Lancaster had accepted the throne, but since he showed little inclination to tackle Manfred, his acceptance was academic. At last in the person of Charles of Anjou, Urban found the man for the job. Charles, the brother of St. Louis, was ready, willing, and able, with a good deal of papal help of course, to take over Sicily. Before a French expedition could materialize, Urban IV died at Viterbo on October 2, 1264.

A former patriarch of Jerusalem, Urban naturally was much concerned about the perilous position of the crusading kingdom. The Tartars overran Palestine, then were chased out by the capable sultan of Egypt, Beibars, while behind their bastions at Acre and Antioch the crusaders trembled. Urban preached a crusade, but the crusade against Manfred prevented much coming of a crusade against the Moslem.

Catholics throughout the world can remember Urban IV when they celebrate Corpus Christi, that beautiful special feast of the Blessed Sacrament. Juliana, the holy nun of Mt. Cornillon, had got Robert, archbishop of Liége, to start the feast in his diocese. Robert's successor, Henry, urged Urban to extend the feast to the whole world, and in a bull filled with glowing praise of the Holy Sacrament, Urban did so on August 11, 1264. To Urban also Catholics owe the very beautiful Mass and office of the feast, for it was at Urban's request that St. Thomas Aquinas wrote them.

Chronologia Summorum Pontificum.

CLEMENT IV

1265-1268

CLEMENT IV HAD A RATHER INTERESTING FAMily history. His father became a Carthusian monk, and the Pope himself had been married and the father of two daughters before he entered the ranks of the clergy. Guy Foulques was born at St. Gilles in France. He followed his father into the profession of law and also into the service of the counts of Toulouse. Later he became a councilor of St. Louis IX. After his wife's death he became a priest and rose rapidly to become bishop of Le Puy, archbishop of Narbonne, and cardinal-bishop of Sabina. Distinguished by a love for justice and an aptitude for conciliation, Guy was much in demand as an arbitrator. Urban IV sent him as legate to England to settle the troubles between Henry III and the barons. The barons, flushed with their victory, refused to let the legate land in England, and nothing much was accomplished. Guy was on his way back from this mission when he learned that he had been elected pope. He tried to refuse, but since the cardinals would not hear of it, he was crowned at Perugia in February 1265. He took the name Clement IV.

Clement IV was holy and capable, but the Sicilian affair consumed most of his short time. He continued the policy of Urban IV and urged Charles of Anjou to hurry his preparations. Charles eluded a Sicilian fleet, slipped past a boom on the Tiber, and entered Rome on May 23, 1265. The Pope and the Guelfs were overjoyed. Months passed in raising a large enough army, but finally Charles was crowned king of Naples-Sicily on Jan-uary 6, 1266. He advanced into his kingdom and defeated Manfred near Benevento. Manfred fell and Charles took over with little more trouble. But Charles, grim and dour, and his Frenchmen grew increasingly unpopular. Soon a revolt broke out and the Sicilians invited Conradin (little Conrad) the son of Conrad IV to take the Sicilian throne. Conradin, a youth of fifteen, accepted the call and invaded Italy. Clement, who had warned Charles against harshness, excommunicated Conradin. But the young Hohenstaufen cared as little for papal censures as his grandfather Frederick II. On he came. Rome fell into his hands and hailed him with joy. Ghibellines all over Italy raised their heads in hope. But joy was turned to sorrow when Conradin's army ran into Charles near Tagliacozzo on August 23, 1268. Once more the Hohenstaufen forces went down before the tough Frenchman. Conradin was captured shortly after. In vain Pope Clement pleaded for mercy. The young Conrad fell under the headsman's axe and with him perished the Hohenstaufens.

Clement sent that first-rate diplomat, Cardinal Ottoboni Fieschi, to England to settle the baronial problem. The barons were not talking big now. Prince Edward had defeated them at Evesham and was pushing them hard. Clement repaid the barons' scurvy treatment of him as legate by urging Prince Edward to have mercy on them.

Clement IV died at Viterbo on November 29, 1268.

Mosaic in the Basilica of St. Paul-Outside-the-Walls, Rome.

BLESSED GREGORY X.

1271-1276

AFTER CLEMENT V DIED IN 1268, THE CARDINALS promptly began election proceedings at Viterbo, but they were decidedly slow to elect a new pope. To help the hopelessly split cardinals come to a decision the people of Viterbo threatened to cut off their food supply and actually did tear the roof off the house in which they were deliberating! Even this vigorous measure did not end matters. Not until almost three anxious years had slipped by did the Cardinals agree to a compromise. Six cardinals were delegated to choose a pope. They chose the archdeacon of Liége, Tedaldo Visconti, who at that very time was on a crusade. If the cardinals had caused much grief by their unconscionable slowness, at least they gave the Church a great leader.

Tedaldo Visconti was born in Piacenza in 1210. Although only archdeacon when elected, Tedaldo had wide experience in the service of the Church. He had been on missions to France, Germany, and England. He attended the First Council of Lyons in 1245. He was a friend of St. Louis and a companion of Prince Edward in the Holy Land. He was consecrated March 13, 1271, and took the name of Gregory X.

Gregory X was a man of large ideas, one of the great medieval popes. He yearned to save the Holy Land so sorely beset by the Moslem. The great-souled Pope strove to promote concord among Christians, and with some notable success. He saw the end of Germany's interregnum with the election of Rudolph of Hapsburg in 1273. He called a general council in 1274. This council, the Second Council of Lyons, might be called a high-water mark of the Middle Ages. St. Thomas died trying to reach it. St. Bonaventure shed luster on it until he died. And at it the Eastern Church returned to Catholic unity.

The Eastern emperor, Michael Paleologus, considerably alarmed by the activity of Charles of Anjou, for several years had entertained thoughts of reunion. Now he sent delegates to Lyons, and there the Greeks agreed to return to Catholic unity. It was a great day for Christians, even though there were not lacking some who doubted the sincerity of the conversion. At all events it was a great step and had the union been as carefully nourished as it was painfully born, it just might have endured.

Pope and council did not neglect reform. Notably they decreed a series of severe regulations regarding papal elections. The Pope, understandably alarmed, planned to make future conclaves finish in reasonable time.

Gregory proved to be an efficient ruler of the Papal States and a charitable father to the poor. He began work on repairing St. Peter's that might have saved the venerable basilica had it been continued. But Gregory's career was cut short. Just after celebrating Christmas the great-souled Pope died, January 10, 1276. He has been beatified. He well deserved the honor.

Firmian Collection of Engravings.
Capodimonte, Naples.

BLESSED INNOCENT V

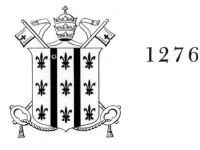

1276

PETER OF TARENTAISE WAS BORN IN SAVOY, PROBably in 1225, of noble and wealthy parents. He grew up good-looking and bright. While still a youngster, he abandoned wealth and position to enter the Order of Preachers. These were stirring times in the intellectual life of Europe and the Dominicans were in the van of progress. To Paris, the thought capital of medieval Europe, went the young Peter to study under St. Albert the Great, and to become a master in theology and a colleague of St. Thomas Aquinas. He wrote much. Indeed his busy pen got him into trouble. His writings were attacked as unsound; but a colleague, quite possibly great Thomas himself, came to his rescue and defended his orthodoxy.

Peter proved to be no ivory-tower scholar. A born ruler of men, he served with distinction as prior provincial of the French Dominicans, then as vicar general of the Order. In 1272 he was made archbishop of Lyons and cardinal. The very next year Pope Gregory X chose Lyons as the site of a general council of the Church. Naturally preparations for the great event kept the archbishop busy, and once the council convened, Peter was in the thick of things. He worked much with St. Bonaventure, and when the lovable Franciscan died, Peter preached his eulogy. He had the consolation of baptizing one of the Tartar envoys to the council. He worked hard and with great joy for the reunion of the Eastern Church.

After the council, Peter's reputation stood high,

and when Gregory X died in 1276, the cardinals thought at once of the charming and capable archbishop of Lyons. He was elected on the first scrutiny.

Peter took for his name Innocent V and for his motto: "My eyes are ever toward the Lord" (Ps. 24:15). He might well have taken "Blessed are the peacemakers," for bringing peace was his favorite task. As archbishop he had put an end to strife between the episcopal palace and the citizens. He had soothed King Philip in a dispute over temporal jurisdiction. He had been instrumental in promoting good relations between the friars and the secular clergy. Now as Pope Innocent he continued this Christlike work. To Genoa, torn with civil war, the Pope sent a letter pleading for peace, and it was consolation to Innocent that on his deathbed word was brought of his success. He removed an interdict from Florence. He strove to keep peace between Emperor Rudolph and the ambitious Charles of Anjou.

Though a man of peace, Innocent was keenly alive to the plight of Christians face to face with the menace of Islam. He sought help for the Spaniards who were having another tussle with the Moors. He urged Philip of France to lead an army to the Holy Land where the old crusaders' kingdom tottered on its last legs.

But his brilliant career was abruptly cut off. Innocent V died after a short illness on June 22, 1276.

Francesco Pacheco. Cabinet of Prints, Uffizi Gallery, Florence.

HADRIAN V

1276

OTTOBONI FIESCHI, OF A NOBLE GENOESE FAMily, was a nephew of Pope Innocent IV. He became Innocent's chaplain, a canon twice over, archdeacon of Rheims and of Parma, and a cardinal. His uncle allowed him to hold many benefices, and he in turn worked busily to provide his own nephews with good pickings among the loaves and fishes.

Dante placed Hadrian in the fifth circle of purgatory because he had become converted from attachment to worldly goods only after he became Pope. But Cardinal Ottoboni was a faithful worker in the vineyard during the reigns of Pope Alexander IV, Urban IV, Clement IV, and Gregory X. He proved his sterling worth when Clement IV sent him on a difficult and delicate mission to England, that of making peace between Henry III and his rebel barons. Ottoboni was sent with such full legatine powers that under the Pope he ruled the Church in England during his mission. His staff, it is interesting to observe, included two future Popes, Gregory X and Boniface VIII. So earnestly and skillfully did he work to bring about peace and to strengthen the Church that F. M. Powicke calls Ottoboni's mission, "the noblest expression in English history in the later Middle Ages of the unity of the two powers, the lay and the spiritual, in a joint recognition of the underlying unity of Christendom" (*King Henry III and the Lord Edward* Oxford, Clarendon Press, 1947, Vol. II, p. 528).

When Blessed Innocent V died in Rome, the cardinals had a bad time of it. Charles of Anjou, as Senator of Rome acting on the regulations of Gregory X, locked up the poor cardinals, and after eight days had produced no pope, reduced them to bread and water. Finally the French cardinals learned that Charles had no objection to Cardinal Ottoboni. He was thereupon elected unanimously. Ottoboni took the name Hadrian V. He was a sick man, indeed hastening toward the grave. Feeling no doubt that the severity of Anjou had hastened his end, he suspended the election regulations of Gregory X. He wished so to amend them as to make it impossible for the cardinals to be again mistreated as they were by the redoubtable Charles.

He had no time to amend them for though he went to Viterbo to escape the deadly Roman dog days, he died on August 18 in the Franciscan friary at Viterbo. Hadrian was never consecrated bishop or indeed, ordained priest. He had been a deacon when elected; a deacon he died.

He was buried in the Franciscan Church at Viterbo.

Chronologia Summorum Pontificum.

JOHN XXI

1276-1277

JOHN XXI IS UNIQUE IN TWO THINGS: HE IS THE only Portuguese pope, and he is the only pope placed in Paradise by that fierce Ghibelline, Dante.

Peter Juliani, the son of Julian a physician, was born probably in Lisbon in 1215. Like so many thirteenth-century leaders, he went to the University of Paris. He became proficient in philosophy, theology and medicine. Indeed, he became a doctor of medicine and wrote treatises in the fields of philosophy and medicine. Dante calls him, "he of Spain in his twelve volumes shining."

Peter became a professor of medicine at the University of Siena. At first, it seems, he was hard pressed to make a living, but later the Sienese seem to have done well by their illustrious professor. The date on which he became attached to the papal curia is not known, but his rise was swift. His services were generously rewarded by a number of benefices, and finally he was made cardinal-bishop of Albano.

Hadrian V had died at Viterbo and it was there that the cardinals gathered for the conclave. The people of Viterbo wanted to enforce the regulations of Gregory X concerning papal elections. These called for an election ten days after the pope's death in the city where the pope had been in residence with his court. The cardinals were to remain secluded from all outside contacts, even their food being passed through a little window or drum. After three days their food was to be cut to a single dish, morning and night for five days. After that it was bread and water for the cardinals until they could give the Church a new shepherd.

Now since Hadrian V had suspended these regulations, the cardinals objected very strenuously to being compelled to observe them. The Viterbese, unmoved by Their Eminences' protests, closed them up and relentlessly cut down their diet as the days dragged on.

Highhanded the Viterbese may have been, but they got results. The cardinals soon agreed on a candidate—the Portuguese physician-philosopher, Peter Juliani. He took the name of John XXI.

One of the new Pope's first acts was to repeal the election decree of Gregory X. This, it seems, caused great scandal, but in view of the harsh treatment just undergone by the Pope and his cardinals, the action, if regrettable, is quite understandable.

John XXI worked hard during his short reign to promote peace among Christian princes. He took measures to correct any abuses in the collection of papal taxes in England. In answer to complaints about this, he ordered his chief collector to look into the matter and punish any offenders. All the papal tax collectors in England were ordered to go to London and there take an oath to perform their duties properly.

Always a man of science as well as a priest, John built for himself a room in the papal palace at Viterbo where he could study the stars, a sort of observatory. This observatory was to be the death of the Pope. One night in the spring of 1277, the roof collapsed on the student Pope. The great beams crushed him horribly. For a while he lingered, conscious and fortified by the last rites of the Church, but on May 20, 1277, the sixth day after the accident, Pope John XXI passed away. He was buried in the Cathedral of St. Lawrence at Viterbo.

National Museum, Florence.

NICHOLAS III

1277-1280

ONE DAY A GREAT ROMAN NOBLEMAN, A WARM admirer of St. Francis, presented his little boy to the saint and offered him for the friars. The gentle saint replied that the boy would never enter the Friars Minor but would become a protector of the order and Lord of the World. Prophetic words indeed, for that little boy was to become Pope Nicholas III. Giovanni Orsini was born in Rome around 1216 of that famous "bear" family whose fighting and achievements filled the chronicles of medieval Rome. Young Giovanni entered the service of the Church and rose rapidly until in 1244 he was made cardinal. He was a fine-looking man of good talents and excellent character. His reputation for justice and tact must have been great, for King Louis IX expressly asked for him to deal with the arrangement of peace between France and England. He became protector of the Franciscan order, even as the saint of Assissi had prophesied, and he served as arch-priest of St. Peter's.

After John XXI's tragic death, the value of the old election regulations of Gregory X became apparent. The cardinals, relieved of pressure, spent months instead of days picking a new pope. Finally, after the people of Viterbo, out of patience with the hesitating cardinals, once more locked them up, the conclave on November 25, 1277, voted unanimously for Cardinal Giovanni Gaetani Orsini. He took the name Nicholas III.

Nicholas proved to be an excellent ruler. He firmly defended the rights of the papal kingdom, and his efforts were rewarded when Rudolf of Hapsburg finally fulfilled his promise to leave the Romagna to the Pope. Nicholas also, though not hostile to Charles of Anjou, was determined to put limits to that prince's power. He asked him to resign as Senator of Rome and was seeking to moderate Anjou's eastern ambitions when he died. He defended the rights of the Church in Hungary and Castile. He took great pains to promote peace and collected money for a crusade. He had been inquisitor general, and as pope he showed a lively interest in the repression of heresy.

His zeal was really apostolic. He had a friendly feeling for the Jews and urged preachers to try to win over the children of Israel. He sent Franciscan missionaries to Hungary to preach to the Cumans, an Asiatic people who had fled from the grim Tartar menace. In 1278 Pope Nicholas sent five Franciscans to preach to the Tartars themselves. They were to preach first in Persia and then go on to China. No limited horizons for Pope Nicholas!

In the history of the Franciscan order Nicholas III looms large. His bull *Exiit qui seminat* is one of the great charters of the friars. In it the Pope strove to end disputes over the kind of poverty to be practiced by the friars, and he forbade anyone to attack the rule of St. Francis.

That Dante placed this great pope in hell is scarcely a tribute to the Florentine's judgment. The only defect that seemed blameworthy in Nicholas was the way he distributed honors and favors among his relatives. Otherwise his character was noble. His achievements were many, and there was great promise of more, but it was not to be. Nicholas' career was cut off by apoplexy in 1280 at Soriano near Viterbo.

National Museum, Florence.

[372]

MARTIN IV

1281-1285

WHEN WORD REACHED ROME THAT POPE NICH-olas had died, the turbulent barons and people swarmed into the streets to attack the Orsini. The late Pope's lavish favors to his family had kindled hate in many a heart, and now that the strong hand of Nicholas was lifeless, that hate exploded into violence.

At Viterbo the cardinals, once more free of Gregory X's election regulations, took plenty of time in conclave. The Orsini faction, too weak to elect one of their own, were yet strong enough to block anyone else. After almost six months had brought no progress, the people of Viterbo stormed the episcopal palace, broke into the conclave and carried off the two leading Orsini cardinals. The deadlock thus rudely broken, the Cardinals elected Simon de Brion who took the name Martin IV. Although actually only the second Martin, Simon assumed the style of Martin IV because in the thirteenth century the two Popes Marinus were listed as Martin.

Simon de Brion was born in Northern France of noble ancestry. He became a priest and distinguished himself in the service of the Church. King St. Louis IX made him chancellor of France. Pope Urban IV created him cardinal and in 1264 sent him as legate to France to persuade Charles of Anjou to undertake the conquest of Sicily. Simon's outlook was strongly French. Unfortunately Pope Martin's did not become much wider.

Martin IV reversed his great predecessor's statesmanlike policy. He gave the go signal to Anjou's ambitions. He excommunicated the emperor Michael Paleologus and precipitated a renewal of the Eastern Schism. The great work of Gregory X and the Second Council of Lyons was undone.

His partiality for Anjou also involved Pope Martin in an affair which cost the papacy much in money and prestige. The French had become hated in Sicily. Anjou was a stern character, the French men-at-arms were arrogant. An incident touched off that explosion of hatred called the Sicilian Vespers when the gutters of Palermo ran with French blood. Soon the whole island had risen against Anjou. The rebels formed a republic, and far from repudiating the feudal overlordship of the Pope, they sent emissaries to acknowledge him as their suzerain. All they asked was that Anjou and his French should not return.

Pope Martin refused to deal with them, and only then did the Sicilians turn to Peter of Aragon, who had married Constance, daughter of Manfred. Peter accepted the throne. The Pope thundered anathema at Peter. He excommunicated the Sicilians. He ordered a crusade preached against Aragon. Money sorely needed for the defense of the last Christian outpost in Palestine flowed into the war chest of Anjou. And all in vain. The Aragonese were in Sicily to stay.

The whole business was a sad one. It cheapened ecclesiastical penalties, irritated non-French Christians, and at a somber moment for the Holy Land did much to weaken the prospect of a general crusade.

Martin IV was carried off by a violent fever on March 28, 1285. His intentions were no doubt good, but his reign was unfortunate. To do him justice he had been most reluctant to become pope.

Mosaic in the Basilica of St. Paul-Outside-the-Walls, Rome.

HONORIUS IV

1285-1287

GIACOMO SAVELLI, A MAN SO CRIPPLED THAT he had to say Mass sitting down, was chosen to succeed Martin IV. But if Giacomo was crippled in body, his mind was vigorous. He was chosen pope the second day after Pope Martin's funeral, a quick election indeed. The cardinals wanted no repetition in Perugia of the mob violence of Viterbo. Cardinal Savelli took the name Honorius IV after his granduncle, Honorius III.

Giacomo Savelli was born of a famous old Roman family. He pursued at least some of his studies at the University of Paris, an institution for which he had the highest regard. Created cardinal in 1261 by Pope Urban IV, Giacomo played a prominent part in top-level papal diplomacy. He was one of the cardinals delegated to invest Charles of Anjou with the crown of Sicily in 1265. He served on the compromise committee of cardinals which chose Gregory X to break the long deadlock after the death of Clement IV. He conducted negotiations with Emperor Rudolf of Hapsburg under Popes Gregory X, Hadrian V, and Nicholas III.

After his election Honorius returned the papal court to Rome, where he was highly popular. A true Roman, he tried to improve the city and to rule the papal kingdom efficiently.

Honorius was a mild man, quick to forgive, quick to remove ecclesiastical censures. He removed an interdict from Venice. He tried to bring peace to bitterly quarreling Genoa and Pisa. His gentle firmness succeeded in bringing about the repeal of objectionable laws in Florence and Bergamo.

This mild policy brought success, but mildness and success both stopped short of Sicily. Honorius continued Martin IV's unrelenting policy toward the Aragonese and the Sicilians, and that policy remained ineffectual and unfortunate.

Martin IV had deposed Peter III of Aragon in favor of Charles of Valois, younger son of Philip III of France. In 1285 Philip led a large army across the Pyrenees. Edward of England pleaded with Pope Honorius to help put an end to this disastrous strife between Christians, but Honorius firmly refused. Philip died; his army accomplished nothing. Peter of Aragon died shortly after. His son James clung to Sicily in spite of Franco-papal force and excommunication and interdict. Edward, eager for a real crusade, tried once more for peace. In vain. By now Charles of Anjou was dead, and his son and heir, Charles of Salerno, a prisoner in Sicilian hands, was willing to renounce his claim to Sicily and content himself with Naples. It looked at last as if peace were at hand; but the Pope would not allow it! And meanwhile money needed for a real crusade was being collected in the face of bitter grumbling to carry on this miserable little fight.

Honorius was not notably pro-French, but he had a strong Guelf background. Above all, he had a legal mind. To him the Sicilians were wrong, and that was all there was to it.

Honorius did show a lively interest in missionary activity. He sent prospective missionaries to study at the University of Paris. He fostered the study of oriental languages. Honorius was not strong enough to check the trend toward the abuse of plurality of benefices. He was a good man, but scarcely a great pope. He died in Rome on April 3, 1287.

Pietro Lorenzetti. "Honorius IV Approves the Carmelite Rule." Panel detail in the Pinacoteca, Siena.

[376]

NICHOLAS IV

1288-1292

After the death of Hororius IV, the folly of abrogating Gregory X's election regulations was starkly evident. For almost a year the cardinals wrangled, quite unable to come to a decision. Finally they elected Jerome of Ascoli, but it took a week and a repeated election to convince the Franciscan cardinal that he should accept. On February 22, 1288, Jerome accepted and took the name Nicholas IV.

Jerome Masci was born on September 30, 1227 at Lisciano, near Ascoli. Although his parents were lowly folk, he formed a strong friendship with a noble boy named Conrad. The two became Franciscans and studied together at Assisi. At Perugia they received their doctorate in theology. Both went to Rome to teach theology, and then their paths separated. Conrad went to Africa to preach to the infidel; Jerome to Dalmatia to serve as minister provincial of Slavonia.

Sent by Gregory X to Constantinople to prepare the way for the reunion of the churches at Lyons, Jerome accomplished his mission work with distinction. He was elected minister general of the Franciscan order in 1274 to succeed St. Bonaventure. Nicholas III made him cardinal priest and sent him on a peace mission to France, where he was joined by his old friend, Conrad. Martin IV made him cardinal-bishop of Praeneste, and there he worked until his election to the papacy. One of his first moves as pope was to call Conrad from Paris to make him a cardinal, but his old friend died.

Nicholas IV, as might be expected of a Franciscan, was intensely interested in missionary projects. He sent the famous Franciscan John of Montecorvino to follow the tracks of Marco Polo and preach Christianity in far-off China. He corresponded with Mongols, Bulgarians, and Tartars.

Nicholas was also interested in art, and he made Rome quite a center for artists and architects. He has been called the Maecenas of his age. He did much to foster universities, helping those already existing and granting charters to new foundations.

The reluctance of Nicholas to accept the heavy duty of ruling the Church may have been due to real self-knowledge. Good, kind, holy, Nicholas was not a successful ruler. He seems to have been too narrow in his views, too slow in transacting business, and too little gifted with a sense of the practical.

The papal states, so well ruled by Honorius IV, were soon in an uproar. The Pope was accused of favoring the Colonna family and the Franciscans. In his relations with Sicily, Nicholas persisted in an intransigent attitude towards the Aragonese. Indeed, he even annulled a treaty which Edward I had negotiated between Charles of Salerno, the rightful king, and James of Aragon, who actually held the island. At a time when all efforts should have been centered on saving the Holy Land, Nicholas was urging the French to attack Aragon. His policy, on the verge of success, crashed in ruin when James of Sicily succeeded his brother as king of Aragon.

The fall of Acre in 1291 caused Nicholas at long last to go all out for a crusade. Earnestly he urged Philip of France and Edward of England to take the cross. He called a council to arrange matters for 1293, but on Good Friday, April 4, 1292, Pope Nicholas IV died.

Domenico Fontana (?). Church of Santa Maria Maggiore, Rome.

ST. CELESTINE V

1294

ONCE MORE THE CARDINALS CRUELLY HURT THE Church as their wrangling left it without a pope for over two years. The deadlock was finally broken in a manner quite startling. Cardinal Orsini told his colleagues that a holy monk had warned him that God had revealed that they would be punished if they did not put an end to their differences and elect a pope. Moved, the cardinals did elect a pope—the holy monk himself, Peter of Murrone!

Peter was the son of poor parents. Born early in the century, he was the eleventh of twelve children. Right from the start he delighted his good parents by manifesting signs of real sanctity. He became a hermit on Mt. Murrone; then to avoid the crowds which flocked around him, he withdrew to even more remote Mt. Majella. Here he lived an austere life, filled with prayer, long fasts, hair shirts, and iron chains. But since crowds still pursued him, he formed a branch of the Benedictine order, later called the Celestines. For lay folk he founded a sort of "third order."

Such was the man elected by the cardinals to rule the Church. One requisite Peter certainly had —sanctity. But could a simple old man who had lived his life in the mountains cope with the complex situations faced by medieval popes?

Peter naturally was overwhelmed when the cardinals' delegates, after a weary climb through the mountains, announced his election. He wanted to refuse, to fly, but his monks told him roundly that it was his duty to end the long vacancy. King Charles of Naples, overjoyed at the election of a friend, hastened to add his pleas to those of the monks. Torn between fear of acting against God's will and of being a mighty poor pope, the old man was sadly distressed. At last he accepted and took the name of Celestine V.

Trouble started at once. Charles of Naples had been a good friend of the monk, but he could not resist taking advantage of the pope. It was as if poor Celestine were his mouthpiece! The cardinals reluctantly had to come to Aquila in the Kingdom of Naples for the consecration on August 29. Celestine then proceeded, not to Rome, but to Naples. He created new cardinals who were all French or Neapolitan. But if the king found Celestine a puppet, unscrupulous curial officials found the simple old man a gold mine. Soon they were selling blank bulls!

Celestine longed only for peace, and if he was no ruler, he was still a saint. He realized that he had made a mistake. More and more he thought of resigning. He made sure he could abdicate. He asked advice of canon lawyers. He renewed— much to the disgust of the cardinals—the badly needed election decree of Gregory X.

A poetical message from the famous Jacopone da Todi proved to be a last straw. The fiery Franciscan warned the Pope of the abuses which were running riot under his feeble old hands.

On December 13 Celestine met the cardinals in the great hall of the palace. Clad in full pontificals, he read them the decree of abdication, then stepped down and stripped himself of all papal insignia. The "great refusal," as Dante called it, had been made.

Celestine was kept in confinement by his successor Boniface VIII, lest he should become the tool of designing schemers and endanger the unity of the Church. He died on May 19, 1296. Pope Clement V canonized him.

16th-century French. "Allegory of the
Coronation of Celestine V."
The Louvre, Paris.

BONIFACE VIII

1294-1303

AFTER ST. CELESTINE'S ABDICATION, THE CARDINALS quickly elected Benedict Caetani, who took the name Boniface VIII. Boniface was a fiery old man, a canon lawyer and a veteran in the papal service. He is said to have given two hours to prayer every day. He certainly needed it, for trouble was his portion.

Those who had profited from the simplicity of Celestine naturally resented his successor. The extremists among the Franciscans joined with the powerful Colonna family to oppose the Pope. Boniface acted forcefully. He deposed the Colonna cardinals and destroyed the Colonna stronghold of Palestrina. But he was to face opponents far stronger than half-cracked friars or turbulent barons.

Edward I of England and Philip IV of France were getting ready for war. Both agreed on one thing: that the Church should provide the sinews of war. Complaints started coming in from bishops who felt that the Church was being squeezed unfairly, and Boniface came to their rescue. In the bull *Clericis laicos* he forbade churchmen to grant money to kings without papal permission. Edward's answer was to outlaw the clergy. Philip forbade the export of gold, a shrewd blow because much papal revenue came from France.

Boniface backed down. He explained that in case of necessity churchmen need not wait for the papal permission. Since the kings could decide when a state of necessity existed, this was quite satisfactory to the crown.

For a short time after this Boniface enjoyed a little peace. He canonized Philip's grandfather, the great Louis IX. He proclaimed a jubilee for 1300. The thousands of devout pilgrims who thronged Rome were a source of consolation, and Boniface needed consolation.

Philip the Fair, surrounded by men like Pierre Flotte, William Nogaret, and Pierre Dubois, who had a superexalted idea of kingly power, was a difficult problem. Soon complaints reached the Pope that Philip was taking very full advantage of the papal relaxation to milk the French church. Furthermore he was harboring the Pope's enemies; and when Boniface delegated the bishop of Pamiers to preach a crusade, Philip had him arrested! To stir up hatred against Boniface, Philip stooped to circulating a forged bull in which the pope was made to claim that he ruled France as a political overlord! Boniface issued a bull warning Philip and summoned the French bishops to meet in Rome in 1302 to discuss ways and means for bringing the king to his senses. Even when his French chivalry was badly mauled by the sturdy Flemish burghers at Courtrais in 1302, Philip continued his opposition. The pope then issued his famous bull *Unam sanctam.* This bull has caused a good deal of commotion, but actually, though Boniface uses some strong language, all he defines is that it is necessary for all to be subject to the Roman pontiff—a thing Catholics held and do hold.

Boniface, seeing Philip so stubborn, prepared to excommunicate him. But the unscrupulous Frenchman took the offensive. His henchman Nogaret and Sciarra Colonna led an armed band into Italy. By forced marches they reached Anagni, where the Pope was staying, and broke into the city. Boniface awaited them seated on his throne. When Colonna and his swordsmen broke in, Boniface greeted them with the words, "Here is my neck, here is my head." Colonna was quite ready to kill the Pope, but Nogaret restrained him. From September 7 to September 9 they held Boniface prisoner. Nogaret wished to carry him off to France, but Colonna refused to allow this. While they were quarreling, Cardinal Nicholas Boccasini rallied the papal forces and rescued the poor old Pope.

Boniface returned to Rome but died shortly after on October 13, 1303.

Arnolfo di Cambio. Petrian Museum, Rome.

BLESSED BENEDICT XI

1303-1304

IT WAS A TROUBLED GROUP OF CARDINALS WHO gathered in conclave after the death of Boniface. Charles II of Naples had entered Rome and was urging them to make a quick election. The aggressive Nogaret was still in Italy trying to raise another armed gang. Under the circumstances there was no dissension. The cardinals quickly elected Nicholas Boccasini, the man who had rescued Pope Boniface at Anagni. He took the name Benedict XI.

Nicholas Boccasini was born at Treviso around 1240 of a poor but pious family. At the early age of fourteen he entered the Dominican order. He loved his order deeply and always acknowledged how much he owed to it. A bright youngster, Nicholas was destined for higher studies and the professorial chair. He became prior, provincial of Lombardy, and finally in 1296, master general of the order. Boniface VIII made him a cardinal in 1298, and used him on peace missions to France and Hungary. When Nogaret and Sciarra Colonna made their swoop at Anagni, it was Cardinal Nicholas who rescued the old Pope from their clutches.

At his election, then, Benedict XI was a man of loyalty, learned, pious, of a sweet disposition, much more ready to forgive than to fight. Faced with the problem of whether to oppose or appease the rough, wily Philip of France, a man like Benedict naturally leaned towards appeasement as far as it was possible without loss of principle. The new Pope absolved right and left. Philip was addressed as "dear son," his excommunication not even mentioned. Even the Colonna family was partially restored. Only the actual perpetrators of the Anagni outrage, who indeed were still working against the Pope, were excluded from the general wave of pardons.

Appeasement, as usual, did not work. Philip, continued to oppress the poor Cistercians because they had been loyal to the Pope. He was to give more trouble later.

Benedict tried to promote peace, vainly in factious Florence, successfully between Venice and Padua. He had friendly relations with King Stephen Urosh of Serbia. Serbia at that time was growing to be the dominant Balkan power. Although Stephen was willing to allow his western Yugoslavs to remain loyal to Rome, he made no move towards uniting Serbia proper to the Holy See.

While staying at Perugia, Benedict was stricken with dysentery on June 22, 1304; on July 7 he died. Many suspected that the Holy Pope had been killed by poison. Stories of how Benedict was given some poisoned figs were quite common. Modern scholars, however, believe that Benedict died a natural death.

Benedict XI was beatified by Pope Clement XIV in 1773. His feast is kept on July 7. Pious and learned, the author of commentaries on various books of both the Old and New Testament, Benedict richly deserved the honor. Whether or not his appeasement policy was justified by future events —and there is some dispute about it—Pope Benedict's sincerity and desire to do the best thing are unquestioned.

Chronologia Summorum Pontificum.

CLEMENT V

1305-1314

WHEN CLEMENT WAS ON HIS SOLEMN PROCESsion to be crowned, a wall crashed down on the cavalcade, knocking the Pope off his horse, sending his tiara flying. When the tiara was recovered, its most precious jewel, a ruby, was missing. This crash was a fitting prelude to a reign which began a time of troubles for the papacy.

After Benedict died, the cardinals wrangled for almost a year before Orsini and Colonna interests agreed on a compromise candidate, Bertrand de Got. Bertrand had been absent visiting his see of Bordeaux. He accepted, took the name Clement V, and summoned the cardinals to Lyons for his coronation. Born at Villandraut in Gascony in 1264, Bertrand rose steadily in the service of the Church to be archbishop of Bordeaux. Though a friend of Philip IV, he had been loyal to Boniface VIII in his struggle with the French monarch. Naturally, however, he welcomed Benedict's appeasement policy and had renewed his friendship with Philip.

Clement, unwilling to face the trouble of living in turbulent Rome, wandered about France. Finally in 1309 he settled at Avignon, a pleasant little town on the banks of the Rhone. Avignon then belonged not to the king of France but to the king of Naples. It was almost surrounded by the papal territory of the Venaissin, and Clement VI purchased the town itself. Thus started the Avignon "exile" or the "Babylonian Captivity" of the papacy which was to last, with a slight interruption, until 1378. These terms mean simply this period in which the popes lived and held their court at peaceful Avignon and exercised their control of Rome through vicars.

Clement V was terrified by Philip IV, a fact of which the monarch was well aware. Philip had his heart set on the condemnation of Boniface VIII as a heretic. He bullied Clement into actually starting a process, but the Pope delayed until to his intense relief Philip told him he could end the affair. The king now had his sights set on living game, the rich order of Knights Templar. The Pope declared Boniface innocent, and then called a general council to meet at Vienne in 1311.

The military Order of the Temple had lost prestige with the final collapse of the crusading kingdom in 1291. Its enormous wealth excited jealous greed. Its international military force was a scandal to the new nationalism and reviving absolutism. Philip seized the French Templars and after a deal of grim work by inquisition torturers secured confessions of all kinds of evil deeds. Clement, evidently not too much impressed by confessions of such dubious value, suppressed the order without condemning it. Its property was to go to the Knights of St. John, but Philip secured the lion's share of the loot in France.

The Council of Vienne was the fifteenth ecumenical council. It censured the errors of a Franciscan, Peter John Olivi, and condemned some wild vagaries associated with the Beghards and Beguines.

Clement V was a canonist of distinction and a man with wide educational interests. He erected universities at Orléans and Perugia. He ordered that chairs of Hebrew, Syriac, and Arabic should be founded at Paris, Oxford, Bologna, and Salamanca. A good-natured man, he was too generous to his relatives and too easy-going with his court. He created a vast preponderance of French cardinals, and when he died on April 20, 1314, French influence was paramount in the papal court.

Mosaic in the Basilica of St. Paul-Outside-the-Walls, Rome.

JOHN XXII

1316-1334

THE POPE IS INFALLIBLE IN MATTERS OF FAITH and morals when he speaks *ex cathedra*, i.e., as supreme teacher. John XXII offers a classic example of a case where the pope is not infallible. John held that the souls of the just do not enjoy God until after the General Judgment, but he made it clear that he was not teaching this *as* Pope. Indeed at last convinced that he was wrong, the humble Pope admitted it.

It was only after a broken and stormy conclave that at long last on August 7, 1316, Jacques d'Euse was elected pope. John XXII, as he chose to be called, was born at Cahors in 1249. He had been a brilliant professor of canon law, bishop of Avignon, and cardinal. Now at seventy-two he was a brisk little man of simple tastes and driving energy. He found the papal court disorganized by the long vacancy, and the papal treasury empty. A good administrator, John got both back in shape. He increased centralization of church government and stepped up papal taxation.

Though a thorough Frenchman, John was no man's tool. Indeed, quite in the tradition of Innocent III he interfered vigorously in a disputed imperial election. After Emperor Henry VII died, Frederick of Austria and Louis of Bavaria fought for the imperial crown. John insisted that he should decide the case, but when Louis won an appeal to arms at Mühldorf in 1322, he did not give the Pope a chance to reverse that decision. Soon the Pope was excommunicating Louis, and the Emperor was appealing to a general council against the Pope. Louis marched on Rome, had himself crowned there by that same Sciarra Colonna who had outraged Boniface VIII at Anagni, and installed as antipope Peter Rainalducci, a Franciscan. Though Louis was soon forced to leave Rome, and the antipope repented, the fight between Pope and Emperor raged on. Around Louis gathered a corps of antipapal writers. Marsiglio of Padua wrote his *Defensor Pacis* and a group of renegade Franciscans, among them the nominalist philosopher William of Occam, blasted the Pope from the pulpit and in books.

The great Franciscan order had been troubled for some time by an extremist group in Southern France and Italy who panted after the pseudo-mystical revelations of Abbot Joachim and the vagaries of Olivi. They were now urging the quite unfounded idea that Christ and his apostles owned nothing even in common. John wished to settle this, but a general chapter of the Order anticipated the Pope by announcing that it was Catholic belief that Christ and his apostles owned nothing even in common. John then dropped the arrangement by which the Pope owned and the Friars used their possessions. He condemned the extremists' theory about Christ's poverty as heretical. This it was which sent a number of rebel friars to serve as volunteers for the Emperor in his struggle with the Pope. The majority of the Order, with true Franciscan obedience and humility, remained loyal.

John XXII died in 1334 at the age of eighty-four. He had been a great organizer and had contributed much to canon law.

Mosaic in the Basilica of St. Paul-Outside-the-Walls, Rome.

[388]

BENEDICT XII

1334-1342

"YOU HAVE ELECTED A JACKASS!" CRIED JACQUES Fournier when to his astonishment he found that he had been elected on the first ballot. But the self-styled jackass was actually the outstanding theologian in the college of cardinals. Jacques Fournier was born at Saverdun in Southern France. He became a Cistercian monk, studied theology at Paris, and rose to be bishop of Pamiers and later of Mirepoix. John XXII made him a cardinal in 1327 and depended upon his theological knowledge in the struggles which marked that Pontiff's stormy reign. Elected unanimously on the first ballot, Jacques chose the name Benedict XII.

At first Benedict toyed with the idea of going back to Rome. From the Eternal City came urgent invitations. But Romans were still turbulent and Avignon was quiet and pleasant. Far from leaving, Benedict began to build that huge fort of a palace which is the landmark of the Avignon exile.

Since Benedict had been a fervent monk, the "spiritual" Franciscan minority hoped that the new Pope would be more favorable to them. But Benedict was a great lover of obedience and orthodoxy, and he soon showed the recalcitrant friars that the monk Pope had much the same ideas as his canon-lawyer predecessor. He worked hard to reform religious orders. One outstanding measure was his determined effort to get wandering monks and friars back into cloister. A number of maladjusted religious had been roaming the roads seeking adventure and, of course, giving no end of scandal.

Benedict did his best to shepherd this wandering flock back into the fold. He enacted other measures which helped the Benedictines, and in general did much to check abuses and foster regularity in religious houses.

Benedict also tried to reform the abuses which were creeping into the Roman court. And he gave to all a shining example of detachment by his steady refusal to enrich his relatives. He loved peace so much that he declared he would not fight even to preserve the papal kingdom. When the storm clouds which warned of the coming Hundred Years' War loomed, Benedict exerted himself to dissipate them. Pro-French he may have been to the extent of creating a great majority of French cardinals, but when war threatened, he showed himself a truly impartial peacemaker. Unfortunately he succeeded only in postponing the terrible war.

Benedict XII has been praised by some of his contemporaries and harshly criticized by others. This is not strange, for he was a pious man and an earnest reformer. Reforms tread on toes and cause anguished outcries. Besides, Petrarch did not like Benedict because he would not come back to Rome, and the fight with Louis the Bavarian still went on. History has done justice to this holy and learned Pope. If he had any weakness it was in the field of diplomacy. His simple monastic outlook was ill-attuned to the complexities of high policy.

Benedict XII died on April 25, 1342.

Paolo da Siena. The Vatican Crypts.

CLEMENT VI

1342-1352

IT IS SAID THAT PHILIP VI OF FRANCE SENT AN envoy to Avignon to secure the election of his favorite, Pierre Roger. The envoy arrived to find that the cardinals had already elected a pope —Pierre Roger. He took the name Clement VI. Pierre was born in 1291 near Limoges of the noble family of the counts of Beaufort. He entered the Benedictine monastery of La Chaise Dieu at the age of ten. He studied at Paris and distinguished himself as a theologian. Abbot, bishop, archbishop, and cardinal—his career was brilliant. The king, like the ecclesiastical authorities, appreciated Pierre's ability and made him chancellor.

Clement VI, like Benedict XII, had been a monk; but while Benedict remained the austere religious bent upon reform, Clement developed into a magnificent prince, scattering largesse with both hands. To Avignon flocked swarms of fortune-hunters and pleasure-seekers. The austere castle built by Benedict was transformed into a princely palace. Abuses, pruned by Benedict, flourished with renewed vitality. The extravagance of Clement hurt the financial position of the papal court even as the sumptuous display lowered its prestige. Not that Clement was a bad man (Petrarch's accusations seem unfounded) but his court echoed to the music of the lute and the lively trumpets of the tournament.

In Clement's reign, Rome saw the meteoric rise and fall of Cola de Rienzi. At first Clement allowed the Tribune to rule Rome, but when Rienzi abandoned good sense, the Pope withdrew his support and Rienzi's regime collapsed. Far from returning to Rome, Clement dug the papacy in deeper at Avignon by purchasing the territory from Joanna, queen of Naples and countess of Provence. He did agree to the Romans' request that the Holy Year should be celebrated every fiftieth year.

Clement tried to stop the disastrous war between France and England. He succeeded only in arranging a truce. Indeed, his partiality for France (he lent large sums to Philip) led to the Statute of Provisors which limited papal financial exactions in England.

Clement did what he could to promote a league against the Turks. The league enjoyed limited success by clearing Turkish pirates from the Archipelago. He also tried to bring back Greeks and Armenians to Catholic unity.

When the Black Death hit Europe, Clement proved that under his rich robes beat the heart of a true vicar of Christ. The dreadful scourge desolated France in 1348. Avignon was hit hard, but the Pope stayed at his post. He took spiritual and temporal measures to check the plague and bolster morale. The stunning blow had numbed men's wits and soon the cry arose that the Jews had poisoned the wells. In German cities mobs rose against the poor Jews. Clement spread the papal mantle around this persecuted folk. He excommunicated those who attacked them and opened the Papal States to Jewish refugees.

Clement VI died rather suddenly on December 6, 1352. St. Brigit of Sweden, the famous mystic, had spoken severely of the Pope, but she believed that by his charity he would be saved.

Chronologia Summorum Pontificum.

INNOCENT VI

1352-1362

CLEMENT VI HAD EASED THE ELECTION REGULA-
tions of Gregory X, but at the next conclave the cardinals did not need the more comfortable conditions, for they quickly elected Etienne Aubert, who took the name Innocent VI. Etienne Aubert was born at Mont near Limoges of parents in moderate circumstances. He became a professor of law at Toulouse, bishop of Noyon and later of Clermont, and a cardinal in 1342. Zealous for reform, he leaned much on the advice of the austere Carthusian Jean Birel. He tried hard to reverse the extravagant policy of Clement. He sent the place-hunters packing, cut down financial abuses, and put a damper on the gaiety of the Avignon court. Financially, however, he could not cut down papal taxation much. Indeed he was so distressed that to make ends meet he actually had to sell paintings, jewels, even the church plate.

In spite of his earnest efforts papal prestige declined. King Edward III of England in 1363 issued the statute of *Praemunire* which hampered relations between Englishmen and the Holy See. In 1356 Emperor Charles IV issued the Golden Bull, which regulated the imperial election—without mention of the Pope. Even at Avignon the Pope was no longer safe. The Peace of Bretigny which put a temporary stop to the war between France and England sent swarms of free companions rampaging into Avignon, and indeed besieging the Pope. The cardinals themselves had shown a disturbing tendency when in the conclave they had all signed an agreement that the man elected pope should give the sacred college a good deal more power than it deserved. A number, among them Etienne Aubert, had signed only with the restrictive clause, "if and insofar as it is according to law." Once pope, Innocent wasted little time in denouncing the mischievous agreement as contrary to the laws of Gregory X and Clement V.

To settle the affairs of turbulent Rome, Innocent first sent Rienzi back to pacify the city, but the people butchered the Tribune. Already in 1353 Innocent had sent as his vicar into Italy the man who would restore order there, the Spaniard Gil Albornoz. Albornoz, cardinal archbishop of Toledo, had fled from the court of Pedro the Cruel, unable to restrain his indignation at that monarch's conduct. He battered and coaxed the Italian barons until he succeeded in making it possible for a pope to live in Rome once more. Unfortunately Innocent was too old and sick to have the necessary energy.

Innocent resumed the work of Benedict XII in reforming religious orders. Though a friend of fervent religious, his legal mind had little sympathy for the remnants of the rebellious "spiritual" Franciscans. His last years were painful, as the Black Death once again struck Avignon. He died September 22, 1362. He had tried hard and had been a good pope. St. Brigit of Sweden declared that "Pope Innocent, more abominable than Jewish usurers, a greater traitor than Judas, more cruel than Pilate, has been cast into hell like a weighty stone." Historians do not endorse this harsh judgment of the Swedish mystic, who, though she was a saint, sometimes said more than her prayers.

Chronologia Summorum Pontificum.

[394]

BLESSED URBAN V

1362-1370

THE LAST TWO POPES HAD BEEN LIMOUSINS, NAtives of the area around Limoges, and created a number of Limousin cardinals. This group was resented by the others and feelings ran so high that there was little prospect of a quick election. But to the general amazement and the discontent of most, the first ballot, taken without consultation as a trial, gave the necessary votes to Hugh Roger, a Limousin and brother of Clement VI! When Hugh greatly relieved the cardinals by refusing, they went outside the Sacred College to elect the holy Benedictine, William de Grimoard. He accepted and chose to be called Urban V.

William de Grimoard was born at Grisac in 1310 of noble parents. His mother was the sister of the holy Elzear de Sabran whom Urban was to canonize. After studies at Montpellier and Toulouse, William became a Benedictine monk. He rose to be abbot of St. Victor and was employed by Innocent VI in various legations. He was distinguished for his holiness and love of learning.

With such a man on Peter's throne, and with Albornoz still strongly ruling the Papal States, hope rose that at last the Pope would go home. And indeed, much as he loved Avignon, Urban felt it his duty to take up residence in the Eternal City. Of course, the fact that he had been compelled to pay a huge sum to Bertrand du Guesclin to rid the county of marauding free companions helped to lessen the grief of leaving. Even so, the cardinals threatened to abandon him if he left Avignon. Urban quelled the cardinals and finally landed in the Papal States on June 3, 1367. Albornoz was there to greet him with joy. Urban made a grand entry into Rome on October 16. The Pope was home at last, but not for long. Urban enjoyed two great moments in Rome. One was when Emperor Charles IV came down to have his empress crowned by the Pope. It was a very love-feast between papacy and empire. Better still was the moment when standing on the stairs of St. Peter's the Pope welcomed the Byzantine emperor, John V, and received him back to the Catholic unity. Unfortunately, however, the Emperor was unable to make his people follow him, and the Pope was unable to rouse Western might to rescue the East from the onrushing Ottomans.

Albornoz had died the year Urban reached Rome, and with his strong hand removed, the papal kingdom rang with clashing swords. Visconti of Milan was on the prowl, Perugia revolted, Sir John Hawkwood attacked the Papal States with his free companions. Discouraged, Urban decided to go back to the quiet gardens of Avignon. Besides, the Anglo-French War was once more flaring up and the Pope felt he could do more for peace at Avignon. The Romans pleaded with their father not to abandon them. St. Brigit of Sweden warned him that if he returned to Avignon he would die shortly after. In spite of pleas and threats, Urban left Rome and reached Avignon September 27, 1370. On December 19 he was dead.

Pius IX beatified this holy Benedictine Pope. His feast is kept on December 19.

Chronologia Summorum Pontificum.

GREGORY XI

1370-1378

IF EVER A YOUNGSTER COULD HAVE BEEN SPOILED by early honors, it was Pierre Roger de Beaufort who became Pope Gregory XI. The nephew of Clement VI, he was skyrocketed to ecclesiastical honors. A canon at eleven, he was a cardinal at nineteen. But Pierre was not spoiled. After receiving the red hat he calmly went to class at the University of Perugia where he made a reputation for goodness and learning. His ability and his sweet disposition probably explain how he, though a Limousin, was elected pope unanimously.

The story of Gregory XI is the drama of his return to Rome. Though Gregory dearly loved France and his family, he was a man of principle and from the start proclaimed his intention of going to Rome. But obstacles and opposition kept piling up as the years moved along. The Pope was desperately hard pressed for means. Papal taxation was bitterly resented, and Gregory actually at one time had to pawn the crown jewels. He tried to make peace between France and England. Bernabò Visconti, the monster of Milan, kept Northern Italy in turmoil until 1375, and then Florence, allied with rebel cities of the Pope's own kingdom, rocked central Italy with warfare.

Meanwhile cardinals and curia officials used every argument and took advantage of every excuse to delay the Pope's going. Charles V of France sent his own brother to plead with the Pope; even more powerfully and steadily Gregory's own family battered at his will with their love. And if Gregory had a fault, it was undue fondness for his family.

On the other hand, to strengthen his good reso-

lution came mystic messages from St. Brigit of Sweden, messages with a double refrain: Rome, Peace. And when St. Brigit died in 1373, St. Catherine of Siena continued to fire the Pope's will with burning words. In 1376 this amazing nun arrived at Avignon as a peace ambassadress from Florence. She treated Pope, cardinals, and courtiers to downright plain speaking. Gregory was upbraided for his inordinate love of his relatives. The good Pope took the scolding meekly, and at long last set September 13, 1376, as the date of departure. When on that day the Pope reached the door, he found his father, the count de Beaufort, waiting for him. In a last desperate gesture of pleading, the Pope's father threw himself across the threshold. Gregory, his heart torn, courageously stepped over the old man. With this act of obedience to Christ's command to hate one's father, the Avignon exile of the papacy came to an end.

Gregory reached Rome on January 17, 1377, but it was to be no haven of peace. Florence, in league with rebellious papal cities, was battling furiously. Gregory had hit back hard with an interdict, but though the Florentines felt the pinch, they fought on. Throughout 1377 Italy ran with blood. Cardinal Robert of Geneva and his Breton mercenaries disgraced the papal arms by the butchery of Cesena. At last in 1378 a congress gathered at Sarzana to bring peace to Italy, but before it could finish Gregory was dead.

Gregory's stay in Rome had not been happy. He longed for the peace of Avignon. Never robust, his health declined rapidly and on March 28, 1378, Gregory XI died.

Vasari. "Gregory XI Returns from Avignon"
(detail of fresco). Sala Regia, the Vatican.

URBAN VI

1378-1389

Not for seventy-five years had Rome seen a conclave. The cardinals met at the Vatican on April 7 in the midst of excited clamoring for a Roman or at least an Italian pope. Oddly enough, in view of the troubles to come, there was little difficulty agreeing on a candidate. Though the French cardinals had a big majority, they were split between the Limousins and the others. As in 1362, they looked outside the Sacred College and chose Bartolommeo Prignano, archbishop of Bari. At first glance he was an excellent compromise. Not a cardinal, he had been closely connected with the curia as acting vice-chancellor. Not a Frenchman, he was a subject of the French queen of Naples and had lived for years at Avignon. Outside the Vatican a mob was roaring, and on April 8 the guards told the cardinals to hurry it up. It was at this point that Prignano was elected by a vote of fifteen to one, Orsini dissenting because he feared the election might be considered invalid. Later on, during a lull in the mob activities, the cardinals once again elected Prignano unanimously. After this, the mob broke in, terrified the cardinals, and pillaged the palace. The excitement subsided and Prignano, informed of his election, accepted and chose to be called Urban VI. The cardinals now enthroned Urban, asked him for the customary favors, and wrote to their six colleagues at Avignon that they had made a free election. Yet within six months they revolted, declared Urban's election invalid and elected an antipope!

Urban VI had been a successful curia official, well-known to the cardinals for his austere goodness and his efficiency. But once pope, Urban's austere but fiery disposition knew no bounds. His plans were excellent, his execution faulty. He promised a thorough reform, but began it by tongue-lashing cardinals and bishops until their souls quivered in angry humiliation. He threatened loudly to end French domination of the Church by creating large numbers of Italian cardinals. But he did not act, and while he raged on, cardinals were slipping away to gather finally at Fondi. There on September 20, 1378, declaring that Urban's election was invalid because of fear, the cardinals elected an antipope, Robert of Geneva, who took the name Clement VIII. Failing to take Rome from Urban, he retired to Avignon.

Europe was torn apart. Most of Italy, the Empire, England, Poland, and Hungary remained loyal to Urban, while France, Scotland, Naples, and the Spanish kingdoms eventually backed Clement. Saints were on both sides. St. Catherine of Siena wrote to Urban, "Those devils in human form have made an election. They have not elected a vicar of Christ, but an anti-Christ." Yet St. Vincent Ferrer supported Clement!

Urban proved to be a difficult ruler. His intemperate harshness embroiled him in quarrels on all sides. His plans for reform were balked by the confusion. His pontificate was unhappy. On October 30, 1389, Urban died with Europe in turmoil and even his own followers disheartened.

Filippo Galle. Cabinet of Prints,
Uffizi Gallery, Florence.

BONIFACE IX

1389-1404

THE GREAT WESTERN SCHISM WAS NOT A SCHISM in the ordinary sense that people revolted from the pope. The Great Western Schism was a split in the Church because it was doubtful to many just who was the legitimate pope. This split caused frightful desolation in the Church. Each claimant excommunicated the other and his supporters. Two papal courts had to be maintained. The popes felt powerless to insist on reform or to fight against the encroachments of the state. In short, the Great Western Schism was stark disaster.

When Urban VI died, a discredited old man, it was hoped that the schism would end. But since Clement VII at Avignon showed no inclination to abdicate, Urban's fourteen Cardinals elected young Pietro Tomacelli, who took the name Boniface IX.

Boniface IX was a Neapolitan of poor but noble birth. As a young man he had been made cardinal by Urban and now at thirty-three he assumed the headship of the Church at a critical time. His reputation was that of a clever and amiable diplomat rather than that of a scholar. Amiable he proved to be. By his winning charm he did much to repair the damage Urban's bitter harshness had caused. But he did not succeed in ending the schism.

Clement excommunicated Boniface and Boniface returned the compliment. He did try to negotiate with Clement, but with no result. Hope flared high when in 1394 Clement VII died. The University of Paris, even the French king himself, urged the Avignon cardinals to hesitate before perpetuating the dreadful schism. But not they! The Avignon cardinals hurriedly rushed through an election and chose the Spaniard Pedro de Luna, who took the name Benedict XIII.

Boniface felt the weakness of his position. He was compelled to tolerate state interference with his rights. He could not cope with abuses. Indeed, in his pontificate abuses multiplied. Papal taxation, already unpopular, was increased. To gain the money he so desperately needed for the expenses of the papal curia Boniface resorted to questionable means. It was during this pontificate that money and indulgences began that close association which was a scandal to many. Yet Boniface did not want the money for himself.

In the political sphere Boniface won a victory over Clement VII when Ladislaus, his candidate for the throne of Naples, ousted Louis of Anjou, the favorite of the Avignon claimant. In general, however, there was a dreary and inconclusive seesaw. Benedict's position was even worse than that of Boniface, for the French, enraged at his stubbornness, withdrew their obedience from him for some years.

Boniface did what he could to help the Eastern Empire, now tottering under the blows of that powerful Ottoman, Bajazet. He also canonized the outspoken mystic, Brigit of Sweden.

In 1404 Benedict sent an embassy to Boniface, but nothing came of it; and shortly after, tormented by stones, Boniface IX died.

Filippo Galle. Cabinet of Prints,
Uffizi Gallery, Florence.

INNOCENT VII

1404-1406

WHEN BONIFACE IX DIED THERE WERE PRESENT in Rome delegates from the Avignon claimant, Benedict XIII. The cardinals asked these delegates if their master would abdicate if the cardinals refrained from holding an election. Only after they were bluntly told that Benedict would never abdicate did the cardinals proceed to an election. Even then, each cardinal took an oath that if elected he would do everything possible, even abdicate, to end the schism. The man they chose was the able and pious Cosimo de' Migliorati, who took the name Innocent VII.

Cosimo de' Migliorati was born at Sulmona in the Abruzzi at some time around 1336. Though of humble origin, he secured a good education at Perugia, Padua, and Bologna. After teaching law at Perugia and Padua, Cosimo went to Rome and entered the papal service under Urban VI. He served as a papal collector in England for ten years. He was made bishop of Bologna in 1386, archbishop of Ravenna in 1387 and a cardinal in 1400. Boniface IX leaned heavily on him in his last painful years, when stones impaired his capacity for business.

Pious as well as learned, Innocent immediately took steps to end the schism. He called a council to discuss ways and means to the desired end; but before the council could meet, Rome was in an uproar. A rebellion broke out which was subdued only with the aid of Ladislaus, king of Naples. But Ladislaus exacted a high price. He insisted that the Pope should make no agreement which might prejudice the rights of Ladislaus to Naples. Since the French still had their eyes on Naples, this might complicate any negotiations to end the schism. Then too, Ladislaus began to encroach on the papal territory. Encouraged by Ladislaus, a Roman faction once more rebelled and sent the Pope flying to Viterbo. Though the Romans welcomed him back, it is easy to see that such broils left little time to work on healing the schism.

Disturbed as was his pontificate, Innocent VII had great plans for restoring the University of Rome. He also tried to reform the curia. But he had neither the peace nor the time necessary to accomplish much, for on November 6, 1406, this able but frustrated Pope passed away. He was a good man whose only fault was nepotism. That he was unable to end the agony of the schism is due more to the stormy circumstances of his reign than to any bad will on his part.

Filippo Galle. Cabinet of Prints,
Uffizi Gallery, Florence.

GREGORY XII

1406-1415

ONCE AGAIN THE CARDINALS BOUND THEMSELVES by oath that the man elected would abdicate to end the schism if Benedict XIII would do likewise. To make doubly sure, the cardinals elected Angelo Corrario, an austere old man in his seventies. He took the name Gregory XII. Angelo Corrario was born at Venice of noble parents. Bishop of Castello in 1380, he became a cardinal in 1400. A pious man, he was outstanding for his desire to end the schism.

At first it looked as if Gregory really meant business about abdicating. He notified Benedict of his election and of his intention to abdicate if Benedict would do so too. Hopes rose when Benedict agreed at least to meet Gregory, but it soon became evident that neither was anxious to abdicate and they never reached agreement. Benedict's conduct is not surprising, but Gregory's was a disappointment. The truth seems to have been that his relatives, of whom he was inordinately fond, badgered the old man into forsaking his good intentions. Ladislaus, king of Naples, added his pressure to that of Gregory's relations.

Gregory's cardinals, growing ever more disgusted, were driven to rebellion when against his word Gregory created four new cardinals—all nephews! Some of his cardinals now left Gregory and began negotiations with equally disgusted Avignon cardinals. Together they called a general council to meet at Pisa on their own—quite inadequate—authority and summoned both Gregory and Benedict to appear. When neither did, the Council of Pisa in 1409 first declared Gregory and Benedict deposed, then proceeded to confound confusion by electing a third pope! Gregory was not idle before this threat. He created ten new cardinals to replace the rebels and held his own council, a small affair, at Cividale. This little gathering denounced Benedict XIII and Alexander V, as the Pisa pope was known.

The condition of the Church was now darker than before, but it was the proverbial darkest hour before dawn. Events marched rapidly. Alexander V died in 1410. John XXIII, who was elected to succeed him by the Pisa cardinals, was put under great pressure to call a new general council. This council, which met at Constance in 1414, finally did end the schism. The heroes of the council were Emperor Sigismund, who did so much to get the council under way, Charles Malatesta, count of Rimini, and Gregory XII. Malatesta, who was Gregory's friend and protector, urged him to live up to his good resolutions and do his part to end the schism. Gregory at last agreed and sent a legate to the Council of Constance, first to convoke the council in Gregory's name and then to announce his abdication. The council accepted Gregory's convocation, thus implicitly recognizing his legitimacy. On July 4, 1415, Gregory abdicated, and the way was open to end the sad business of the schism. John XXIII accepted deposition; Benedict XIII, stubborn to the bitter end, refused to abdicate. Abandoned by all the powers and all but three of his cardinals, he was passed over.

Gregory XII had been treated by the council as legitimate pope, and after his abdication he was made bishop of Porto and perpetual legate of Ancona. He died piously at Recanati on October 18, 1417.

Taddeo di Bartoli. State Archive, Siena.

CCXXXIX.

Gregorius   papa duodecimus :·'

Summus pontifex Gregorius papa duodecimus Intrauit ciuitates
Senar die quarta Settembris in die dnica m.cccvij. hora xxij
fex Johanne francisci de asciano existente notario consistorij
te mensibus Settembr et ottobr dci anni sud xv z plurib2 pcuria.
z vij uice :·)

MARTIN V

1417-1431

AFTER YEARS OF AGONY THE GREAT WESTERN Schism drew to its end. Gregory XII, the legitimate pope, after convoking the council already gathered at Constance, had abdicated. John XXIII, the Pisa claimant, had been deposed. Only the Avignon claimant, Benedict XIII, remained, and the council, kings, and churchmen strove to persuade him to abdicate. Not he! Even when abandoned by the powers and by his staunch supporter and friend St. Vincent Ferrer, he retired to Peniscola and continued to denounce all opponents. When the Spanish kingdoms abandoned him and made their submission to Constance, the way was open for an undisputed election.

After three days of conclave, Oddone Colonna was elected unanimously on November 11. He took the name Martin V. Christendom once more recognized the same pope. As an old chronicler put it, "Men could scarcely speak for joy."

Oddone Colonna was born at Genazzano in 1386. After studies at Perugia he entered the diplomatic service of the Church. He became a cardinal in 1405 and abandoned Gregory XII to take part in the Council of Pisa. A subdeacon at his election, he was rapidly ordained deacon, priest, and bishop before his coronation on November 21.

Martin V was a vigorous man, virtuous, able, and gracious. He needed all his good qualities, for the difficulties he faced were immense. Though the schism had ended, it left a rich legacy of evils. At first Martin could not even get to Rome, but by skillful diplomacy he entered the city in 1420. He found it in dreadful shape and worked hard to restore it.

Martin was much less successful in launching the needed reform. His energy was diverted from this task by his fear of a council. The Council of Constance in a revolutionary series of decrees had declared that a general council is above the pope. Martin was unable to approve this, but he feared to provoke a fresh schism. Consequently, he cleverly approved whatever the council had done in a conciliar manner. Since the revolutionary decrees had been carried in a manner far from conciliar they were implicitly excluded from the papal approval. Constance had also decreed that councils should be held at stated intervals. These councils might have been helpful to promote reform, but under the troublesome circumstances it is no wonder that Martin feared them. Martin indeed called a council for Pavia in 1423, but when the plague sent it to Siena, so few were present that the Pope dissolved it. This council decreed that another should meet at Basel in seven years. Though Martin convoked it in 1431, his successor had to face it. Martin died February 29, 1431.

Martin V did not start the thorough reform so much needed, but he did accomplish something. He supported the great Franciscan St. Bernardino of Siena in his propagation of devotion to the Holy Name of Jesus. He created excellent cardinals. He did so much for Rome and the Papal States that he is known as "the second founder of the papal monarchy and the Restorer of Rome."

Pulzone Scipione. Basilica of St. John Lateran, Rome.

EUGENE IV

1431-1447

GABRIELE CONDULMER WAS BORN IN 1338 OF A noble and wealthy Venetian family. He gave away his wealth and joined the canons regular of St. Augustine. His uncle, Pope Gregory XII made him a cardinal in 1408. He remained loyal to his uncle at the time of Pisa, and went to Constance only after Gregory's abdication. He was elected pope on the first ballot and took the name Eugene IV.

Tall, thin, austere, Eugene's very presence inspired reverence. Generous and religious, he made an amiable pope. He had something to learn about diplomacy and did improve as he grew older. He had agreed to an election capitulation which gave the cardinals more power than they deserved. He took harsh measures against the family of Martin V, but the powerful Colonna fought back so furiously that it took the aid of Florence, Venice, and Naples to beat them down to terms. A revolution broke out in Rome which sent Eugene flying to Florence, but soon the papal government was re-established.

Eugene's greatest problem was the council that Martin had convoked at Basel in Switzerland. The council got out of hand and by a series of revolutionary decrees tried to make a limited monarchy out of the papacy. For a while the situation was dark, but fear of another schism so frightened the best men that when the Pope moved the council to Ferrara, the leaders all obeyed. One cardinal, a few bishops, and a rabble of theologians defied the Pope to remain at Basel and go from absurdity to worse. This rump council deposed Eugene and elected an antipope, Amadeus of Savoy, who took the name Felix V. For a short time this pocket-size schism had some support, but meanwhile great things were in the making at Ferrara and Florence where the council moved in 1439.

The Eastern emperor, John VII, eager for Western help against the Turks, led an imposing array of dignitaries to the council at Ferrara to seek reunion with Rome. At Florence the union was solemnly proclaimed. There was great rejoicing that the Eastern Schism was now healed, but the union, though accepted sincerely by men like Bessarion and Isidore of Kiev, was not popular at Constantinople and lasted only until the fall of the Empire in 1453.

To the council also came an Armenian delegation to renounce the Monophysite heresy and return to Catholic unity. Copts and Abyssinians soon joined the Armenians. These unions, though short-lived, were important, because since Florence there had been at least small groups which stayed faithful to Rome. These are called Uniates. At Basel also the Hussites of Bohemia, having soundly trounced crusading armies, became freely reconciled to the Church. The results of this Basel-Ferrara-Florence Council are highly significant. The excesses of the rebellious Basel group struck a blow at the conciliar theory while the return of the Eastern Churches to unity enhanced the prestige of the papacy.

Eugene did try to reform the Church, but he was preoccupied with the council. He did encourage St. Frances of Rome in her noble work. He himself gave good example by his piety and charity. He tried to get a crusade under way against the Turks, but it was drowned in blood at Varna. He did succeed in negotiating a concordat with the Byzantine Empire.

Now the Renaissance was blooming, and the Pope did his part to encourage art. He ordered the bronze gates which still stand at the entrance to St. Peter's. He also commissioned the famous Fra Angelico to decorate a new chapel in the Vatican.

Eugene IV died February 23, 1431. He had guided the Church through a tempestuous time.

Filippo Galle. Cabinet of Prints,
Uffize Gallery, Rome.

NICHOLAS V

1447-1455

IN THE PERSON OF NICHOLAS V THE RENAISSANCE mounted the fisherman's throne. An enthusiastic patron of artists, scholars, and men of letters, Nicholas did much to create a humanist atmosphere around the papal court.

Thomas Parentucelli was born November 15th, 1397, probably at Sarzana in Liguria. The son of a poor physician who died while Thomas was yet a youngster, he was forced by lack of funds to interrupt his studies at the University of Bologna to serve as tutor to Florentine noble families. This stay at the capital of the Renaissance during two formative years probably did much to make him the humanist he was. He finally finished his course at Bologna and joined the staff of Bologna's holy bishop Nicholas Albergati. Ordained priest soon after, Thomas followed his master to Rome when Albergati was made a cardinal. His wide reading stood him in good stead when he was employed in delicate negotiations with the Greeks at Florence. After this his rise was rapid. Bishop of Bologna in 1444, cardinal in 1446, he was elected pope in 1447. He took the name Nicholas V.

Nicholas achieved some brilliant successes. He arranged the Concordat of Vienna with the Emperor Frederick III in 1448 and put an end to any possibility of imperial support for the Basel schismatics. In 1449 that ghost of a gathering, now in session at Lausanne, wheezed its last. Antipope Felix V resigned. Nicholas by his kindness made submission easy for all.

Emperor Frederick III came down to Rome in 1452 to be crowned by Nicholas. He was the last emperor to be crowned at Rome. In 1450 Nicholas had proclaimed the jubilee and once more Rome was filled with pilgrims.

Nicholas did much to promote reform. He sent out excellent legates like the great Cardinal Nicholas of Cusa and the Franciscan St. John Capistrano to work for reform in Germany. Unfortunately on the other hand, Nicholas contributed to creating a decidedly worldly atmosphere around the papal court by employing such men as Lorenzo Valla, Pozzio, and Filelfo, brilliant scholars, to be sure, but also downright filthy writers.

A true child of the Renaissance, Nicholas was enthusiastic about all forms of culture. His reign was a real golden age for hungry artists. While humanists like Valla were put to work translating Thucydides, artists like Fra Angelico were painting masterpieces on Vatican walls and architects like Alberti were working on the Belvedere. Meanwhile, spurred on by lavish papal rewards, searchers were combing ancient monasteries for classical manuscripts. And here, perhaps, is the chief title of honor for Nicholas V. He was the founder of the Vatican Library.

Two events saddened the last years of the humanist Pope. In 1453 his heart was wrenched by the fall of Constantinople. While the West supinely stood by, Mohammed II broke through the walls and put a final period to the Roman Empire of the East. Nicholas had given what help he could. It was not enough and it was not in time.

Early in 1453 a gentleman named Stephen Porcaro, on fire with humanist ideals of ancient republican Rome, launched a conspiracy to overthrow the Pope. Though the plot was foiled, Nicholas was badly shaken. From 1453 to his death in 1455 Nicholas was tormented by gout and other sicknesses. On November 15, 1455, the humanist Pope died, his eyes fixed on the crucifix.

La Hyre. "Pope Nicholas V Opens the Vault of St. Francis of Assisi." The Louvre, Paris.

CALIXTUS III

1455-1458

ALONSO BORGIA WAS BORN IN XATIVA NEAR Valencia of an old Catalan family, January 13, 1378. A brilliant professor of canon law at the University of Lerida, he was made canon by Antipope Benedict XIII. After that obstinate Spaniard died, Alonso used his influence to reconcile his shadow successor, Antipope Clement VIII, to Pope Martin V. Martin made him bishop of Valencia, and Alonso showed his loyalty by refusing the position of royal Aragonese envoy to the schismatic Council of Basel. Eugene IV thereupon made him cardinal and invited him to join the papal curia, where he served with credit.

Alonso was a dark horse in the conclave which followed the death of Nicholas V. Only after the cardinals failed to unite on the outstanding Capranica or Bessarion, the learned and pious Greek, did the votes swing in compromise to Alonso Borgia. Alonso accepted and took the name Calixtus III.

Although seventy-seven years old, Calixtus still had abundant energy. His great objective was to save Christendom from the Turks. To this end he subordinated everything else. Humanists and artists wailed for the good old times of Nicholas V. Money still flowed, but to generals and munition makers rather than to poets and artists. The careers of Calixtus III and of his successor Pius II prove that if a large part of Eastern Europe went under the Turkish domination the fault was not the

popes. The failure of Calixtus proves how far papal prestige had already declined. Calixtus pleaded, urged, threatened the monarchs of Europe—in vain.

Calixtus had one moment of triumph when that great Hungarian, John Hunyadi, accompanied by St. John Capistrano, saved Belgrade from the mighty grasp of Mohammed II. It was a great victory, but unfortunately Hunyadi died shortly after it. He had no successor, and even the glory of the Belgrade victory could not infect the cold monarchs of Europe with crusading enthusiasm.

Absorbed as he was with the crusade idea, Calixtus still found time for an act of justice. It was he who ordered the posthumous re-examination of Joan of Arc's case which resulted in the glorious vindication of that heroine.

A man of austere life, Calixtus was in many ways a good pope. Unfortunately he had one defect, dangerous in a spiritual leader. He was overfond of his family. Catalans flooded to Rome to enjoy papal favor—much to the disgust of the Romans. Calixtus created two of his nephews cardinals at an early age. One of these, Rodrigo Lanzol-Borgia, was later, as Pope Alexander VI, to overshadow Calixtus by his reputation—a reputation that was quite unsavory.

Calixtus III died still full of plans for the future on August 6, 1458. His death was the signal for popular outbreaks against the hated Catalans.

Sano di Pietro. "The Madonna Appears to Calixtus III." The Academy, Siena.

PASTOR · DESNIO · ALMIO · POPOL · XPIANO
A · TE · DI · SIENA · ORMAI · LACURA · REL · DO
FA · CH · ALLEI · VOLRA · OENI · TVO · SENSO · HVMANO

OREI · NE MADRE · ADIO · LARA · CONSORTI
LO · CALISTO · E · DESNIO · ATANTO · DONO
ASIENA · NO · TORAMI · ALTRO · CHE · MORTE

CALISTVS · III · SANVS · PETRI · DE SENI · PIXE

PIUS II

1458-1464

THE MAN CHOSEN TO SUCCEED CALIXTUS III WAS the humanist, historian, statesman, and reformed rake, Aeneas Sylvius Piccolomini. Aeneas Sylvius was born at Corsignano near Siena of poor but noble parents. He studied at the University of Siena and later sat at the feet of Filelfo in Florence. Aeneas Sylvius combined hard study with loose living. Though he took canon law and entered the ecclesiastical service, he had too much respect for holy orders to become a priest living as he was. He served various princes of the Church, including Capranica and Albergati. On a mission to Scotland when his ship was threatened by a storm, Aeneas Sylvius vowed to walk barefoot to the nearest shrine of Our Lady if a landfall was safely made. The nearest shrine was ten miles away from the landfall, but Aeneas Sylvius resolutely trudged barefoot through bleak Scottish snow to pay his debt. It cost him dearly, for he contracted gout, a disease which tormented him the rest of his life.

His conversion, however, did not yet take place. He joined the schismatic Council of Basel and formed one of a rebellious and loose-living circle there. He wrote tracts against the Pope, and filthy prose and poetry which would cause Pius II much bitter regret. Having a keen sense of the wind's direction, Aeneas abandoned the moribund Basel council for the service, first of the Emperor Frederick III, then of the Pope. He served the papacy well, taking a large part in the negotiations which led to the Concordat of Vienna. Calixtus III made him cardinal in 1456, and in 1458 after a somewhat difficult conclave, Aeneas Sylvius emerged as pope. He chose the name Pius II.

Pius had already turned over a new leaf when he had become a priest. Now he strove to live up to his chosen name. He publicly retracted his youthful errors and bade the Christian world to reject Aeneas but accept Pius. As pope, he led a simple life more like that of a monk than of a Renaissance prince. He loved nature, and whenever possible he worked outdoors. He was accustomed to give audiences sitting under the chestnut trees or beside some splashing fountain.

If the humanists expected a return of the golden age of Nicholas V, they were disappointed. Pius did not altogether neglect the arts, but his main concern was to carry on the crusading policy of Calixtus III. The necessity of a crusade was impressed upon him by the piteous complaints of princes driven from Greece and the Eastern islands by Ottoman might. Pius called a congress of the powers to meet at Mantua in 1459, but the congress did little else than prove the Pope's zeal. Power politics, and narrow power politics at that, prevailed among the monarchs of Renaissance Europe.

Pius enjoyed one great triumph when he succeeded in getting Louis XI of France to abrogate the Pragmatic Sanction of Bourges. Even this, however, was spoiled by future encroachments of the spider king.

Although he saw the need for a thoroughgoing reform, Pius undertook only partial reforms. He concentrated on the crusade. He even wrote a letter to Sultan Mohammed II, urging him to become a Christian. No answer. At last, as if to shame the sluggard kings, Pius, old and sick, dragged himself to Ancona, where he had assembled a small crusading army. Fever struck him down, and on August 14, 1464, he died on the shores of the Adriatic, looking towards the East he had so much desired to help.

The Borgia Apartment, the Vatican.

PAUL II

1464-1471

WHEN A YOUNG VENETIAN HEARD THAT HIS uncle had been elected pope, he promptly abandoned his business career for the service of the Church. His foresight was justified. He advanced steadily until he became Pope Paul II.

Pietro Barbo was born in Venice on February 23, 1417, of a wealthy Venetian merchant family. His mother, Polixena Condulmer was the sister of Pope Eugene IV. A very pious woman, she brought up Pietro carefully. Her brother the Pope saw to it that Pietro had the best teachers, once he embraced the ecclesiastical state. Pope Eugene made him a cardinal in 1440.

After Pius II had died at Ancona, the cardinals hurried back to Rome and proceeded to hold an election. The conclave was short; after the first ballot the cardinals elected Pietro Barbo. He wished to take the name Formosus II, but since that name means handsome, the cardinals dissuaded him out of fear that the people would consider it a vulgar allusion to Pietro's striking good looks. He next chose Mark, but since the second evangelist's name was used as a war cry by the armed forces of Venice, the cardinals likewise vetoed it. Finally he chose Paul II. No one objected to the apostle of the gentiles.

Paul II refused to ratify an election capitulation which the cardinals had signed. Indeed, no pope could in justice ratify such a document, for it unduly exalted the power of the cardinals.

Paul's election was popular, and with reason. He was a large-hearted man who loved to do things for the people. He took very good care of Rome itself. He saw to it that adequate provisions reached the city. He made war on robber barons. He tried to stamp out the vendetta which disgraced the section. Other rulers had done as much, but Paul stands out as a pope who provided not only spiritual and temporal care for the people, but even saw to it that they had fun! Pageants, glowing with all the color of the Renaissance, delighted the Romans. Games, races, fun for every class marked the holiday season under this genial pontiff. The Pope himself loved to stand at the window of his palace and watch the merrymaking. But Paul was no playboy pope. Quite alive to the danger from the Moslem, he welcomed the epic Albanian hero Skanderbeg and sent him home to renew the fight, with a blessing and a substantial sum of money. Like his predecessors, Paul tried to arouse Europe to a sense of its danger, but like his predecessors, he failed. He was very good to those poor refugees from the Ottoman onslaught who had come to Rome for a refuge.

Nor was he blind to the need for reform. Though he failed to launch the root-and-branch reform which was needed, he did limit financial abuses.

Yet Paul II had a bad press. And why? Because he dared to clear out some humanists from the papal curia, they gave the pope a bad reputation. His unpopularity with the humanist extremists was heightened when he swooped down on an academy presided over by an eccentric named Pomponio Leto. At this academy, atheism and sedition were discussed—somewhat academically to be sure. Still, the Pope had the Porcaro conspiracy to remember.

Paul also had trouble with some people quite other than pedants—the shrewd Louis XI of France and the cold Venetian oligarchs. George Podiebrad, king of Bohemia, with his Hussite tendencies was also a vexation to Paul II.

Paul II died suddenly of a stroke on July 26, 1471.

Bellano. The Palazzo Venezia, Rome.

SIXTUS IV

1471-1484

FRANCESCO DELLA ROVERE WAS BORN AT CELLE ON July 21, 1414, of poor parents. He was a sickly youngster, and his mother consecrated him by vow to St. Francis. At the age of nine he was put under the care of a Franciscan schoolmaster, and later on he entered the Franciscan order. He proved to be a talented student at the universities of Pavia and Bologna. Ordained, he taught theology with an extraordinary success. Even the learned Cardinal Bessarion sat in on his lectures.

As provincial of the Ligurian province of his order, Francesco worked hard for reform, and after 1464 when he was elected minister-general of the order, he extended his efforts to the whole order. He so ably defended his friars before Paul II that not only was the Pope appeased but he made Francesco a cardinal in 1467. Cardinal Francesco continued to live as simply as Fra Francesco. He devoted his leisure to study and produced a number of volumes which earned him considerable notice, especially a work defending Mary's Immaculate Conception. With perhaps less success he strove to show that Aquinas and Duns Scotus differed only in words!

Such was the man the cardinals chose to succeed Paul II on August 7, 1471—a friar, zealous for reform, a hard-working scholar learned in theology. Surely now it would seem that the church had a leader who would undertake the root-and-branch reform so long desired. But not since Urban VI had a pope been more of a disappointment.

It is true that Sixtus IV, as Francesco chose to be called, accomplished some good in his pontificate. He tried to regulate abuses in the inquisition. He made Rome more sanitary. He could be called

a second founder of the Vatican Library. He was a great patron of art, and for this he will be remembered whenever men look at the Sistine Chapel.

In spite of all this his pontificate must be considered a dismal failure. At a time when the Church needed reform and rightly expected vigorous leadership in that direction, Sixtus IV caused the moral tone of Roman ecclesiastical life to dive sharply. Not that he was crudely immoral: the Franciscan pope, devoted to Mary, lived a private life which is attacked only by gossipy enemies whose testimony is of no value. The crime of Sixtus was nepotism. From Liguria came numerous relatives to fatten on church wealth and to lower church standards. He created youthful nephews cardinals and loaded them with ecclesiastical plums.

The moral tone of Rome sank as parties, gambling, and loose living became commonplace. The older cardinals looked on with dismay at these manifestations of a new spirit, but they were dying off, and the future remained with the numerous cardinals created by Sixtus IV, the cardinals who did much to pave the way for the success of the Protestant revolt.

Sixtus lowered the prestige of the papacy also by becoming involved in a shabby conspiracy to overthrow the Medici in Florence. To do him justice the Pope insisted that no blood be shed, but still any connection with the Pazzi conspiracy, which was climaxed by a murder on the altar of the cathedral in Florence, is a disgrace to a Pope.

Sixtus IV died August 12, 1484, in the midst of diplomatic and military failure. It was fitting, for the keynote of his pontificate is failure.

Titian. Uffizi Gallery, Florence.

INNOCENT VIII

1484 - 1492

THE DEATH OF SIXTUS IV WAS THE SIGNAL FOR A general outbreak against his pushful and greedy relatives. Once more Orsini and Colonna stood to arms while Caterina Sforza, the redoubtable wife of Girolamo Riario, the late Pope's favorite lay nephew, seized the Castle of St. Angelo. It looked as if blood would wash Roman gutters, but cooler heads prevailed, and the cardinals were able to proceed to an election.

The conclave, like Rome itself, was torn by factions. The chief rivals were Giuliano della Rovere, the most able of the late Pope's nephews, and Rodrigo Borgia, the nephew of Calixtus III. Bargaining seems to have been quite open, and the election was decided when Della Rovere and Borgia got together on a compromise candidate, a weak, good-natured man whom the ambitious cardinals hoped to dominate, Giovanni Battista Cibo.

Giovanni Battista Cibo was born in Genoa in 1432, the son of a Roman senator. As a young man he was somewhat licentious and had two illegitimate children, Franceschetto and Teodorina. But after young Cibo took orders he settled down. He became bishop of Savona in 1467, and in 1473 exchanged Savona for the see of Olfetta in Naples. He was created cardinal in 1473 by Sixtus IV. He chose the name of Innocent VIII.

The first part of his reign was dominated by Cardinal Giuliano della Rovere, that most able and energetic of Sixtus IV's nephews, but the easy-going Innocent soon tired of power politics and allowed Lorenzo de' Medici to guide his policy during the latter part of his pontificate. He made Lorenzo's teen-age nephew a cardinal, but stipulated that he should not assume the robes and obligations of the cardinalate until he was eighteen.

Innocent summoned a congress to meet at Rome in 1490 to discuss a crusade against the Turks. Interest in the proposal was heightened by the presence of the Sultan's brother, Prince Jem, in Rome. But as usual, nothing came of the congress.

Although Pope Innocent meant well, he contributed to the decline of papal prestige by his open acknowledgment of his illegitimate children in the Vatican. His son Franceschetto, who was living a dissolute life, was no help to the Pope.

Then too, Innocent was very hard pressed for funds. To get them he increased the number of purchasable offices. This in turn caused graft and corruption among officials. Innocent had the bitter experience of seeing forged bulls sold under his very eyes. When the culprits were discovered, death was their portion, but great damage was done before the forgeries were discovered.

Innocent had the consolation of hearing of the fall of Granada to the arms of Ferdinand and Isabella. But his pontificate, on the whole, did little for the Church. He himself seemed to realize this, and on his deathbed he asked the cardinals' forgiveness for having done so little and begged them to elect a better successor. How they answered this appeal is a matter of history.

Innocent VIII died devoutly on July 25, 1492.

Detail of Monument to Innocent VIII.
Basilica of St. Peter, Rome.

ALEXANDER VI

1492-1503

ORGIA POISON IS ALMOST CERTAIN TO FIGURE largely in any Renaissance novel. It does not figure in history. Yet, though hostile exaggeration and downright lies did much to create it, there was unfortunately, some basis in fact for the miasma of scandal which surrounds the name of Alexander VI.

Rodrigo Borgia Lanzol was born at Xativa in Spain on January 1, 1431. His mother was the sister of Pope Calixtus III. A cardinal at twenty-five, Rodrigo reached eagerly for the ecclesistical plums his uncle shook down for him. His eagerness did not extend to ecclesiastical morals. Though rebuked by Pius II, young Rodrigo continued to live evilly.

Such was the man the cardinals elected in answer to poor Innocent's plea that they elect a better pope. Yet Rodrigo's election was hailed by the Romans with enthusiasm. Alexander VI, as Rodrigo chose to be called, was still a fine figure of a man when elected at the age of sixty-one. He was talented, generous, a wise patron of art. He performed the exterior ceremonies of his office with decorum and dispatched the routine business of the papacy with ability. He promoted peace between Spain and Portugal, putting a rein on their fierce competition for empire by his line of demarcation. He treated Jewish refugees from Spain with kindness. In Rome he made considerable improvements and did much for the university.

Alexander had to face a difficult problem when the French king, Charles VIII, came storming down into Italy to make good his claim to Naples. It was a touchy moment for Alexander when the French approached Rome. His enemies—Giuliano della Revere, the Orsini, Savonarola—clamored for his deposition as a simoniacal prelate. But Alexander, no fool when it came to diplomacy, outmaneuvered them all and escaped scot-free from the French menace. He was not done with Savonarola. The friar of San Marco continued to denounce Alexander, but in 1498 the people of Florence turned against him and put the bold preacher to death.

There was a moment when it looked as if Alexander might turn over a new leaf. One night his favorite son, Juan, disappeared after a party. After days of anxious search, his body, pierced with wounds, was fished from the Tiber. The grief-stricken old Pope was crushed and gave much thought to reform. A commission drew up a plan full of promise. But the mood passed, and soon Alexander was deep in plans to push his son Caesar's career.

Caesar abandoned the ecclesiastical state (though a cardinal, he was not a priest) and to him Alexander allotted the turbulent semi-independent northern section of the Papal States known as Romagna. Caesar smashed his way into his duchy and held it with a mixture of skill, energy, and ruthlessness which made him Machiavelli's idol. But his activity was in vain. His sickness and the Pope's death were to rob him of a principality.

After dining at a cardinal's villa the Pope and Caesar defied the treacherous night air of a Roman August. Soon both were down with malaria. Caesar managed to pull through, but Alexander, now seventy-three, succumbed. It was six o'clock on August 13 that Alexander VI went to meet Him as his judge Whose vicar on earth he had been.

Pinturicchio. The Vatican.

THE MAKING OF A POPE

THE SPLENDOR AND MAJESTY WHICH ATTEND THE coronation of a pope reflect not the glory of the individual being crowned, but the glory of Jesus Christ. The pope is bishop of Rome. This is his basic title. As bishop of Rome he is the successor of St. Peter and Christ's representative or vicar on earth.

It is not clear how a pope was chosen in the very early days of Christianity, but soon the custom developed that the clergy and people of Rome should choose their bishop. This democratic system worked well enough for a time, but after the popes became temporal rulers in the eighth century, the system broke down. Power-greedy nobles controlled too many elections and placed relatives or friends on the papal throne. This was not good and led to the so-called Iron Age of the papacy. No wonder that in the eleventh century when the great movement for ecclesiastical reform arose, this system was one of the first targets for reforming popes. Pope Nicholas II in 1059 decreed that henceforth only the cardinal-bishops should elect the pope. (Cardinal-bishops are the bishops of small areas near Rome.) Later Pope Alexander III and the Third Lateran Council in 1179 extended the privilege of electing the pope to all the cardinals. This custom endures to the present.

The conclave, or the practice of enclosing the cardinals during the papal election, began in the thirteenth century. After an election which took almost three years, Blessed Gregory X at the Second Council of Lyons in 1274 ordered that the cardinals should be locked up and kept in seclusion until they had chosen a pope. St. Celestine V restored the conclave after it had been discontinued, and Boniface VIII placed Gregory X's decree in the code of canon law.

There are three methods of electing a pope: inspiration, compromise, and election by secret ballot. A pope is elected by the method of inspiration when the cardinals on the first day of the conclave without any ballot unanimously proclaim one man as pope. A pope is elected by compromise in case of a deadlock. The cardinals agree to allow a committee of no fewer than three nor more than seven members to choose a pope. By far the most common method of election is the method of secret ballot. In this method the successful candidate must secure two-thirds plus one of the possible votes.

Once elected, the pope is crowned in a ceremony which marshals ages of traditional pageantry. Underneath all the pomp, the *sedia gestatoria,* the *flabelli,* the ceremony consists chiefly in the pope offering the most Holy Sacrifice of the Mass. The coronation takes place after the pope's Mass, and is quite simple. When the Mass is concluded, the pope goes in procession to the balcony of St. Peter's. There in the presence of thousands assembled in the square he takes his seat on the papal throne. An ancient hymn is sung and the Dean of the College of Cardinals says the Our Father. A cardinal removes the pope's mitre and the Dean of the College of Cardinals approaches with the tiara. He kneels and says: "Accept this ornate tiara of the three crowns and remember that you are the Father of the Princes and Kings, Pontiff of the World, and Vicar of Our Saviour Jesus Christ on this earth, Whose honor and glory will last through centuries and centuries."

The newly crowned pope arises and gives his first blessing to the City and the World.

*Pope John XXIII celebrates
the Coronation Mass in
St. Peter's.*

ST. PETER'S BASILICA

SAINT PETER'S, EVEN IN PICTURES, STRIKES THE imagination so forcibly that one is not surprised at Byron's beautiful tribute in *Childe Harold's Pilgrimage*:

"But lo the Dome, the vast and wondrous Dome,
  To which Diana's marvel was a cell—
  Christ's mighty shrine above his martyrs' tomb."

Spectacular as the great building is, its historical background is even more striking. The Vatican Hill, on which St. Peter's stands, lies outside the old city of Rome; but the Romans seemed to have loved the neighborhood. There Agrippina laid out her gardens. There her son, the mad emperor known as Caligula, built a circus or arena. There in that very circus Nero made living torches out of early Christians. There St. Peter was beheaded and when his head touched the ground, that ground became sacred. Peter was buried on the Cornelian Way which ran past the Circus of Caligula, and to his tomb, even in times of persecution, flocked thousands of pious Christians.

After Constantine freed the Church from persecution, he decided to build a great basilica over the tomb of St. Peter. And so in the early fourth century the first St. Peter's rose on the Vatican Hill. Pope St. Sylvester consecrated it in 326. This church was not the cathedral of the bishop of Rome: St. John Lateran enjoys that privilege. St. Peter's belongs to the world. The basilica of Constantine stood for over a thousand years, and in it were buried scores of popes. In it were crowned emperors and kings: Charlemagne and Alfred and Frederick Barbarossa. Its great walls looked down on good days and bad days. They echoed to tri-

umphant shouts of ravaging Moslems. They saw saints, founders of religious orders, holy men and holy women, they saw riots and disturbances. This Church was history.

Yet it had to go. During the fifteenth century the basilica began to show its age. In spite of huge sums spent to prop it up, the time came when its destruction was decreed. This was no sudden decision. Many fifteenth-century popes had concerned themselves with the venerable basilica, but it was left to that vigorous man of the Renaissance, Pope Julius II, to begin the work of destruction and rebuilding.

The new St. Peter's was the work of many men and many generations. Julius II laid the cornerstone in 1506. Urban VIII dedicated the new basilica in 1626. The greatest artists of the age gave their genius to this church. Bramante began the building. Raphael succeeded him but actually did little work on the basilica. The mighty Michael Angelo lifted its great dome to the sky. Carlo Maderna built the façade and gave the basilica its final form of a Latin Cross. Bernini built that colonnade which in the words of Robert Browning stands

"With arms wide open to embrace
  The entry of the human race."

St. Peter's is huge, the largest church on earth. With its adjuncts the basilica covers six acres, has an over-all length of 700 feet and a width of 500 feet. Its height reaches 448 feet to the top of the cross on top of the dome. No wonder Horace Greeley called St. Peter's "Niagara of buildings."

St. Peter's: The square and the basilica
Vatican City.

PIUS III

1503

THOUGH ALEXANDER WAS DEAD, CAESAR STILL lived and lived in Rome where he could keep an eye on the conclave. But it was a sick Caesar, a Caesar still shaky from his bout with fever that all eyes watched anxiously. Even so, the cardinals were frightened enough to plan to hold the conclave in the Castle of St. Angelo rather than the Vatican. But when the ambassadors of the Empire, France, Spain, and Venice joined the cardinals in urging the terrible duke to withdraw, the convalescent Caesar agreed to do so. With his litter disappeared his chance to dominate the conclave. The Borgias were on the way out.

Three candidates led the field in this conclave—the great enemy of Alexander VI, Giuliano della Rovere, the wealthy and powerful minister of Louis XII, Georges d'Amboise, and the raffish Ascanio Sforza. When none of these could gain the necessary majority, they turned to a compromise candidate, Francesco Piccolomini, a sick old man. On September 22, Francesco was elected and took the name Pius III. It was a popular choice.

Francesco Todeschini Piccolomini was born May 9, 1439, in Siena. His father was a man of great wealth. His mother, Laodinica Piccolomini, was the sister of Pope Pius II. Pius adopted young Francesco and gave him his name and coat of arms. He proved to be a bright student, and took his doctorate in law at the University of Perugia. Although Pius II made him a cardinal and archbishop of Siena at the age of twenty, he did not take priest's orders until elected pope as an old man of sixty-four. Pius II, however, took good care to give him a holy and able coadjutor to act as bishop in his place.

Young as he was, Francesco proved worthy of the sacred college by his excellent life. During the worldly times of Sixtus IV and Alexander VI, Cardinal Piccolomini stayed away from Rome as much as he could. He served the Popes as legate on various occasions, with skill and usually with success. The election of such a man, as able as he was religious, delighted those who yearned for a thorough reform. But Pius was not to be given the opportunity for accomplishing great things.

Although only sixty-four when elected, Pius was a sick man. Tormented by gout, he suffered severely, but bravely went through the ceremonies of ordination, consecration as a bishop, and coronation as pope. So sick that he had to say Mass sitting down, the courageous Pope tried desperately to carry on the business of the papacy. He planned to call a general council. He announced that he was to be a pope of peace. But the pressure was too much for his tired old frame. He fell into a fever and by October 17 his doctors were in despair. After receiving the viaticum and extreme unction, the noble old man died peacefully on the evening of October 18. He had been pope for less than a month.

Mosaic in the Basilica of St. Paul-Outside-the-Walls, Rome.

JULIUS II

1503-1513

GIULIANO DELLA ROVERE, BORN IN POVERTY AT Albrissola in Liguria, became one of the most powerful Renaissance popes. His fortune was made when his uncle became Pope Sixtus IV. Sixtus made Giuliano (who had been a Franciscan) a cardinal and heaped honors upon him. At his uncle's death Giuliano eagerly competed for the tiara with Rodrigo Borgia. Though forced to accept Innocent VIII as a compromise, Giuliano soothed his ambition by doing much of the governing for that easy-going pontiff. At the next conclave Giuliano and Rodrigo once more strove for election. This time Rodrigo won, and as Alexander VI he had little use for his rival. Giuliano, on his part, eyed the Borgia Pope with suspicion and busied himself with intrigue. He even worked on Charles VIII of France to invade Italy. At Alexander's death Giuliano once more tried for the tiara, once more failed. But when Pius III quickly passed away, Giuliano finally succeeded. He took the name Julius II.

Julius was fifty when elected. He was vigorous, irascible, a man of his own counsel, very much a man of his own age, an outstanding personality in an age of individualists. He is chiefly remembered for two things: he rebuilt the papal kingdom, and he made Rome a Mecca for artists and art-lovers.

Julius devoted himself to the task of becoming master in the papal kingdom. He managed to get Caesar Borgia out of the country. He drove the Baglioni out of Perugia, and when the Bentivogli of Bologna proved stubborn, he excommunicated them and their supporters, and battered his way into the city. Venice, insolent on its lagoons, defied the Pope and held on to portions of Romagna. Julius formed the League of Cambrai with Em-

peror Maximilian and Louis XII of France. League forces soon compelled the proud republic to disgorge its ill-gotten gains. This pleased the Pope, but another result of the war did not. France got hold of Milan. The stormy but shrewd Julius now raised the cry "Out with the barbarians." Against France he formed the "Holy League" with Ferdinand and his old enemy Venice. Again the Pope was successful, and the French retreated beyond the Alps.

Louis XII had countered this political "Holy League" by inspiring a church council at Pisa in 1511 with the help of a few rebellious cardinals. As usual Julius acted decisively. He called a true council to meet at the Lateran. This Fifth Lateran Council left the French council at Pisa to wither on the vine. Unfortunately, though the Lateran Council checkmated the French, it did not produce the thoroughgoing reform so badly needed.

Julius II was a truly great patron of art. He set Michael Angelo to work on the Sistine Chapel, Raphael on the Vatican, and Bramante to plan St. Peter's. In his reign the capital of the Renaissance may be said to have moved from Florence to Rome.

After ailing for some time Julius II died peacefully on February 21, 1513. His death was regretted by the Romans, for if he had not been a great Pope, he had been a good king. Julius II shocked many by his open display of power politics, but it must be said that if Julius worked like a secular prince, it was not to promote the glory of his own family, but the welfare of the papal kingdom. He has been called the second founder of the papal states.

Raphael. Pitti Gallery, Florence.

[432]

LEO X

1513-1521

IF EVER A MAN WAS PRODUCED BY THE ITALIAN Renaissance it was Giovanni de' Medici. He was born at Florence in 1475, the son of the magnificent Lorenzo. Marsilio Ficino and Politian saw to his humanist education. Destined for the Church, he was tonsured at the age of seven or eight and soon became abbot of several monasteries. A cardinal at thirteen, he was pope at thirty-eight.

Yet Giovanni had his troubles too. His family was expelled from Florence in 1494. Appointed legate in Romagna by Julius II, Giovanni was taken prisoner by the French in the War of the Holy League. But then fortune's wheel spun. The Medici recovered control of Florence in 1512, and the very next year Giovanni entered the conclave a dark horse to emerge as Pope Leo X.

Leo faced the crushing responsibility of spiritual leadership with a light heart. He loved shows and games, and many a play and ballet was performed for the Pope's amusement. A keen sportsman, Leo spent much time hunting. He was careless of the morals of the humanists he patronized as long as their Latin was Ciceronian. Yet Leo had no scandal in his own life, before or after becoming pope. He was charitable, said his prayers regularly, and even fasted three times a week.

His open-handed extravagance made Rome a happy hunting grounds for humanists, but it so seriously embarrassed the papal treasury that Leo was forced to stoop to unworthy devices to secure necessary funds. In politics Leo played a shifty game without much ability and usually reaped only embarrassment.

He completed the Fifth Lateran Council called by Julius. But, though excellent reform decrees had been passed, little enough came of them. Leo's most famous achievement was the Concordat of Bologna, an agreement with Francis I of France signed in 1516 which put an end to the semi-schismatical policy intermittently followed by the French since the Council of Basel. This agreement, which allowed the king to name bishops and abbots, gave him so great a stake in French church wealth that greed would not tempt the French monarchs, as it did others, to leave the Church so that they could confiscate its wealth. These advantages, however, were dearly bought, for the concordat left an open avenue to corruption in the French church.

Leo X had been elected by the younger cardinals, and these made so many demands on him that he could not satisfy all. One of the disgruntled dignitaries, Cardinal Petrucci, plotted to poison the Pope. Leo discovered the plot, had Petrucci executed, and then at one sitting created thirty-one new cardinals, a wise step which ensured a loyal college.

Leo had appointed Raphael to proceed with the building of St. Peter's, but lack of funds forced the great artist to chafe in idleness. The Pope granted an indulgence to all who under the usual conditions contributed to the building of the basilica. Tetzel, preaching this indulgence in Germany, stirred a stormy Augustinian to challenge him and indulgences on October 31, 1517. From 1517 to 1521 Martin Luther drifted into open rebellion against the Catholic religion. Leo was quite patient with him, but at last in 1520 he condemned Luther's errors by the bull *Exsurge Domine*.

Condemnations were not enough. By December 1, 1521, when Leo X died, Germany was aflame. It was the time's misfortune that when the Church needed a Hildebrand on the papal throne all it got was a Medici.

Bugiardini. The Palazzo Corsini, Rome.

[434]

ADRIAN VI

1522-1523

AFTER LEO'S DEATH HIS COUSIN GIULIO WAS THE dominant figure in the conclave, but unable to control the necessary majority, Giulio proposed a compromise candidate, Cardinal Adrian Florensz, absent in Spain serving as viceroy for Charles V. Cajetan, the famous Thomist, earnestly seconded this proposal; and almost before they knew it, the cardinals elected the grave Dutchman. Adrian accepted and chose to be called Adrian VI.

Adrian was born in Utrecht, on March 2, 1459. His parents, poor and pious, gave him a good religious foundation which was deepened by his early schooling with the Brothers of the Common Life. Helped financially by Margaret of York, dowager duchess of Burgundy, he took his doctorate in theology at Louvain in 1491. He taught theology there and published two books. Among those who came to his lectures was the famous Erasmus.

Chancellor of the university, twice rector, councilor of Duchess Margaret, he was chosen by Emperor Maximilian to be tutor to his grandson and heir. Adrian's work with the young prince paid dividends in the sturdy Catholicism of Emperor Charles V.

Sent to Spain on a delicate mission in 1515, he found himself the next year co-viceroy with the great reformer Ximénes. He was made Bishop of Tortosa, a cardinal, and grand inquisitor. After Ximénes died, Adrian carried on as sole viceroy.

The election of this Dutchman, this great friend of Charles V, stunned everyone including the cardinals, but by his firm though tactful dealings with Charles, Adrian soon showed that he would be no tool in imperial hands. It was not until late August that Adrian reached Rome, a decidedly hostile Rome. All the pagan humanists, all the swarm of place-hunters and job-buyers, feared the stern theologian. And with reason, for Adrian was determined to reform the Church and to start right in at Rome.

Adrian faced a serious situation. In the East the Turks were about to batter their way into Rhodes, in Germany Luther's revolt still blazed, and at home the Church needed reform. Adrian tried to get adequate help for Rhodes, but had to see it fall. Against Luther he tried to get Erasmus to use his golden pen, but that timid humanist still hung back. With rare moral courage Adrian, in his instruction to Chieregati, his nuncio in Germany, fearlessly acknowledged the existence of abuses, abuses he was determined to stamp out.

Adrian devoted himself to this task. He ruthlessly slashed the expenses of his court. He suppressed useless offices. He avoided even the suspicion of favoring his own family. But it takes time to overcome the resistance of vested interests and the inertia of human weakness. And time was running out on the sexagenarian Pope. A fierce outbreak of plague sent the cardinals on the run for a safer climate, and though the indomitable old Dutchman stayed on and survived, he lost six precious months because little could be done in the absence of the cardinals; and then when the plague died down and the cardinals came back, Adrian fell sick. He died September 12, 1523. The frivolous rejoiced at his passing, but it was a tragedy for the Church.

Filippo Galle. Cabinet of Prints,
Uffizi Gallery, Florence.

CLEMENT VII

1523-1534

AFTER ADRIAN, ANOTHER MEDICI. AT THE CONclave Leo's cousin Giulio won the tiara after stubborn competition from cardinals Farnese and Wolsey. He took the name Clement VII.

Giulio de' Medici was born in Florence in 1478. Created cardinal in 1513, he was considered the architect of Leo's foreign policy. Giulio was a handsome man of good morals, and quite free from the frivolity of Leo X, but he was not very able and was tortured with a dangerous inability to make up his mind. In short, he was scarcely the pope for troubled times.

Two tragedies mark the reign of this second Medici pope: the sack of Rome and the loss of England.

After trying vainly to bring about peace between the Emperor and Francis I, Clement, unlucky and improvident, made an alliance with the French even as they were on the march for Pavia and disaster. The Emperor, really angry, made himself disagreeable to the Pope. Clement, frightened more than ever, formed the League of Cognac against him. In return the imperialists egged on the Colonna to make trouble for the Pope. These ruffians burst into Rome, sacked the Vatican, and desecrated St. Peter's, a grim prelude to next year's frightful tragedy. The next year, 1527, the imperialist army in North Italy, infuriated by lack of pay and longing for plunder, marched south. Florence, threatened, was saved by the Cognac League Army. The mercenaries, however, had fixed their greedy eyes on a greater prey, rich Rome itself.

Abandoning even their guns, the motley horde of Spaniards, Italians, and Germans hastened toward the city. On May 5, even without artillery, the wild throng broke through the feeble defenses of the papal capital. Clement, who had only just reached the safety of the Castle of St. Angelo, had to listen to the agonized screams of his poor flock. A nightmare followed as pikemen butchered men, women, and children, plundered and desecrated to their hearts' content. The glory of Renaissance Rome was extinguished in blood. Clement finally made peace with the Emperor, indeed, even crowned him at Bologna in 1530; but a greater disaster than the sacking of Rome was in the making.

Henry VIII of England had written against Luther, and even in politics was quite pro-papal; but a lustful attachment to Anne Boleyn showed how weak his principles were. Eagerly he bombarded Clement with requests for an annulment of his marriage with Catharine of Aragon. Clement, reluctant to displease the friendly monarch and hoping that something would turn up to change the situation, stalled and delayed. But he was waiting for a break that never came, and when all the facts were in, there was only one decision possible: that Henry's was a good marriage. Henry did not wait for the final decision. In 1534 he climaxed a series of anti-Catholic acts by forcing the Church in England to break from Catholic unity.

Clement VII died shortly after on September 26, 1534.

Frà Sebastiano del Piombo. National Museum, Naples.

PAUL III

1534-1549

PAUL III, LIKE THE FABLED JANUS, LOOKS TWO ways, back to the bad old times of Renaissance Rome, forward to the glory of the Catholic Reform.

Alessandro Farnese was born of a noble family in 1468. Educated by Pomponio Leto in the house of Lorenzo de' Medici and at the University of Pavia, he was steeped in Renaissance culture and Renaissance morality. Though he entered the service of the Church and was created cardinal in 1503 by Alexander VI, he lived a loose life. But he gradually improved, and when in 1519 he decided to become a priest, he turned over a new leaf and thenceforth lived chastely. Agreeable and competent, he got along with the variety of popes he served from Alexander VI to Clement VII. And when Clement died, Alessandro's election was achieved with ease and hailed with delight.

Paul III, as he chose to be called, was a good pope, a strong pope, sagacious, energetic, and largely devoted; not entirely devoted, for he was guilty of favoring his relations. But he compensated for this dangerous fault by his great work in promoting the Catholic Reform.

Paul III began to do what Adrian VI had been prevented by death from doing. Paul did not merely talk reform, he reformed. There was a crying need for spiritual cardinals to replace the worldly Renaissance princes of the last generation. Paul filled the sacred college with earnest reformers, men like Gian Pietro Caraffa and Reginald Pole.

There was a crying need for reform in the papal curia. Paul began that work over the agonized protests of vested interest. There was a crying need for reform of the clergy and the religious orders. Paul gave strong support to new orders and reforms of the old orders. He backed up reforming bishops who put their dioceses in order. On September 27, 1540, Paul approved of the Society of Jesus, and before his pontificate was over, Ignatius and his followers were spreading throughout Europe and Xavier had left for India and spiritual conquest. Paul favored the Theatines, the Barnabites, and the Ursulines, and in a time of trial, his wisdom protected the great reform order of the Capuchins.

Above all, Paul after most vexing difficulties got the long-desired general council under way. On December 13, 1547, his legates opened the Council of Trent. And Trent is a watershed in church history.

Paul III forbade the enslavement of the Indians. He rebuked Francis I for his ferocious cruelty toward the Protestants, while, on the other hand, he established the Index of Forbidden Books to check heretical tendencies. He was a great patron of art. Under him Michael Angelo began that dome of St. Peter's which today is a landmark of Rome.

But Paul's great glory lies in the fact that when he died on November 10, 1549, a new era had been born, the era of the Catholic Reform.

Titian. National Museum, Naples.

JULIUS III

1550-1555

PAUL III HAD MOVED THE ECUMENICAL COUNCIL from Trent to Bologna. This enraged the Emperor, who forbade his subjects to leave Trent. With some members at Trent and others at Bologna, the council was at a standstill. But after Paul's death the man chosen to succeed him was Cardinal del Monte who, as senior papal legate, had opened the council. Now he ordered the fathers back to Trent and once more the great work of the council went forward. Unfortunately, however, the defeat of the Emperor by the Schmalkaldic army and lack of French cooperation forced the Pope to suspend the council in 1552.

Giovan Maria Ciocchi del Monte was born in Rome on September 10, 1487, the son of a brilliant lawyer. After studies in law and theology he became archbishop of Siponto. He served Clement VII as prefect of Rome and, less agreeably, as a hostage to the wild men who had sacked the city. Indeed, when poor Clement could not keep up the exorbitant payments demanded, the future pope was very close to being hanged! Created cardinal by Paul III, he served on the commission to prepare for the great council and then as the council's first president. His election on February 7, 1550, was the result of a compromise. He took the name Julius III.

Julius was a well-meaning but easy-going man. He favored his relatives, spent money lavishly, and loved good times. But on the other hand, he did continue Paul III's work in favoring the forces of reform. At the instance of St. Ignatius he founded the famous German College to provide zealous and learned priests for the afflicted Empire.

Julius showed excellent good sense and tact in his dealings with England. Mary, now on the throne, was negotiating for the return of England to Catholic unity. Julius appointed her kinsman Cardinal Pole to be his legate in the matter and gave him the widest faculties to ease troubled consciences. He did not insist on the return of stolen monastic property. He was rewarded by seeing England once more a Catholic country.

Julius III, greatly interested in learning and art, promoted the development of the Vatican Library and of the Roman and various German universities. He favored Michael Angelo and the historian of art, Vasari. Pierluigi Palestrina, the great composer, he placed in charge of St. Peter's choir.

Julius might have been more fond of ease and jollification than suited either his state or the times, but it is to his credit that the work of reform did continue. By the time Julius died on March 23, 1555, St. Peter Canisius was spearheading a Catholic reaction in Germany, St. Francis Xavier had died trying to get into China after an epic sweep through the Indies and Japan, and zealous Franciscans and Dominicans were spreading the gospel in the Americas.

Pulzone Scipione. The Palazzo Spada, Rome.

MARCELLUS II

1555

THERE ARE A FEW CHARACTERS IN WHOM THE Renaissance spirit and the Christian spirit met in so harmonious a blending that in them the best spirit of the age seemed incarnate. St. Thomas More was one such. Pope Marcellus II was another.

Marcello Cervini was born May 6, 1501, of a noble family of Montepulciano. His father Ricciardo, a scientist, started Marcello on the path to knowledge. Marcello was a serious young man, yet so agreeable that he was liked everywhere. At Siena, where he continued his education, he was so respected that his presence was enough to cut off evil conversation. He completed his education at Rome, where he made such an impression on Clement VII that the Pope ordered Marcello to collaborate with his father on a book dealing with calendar reform. He helped his father not only on the book but on his estates. Marcello proved to be a practical farmer as well as a scholar, a conjunction not always found.

After his parents' death he settled the family, then went to Rome where he served first in the papal chancery, then in the diplomatic corps. Cardinal Farnese, who had studied under Marcello and liked him, used him a great deal in affairs of state. His advancement was swift. Bishop of Nicastro and administrator of Reggio and later of Gubbio, he took great pains to reform those dioceses. Created cardinal in 1539, he served as legate at Trent, where he did valuable work on the decrees on scripture, tradition, and justification.

Marcello is remembered by scholars as one of the great directors of the Vatican Library. By his cataloguing, his acquisition of new manuscripts and his printing of old ones he contributed a great deal to scholarship. He was a friend to young writers and such scholars as Seripando, Sirleto, and Panvinio owed much to him.

Such then was the man the cardinals chose to succeed Julius III. His election on April 10, 1555, was hailed with joy, especially by those eager for reform. Marcellus II (he retained his own name) wasted no time. He cut down the display of the coronation. He rigidly refused to favor his relatives. He issued severe regulations for his household. He proclaimed his intention of resuming the Council of Trent. Men felt a golden age of the papacy was dawning; but the greater the hope, the greater the disappointment.

The long ceremonies of the coronation and Holy Week had so exhausted the delicate Pope that he fell into a fever. In spite of doctors' orders he continued to work. Although the fever persisted, the doctors were not alarmed; but on May I, 1555, after a pontificate of only twenty-two days, Pope Marcellus died in his sleep.

His memory is enshrined in Palestrina's great Mass of Pope Marcellus, and still more in the hearts of those who reverence goodness and scholarship.

Mosaic in the Basilica of St. Paul-Outside-the-Walls, Rome.

PAUL IV

1555 - 1559

UNDER MARCELLUS REFORM HAD BEGUN TO STIR Rome like an insistent but gentle breeze. Under his successor reform roared through the city with all the violence and some of the freakishness of a tornado.

Giovanni Pietro Caraffa was born near Benevento on June 28, 1476, of a noble Neopolitan family. With his connections advancement was easy. He served Leo X as diplomat in England and Spain. He was a zealous bishop of Chiete; but dissatisfied with the comfortable life of a Renaissance prelate, he yearned to be a Camaldolese monk or a Dominican friar. He finally persuaded Clement VII to let him join the new order of Theatines founded by his friend St. Cajetan. Caraffa became general of the order, the object of which was to promote the welfare of the secular clergy. Paul III used both the order and Caraffa to further his reform projects. Indeed Caraffa became Paul's right-hand man in matters of reform. Created cardinal in 1536, and archbishop of Naples soon after, Caraffa worked furiously to carry out the reform plans of his chief.

Caraffa was chosen Pope after a stubborn election May 23, 1555. He was an old man of seventy-nine, but a vigorous old man, full of fire and fight. He took the name Paul IV. Though deeply religious, Paul IV was hot-tempered, had small understanding of human nature, and was too fond of his relatives. These relatives caused him grief, for they disgraced the high positions he gave them. But to do Paul justice, when his eyes were opened, he ruthlessly disgraced them.

Paul was extremely anti-Spanish, and soon was involved in a disastrous war with Philip II. By 1557 the Pope was soundly beaten, and when let off with easy terms, he prudently decided to spend more time on spiritual activities. Paul IV had already begun to work on reform. With furious zeal he swung the axe, cutting down expenses and his own revenues. He gave good example too by his private life, which was pious and austere.

Paul had a horror of heresy which surpassed even his horror of abuses. As cardinal he had urged Paul III to reestablish the Roman Inquisition, and now under his eager hands it leaped into high gear. When he extended its competence to cover moral cases as well as heresy, Rome trembled. When it came to heresy, Paul had an enormous capacity for suspicion. He jailed Cardinal Morone, a truly great prelate, on suspicion of heresy. He recalled Cardinal Pole from England where he had just reconciled that country with the Church to answer the same charge! Small wonder ordinary men shook.

Paul IV died August 18, 1559, admitting his faults. But in spite of them, he did much for the Church. Many of his reform decrees were adopted by the Council of Trent. His harshness was resented by the Romans, who threw down his statue and attacked the Inquisition Office to celebrate his death. But this very harshness cleared away any last remnants of the pagan miasma which afflicted Renaissance Rome. The best epitaph for the fierce old reformer was the statement of the Venetian ambassador—that in his reign Rome had been turned into a monastery.

Filippo Galle. Cabinet of Prints, Uffizi Gallery, Florence.

Filippo Galle. Cabinet of Prints, Uffizi Gallery, Florence.

PIUS IV

1559-1565

AFTER THE STORMY CARAFFA CAME THE PEACE-ful Medici. The conclave, so bitterly split between French and Spanish factions that it dragged on for months, finally settled on Gian Angelo Medici as a compromise. Elected Christmas Day 1559, he took the name Pius IV.

Gian Angelo Medici was born March 31, 1499, of a struggling Milanese family which had no connection with the wealthy Florentines. He started his university education at Pavia as a charity student. After 1521 things improved, and he concluded his education at Bologna and entered the papal service. His progress was slow because he was neither of high enough birth to gain honors by influence nor of high enough morality to gain them by merit. At last created cardinal by Paul III in 1549, he enjoyed some favor under Julius III, but faded into the background under Paul IV.

Pius IV was a good-natured, cheerful Lombard. He quickly curbed the power of the Inquisition and removed some names from the Index. But for all his mildness, Pius was determined that the work of reform should proceed. With less hubbub he continued Paul's reform of the papal court, but his great achievement was the successful ending of the Council of Trent.

The council had not met since 1552, and the obstacles to its resumption were enormous. It took patient and persevering diplomacy to accomplish its resumption and conclusion. Aided by brilliant legates, especially Morone (the same Morone who languished in an Inquisition jail under Paul IV!)

the council jerked its way forward through the thorny obstacles which sprang up in its path. At last on December 3, 1563, it held its final session. When early the next year Pius confirmed the council's decrees, he could justly feel that he had accomplished a great work.

Pius, however, had something of the Renaissance prelate in him. He heaped favors on his numerous relatives in the grand manner, but even here he touched gold. One nephew, quickly raised to the purple, proved to be St. Charles Borromeo, the very model of a reform bishop, and the good angel of the reign.

As a diplomat, Pius renewed relations with Emperor Ferdinand which had been broken off by the impetuous Paul. He worked steadily for peace among the princes. As a patron of art and learning Pius was in the best Renaissance tradition. He supported old Michael Angelo, and under him the work of St. Peter's went forward. He fostered the University of Rome with warm patronage.

In 1564 a crack-brained fellow named Accolti planned to murder Pius to make way for an angelic successor! The plot was betrayed and Pius suffered nothing worse than a scare. But by the end of 1565, he was tormented by gout, and on December 9, 1565, a fever struck him down.

Pius IV had his faults, but his name will ever be remembered with two glorious names in the history of the Church: the Council of Trent and St. Charles Borromeo.

Filippo Galle. Cabinet of Prints, Uffizi Gallery,
Florence.

ST. PIUS V

1566-1572

A REPORT CIRCULATED IN ROME THAT PIUS IV would be succeeded by an angelic pastor. For once such a report proved true. The next pope was the great St. Pius V.

Antony Ghislieri was born of poor parents near Alessandria on January 17, 1504. Educated by the Dominicans he entered the order and took the name Michael. He was ordained in 1528 and for years taught philosophy and theology. He served his order in several high offices and the Church as an inquisitor. A man of great austerity and prayer, he caught the eye of the reforming Caraffa. When Caraffa became Paul IV, he made the holy Dominican a bishop, cardinal, and grand inquisitor. Under the easy-going Pius IV, Ghislieri found himself out of favor, and it was a surprise when on January 7, 1566, he was elected pope. He took the name Pius V.

Pius set his heart on carrying out the reforms of Trent, extirpating heresy and promoting peace among princes to unite them against the Ottoman menace. He accomplished the reform objective to a large extent. One department after another felt the force of his zeal. Religious orders bloomed anew under his fostering hand. He published the catechism of the Council of Trent, and an improved edition of the missal and breviary. Pius tried to make Rome truly a holy city. Immorality he punished severely. Bull fights were forbidden. He actually tried to stop bull fighting in Spain, but that was too much even for a pope!

A former grand inquisitor, Pius dealt harshly with heretics. Queen Elizabeth he excommunicated in 1570, an act which, while it heightened the persecution of Catholics in England, also did much to strengthen them.

The great concern of the Pope's last years was the Ottoman's fierce onslaught. When in 1570 they tore Cyprus from the Venetians, the Christian outposts in the Levant shook with fear. Then Pius, in Chesterton's words, "called the kings of Christendom for swords about the cross." But "the cold Queen of England is looking in the glass. The shadow of the Valois is yawning at the Mass." The Venetians, however reluctantly, had to fight because the Turks were attacking them, and Philip of Spain alone joined the Pope and the Venetians in a crusading league. After disappointing delays, the league fleet under Don John of Austria smashed the big Turk fleet at Lepanto in 1571. The delighted Pope established the feast of Our Lady of Victory to commemorate this astounding victory, which he attributed to Mary's intercession.

It had been weary work getting this crusade going, work that took a good deal out of the old Pope. Though he suffered much from stone, his prayer was: "Lord increase my pains, but increase my patience too." Pius died joyfully on May 1, 1572. Venerated at once by the Roman people, he was beatified by Clement X in 1672 and canonized by Clement XI in 1712. His feast is kept on May 5, and on this day Romans still gather at his shrine to venerate a great pope and a holy man.

Leonardo da Sarzana. Church of Santa Maria Maggiore, Rome.

GREGORY XIII

1572-1585

ON MAY 13, 1572, UGO BONCOMPAGNI WAS elected Pope without delay or difficulty. He chose to be called Gregory XIII. Born at Bologna on January 1, 1502, he studied and then taught law at the city's famous university. In 1539 he entered the papal service. He served Paul III and Pius IV at the Council of Trent. He was made a bishop by Paul IV and a cardinal by Pius IV.

He had not always lived up to Christian standards, but after his ordination he proved to be an excellent prelate. At the papal court he was closely associated with St. Charles Borromeo, whose example was a shining beacon.

Gregory XIII was not particularly successful in his political ventures. He hailed the massacre of St. Bartholomew with a Te Deum and a medal, but what the Pope celebrated was the news that the king had been preserved from a Huguenot conspiracy. The butchery he deplored even with tears. He tried hard to put new life into the league against the Turks, but Venice made a separate peace with the Sultan. He tried to help poor Ireland groaning under the Elizabethan terror, but again he failed. The erratic Stukely, sent to Ireland, ended up in Africa, and the gallant Fitzmaurice expedition was bloodily crushed.

Nor was Gregory a great success as ruler of the papal kingdom. His financial policy was a failure, and he was quite unable to cope with the impudent bandits who plagued the territory.

Gregory gave a great gift to civilization when in 1578 he introduced the reformed calendar which bears his name. He also did much to beautify Rome.

But a pope's interests are chiefly spiritual, and here Gregory shone. His life, simple and pious, gave great edification. He devoted himself to carrying out the reforms of Trent. Gregory especially interested himself in the training of good priests. He personally either founded or supported twenty-three seminaries, including the English College and the German College. He erected a fine new building for the Jesuits' Roman College, thenceforth known as the Gregorian University.

Gregory was a careful watchman over the purity of the faith. He condemned the errors of Baius, a Louvain professor, and kept a sharp eye on heresy. But his wide vision made him keenly interested in the positive spreading of the faith. In Europe he sent missionaries to England and Sweden. To Ivan the Terrible in far-off Muscovy he sent a legate. On the global front the Pope was consoled by favorable reports from Japan, the Philippines, India, Mexico, and South America. A picturesque event highlighted the intense missionary activity of the reign when Japanese envoys from the Daimios of Bungo, Arima, and Omura visited Rome to venerate the Holy Father. Gregory was delighted, and the envoys edified all by their sincere piety and charming manners.

Gregory XIII died April 10, 1585. His name is enshrined in the calendar we use today and the university which has alumni all over the world.

Civic Museum, Bologna.

SIXTUS V

1585-1590

FEW POPES HAVE SO CAPTURED THE IMAGINATION as Gregory's successor, the Minorite Conventual Felice Peretti who took the name Sixtus V. A vigorous sixty-four on his election, with sharp eyes gleaming from under bushy brows, Sixtus ruled the Church with intelligence and vigor.

Felice Peretti was born December 13, 1521, at Grottamare of poor parents. He did the usual chores of a peasant lad until a Franciscan uncle sent him to the Conventual friary at Montalto to get an education. Felice loved the friars and soon entered the order. He became a learned theologian and an eloquent preacher. In 1552 he preached the Lent in Rome and gained the friendship of such reform leaders as Cardinals Caraffa and Ghislieri, St. Ignatius and St. Philip Neri. Though his severity as an inquisitor at Venice led to his recall, his rise in the hierarchy was rapid. Procurator-general of the Franciscans, bishop and cardinal, he was confessor to St. Pius V. But Gregory XIII had little use for him, and during Gregory's reign, Felice devoted himself to scholarly pursuits. In spite of his absence from the center of power he was quickly elected to succeed Gregory on April 24, 1585.

Sixtus proved to be both a good king and a good pope. He fearlessly grappled with the bandit problem which had plagued so many popes. First, he secured extradition treaties with neighboring states, then he pursued the criminals with ruthless severity. The knowledge that neither noble blood nor powerful protectors could shield rascals from the noose or the axe made robbery a less popular pastime in the Papal States.

Horrified at the state of papal finances, Sixtus by new taxes, by increasing the number of salable offices, and by other devices, managed to amass a huge treasure in Castle of St. Angelo, while at the same time he spent much on public works. He finally got the dome of St. Peter's finished, built a new Lateran Palace, erected four obelisks and a large aqueduct to bring water for Rome's many fountains. Keenly interested in the welfare of the poor, he planned to drain the Pontine Marshes and strove to keep the price of bread low.

Sixtus V might be called the great organizer of the papacy in modern times. With lucidity and vigor he so efficiently reorganized the papal curia that essentially his system still prevails. He grouped the cardinals into fifteen congregations, each of which assisted the pope in a special phase of Church business. The number of cardinals he limited to seventy. Sixtus also restored the custom that bishops should visit Rome at regular intervals.

Sixtus admired Elizabeth of England and longed for her return to the old faith, but the execution of Mary Stuart did much to disillusion him, and he helped Philip send his anything but invincible armada against Elizabeth. He was, however, no court chaplain to Philip. In France where the murder of Henry III had left the throne open to Huguenot Henry of Navarre, the Pope, though at first hostile to Navarre, adopted a cautious policy which disgusted the Spaniards but paid dividends later.

Sixtus V died August 27, 1590. One of his last acts was to take half a million ducats from his St. Angelo treasury to help the poor during a bad harvest.

Silla da Vigiù. Monument of Sixtus V, detail.
Church of Santa Maria Maggiore, Rome.

URBAN VII

1590

U RBAN VII WAS THE FIRST OF THREE POPES whose combined reigns did not last a year and a half.

Giambattista Castagna was born in Rome on August 4, 1521, of a noble family. He studied at Perugia and Padua and finally took a doctorate in canon and civil law at Bologna. He entered the service of his uncle, Cardinal Girolamo Verallo, and started his diplomatic journeyings by going with him on a legation to France in 1551. In 1553 he was made archbishop of Rossano in the Kingdom of Naples. Though he served his diocese for twenty years before resigning it in 1573, Castagna made his chief reputation as a brilliant diplomat. Pius IV sent him into Spain with Cardinal Buoncompagni in 1564 and then left him there as nuncio. He got along well with the Spaniards, and it was during his nunciature that the League, which resulted in the victory of Lepanto, was formed.

Under Gregory XIII Castagna served as nuncio in Venice and legate in Bologna. He represented Gregory at the peace conference between the Spaniards and the Dutch held at Cologne in 1579-1580. Gregory made him a cardinal in 1583, and only two years later at the conclave held after Gregory's death, Castagna was considered a likely candidate for the papacy. Sixtus V, like his predecessors, had a high regard for Castagna and used him as legate in Bologna. Besides all these diplomatic offices, Castagna had played a distinguished part in the last sessions of the Council of Trent.

After Sixtus died there was some civil commotion, but the cardinals got matters under control, and the conclave went smoothly enough. Contrary to what often happens, Castagna went into the conclave the favorite and came out pope. He was elected September 15, 1590, and took the name Urban VII.

Urban showed his kind and sympathetic nature at once. He promptly told the pastors of Rome to draw up for him lists of their needy parishioners. He ordered the bakers to keep the price of bread low and told them that he would make up any loss they might thereby suffer—an early and very Christian example of price subsidy!

Although seventy when elected, Urban was quite vigorous, and it was hoped that this kind and capable man would live to do much for the Church. But that terrible scourge of old Rome, the malarial mosquito, struck the new Pope down. Within three days of his election, Urban was shaking with fever. The people of Rome, frantic at the thought of losing so good a shepherd, multiplied prayers as 30,-000 men marched in procession. The Jews, too, are said to have fasted and prayed for the good Pope's recovery.

But it was not to be. Urban had Mass celebrated every day in his room and just as the Mass was ending on September 27, he died peacefully. Charitable to the last, Urban left his private fortune to provide endowment for poor girls.

Mosaic in the Basilica of St. Paul-Outside-the-Walls, Rome.

GREGORY XIV

1590-1591

THE ELECTION OF GREGORY XIV MARKED A HIGH point in Spanish interference in papal elections. With Henry of Navarre rapidly gaining ground in France, Philip was determined to have a Pope who would be stern with Navarre. His ambassador, the haughty Olivares, bluntly told the cardinals that of their number, only seven were acceptable to Spain's monarch. Resentment at such barefaced dictation flared and for two months the conclave was deadlocked. But the Spanish forces prevailed, and finally on December 5, 1590, the cardinals elected Niccolo Sfondrati, one of Philip's seven. He took the name Gregory XIV.

Niccolo Sfondrati was born near Milan on February 11, 1535. His father, a Milanese senator, became a cardinal after his wife's death and was considered a possible choice for the papacy in the conclave of 1550. Niccolo studied law at Perugia and Padua, then entered the service of St. Charles Borromeo. Pius IV made him bishop of Cremona in 1560. The following year he went to Trent, where he did some good work at the last sessions of the Great Council. He ruled his diocese wisely, and though Gregory XIII made him a cardinal in 1583, he remained a working bishop and only went to Rome when necessity demanded.

Gregory XIV was a man of deep piety. The friend of St. Charles Borromeo and St. Philip Neri, he had been a true reform bishop. But now his health was poor and he had little experience in po-

litical and diplomatic affairs. Unfortunately he chose as his secretary of state Paolo Emilio Sfondrati, a young nephew, pious, but even less experienced than the Pope.

Gregory quickly abandoned the cautious policy of Sixtus V with regard to the complex French situation. Sincerely convinced that the Spaniards and the League (formed to fight for Catholic interests in France) were right in mistrusting Henry of Navarre, he hurled spiritual thunderbolts at Navarre's numerous ecclesiastical supporters. More, he sent money and even a papal expeditionary force to aid the embattled Leaguers and their Spanish allies.

Plague and famine ravaged Rome during Gregory's pontificate. The kind Pope did what he could for his people. Ecclesiastics from the cardinals down to simple religious worked to help the stricken. Prominent was St. Camillus de Lellis, the founder of the Fathers of the Good Death. At this time also that remarkable young man Aloysius Gonzaga died caring for the plague-stricken.

Gregory XIV, ill at ease in political affairs, interested himself in all reform projects. He approved the Order of the Fathers of the Good Death and encouraged reformers everywhere. He had not time to accomplish much, for his health, always bad, soon failed completely, and on October 16, 1591, Gregory XIV died.

Mosaic in the Basilica of St. Paul-Outside-the-Walls, Rome.

INNOCENT IX

1591

EVEN BEFORE GREGORY XIV BREATHED HIS LAST, Spanish and anti-Spanish factions were hard at work electioneering for the next pope. Many churchmen were angry at King Philip's high-handed interference when at the last conclave he had excluded all but seven cardinals. This time the Spaniards did not go so far, but they still controlled a majority and after a quick conclave the cardinals chose another of Philip's seven, Gian Antonio Facchinetti. He accepted and took the name Innocent IX.

Gian Antonio Facchinetti was born at Bologna on July 20, 1519. He studied at his birthplace's famous university and took his doctorate in law there. He entered the service of the powerful Cardinal Alessandro Farnese, held several diplomatic posts, and then was made bishop of Nicastro by Pius IV. As bishop, he attended the Council of Trent and then returned to his diocese to rule it according to the reform decrees of the Council. St. Pius V sent him as nuncio to Venice in 1566. There he worked hard and successfully to forge the Venetian link in the alliance which led to the brilliant victory at Lepanto. When in 1575 he resigned his diocese because of ill health, Gregory XIII made him titular Patriarch of Jerusalem. Gregory used him a good deal and made him a cardinal in 1583.

Gian Antonio Facchinetti was a quiet, studious man who lived a holy and retired life. He devoted himself to his business and his books. He wrote several, including a treatise on the *Politics of Aristotle* and an attack on Machiavelli. Admired as a holy and learned man, he made few enemies and had been among the favorites at several conclaves.

Innocent IX was crowned on November 3, 1591, by Cardinal Andrew of Austria, a Hapsburg prince who had entered the service of the Church. Innocent's election was hailed with joy by the Romans, and the new Pope added to his popularity when his first measures were an attempt to end the food scarcity in Rome and to put down the bandits. Though old and sickly, Innocent threw himself into the work of being pope with youthful vigor and enthusiasm. He plunged into considerations of reform and administration. But he was to be denied the time to do much. He did make one important administrative change when he broke the secretariat of state into three divisions. He reasoned that it was too much work for one cardinal and now appointed a cardinal for France and Poland, another for Spain and Italy, and a third for Germany. Showing great interest in Germany, he re-established the German Congregation and lowered certain papal taxes for Germans.

Innocent was especially insistent on orderly finances. He demanded an efficient administration and rigid economy. Toward Henry of Navarre he maintained the same general attitude as Gregory XIV. It is true that he cut down the sum of money he had been spending on the war against Navarre, but he kept the papal army at the side of Spanish and League forces.

Though feeble, Innocent insisted in making a pilgrimage to the chief churches in Rome during bleak December. He caught cold, and by December 30 he was dead. His body, exposed in St. Peter's, was venerated by the Romans.

Mosaic in the Basilica of St. Paul-Outside-the-Walls, Rome.

CLEMENT VIII

1592-1605

AMONG THE POPES THERE HAVE BEEN POOR MEN in plenty, but Clement VIII was the first bank clerk to obtain the tiara. Ippolito Aldobrandini was born in 1536 at Fano. His father was a political exile from Florence. Ippolito, rescued from the bank by Cardinal Farnese's kindness, studied law at Padua, Perugia, and Bologna. He entered the service of the Church, but his advancement was slow until the reign of Sixtus V. That energetic Pope promoted him rapidly. A cardinal in 1585, Ippolito made a great reputation as legate to Poland in 1588. Thereafter he was considered a possibility for the papacy. Elected on January 30, 1592, he took the name Clement VIII.

Clement was above all a spiritual pope. For years Philip Neri had been his confessor, and now every night the great Oratorian Baronius came to hear the Pope's confession. As zealous as he was devout, the busy Clement would often take a confessional in St. Peter's so that anyone who wished could go to the Pope himself. He did much to promote the forty hours' devotion. He often visited hospitals, not only to comfort the sick and distribute alms, but to check on the food! He was a truly humble man who could accept criticism. His only defect was nepotism.

Clement's great achievement was the settlement of the French problem. Henry of Navarre was gaining steadily. Now that he had accepted Catholicism, opposition melted away. French bishops absolved him, but still at Rome the Spaniards grimly struggled to prevent the Pope from granting Henry absolution. Influenced by spiritual men like St. Philip Neri, the historian Baronius, the the-ologian Toledo, Clement at last on September 17, 1595, solemnly absolved Henry IV. The way was open for peace in France and men felt that the danger of Spanish domination over the papacy was on the wane.

Clement was a great mission pope. Under his vigorous leadership, the enterprising Ricci entered China, the Japanese withstood the first shock of persecution, and Franciscans, Dominicans, and Jesuits reaped rich harvests in the Philippines, Mexico, and South America. The Pope sent missionaries to Persia and Abyssinia and even to the court of the Great Mogul. He strove to reunite the Copts of Egypt and the schismatics of Serbia. He succeeded in bringing some Ukrainians back to the Church by the Union of Brest in 1598. And at home in Europe the tide of Catholic reform was winning back much that had been lost in the bad days. It was a great outpouring of zeal, and to channel and control it Clement set up a congregation of cardinals.

Two famous executions took place in Clement's reign—that of the parricide Beatrice Cenci about whom legend and Shelley have woven an unmerited spell, and that of Giordano Bruno. Clement forbade dueling, revised the breviary, and found time to encourage the poet Tasso and set on foot many works of art. To judge the case of the great Jesuit theologian Luis Molina, whose doctrine on grace had been assailed by Dominicans, the Pope set up a special congregation. Clement took great interest in this matter, but before it could be settled, he was struck down by apoplexy, March 5, 1605.

C. v. d. Passe. Boymans Museum Rotterdam.

LEO XI

1605

LEO XI WAS A MEMBER OF THE FAMOUS MEDICI family and a grandnephew of Leo X. But while Leo X was a thoroughgoing Renaissance prince, his grandnephew was a true Counter-reformation pope. One typical Medici quality was shared by both, a love for literature and art.

Alessandro de' Medici was born in 1555. He was a pious lad and was so fond of the Dominican friars of San Marco that it was thought that this Medici would enter the family of Savanarola. But he chose to become a secular priest and worked quietly in a country parish until 1569, when his relative, Duke Cosimo, sent him as Tuscan ambassador to Rome. At Rome he became a disciple and close friend of St. Philip Neri. In 1573 Alessandro was made, first, bishop of Pistoia, then archbishop of Florence. Though he was forced to remain at Rome, Alessandro saw to it that the reform decrees of Trent were carried out in his archdiocese. Made a cardinal by Gregory XIII in 1583, he was sent by Clement VIII as legate to France in the crucial years 1596-1598. There he became a friend of Henry IV.

Naturally the Spaniards were opposed to him, and his chances for the papacy were so lightly esteemed that Cardinal Avila, King Philip's mouthpiece, did not bother to publish his monarch's veto until too late. Baronius, the great historian, was the favorite at the conclave which began on March 14, 1605; but Baronius had told too much truth too impartially in his history to suit Spanish susceptibility, and so this holy and learned man, to his own joy and relief, was kept from becoming pope. At last after several weeks the majority swung to Medici. Too late Cardinal Avila protested bitterly, but even his own party told him to quiet down. Alessandro accepted and chose to be called Leo XI. The French were jubilant but Leo quickly showed that he intended to be the tool of no ruler.

Easter Sunday, April 17, the coronation day of Leo, was a gala occasion for the Romans, but for Leo himself it was deadly. The old man caught a chill during the ceremonies and soon was in bed fighting vainly for his life. When it became evident that he was going to die, appeals rained on him to make a nephew a cardinal. Although the candidate was worthy, Leo had so great a horror for this rather common papal failing, that he repeatedly refused. Indeed when his confessor added his voice to the general pleading, Leo exchanged his confessor for another more prudent or detached.

Leo XI died piously on April 27, 1605. Although he had ruled so short a time, he managed to lower taxes and send help to the Hungarians in their struggle against the Turks.

Algardi. Church of St. Peter, Rome.

PAUL V

1605 - 1621

B ARONIUS AND ST. ROBERT BELLARMINE WERE among those considered as successors of Leo XI, but finally the cardinals chose Camillo Borghese, who took the name Paul V. Camillo Borghese was born at Rome on September 17, 1550. His family, originally from Siena, claimed relationship with the great mystic, St. Catherine. Trained at Perugia and Padua, Camillo became an expert canon lawyer. In 1596 Clement VIII made him a cardinal and vicar of Rome. No party man, he was agreeable to all factions.

Paul V was a vigorous fifty-two when elected. Pious and learned, charitable and hard-working, he made an excellent pastor. Being a canon lawyer, he believed rules were made to be kept, and his rigorous enforcement of Trent reform decrees caused a deal of rustling in Roman ecclesiastical circles. The same respect for law made him a terror to evildoers. Like Sixtus V he was concerned to put down banditry.

Paul V had a hard time with Venice. The republic's pride seemed to swell in proportion as its power decreased. It had defied church law to forbid the erection of new church buildings and to arrest two clerics. Paul tried to bring the republic to reason, but when the oligarchs stubbornly defied all threats, the Pope excommunicated doge and senate and placed Venice under interdict. The Venetian government defied the interdict by ordering priests to go ahead with services, and when Capuchins, Jesuits, and Theatines refused, the oligarchs expelled them. This quarrel almost flamed into a European war. When Paul tried to raise an army, England and Holland threatened to intervene in favor of Venice. Meanwhile a war of words was bitterly fought. Paolo Sarpi, a Servite who combined brilliant scholarship with a most peculiar notion of Catholic loyalty, wrote furiously against the Pope, while Baronius and St. Robert Bellarmine brought their vast learning into play to defend him. After a year of struggle, shrewd King Henry IV of France mediated to bring peace. Venice gave in as little as possible but enough to justify the Pope in releasing the republic from censure.

Wily King James of England also gave trouble to Paul. He issued a new oath of allegiance which, cunningly worded, was considered acceptable by some Catholics. Paul V had to condemn this oath twice, and even so, it made for division among the English Catholics.

A great patron of art, Paul V succeeded in having Carlo Maderna finally bring the construction of St. Peter's to a grandiose finish. Paul had one defect, nepotism Too fond of his relatives, he made the fortune of the Borghese family. He was, however, a broad-minded and energetic leader in mission activity. He did not discourage the daring innovations of men like Matteo Ricci and Robert de Nobili.

Paul V died of a stroke on January 28, 1621.

Bernini. Borghese Gallery, Rome.

GREGORY XV

1621-1623

IT WAS ALESSANDRO LUDOVISI, AN AMIABLE OLD gentleman of sixty-seven, that the cardinals finally chose to succeed Paul V. He took the name Gregory XV. Alessandro Ludovisi was born of noble parents in 1554 at Bologna. After studies under the Jesuits at the Roman and German Colleges, he took a degree in law at Bologna. After distinguished service in the legal department of the papacy, Alessandro was made a cardinal and archbishop of Bologna by Paul V.

Though Gregory XV was a sick old man and had only a short pontificate, he had great ability, and it had distinction. He began by securing a valuable helper. He made his young nephew Ludovico a cardinal and his right-hand man. Ludovico proved to be a real staff to his old uncle. He was a pious, hard-working, and loyal servant.

There had been much dissatisfaction with the conduct of papal elections. Reform-minded men felt that politics had too much scope in the conclaves. Other popes had given thought to the matter, but sick old Gregory provided a solution. He made a series of regulations so sound that to this day, in essentials at least, they govern the conduct of papal elections. Other popes had set up congregations to regulate missionary activity, but to Gregory XV goes the honor of having established on a permanent basis the great Congregation for the Propagation of the Faith. A congregation is a committee to assist the pope in ruling the Church. This committee oversees, regulates, and fosters mission activities all over the globe.

Gregory XV encouraged the Catholics of Germany, now engaged in the grim Thirty Years' War. He did much to obtain the electorate for Maximilian of Bavaria. By diplomacy he averted war between France and Spain over the Valtelline Pass. Gregory's foreign policy was wholeheartedly Catholic and supranational, and by it he increased the prestige of the papacy.

A pious man himself, Gregory XV did much to promote devotion to the saints. Devotion to St. Joseph and St. Anne, so popular in modern times, received great impetus from Gregory. He also defended the doctrine of Mary's Immaculate Conception, though he did not feel that the time was ripe for declaring it a dogma. In a great ceremony at St. Peter's he canonized Ignatius Loyola, Teresa of Avila, Francis Xavier, Philip Neri, and a Spanish farmer named Isidore. Naturally, so devout a pope was interested in enforcing the reform decrees of Trent.

Gregory XV suffered a great deal from gout and from stone. A fever carried him off on July 8, 1623. His pontificate was short but glorious.

Church of St. Ignatius, Rome.

URBAN VIII

1623-1644

WHEN MAFFEO BARBERINI BECAME POPE Urban VIII in the conclave of 1623, his comparative youth, his vigor, his talent, his goodness, all seemed to indicate a long and successful pontificate. Urban's pontificate was indeed long, but it was scarcely successful.

Maffeo Barberini was born at Florence in 1568 of wealthy parents. Educated by the Jesuits, he dabbled in literature, but for a profession turned to law. After taking his degree at Pisa, Maffeo joined the pope's legal staff and rose to be archbishop of Nazareth, cardinal and bishop of Spoleto. He twice served as nuncio to France, did much there for reform, and won the friendship of Henry IV.

Urban VIII faced a difficult situation. The Thirty Years' War was going full blast when he was elected, and it was still dragging on at his death. Urban has been criticized for not giving sufficient support to the Catholic-Hapsburg side, but it must be remembered that the situation was not simple. At that, Urban did give support to the Hapsburgs, though he probably could have given more. To have excommunicated Louis XIII or his powerful minister, Richelieu, might have had dangerous results. Still, whatever Urban's responsibility or lack of it, the fact remains that at the outset of his pontificate the tide of the Catholic Counterreformation slapped menacingly at Protestant bastions. At his death that tide had receded.

Urban had small success in other fields also. He started and lost a war with the Farnese family over the territory of Castro, a proceeding which did not enhance the papacy's prestige. He is connected with the famous condemnation of Galileo. The imprudent astronomer had been lured by his enemies on to the field of theology and as a result had been condemned by a commission of the Holy Office. He gave in, however, and suffered small inconvenience in a sort of house arrest. The affair was unfortunate; for though papal infallibility was not involved, papal prestige was. And the more the Copernican theory was accepted, the more the condemnation of Galileo gave a pretext to rationalist calumnies that the Church is opposed to science.

Urban "reformed" the breviary, a reform that brought anguished cries from many quarters. Even his magnificent baroque building program under the directing genius of Bernini is somewhat overshadowed by Pasquino's cruel pun. Urban had taken bronze from the Pantheon to make cannons and to build the baldachin of St. Peter's. And to this day his name is "immortalized" in Pasquino's words "What the barbarians spared the Barberini destroyed."

Urban, however, was a good pope and did accomplish something. He condemned Jansen's dangerous book, *Augustinus*. He encouraged foreign missions. He favored the beautiful forty hours' devotion. He severely curtailed unofficial canonizations. He missed the chance of becoming a great leader in the field of religious orders for women when he discouraged Mary Ward and her English ladies.

Urban VIII died on July 29, 1644.

Bernini. Palazzo dei Conservatori, Rome.

INNOCENT X

1644 - 1655

WHEN GIAMBATTISTA PAMFILI BECAME POPE Innocent X, he was promised thorns; and the promise was kept. Innocent's was indeed a thorny pontificate.

Giambattista Pamfili was born in Rome on May 6, 1574, of noble parents. After taking a degree in law at the Roman University, he entered the papal service. Appointed nuncio to Naples, he displayed a great talent for diplomacy. Urban VIII made him a cardinal and sent him as nuncio to Spain. Though seventy years old, he was a favorite in the conclave of 1644. Elected, he chose the name Innocent X.

Innocent X was a healthy old gentleman who was pious and capable. His charity was outstanding; during a famine which afflicted Rome in 1649, he outdid himself in centering efforts to give bread to his people. But Innocent, like Urban, was given to nepotism. Since none of his nephews proved to have much ability, he came to depend on his sister-in-law, the grasping Olimpia Maldaichino.

In 1648 the miserable Thirty Years' War was finally ended by peace congresses at Münster and Osnabrück. Innocent sent the capable Fabio Chigi to safeguard Catholic interests, but the nuncio was not listened to in the congress, and when Innocent himself protested against unjust measures in the treaties, he was unheeded. A new era had begun, the era of secularism.

Innocent had trouble in Portugal too. In 1640 a rising had chased out the Spanish Hapsburgs and re-established the House of Braganza. Fearing to offend Spain, neither Urban VIII nor Innocent X acknowledged John of Braganza in any way, even by confirming his appointments to Portuguese bishoprics. The result was that soon Portugal had only one bishop left—a sad state of affairs.

Innocent X is a pope who helped Ireland. To the embattled Irish grimly fighting for faith and fatherland, Innocent sent the capable nuncio Rinnuccini. In return the Irish sent to the Pope the banners captured by Owen Roe O'Neill at Benburb. But the shrewd Rinnuccini was unable to prevail over Anglo-Irish folly, and Innocent lived to hear of the victories and butcheries of Oliver Cromwell and of the sad fate of the Irish Catholics.

The Pope had more success in his efforts to help Venice against the Turks. To aid the Venetians in their fight to hold Crete, Innocent sent them ships, men, and money.

The Jansenists, although Jansen's *Augustinus* had been condemned by Urban, still gave trouble. Innocent took five propositions from Jansen's book and condemned them, but even this did not quash these peculiar heretics.

Innocent, though an old man, enjoyed good health and was a hard worker. Not until December 1654 did his health give way, and even then he tried to keep going. On January 7, 1655, Innocent X died. His burial was cheap and simple because the sister-in-law, whom he had enriched, refused to pay for the customary pomp.

Velasquez. Doria Gallery, Rome.

ALEXANDER VII

1655-1667

IN THE CONCLAVE OF 1655 APPEARED A GROUP OF cardinals who pledged themselves to remain independent of personal ties and political connections. This group, called by the Spanish ambassador "the flying squadron," did much to preserve the independence of the Church for many a conclave. On April 7 after a long conclave, Fabio Chigi was elected. Fabio took the name Alexander VII.

Fabio Chigi was born in Siena on February 13, 1599. Like Urban VIII he wrote verse, but adopted the law as a profession. He rose to be vice-legate of Ferrara, bishop of Nardo and apostolic visitor to Malta. He made a great reputation as a diplomat when Urban VIII sent him to Cologne as nuncio in 1639. Innocent X made him envoy to the peace congress at Münster in 1648, and though Fabio could accomplish little of what the Pope wanted, he so pleased Innocent that he made Fabio secretary of state and cardinal.

Alexander VII was a sincere man, gifted with ability and endowed with piety. He tried to avoid nepotism, but he later relaxed his great strictness toward his relatives. He proved his charity when the plague hit Rome in 1656. Alexander, who had been staying at healthy Castel Gandolfo, hastened back to Rome to take personal charge of his people. He not only adopted sensible sanitary measures but calmed the people by frequent public appearances.

Alexander helped Venice and the Empire in the fight against the Turks. He succeeded in prevailing upon Venice to allow the return of the Jesuits, banished for their loyalty to Paul V. His relations with young Louis XIV were not so happy. When some Corsican papal soldiers, not unprovoked, attacked the French embassy in Rome, Louis took advantage of the occasion to humiliate the Pope. Alexander was most conciliatory, but when he resisted demands which he could not in justice grant, Louis annexed Avignon and prepared to march on Rome. Poor Alexander had to give in; with the Grand Duke of Tuscany mediating, peace was signed at Pisa.

Alexander also had trouble with the Jansenists. The French appealed to him for a formula of submission which the Jansenists should sign. Alexander sent them the formula, but a number of Jansenists including the nuns of Port Royal refused to sign it. The Pope also rebuked a few moral theologians who had advanced laxist opinions.

In 1655 Alexander had received the most celebrated convert of the age, Queen Christina of Sweden. This talented daughter of Catholicism's great enemy Gustavus Adolphus had given up a throne for the faith.

Alexander VII died on May 22, 1667. His memory is kept fresh by Bernini's magnificent colonnade, for it was Alexander who is responsible for its erection.

P. v. Schupper. Boymans Museum, Rotterdam.

VNVS ALEXANDRO NON
SVFFICIT ORBIS.

P. Mignard pinx. Roma.   P. Van schuppen, sculpebat Parisius 1661.

CLEMENT IX

1667-1669

CLEMENT IX MIGHT BE CALLED THE PLAYWRIGHT pope because before his elevation to Peter's throne he had been a successful dramatist. Giulio Rospigliosi was born at Pistoia in 1600. Educated at the Jesuit Roman College, he went on to take doctorates in philosophy and theology. But he loved poetry and letters. His plays, which reflected the influence of the great Calderón, seem to have been quite successful. His creative pen did not hinder his rise in the papal service. The cultured Urban VIII and his powerful nephews made much of him. Giulio went to Spain as nuncio and served there with distinction for nine years. On his return his fortune paled, for he had been too closely attached to the family of Urban VIII to receive honors from Innocent X. Alexander VII, however, made him secretary of state and cardinal. Amiable, gifted, and popular, Giulio was a favorite in the conclave of 1667.

He chose to be called Clement IX and with reason, for he was clement by nature. This pope loved conciliation. His favorite expression seemed to have been, "We concede." His relations with the cantankerous Jansenists go far to prove this. Four French bishops had refused to sign the formula of faith drawn up by Alexander VII. These peculiar heretics did not want to leave the Church but neither did they want to leave their erroneous opinions. The result was a series of mental gymnastics and contortions. At this time they were accepting the Pope's condemnation of the five propositions taken from Jansen's book, but refusing to believe that the propositions had been maintained by Jansen—at least in the sense the Pope had condemned them. Since Jansenism had become fashionable, it was thought best to allow the stubborn four bishops to sign a less explicit formula of faith. This face-saving device was adopted by Clement, who was served poorly by his less than shrewd French nuncio. This compromise, which produced only a lull in the Jansenist storm, is called the Clementine Peace.

Clement also tried hard and finally with success to end the war between aggressive Louis XIV and Spain. The Pope wanted all Christians to help the Venetians save Crete. He himself made great efforts but in vain. Candia, the last Christian stronghold, fell in 1669.

Clement was a very attractive character. Free from nepotism, he was devoted to his flock. He personally heard confessions in St. Peter's. He lowered the tax on flour, and he reorganized papal finances. Stingy only with himself, he spent much to help the Venetians and was a generous patron of artists, and a kind father to the poor.

Clement IX died on December 9, 1669.

Maratta. Rospigliosi Gallery, Rome.

[476]

CLEMENT X

1670 - 1676

I N THE CONCLAVE WHICH FOLLOWED THE DEATH of Clement IX, Emilio Altieri was scarcely an outstanding favorite. He had been made a cardinal only a few weeks before, and he was an old man of almost eighty. Yet it was Emilio Altieri who emerged from this long and stubbornly contested conclave as Pope Clement X. The conclave which had begun on December 20, 1669, ended only when there was a general swing to Altieri on April 29, 1670. Even then Altieri objected that he was too old, but he was overruled and installed as Pope Clement X.

Emilio Altieri was born at Rome on July 13, 1590, of a noble and pious family. Educated at the Roman College, he went on to take his law degree at the Roman University. Although he became a brilliant attorney, Emilio entered the ranks of the clergy and rose to be bishop of Camerino in 1627. Urban VIII made him governor of Loreto and apostolic visitor for the Papal States. Innocent X sent him as nuncio to Naples, where he ran into the torrid situation created by Masaniello's rising against Spain. He fell into disfavor with Innocent and returned to his diocese, but Alexander VII recalled him to Rome, and Clement IX made him a cardinal at long last on November 27, 1669.

Clement X, though an octogenarian, was able to work hard. Indeed his hours dismayed the members of his household, for he always rose two hours or more before daybreak and was often at work by five o'clock in the morning. Clement was very charitable and did much for the poor, not only by generous alms but by social legislation. He tried to improve agriculture and foster industry in the Papal States. At first Clement did not do much for his relations, but as he grew older he grew softer toward them.

Clement was much preoccupied with the problem of Poland. That fair land was not only invaded by Turks but torn with civil dissension. The Pope despatched a nuncio to work for unity. At the death of the weak young King Michael the Pope worried lest a Protestant mount the Polish throne. Clement was relieved when the fighting nobleman John Sobieski was elected. To help Sobieski the Pope sent a subsidy, and he had the satisfaction of hearing that Sobieski had defeated the Turks near Lvov. Clement tried hard to get the Powers to help the hard-pressed Poles.

Clement had to suffer from French arrogance, but he entertained hopes that the French invasion of Holland would aid the Church. He sent a legate to the peace congress of Nijmegen.

The octogenarian Pope had celebrated the jubilee of 1675, but in 1676 dropsy attacked Clement, and on July 22, 1676, a fever carried him off.

The British Museum, London.

BLESSED INNOCENT XI

1676-1689

WHEN THE CARDINALS CHOSE BENEDETTO ODEscalchi to be Pope Innocent XI, they chose a man of piety, ability, and firmness who was to be one of the greatest seventeenth-century pontiffs.

Benedetto Odescalchi was born at Como on May 16, 1611. After studies at the local Jesuit school, Benedetto took law at Rome and Naples. His ability caused him to rise in the papal service. He loved his work at Rome so much that he even resigned his bishopric of Novara to work on at Rome.

Innocent XI devoted himself to saving Austria from the Turks. He pleaded with the kings of Europe to help distressed Austria, but that Christian monarch, Louis XIV, actually encouraged the Turks! Poland's fighting King John Sobieski was of nobler stuff, but it took an incredible amount of patient diplomacy on the Pope's part to get help for the Emperor. Innocent's work was rewarded. Sobieski and his Poles, Lorraine and his Germans smashed the Turks as they were about to break through Vienna's walls. It was a great victory and a decisive one. After 1683 the Turks will be on the defensive.

Innocent XI was strong yet prudent. He needed both virtues in his dealings with Louis XIV. The Sun Monarch was riding too high to brook opposition even from a pope. He had extended the *regale* in an unfair and illegal manner. The *regale* was an ancient privilege the French kings had of taking over the revenue and the right of appointments to benefices in vacant dioceses. Though this dangerous custom had been restricted far back in the Middle Ages, Louis was now extending it in an arbitrary manner. Innocent protested in three successive briefs, but Louis answered by having an assembly of subservient clergymen pass the famous Four Articles of 1682. This manifesto of Gallicanism was, to say the least, highly objectionable. Innocent was put out, and relations were badly strained. Nor were they eased by the petty and arrogant resistance of the French king to Innocent's attempt to confine ambassadors' right of asylum to reasonable limits. And the Pope was not impressed by the clumsy and highhanded treatment of French Protestants which culminated in the revocation of the Edict of Nantes. Innocent also was too prudent to encourage James II in his well-meant but untimely actions in favor of English Catholics.

Although the pious Pope was for a time fooled by the Spanish pseudo-mystic Miguel de Molinos, he soon condemned quietism. He also condemned a number of laxist propositions. As an administrator Innocent XI was outstanding. By the practice of severe economy he soon managed to balance the papal budget, indeed even to produce a surplus, and on top of that to lower taxes! Rigidly conscientious, Innocent avoided nepotism.

Innocent XI died on August 12, 1689. He was beatified by Pope Pius XII on October 7, 1956.

Monnot. Church of St. Peter, Rome.

ALEXANDER VIII

1689-1691

CARDINAL PIETRO OTTOBONI ENTERED THE CONclave of 1681 a favorite. At first, however, the Austrian and French monarchs objected to him. The French tried to force Pietro to promise certain concessions before they allowed his election. But Pietro replied that while he wished to have peace with France, he would make no sacrifice of his honor. The French gave in, and Pietro was elected. He took the name Alexander VIII.

Pietro Ottoboni was born in Venice on April 22, 1610. After studies in law at Padua, Pietro entered the papal service. He distinguished himself at Rome by his ability to get business done quickly. Made a cardinal by Innocent X, Pietro joined the "flying squadron," that group of Cardinals who remained independent of countries or persons in the conclaves. One reason why the French were slow to accept him was the loyalty with which he had backed Innocent XI in his struggle with Louis XIV.

Alexander VIII was a man of great charm. Kind and affable he was somewhat a contrast to the rather severe Innocent XI. Festivals which Innocent had frowned on once more delighted the Romans. Unfortunately, he was also a contrast to his predecessor in the way he treated his relatives. Innocent had been rigid against nepotism. Alexander loved to shower favors on his family. But at least he did not allow his relatives to influence papal policy.

A Venetian, Alexander was naturally interested in helping the Republic of Venice in its fight against the Turks. This was in line with usual papal policy and presented only the problem of raising the necessary money. The War of the League of Augsburg, however, made the Pope's position delicate. On the one side was Catholic France; on the other, Catholic Austria. Since Louis was helping exiled King James II, French propagandists loudly proclaimed the struggle a holy war. Alexander, not impressed, was careful to observe neutrality. Indeed relations between the Sun Monarch and the Pope were far from good.

Innocent XI had secretly excommunicated Louis XIV and Louis in turn had once more taken Avignon from the Pope. Worse still, Louis insisted on appointing to vacant bishoprics the subservient clergymen who had signed the objectionable Four Articles of 1682. Since Innocent XI and Alexander VIII refused to confirm these appointments, the number of vacant French bishoprics began to mount. Alexander's last act undertaken on his deathbed was a brief which declared the Four Articles null and void, and pleaded with Louis to act like a Catholic.

Alexander also condemned two odd propositions held by two individual Jesuits, and thirty-one Jansenist propositions.

Though seventy-nine when elected, Alexander was still vigorous. In 1691, however, he failed rapidly and by February 1, 1691, Alexander VIII was dead.

Sanmartino. Church of St. Peter, Rome.

INNOCENT XII

1691-1700

"INNOCENT BY NAME AND NATURE TOO." THUS Robert Browning describes the last seventeenth-century pope in *The Ring and the Book*. In saying this, Browning spoke not only as a poet but as a historian, for Innocent XII was indeed a man of deep piety. Elected as a compromise after a heated conclave had gone on for five months, Antonio Pignatelli accepted and chose the name Innocent XII.

Antonio Pignatelli was born at Spinazzola near Naples on March 13, 1615. Educated by the Jesuits at the Roman College, Antonio early earned a striking reputation for goodness. After taking a degree in law, Antonio entered the papal service and under a succession of popes served brilliantly. Under Clement X, however, Antonio's career was checked. He was recalled from the nunciature at Vienna to be made bishop of Lecce. But the check was only temporary. Antonio went on to become a great cardinal-archbishop of Naples.

Innocent XII was seventy-six when elected, but he had a commanding appearance and excellent health. He accomplished much in his nine years' pontificate. First of all, he put through a reform which, though excellent, was acutely painful to papal finances. He abolished the purchase of offices. Then Innocent, completely free from nepotism himself, struck a great blow at this occupational failing of many popes. By a bull of 1692 Innocent made nepotism very difficult, a reform which increased papal prestige even with Protestants.

Innocent had some trouble with Jansenists both in France and Holland. He also had to condemn the quietism of Madame Guyon and a book by the noble archbishop of Cambrai, Fénelon.

Innocent XII reaped the fruit of the noble firmness of Innocent XI and the firm patience of Alexander VII in dealing with the arrogant Sun Monarch. Louis, now contending in arms with half Europe, felt the need of coming to an agreement with the Pope. After a deal of backing and filling, Louis finally in 1693 revoked his order enforcing the Four Articles of 1682 on the French clergy. This was a triumph for papal rights over royal absolutism.

Innocent showed moderation in his foreign policy. He did not protest when Ernest Augustus of Hanover became a ninth imperial elector. He gained a diplomatic triumph at the Peace of Ryswick when a clause safeguarded Catholic rights in restored territories. He welcomed the conversion of Frederick Augustus, elector of Saxony and king-elect of Poland. He deplored the persecution in Ireland and begged funds for the distressed Irish.

Innocent XII approved of the fateful step by which Charles II of Spain passed over his Austrian kinsmen to choose Philip the grandson of Louis XIV as heir to his far-flung Spanish possessions.

Innocent XII died piously on September 27, 1700.

Mosaic in the Basilica of St. Paul-Outside-the-Walls, Rome.

CLEMENT XI

1700-1721

WITH CHARLES II OF SPAIN ABOUT TO DIE childless, leaving his vast dominions behind him, it was only human that the great Catholic powers should strive to secure a friendly pope. The conclave of 1700 dragged on, lost in mazes of Bourbon and Hapsburg intrigue, until the news that Charles of Spain had at last died spurred the cardinals into a feverish search for a compromise. They elected Gian Francesco Albani but Albani refused to accept the burdensome honor, and it took several days and the combined arguments of four theologians to overcome his reluctance. He chose to be called Clement XI.

Gian Francesco Albani was born at Urbino on July 22, 1649. Educated at the Roman College, he became a distinguished scholar and a prominent member of Queen Christina's Academy. He made a number of translations from Greek into Latin. Not until he was twenty-eight did Gian Francesco enter the papal service; indeed he did not become a priest until a few months before his election. Secretary for briefs under Innocent XI, he was made a cardinal by Innocent XII. He was a strong right hand to Alexander VIII in his struggle with Louis XIV and to Innocent XII in his war on nepotism.

Clement XI was only fifty-one when elected, and his vigorous health, great talents, and sincere piety promised a long and successful pontificate. Clement's pontificate was indeed long, but it was not too successful. The age was turning irreligious. Bayle and Fontenelle were already writing, Voltaire and Rousseau were growing up. Clement worked hard, but even a capable pope can do only so much.

Clement's first problem was to guide the Church through the stormy War of the Spanish Succession. Although he tried to remain neutral, he was at heart an adherent of the Bourbons, and had advised Innocent XII to approve the will of Charles II leaving Spain to Philip of Anjou. When the Austrians invaded the Papal States, the Bourbons gave no aid, and Clement was compelled to halt the Austrians by acknowledging Charles of Hapsburg as king of Spain. Now, of course, Louis and grandson Philip grew indignant, but Clement could do nothing about it. The war ended at Utrecht and Rastatt with the Pope pretty much ignored.

Another vexing problem was that of the revived Jansenists. Under the leadership of Pasquier Quesnel, the Jansenists were becoming a source of great alarm. By his bulls *Vineam Domini* in 1705 and especially the famous *Unigenitus* in 1713, Clement XI struck a mighty blow at the cat-lived sectaries.

Clement XI also took measures against the Malabar and Chinese rites, but the vexed question dragged on. Keenly interested in missionary activity, this zealous Pope fostered numerous seminaries to provide workers for the foreign missions. He tried to win over Czar Peter the Great, but was not too severely disillusioned when Peter's interest in Roman Catholicism died out after his decisive victory at Poltava.

Clement XI died March 19, 1701.

Maratta. The Prado Museum, Madrid.

[486]

INNOCENT XIII

1721-1724

THE ELECTION OF MICHELANGELO DE' CONTI aroused nostalgic memories of the Middle Ages, for Michelangelo was of the same family which had produced three thirteenth-century popes: Innocent III, Gregory IX, and Alexander IV. Yet the very circumstances of the election showed how wide was the chasm which separated the politically powerful papacy of Innocent III from the badgered papacy of Innocent XIII. The favorite in the conclave had been Cardinal Paolucci, the late Pope's secretary of state; but when his election seemed near, Cardinal Althan in the name of Emperor Charles VI declared him excluded. Then the cardinals turned to Michelangelo de' Conti, who took the name Innocent XIII.

Michelangelo de' Conti was born May 13, 1655, in the family's ancestral castle at Poli. He studied first with his uncle, the bishop of Ancona, and then with the Jesuits at the Roman College. In the papal service he rose to be governor of Ascoli, Frosinone, and Viterbo. In 1695 he was sent as nuncio to Switzerland and made titular archbishop of Tarsus. From 1698 to 1709 he served as papal ambassador to Portugal, where he won the esteem of Lisbon court. In 1706 he was made a cardinal. After his return from Portugal he became bishop of Osimo, and later was given the see of Viterbo. Sickness compelled him to resign his see in 1719.

A stout old gentleman of sixty-six, Innocent XIII was known for his blameless life, his ability, and his strong sense of dignity. This sense of dignity added to ill health tended to make the Pope somewhat hard to see. But if officials and envoys found Innocent difficult, the poor discovered in him a father.

Innocent XIII granted the investiture of Naples-Sicily to Emperor Charles VI, but his kindness was not rewarded. The Hapsburgs continued to encroach on ecclesiastical rights, refused to restore Comacchio, and ignored the Pope's rights in Parma.

The irrepressible Jansenists hoped that Innocent would not be as firm against them as had been Clement XI. They were disappointed. Innocent insisted on submission to the bull *Unigenitus.* Though he met with much insubordination in France, the old Pope stood firm. Even worse was the situation in Holland, where stubborn Jansenists got themselves a bishop and revolted from the Pope. To this day a small Jansenist sect exists in Holland.

The sore problem of the Chinese rites remained to vex Innocent. The Pope misled by a volley of attacks on the Jesuits, actually threatened to forbid the order to receive novices. The Jesuit General Michelangelo Tamburini, however, presented a convincing defence; but before Innocent could act on the matter he was dead. Meanwhile the Church in China reeled under persecution.

Never well, Innocent was attacked by dropsy in February 1724. On March 7 Innocent XIII died.

BENEDICT XIII

1724-1730

IF PIETRO FRANCESCO ORSINI WAS BORN WITH A silver spoon in his mouth, he did not wait long to throw it away. Born February 22, 1649, at Gravina, Pietro Francesco was the heir not only to his father, the duke of Gravina, but to his uncle, the duke of Bracciano. But the noble young man spurned these great Orsini titles for the white habit of a son of St. Dominic. Though he overcame family opposition to become a Dominican friar, it was difficult in that aristocratic age for a highborn ecclesiastic to escape honors. Clement X forced the red hat on the reluctant young friar, and soon he was ruling the see of Manfredonia, then Cesena, and finally Benevento, where he spent thirty-eight years. He loved Benevento and earned the title of the city's second founder by his loving charity after the disastrous earthquakes of 1688 and 1702.

When the conclave of 1724 was worn out with over two months of ineffectual wrangling, the cardinals turned to the spiritual-minded Dominican archbishop. But Orsini refused, and it took a great deal of argument and the pressure of the Dominican general to bring him to accept. He chose to be called Benedict XIII.

One of the first problems faced by Benedict was the accusation against the Jesuits of insubordination in the matter of the Chinese rites. Benedict, after mature consideration, convinced by Jesuit General Tamburini's defence, acquitted the Jesuits and quashed the stern decree of Innocent XIII.

The Jansenists, disappointed in Innocent XIII, had great hopes in Benedict. These sectaries tried to shelter themselves behind the massive form of St. Thomas and claimed that they held Dominican doctrine on grace. The Dominican Pope disabused them. He issued a bull filled with praise of St. Thomas and of the Dominicans, but of words of encouragement for Jansenists there were none. Benedict insisted on submission to Clement XI's bull *Unigenitus,* and what is more, he secured the submission of the Jansenist's champion, Cardinal de Noailles, archbishop of Paris. At long last it was the beginning of the end for Jansenism.

Benedict was less happy in his dealings with the Powers. The shrewd politicos of the despots' courts wrung extreme concessions from the good-natured and inexperienced Pontiff. Even less happy was Benedict in routine government. Though he tried hard to improve ecclesiastical discipline and was most devoted to the spiritual side of his work, he was too loyal to his friends. He placed implicit confidence in a cleric he had brought from Benevento, Cardinal Coscia. Coscia was a grafter, and under him the papal curia deteriorated. Benedict, busy insisting that priests should not wear wigs and blessing altars, was deaf to the clink of gold talking loudly to Coscia and his associates.

Benedict XIII died February 23, 1730. His virtues were his own, his defects were due to inexperience and lack of aptitude for government. After all, he had not wanted to be pope. Benedict left the Church a legacy most precious. He first approved of the Congregation of the Cross and Passion of Our Lord founded by St. Paul of the Cross.

Church of Santa Maria sopra Minerva, Rome.

[490]

CLEMENT XII

1730-1740

ANOTHER CONCLAVE IN WHICH THE REPRESENTAtives of the Great Powers battled through weary months ended on July 12, 1730, with the election of feeble old Lorenzo Corsini, who took the name Clement XII.

Lorenzo Corsini was born at Florence on April 7, 1652, of an ancient family, the most famous member of which was St. Andrew Corsini. Lorenzo passed up the paternal estates to enter the clerical ranks. After studies at the Jesuit Roman College, he took a doctorate in law at the University of Pisa. He proved to be a hard-working, capable papal official and was made treasurer by Innocent XII and a cardinal by Clement XI. His experience in papal government made him shrewder than his predecessor, but his age and health greatly handicapped him. Seventy-nine at his election, Clement soon went completely blind and for a large part of his pontificate had to rule from his bed. But there was still plenty of mental vigor in the old man, and he had the happy faculty of choosing honest and competent officials.

Clement began by making a clean sweep of the corrupt Beneventan officials and an example of the chief offender, Cardinal Coscia. He imposed a large fine and a prison sentence on that grafter, an act of salutary severity. Under Clement XII the government of the Papal States improved, though some may object to his use of the lottery as a painless way of raising money.

In dealing with the Great Powers, Clement suffered the same humiliations as most eighteenth-century popes. His suzerain right over Parma was ignored, and Bourbons vied with Hapsburgs in putting pressure on the old Pope. The Pope did not find the eighteenth-century despots particularly benevolent.

Clement continued to insist on Jansenist submission to the bull *Unigenitus*, and he had the satisfaction of receiving the submission of a group of French monks. But while the Jansenist menace subsided, another and greater evil loomed up over the age, the onrush of infidelity. Clement struck at this new enemy by his bull of 1738 which condemned Freemasonry. This he did because all too often the un-Christian and anti-Christian tendencies of the age were channeled into the lodges. Masonic religiosity was well suited to the deism of the age. Clement did much to further mission activity. He had the joy of receiving back to Catholic unity a large number of Monophysite Copts.

As pope, Clement continued the patronage of art and letters he had begun as cardinal. He did much to beautify Rome.

Cardinal Alberoni, the one-time ambitious and all-powerful prime minister of Spain, was now like Napoleon in Elba as a papal official. He attacked little San Marino and annexed it to the Papal States. Clement XII, learning that this was unjust, restored its liberty to the mountain republic.

After almost ten years Clement XII finally succumbed to a number of diseases on February 6, 1740.

Bracci. Borghese Museum, Rome.

BENEDICT XIV

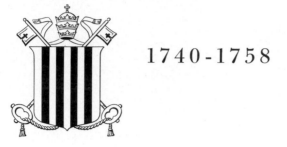

1740-1758

"IF YOU WANT A SAINT, TAKE GOTTI; IF YOU WANT a statesman, take Aldovrandi; if you want a good fellow, take me." Thus spoke Prospero Lambertini in his jocose way at the painfully long conclave of 1740. When the cardinals took Lambertini at his word, they got a good fellow, all right; but much more, a good priest and a good pope. Lambertini accepted and chose to be called Benedict XIV.

Prospero Lambertini was born March 31, 1675, at Bologna of an ancient family which had produced two members worthy of beatification. After studies under tutors and the Somaschi Fathers, Lambertini took doctorates in law and theology when only nineteen. He entered the papal service and rose to be titular archbishop of Theodosia, archbishop of Ancona, and finally of Bologna. As archbishop he proved to be a great spiritual leader. A cardinal in 1728, he became a trusted adviser of the popes. Yet his power to work was so great that with all his work he was able to be a scholar and at the same time to enjoy the company in which his good humor and brilliant wit made him popular.

Even as cardinal, Benedict XIV had been known for his tendency to conciliation. As pope he went the limit in his efforts to appease the power-greedy monarchs. If Benedict's extensive concessions to Spain, Naples, and Sardinia aroused criticism, at least they proved his deep desire for peace and harmony.

Since Benedict was known to be so conciliatory, Jansenists and infidels hoped much from him. Of course they were disappointed. Although he was a little easier on the Jansenists, he continued to demand submission to the bull *Unigenitus.* When Benedict accepted Voltaire's dedication of his drama *Mahomet,* infidels hoped that at last they had a pope suitable to the eighteenth century. But Benedict soon showed his awareness of the time's danger by condemning the works of Voltaire and other infidels and by renewing Clement XII's prohibition of Freemasonry.

Benedict XIV stands out among modern popes as a great legislator. Many-sided, he improved not only canon law but liturgy and ecclesiastical discipline. A scholar himself, he founded four academies in Rome and worked hard to improve the University of Rome. He gave the Church a glorious new order when in 1749 he approved the rule of St. Alphonsus Liguori's Redemptorists.

In the field of mission activity Benedict put a definite end to the arguments about the Chinese rites by ordering all missionaries to take an oath against the forbidden practices. Benedict secured the reunion of the Egyptian Melchites, and by skillful diplomacy averted a storm among the Maronites.

Since his pontificate had begun with the War of the Austrian Succession and ended with the Seven Years' War still raging, Benedict's diplomatic problems were many and delicate. Through them all he so conducted himself that at his death on May 3, 1758, Benedict XIV was mourned even by Protestants. The English Protestant Horace Walpole observed that Benedict "restored the lustre of the tiara. By what art did he achieve that glory? Solely by his virtues."

CLEMENT XIII

1758-1769

STORM SIGNALS WERE FLYING AS THE CARDINALS met in conclave on May 15, 1758. The spirit of the age which frowned on religious orders and papal control had entered the courts of the Catholic kings. A strong pope was needed, but the Powers wanted a compliant one. When France vetoed the capable Cardinal Cavalchini, the conclave chose Carlo Rezzonico. Rezzonico unwillingly accepted and chose to be called Clement XIII. Rezzonico was known to be good and capable, but somewhat timid and indecisive. What the Powers did not take into consideration was the man's deep spirituality. Timid perhaps by nature he was fearless when principle was at stake.

Carlo Rezzonico was born at Venice on March 7, 1693, of a noble family. Educated by the Jesuits at Bologna, he took his degree in law at Padua. In the papal service Carlo rose steadily. He became cardinal-deacon in 1737, bishop of Padua in 1743, and cardinal-priest in 1747. As bishop he distinguished himself by his spiritual leadership. He held an important synod in 1746, and he issued a beautiful pastoral on the priestly life.

Clement XIII had to face the terrible onslaught of the Catholic powers on the Jesuits. This order, with its fourth vow of special obedience to the Pope and its insistence on solid Christian education, was a cinder in the eye of "enlightened" despots and their ministers. As followers of a false "enlightenment" they were offended by the Jesuits' staunch Christianity; as believers in the all-powerful state, they objected to an order so devoted to the Pope. Regalists and Jansenists, Gallicans, and infidels found one common hate—the Jesuits.

The opening gun of the anti-Jesuit attack was fired by Carvalho, the powerful minister of weak King Joseph of Portugal. In 1759, with great brutality, he suppressed the order in Portugal. Clement XIII objected, but his remonstrances only provoked a rupture of diplomatic relations between Portugal and the Vatican. France suppressed the Society of Jesus in 1763 and Spain drove the Jesuits out in 1767. Spain's puppets, the king of Naples and the duke of Parma followed suit. Parma's action, coupled with other anticlerical decrees, especially irritated Clement XIII because the Pope was rightfully the suzerain of Parma. Consequently the courageous Clement issued a monitorium declaring the Parma decrees null and void. This act of justice aroused the despots to frenzy. France seized the papal territory of Avignon. Naples took Benevento. Then in a joint note the Bourbon and Portuguese courts bluntly and forcefully demanded that the Pope withdraw his monitorium and suppress the Society of Jesus.

Greatly upset by these broils, Clement's health gave way and on February 7, 1769, the brave but gentle Pope died. Clement XIII has been called the eighteenth-century Hildebrand, and he deserves the title. While Clement's memory is held in honor by all who admire courage and adherence to principle, it is especially revered by Catholics because Clement XIII is the pope who, against much opposition, established the beautiful feast of the Sacred Heart of Jesus.

Mengs. Royal Pinacoteca, Bologna.

CLEMENT XIV

1769-1774

THE POWERS BALKED BY COURAGEOUS CLEMENT XIII were determined that this time they would get a pope they could handle. The pressure put on the conclave was overwhelming. Lists were prepared rating the cardinals according to their acceptability to the kings. And pressure was necessary, for most of the cardinals were independents who thought first of the good of the Church. The man who emerged from all this as pope was the Conventual Franciscan, Cardinal Lorenzo Ganganelli. As the only religious in the college of cardinals, and a man who had been fond of the Jesuits, Ganganelli was acceptable to the independents. But he had also won the favor of the Crowns by assuring them that in his opinion a pope could suppress the Jesuits with a good conscience and that a pope should try to please the Powers.

Giovanni Vincenzo Ganganelli was born October 31, 1705, at Sant' Arcangelo near Rimini. In 1723 he became a Friar Minor Conventual, taking the name Lorenzo. Fra Lorenzo showed excellent talent and rose to a high position in his order. He was made a consultor of the Holy Office by Benedict XIV and a cardinal by Clement XIII.

Clement XIV, as Ganganelli chose to be called, promptly threw over the firm policy of Clement XIII. He fairly rained concessions on the greedy despots. But though mildly pleased, the courts were not satisfied with the new Pope, because Clement showed no eagerness to suppress an order so devoted to the Pope, so praised by popes down to his predecessor, Clement XIII. Years went by

—no suppression. Now the Bourbon courts had made it a point of honor to force the Pope to prove that they were justified in their tyrannical acts against the Jesuits by suppressing them. Charles III of Spain was especially insistent, and in 1772 to bring about the suppression he sent the aggressive and capable Jose Moñino as ambassador to the Holy See. This determined driver was given one task—to secure the suppression of the Jesuits. Coldly, insistently, he cajoled, badgered, and bullied poor Clement until the harried Pope cried out in distress. When Maria Teresa, busy marrying off her daughters to Bourbons, abandoned the Jesuits, Clement gave in.

In the words of Pius XII: "Under the pressure of the unjust and envious secular forces of the times, in a sea of dark forebodings, a Father's hand sacrificed it [the Society of Jesus] for the tranquility of the bark of Peter."

By the brief *Dominus ac Redemptor*, Clement suppressed the Society of Jesus. Appeasement rarely works, and though France restored Avignon and Naples Benevento, Clement soon found that the monarchs' arrogant interference with Church rights only mounted after the destruction of the Jesuits.

Clement did enjoy some gleams of consolation, especially when Mar Simeon, a Nestorian patriarch, led six bishops back to Catholic unity.

Clement XIV felt his unhappy position keenly, and under the strain his health gave way. He died September 22, 1774.

Christopher Hewetson. Victoria and Albert Museum, London.

[498]

PIUS VI

1775-1799

"AS HANDSOME AS HE IS HOLY," THUS THE RO-mans described Gianangelo Braschi, who as Pius VI succeeded Clement XIV. Gian-angelo Braschi was born December 25, 1717, at Cesena of noble parents. After studies with the Jesuits, the bright young man took his degree in law when only seventeen. Braschi caught the eye of Benedict XIV, who offered him a canonry in St. Peter's, but the handsome lawyer was engaged to be married. At last he decided to become a priest; his fiancée entered a convent. Braschi became pa-pal treasurer, and in 1773 a cardinal. Not yet sixty and full of vigor, Pius VI was to need all his reserves of holiness and strength to face what was coming.

Pius found the Jesuit problem still haunting the Vatican. He released some Jesuits imprisoned by Clement, but friendly as he was, he dared not do more. When he showed an inclination to allow the Society of Jesus to remain alive in Russia, the Bour-bons stormed at him so fiercely that he had to in-sist on breaking up this last Jesuit province. Cath-erine of Russia, however, refused to allow the brief of suppression to be published in her dominions, and since Clement had so arranged matters that the suppression brief would become law in a dio-cese only when the bishop published it, the Jesuits lived on in Russia. In 1780 Pius VI, by word of mouth, approved of their existence.

The Jesuit problem was the least of the Pope's worries. Emperor Joseph II, flailing about in a frenzy of misdirected zeal, was limiting papal power, suppressing monasteries, and changing church regulations in a manner which led sardonic Frederick II to call him "my brother the sacristan." However amusing to old Fritz, Joseph's vagaries were more than an annoyance to Pius. He actually made the long trip to Vienna to try to talk sense into the imperial meddler, but in vain. Joseph's brother, Leopold, Grand Duke of Tuscany, was just as bad, and one of his bishops, Ricci of Pistoia, held a synod in 1786 which passed some outrageous decrees. Pius condemned these in 1794. The ec-clesiastical electors—the prince-bishops of May-ence, Trèves, and Cologne—got into the act in 1786 by issuing a Febronian manifesto known as the Punctuation of Ems. Febronianism was the doc-trine taught by Von Hontheim (who wrote under the pen name Febronius) which claimed that the pope was not superior to all bishops and that Cath-olic kings should reduce the papal power.

The king of Naples saw to it that Bourbons con-tributed to the Pope's misery, but all these troubles faded in the intense glare of the French Revolu-tion.

Pius grew increasingly alarmed as the revolution-ists multiplied anti-Catholic measures. The con-fiscation of Church property, the suppression of papal taxes, the patient Pope let go by, but he se-cretly protested against the suppression of religious orders, and he had to speak out when the little bunglers of the Constituent Assembly tried to drive France into schism with the Civil Constitution of the Clergy. Pius saw the Church in France driven underground as blood-drunk Jacobins drove priests and nuns to the knife. Soon the Revolution flowed over the Alps and Napoleon forced the Pope to ac-cept the harsh Treaty of Tolentino in 1797. But the Directory, more cruel than Napoleon, soon took over Rome and made the old Pope a prisoner. Dragged to France, Pius was greeted by the people with affectionate enthusiasm. His health gave way at Valence, and a prisoner and an exile, Pius VI died August 22, 1799. His last words were: "Lord forgive them."

Canova. Church of St. Peter, Rome.

PIUS VII

1800-1823

W HEN PIUS VI DIED A PRISONER IN FRANCE, there were those who sneered that Pius VI would be Pius the Last. But the cardinals got together at Venice and elected another and great Pius in the person of Barnaba Chiaramonti, who took the name Pius VII.

Barnaba Chiaramonti was born at Cesena, August 14, 1740, of noble parents. At the age of sixteen Barnaba entered a Benedictine monastery and took the name Gregorio. He became abbot of San Callisto in Rome, but Pius VI took him from the monastery to make him bishop of Tivoli, then bishop of Imola, and in 1785 a cardinal. When the French overran Imola in 1797, Cardinal Chiaramonti earned the admiration of Napoleon by sticking to his post. By interceding with Generals Augereau and Macdonald, he saved his flock from misery; and in a Christmas address he said: "The democratic form of government is not . . . repugnant to the Gospel. On the contrary it exacts all the sublime virtues which are learned only in the school of Jesus Christ." These words, now commonplace, took vision and courage to utter in 1797 with the smell of blood still rank on French "democracy."

Pius VII had the great joy of restoring religion in France. After difficult negotiations a concordat was signed in 1801 between the Holy See and the French Republic. Pius had the gift of choosing and trusting capable assistants, and it was one of these, the outstanding diplomat Cardinal Consalvi, who went to Paris and pulled the concordat through tight places. In spite of the fact that Napoleon played the weasel with his "organic articles," the concordat was a great blessing. No wonder Pius VII took the extraordinary step of going to Paris for Napoleon's coronation in 1804.

Napoleon, however, soon gave the Pope plenty of trouble. He kept insisting that Pius take sides in the war against England. Bitterly disappointed at the Pope's neutrality, he finally seized the Papal States in 1809. When Pius boldly excommunicated him, Napoleon had the Pope carried off a prisoner to France. In 1813 Napoleon first isolated Pius from his trusted advisers and then bullied him into making concessions which the Pope bitterly regretted. It was not long before Pius withdrew these, and not long either before Napoleon, with his empire collapsing, freed the Pope. By May 27, 1814, Pius was back in Rome.

Two events show the prestige and independence Pius had gained for the papacy. On August 7, 1814, Pius VII restored the Society of Jesus throughout the world. The second act was in the temporal sphere. Cardinal Consalvi represented the Pope at the Congress of Vienna, and from that assembly of the Powers he brought back the entire Papal States to Pius VII. Only the outside territories like Avignon in France and Benevento in Naples were excepted.

A third act shows why Pius deserved so much prestige. A true Vicar of Christ, he sheltered the broken family of Napoleon, and he even interceded with the British to soften the lot of his old persecutor on St. Helena.

When Pius VII died on August 20, 1823, Gallicanism and Jansenism were becoming historical memories. It is true that infidelity still threatened, but many intellectuals were now reading Christian apologists like Chateaubriand and Lammenais rather than Voltaire and Rousseau.

David. The Louvre, Paris.

LEO XII

1823-1829

"WILL YOU ELECT A SKELETON?" ASKED GAUNT old Cardinal Della Genga when the conclave of 1823 swung toward him. But the skeleton proved to have plenty of life, and as Leo XII gave the Church guidance for almost six years.

Annibale della Genga was born of a noble family at Castello della Genga near Spoleto. After studies at Osimo and Rome, Della Genga was ordained priest in 1783 at the age of twenty-three. Pius VI took the young priest into his service, and he soon showed his tact by preaching a funeral oration for Emperor Joseph II. To give a sermon on Joseph without compromising the Church or offending Hapsburg ears was no easy task, but Della Genga managed it. In 1792 he became a canon of the Vatican, and in 1793 titular archbishop and nuncio to Lucerne, then nuncio to Cologne, and in 1805 nuncio extraordinary to the Diet of Ratisbon. Napoleon did not care for Della Genga and tried to have him removed, but Pope Pius refused to recall his faithful envoy. In 1808 Della Genga accompanied Cardinal Caprara to Paris on a mission to see if Napoleon could be brought to see reason. But the Emperor was in no mood for compromise. After Napoleon carried off the Pope to France, Della Genga retired to a monastery and spent some quiet years drilling a choir of peasants in plain chant. Recalled from rustic obscurity when Pius returned to Rome, he was sent to Paris to convey the Pope's congratulations to Louis XVIII. Consalvi, who was already representing the Pope in Paris, imagined that Della Genga's mission was an insult, and this caused some unpleasantness.

A few years later Pius made Della Genga a cardinal and bishop of Sinigaglia. Since he could not stand the Sinigaglia climate, Della Genga soon resigned his see and became vicar of Rome.

At the conclave the Powers favored Castiglioni, but among the cardinals Severoli was the favorite. Cardinal Albani in Austria's name declared Severoli excluded, but this barefaced interference boomeranged. At once the independent cardinals elected the "skeleton."

Leo XII showed that he was a big man by making use of Consalvi's advice until the great diplomat died. Much alarmed by the march of infidelity, Leo took measures against indifferentism. He also condemned societies which distributed unauthorized editions of the Bible. Secret societies were a thorny problem for the old Pope. Though he condemned them, they continued to flourish right under his eyes. To crush them Leo sent Cardinal Rivarola to Ferrara and Rivarola ruled with an iron hand. But down to his death the secret societies, especially the Carbonari, troubled the Pope.

Though Leo was a conservative old gentleman, his pastor's heart could not endure the sight of empty bishoprics in South America. In spite of his own inclinations and of Bourbon wrath, he implicitly recognized the independence of the South American republics by treating with them about the appointment of new bishops.

Leo XII had tried to rule the Romans like a strict old-fashioned father, and his strict old-fashioned methods were resented. Leo XII died February 10, 1829, a good priest, if not a great ruler.

Church of St. Peter in Vatican, Rome.

PIUS VIII

1829-1830

A MILD, MODERATE MAN, FRANCESCO XAVERIO Castiglioni had been the favorite of the Powers in the conclave of 1823. He was again the favorite in 1829, and this time he was elected. He chose the name Pius VIII.

Francesco Xaverio Castiglioni was born of a noble family at Cingoli on November 20, 1761. Educated by the Jesuits, he took law at Bologna and Rome. At Rome he worked with his professor, Devoti, on his book dealing with canon law. When Devoti became bishop of Anagni, he took his promising pupil along as vicar-general. Castiglioni later served as vicar-general for Bishop Severoli of Angoli, an interesting association because in the conclave of 1823, Severoli was vetoed by Austria in an effort to help Castiglioni become pope. Bishop of Montalto and later bishop of Cesena, Castiglioni ran into trouble with the occupying French forces when he refused to swear allegiance to Napoleon as king of Italy. He was arrested by the French for his boldness, but after Napoleon's downfall, Pius VII made him a cardinal and bishop of Frascati.

Pius VIII was a spiritual man of deep conscientiousness. To avoid the least suspicion of nepotism, he refused to allow his relatives even to come to Rome. He abandoned Leo's repressive policy in running the Papal States, but he repeated Leo's condemnations of indifferentism, unauthorized Bible societies, and secret societies.

Although it lasted for less than two years, the pontificate of Pius VIII saw some outstanding events. Rome was overjoyed to learn in 1829 that the great Daniel O'Connell had at last overcome mountains of bigotry and walls of prejudice to wrest from a reluctant government freedom for British and Irish Catholics.

Prussia, however, gave the Pope cause to worry. That country on its march to empire had gobbled up large sections in the Rhineland, Silesia, and Poland with Catholic populations. It was now trying to prevent children of mixed marriages from being brought up as Catholics.

Pius, faced with weak German bishops and a bullying government, went to the utmost limits in concession by allowing priests to assist passively at mixed marriages in which the proper promises had not been given. But even this rather amazing concession did not satisfy the Berlin bureaucrats.

Pius was greatly alarmed by the revolutions of 1830. It was only with reluctance that he brought himself to recognize the revolutionary government of France's King Louis-Philippe. The revolution in France set up tremors throughout Europe, but the gentle Pius VIII did not have to worry about the situation, because on December 1, 1830, he died.

Mosaic in the Basilica of St. Paul-Outside-the-Walls, Rome.

[506]

GREGORY XVI

1831-1846

GREGORY XVI HAS BEEN PILLORIED AS THE POPE who so hated modern developments that he would not allow railroads in his dominions! There is some truth in that. As a temporal ruler Gregory was reactionary—no doubt about it. But as a spiritual ruler Gregory carried on a pope's real work with distinction.

Bartolommeo Cappellari was born of a noble family at Belluno in Northern Italy on September 8, 1765. Against family opposition he entered a Camaldolese monastery in 1783, taking the name Mauro. Ordained a priest in 1787, he taught philosophy and theology to the young religious. In 1799 he wrote a defense of papal rights and papal infallibility. Pius VII made him abbot of St. Gregory's Monastery on the Coelian Hill, but when the French took over Rome, Cappellari retired to a Camaldolese monastery and once more taught philosophy.

Called to Rome by Pius VII after his restoration, Cappellari twice refused bishoprics. Leo XII made him a cardinal in 1825 and prefect of the Congregation for the Propagation of the Faith. In the conclave of 1830 Cardinal Giustiniani was the favorite, but when Spain vetoed him, the cardinals elected the pious Camaldolese Cardinal Cappellari. He took the name Gregory XVI.

Gregory XVI continued to live like a monk. It was his cross that, a simple pious religious, he was plunged into the vortex of a revolutionary storm which was rocking Europe. In the Papal States, revolutionists were triumphant in Bologna, and in Rome itself a rising was barely nipped in the bud. Unable with weak papal forces to put down the rebels, Gregory called on Austria, and Austrian bayonets restored order in Bologna. Jealous of Austrian intervention, the French seized Ancona. It took years to get the French and the Austrians out again. The Powers took this opportunity to read the Pope a lecture on government and to urge certain reforms on him. Gregory, however, could scarcely take seriously such requests from notorious despots like Metternich and Czar Nicholas I. Indeed, down to the last Gregory believed in ruling his States with a strong hand. Impatient with his own liberals, Gregory had little sympathy even for Catholic rebels like the Belgians and Poles. Yet he did what he could to soften the lot of the oppressed Poles, even speaking very bluntly to Czar Nicholas when that despot visited Rome. Gregory condemned the slave trade in 1839, and he adopted a sane policy of dealing with *de facto* governments which was to save much embarrassment for the Holy See.

In 1832 Gregory had the unpleasant task of condemning a number of errors connected with the brilliant Catholic periodical *L'Avenir*. He disliked doing this because the writers were great defenders of papal rights against statism. He also condemned a synthesis of Kantian and Catholic thought dreamed up by a Bonn professor named Hermes, and when another professor, Bautain of Strasbourg, attacked the proper sphere of reason, the vigilant Gregory condemned him.

Though Gregory suffered much from political troubles and from the persecution of his children in Spain, he enjoyed the consolation of seeing the Church win a great fight with Prussian bureaucracy in the mixed-marriage question.

Gregory XVI died June 9, 1846.

Gaillard. Boymans Museum, Rotterdam.

GREGOR. XVI. PONT. MAX.

PIUS IX

1846-1878

THE CARDINALS, WHO FELT THAT GREGORY XVI had been a little severe, fixed their eyes on the amiable Cardinal Mastai-Ferretti, but the Austrians also had their eyes on him—cold eyes. Austria's representative Cardinal Gaysruck reached the conclave with a veto for Mastai-Ferretti, but it was too late. He had already been elected and had chosen the name Pius IX.

Giovanni Mastai-Ferretti was born at Sinigaglia on May 13, 1792. Refused admission to the pope's noble guards because of epileptic attacks, he turned to the study of theology, and when his epilepsy passed away, Giovanni was ordained a priest. In 1823 he accompanied the apostolic delegate to Chile, and thus became the first pope to have visited the new world. As archbishop of Spoleto, he handled the revolt of 1831 with kind diplomacy. He persuaded the rebels to down arms and the avenging Austrians to be merciful. Transferred to Imola in 1832, he became a cardinal in 1840.

Pius IX at once started to live up to his liberal reputation. He promptly issued an amnesty for political prisoners and made numerous reforms in the Papal States. The delighted Romans took the horses from his carriage to pull it themselves, while girls strewed flowers in the way. But, however numerous his concessions, they were not sufficient to please the radicals, and when Pius refused to join the war against Austria in stormy forty-eight, his popularity plummeted. On November 15 the radicals stabbed the Pope's prime minister, Rossi, and practically besieged Pius himself. Disgusted, Pius fled to Gaeta, leaving Mazzini and his minions to take over at Rome. In 1849 a French army restored papal authority in Rome, and in 1850 back

came Pius IX, thoroughly cured of liberalism.

The restoration was not to last. In 1860 Cavour and Garibaldi wrested most of the Papal States from Pius, and in 1870 when the French garrison was withdrawn from Rome, the Piedmontese moved in. Pius, after making a token resistance, confined himself to the Vatican. He refused to accept the situation, and Italo-papal relations remained fundamentally strained until 1929.

If Pius was unfortunate in the temporal sphere, he showed himself a vigorous leader in spiritual matters. In 1854 he declared it a dogma that Mary was conceived without original sin. This was an assertion of papal infallibility and a challenge to a materialistic age which had little belief in original sin. In 1864 Pius issued the encyclical *Quanta cura* and with it a syllabus of seventy errors. This was no sudden whim of the Pope's, but a measure which had been widely discussed and long pondered. Since it was an outspoken and even harsh indictment of many nineteenth-century trends, it caused a sensation. Indeed the syllabus has been an arsenal of anti-Catholic arguments for many who misjudged or misinterpreted it.

The greatest event of the pontificate of Pius IX was the Vatican Council. This, the twentieth ecumenical council, proclaimed as a dogma that the pope when speaking *ex cathedra*, that is, as pope, can make no mistake in solemn declarations of what must be believed in matters of faith and morals. Pius had to adjourn the council in the summer of 1870 owing to the outbreak of the Franco-Prussian War.

Pius IX died, a very old, tired man, on February 7, 1878.

Mosaic in the Church of St. Lawrence, Rome.

LEO XIII

1878-1903

IT WAS IN A GLOOMY ATMOSPHERE THAT THE first conclave since the fall of Rome gathered, but that conclave produced a pope who would lift up the hearts of Catholics, and indeed of all men of good will throughout the world, the great Leo XIII.

Gioacchino Pecci was born at Carpineto on March 2, 1810. After education at the Jesuit college in Viterbo, the Roman College, and the College for Nobles, Pecci hesitated about becoming a priest; but in 1837 he made his decision and plunged wholeheartedly into the priestly life.

In 1838 Gregory XVI sent Pecci to rule Benevento as a legate. He gave the district a taste of good government by running down the bandits who infested the area. Moved to Perugia in 1841, Pecci started a bank for the poor and introduced other reforms. In 1843 he went as nuncio to Belgium, and when recalled in 1845 he was made bishop of Perugia. Pius IX made him a cardinal in 1853. Pecci ruled his diocese in such a manner as to foreshadow his career as pope. He insisted on religious instruction and on the study of Aquinas. He spoke out against the social evils of the day. When the Piedmontese took Perugia from the Pope in 1860, anticlerical politicians made life miserable for Catholics. Pecci stood up to them, registering eighteen protests; yet such was his diplomacy that despite his manly defense of church rights, he got along with the government. In 1877 Pius IX called him to Rome and made him *camerlengo*. After Pius died Pecci succeeded him as Leo XIII.

Leo found the Church under fire in many countries, and except for Italy, his policy was one of conciliation. He made the road to Canossa easy for Bismarck, who called off his anti-Catholic campaign. He tried to get French Catholics to come down from a royalist dream world to republican reality. He soothed the English by frowning on the vigorous methods of Irish agrarian reformers. He even won a few concessions for the Czar's oppressed Catholic subjects. When in 1885 Germany and Spain accepted Leo's arbitration in a dispute over the Caroline Islands, it was a token of the Pope's new prestige.

It was as a leader in ideas that Leo is truly great. He saw the need for emphasizing the value of St. Thomas, and he recalled Catholic thinkers to the study of Aquinas. He encouraged biblical studies, and while rightly cautious about certain "critical" tendencies of the age, he left the way open to continued improvement. To historians Leo was a true friend. He opened the Vatican archives to research, and he urged scholars to tell the truth and tell it whole.

Above all, by his encyclical *Rerum novarum*, Leo brought Christ into the factories and slums. As Christ once scourged the buyers and sellers in the temple, so now did His Vicar flail those who defiled God's human temples by cruel economic and social measures. Critical of both extreme socialist and capitalist solutions to the day's problems, Leo laid down Christian norms to guide men to a better social system. Published in 1891, *Rerum novarum* was hailed by Catholics and non-Catholics alike.

Though Leo XIII died on July 20, 1903, his influence lives on.

A. Chartran. Portrait, 1891.
St. Joseph's Seminary, Yonkers, New York.

ST. PIUS X

1903-1914

SHORTLY BEFORE HIS DEATH, WISE OLD LEO XIII told Cardinal Sarto that he would be the next pope and would do much for the Church. Leo was right on both counts.

Giuseppe Sarto was born at Riese on June 2, 1835. His father, a cobbler, also served as janitor in the parish church and postman. A bright, pious lad, Giuseppe studied under his pastor, then at a nearby secondary school, and finally at the seminary in Padua. Ordained in 1858, Sarto worked hard and well as parish priest. In 1884 he became bishop of Mantua and did so much for that run-down diocese that Leo XIII made him a cardinal and moved him to Venice. Both as bishop of Mantua and patriarch of Venice, Sarto proved to be a zealous pastor and a highly capable administrator. In the conclave of 1903 Rampolla took an early lead, but Austria vetoed him and the cardinals turned to Sarto. He accepted unwillingly and took the name, Pius X.

Pius was not to enjoy peace. The French Republic was waging bitter war on the Church. The government suppressed religious orders, attacked religious education, and in 1905 unilaterally denounced the concordat, separated Church and State, and confiscated Church property. When Pius forbade Catholics to form the associations required by the government to run the churches, things looked desperate; but the government backed down from its extreme position, and though extremely poor, the French Church struggled on. In Spain and Portugal, too, Pius had the grief of seeing the Church attacked.

Attack from outside was not the greatest danger.

Some priests, infected with bad philosophical ideas and worse theological ones, were striving to make modernism prevail within the Church. Modernism does not mean a devotion to television or atomic research, but a very dangerous adaptation of the dogmas of faith to fads of the day. Pius banned the works of leading modernists, and by his encyclical *Pascendi* and his decree *Lamentabilis*, published in 1907, he struck hard at modernism. Determined to tear it out by the roots, Pius followed these measures by demanding from every priest an oath against modernism. Under this attack the dangerous movement wilted, and the Church was saved much trouble by the saintly Pope's alert vigilance.

Pius took as his motto Paul's expression: "to restore all things in Christ." He made every effort to live up to it. He reformed Church music. He reorganized the papal court and Italian seminaries. He reformed the breviary. He started the tremendous work of codifying canon law. But above all, Pius will be remembered as the Eucharistic Pope. He wished children to receive Holy Communion when they reached the age of reason, and in a return to the early Christian practice he begged Catholics to receive Holy Communion frequently.

Pius X predicted that a great war would break out in 1914, but when it came it nearly broke his great heart. He died on August 20, 1914. The people, with touching devotion, kept thronging around the kind-hearted Pope's tomb. Miracles were worked. In June, 1951, Pius XII beatified and on May 29, 1954, canonized this great Pope of the Eucharist.

BENEDICT XV

1914-1922

WITH BATTLE SMOKE HANGING HEAVY OVER Flanders fields and Carpathian Mountains, the Cardinals realized that the next pope should be a diplomat. The man chosen was Giacomo della Chiesa, who took the name Benedict XV.

Giacomo della Chiesa was born at Genoa on November 21, 1854. He studied law at Genoa and theology at Rome's Gregorian University. Ordained in 1873, he became a doctor of sacred theology in 1879. Giacomo entered the papal diplomatic service and soon caught the eye of the great diplomat Rampolla. When Rampolla became secretary of state, Giacomo joined him as a valuable assistant. In 1901 he was made under-secretary of state. Pius X continued him in this office until 1907, when he made Giacomo archbishop of Bologna. Here Della Chiesa proved to be a capable and excellent spiritual leader. Pius X made him a cardinal in 1914.

Benedict XV faced a difficult task. As father of all Catholics he had to maintain strict neutrality. He succeeded so well that while excitable Allies called him pro-German, excitable Germans called him pro-Ally. Benedict constantly pleaded for peace, but not until 1917 did he judge the time ripe for a formal attempt to mediate between the Powers. Certain German elements welcomed the papal overtures, but after a good deal of excited buzzing and rumor mongering, it became sadly evident that not even the hideous blood bath of three years had brought either side to be really earnest in a desire for a fair and square peace. The Pope did his best to lessen the miseries of the frightful conflict. Thanks to Benedict, disabled prisoners were exchanged through neutral countries, and later, after weary efforts, Benedict succeeded in getting wounded and sick prisoners sent to recuperate in the comparatively well-off neutral countries. The Pope also tried to help suffering civilians. His intercession enabled deported Belgians to return home. He begged mercy for the poor Armenians, and he donated money freely to the suffering all over war-torn Europe.

After the armistice Benedict continued his good work. He pleaded with the Allies to stop the murderous blockade of Germany which was causing so much suffering to women and children. At the Pope's command a collection was taken up in Catholic churches throughout the world to help hungry children.

Benedict urged Wilson to use his great influence for a just peace, but the Pope expressed disappointment at the results of the Paris Peace Conference. Although excluded from the League of Nations, the Pope praised the idea behind it, and at a time of excited nationalist hate, he pleaded for recognition of human solidarity.

In 1917 Benedict promulgated the great new Code of Canon Law but he gave the credit to his illustrious predecessor, Saint Pius X.

Influenza carried off this man of peace on January 22, 1922. Among his last words were "We offer our life to God on behalf of the peace of the World." Rightly has Benedict XV been called "The good Samaritan of humanity."

Fabres. The Vatican.

PIUS XI

1922-1939

ACHILLE RATTI, LIKE PIUS X, HAD PARENTS WHO were just plain folks. Born at Desio on May 31, 1857, he went to the seminary at Milan and then on to the Gregorian University to take his doctorate in theology. After a few years in a parish, Father Ratti was put to work at the Ambrosian Library in Milan. Here he made such a reputation that Pius X in 1912 made him assistant librarian at the Vatican and soon after head of the great Vatican Library. Scholar that he was, Ratti was no pale bookworm. He was an expert, indeed something of a champion, in a difficult and dangerous sport, mountain climbing.

In 1918 Benedict XV sent Ratti from his research to serve first as visitor and then as nuncio to stormy Poland. For a scholar in his sixties to go on his first diplomatic mission to a country coming to life after over a century of partition was something of a task. But the old historian successfully handled a situation perplexing enough to trouble a supreme court full of Solomons. He showed courage too. When other diplomats fled before Trotsky's onrushing Red Army, Ratti remained to hear the thunder of Soviet guns in threatened Warsaw. He had the satisfaction of seeing the heroic Poles strike back and rout the Communists.

In 1921 Benedict made Ratti a cardinal and archbishop of Milan. A few months later Benedict was dead and Ratti succeeded him. He chose the name Pius XI.

Pius XI faced a sadly disturbed postwar world, a world threatened and tempted by fascism and communism. Far from yielding to discouragement Pius strove mightily to rally the forces of good and to remedy the times' evils. To remind a material-istic world of the primacy of the spiritual, Pius established the beautiful feast of Christ the King. In thirty encyclicals he shed light on the difficulties of the day. Outstanding were his encyclicals on education, marriage, and above all, on the social problem.

Though he fought manfully for principle, Pius was quick to extend the hand of friendship, and his pontificate is notable for a whole series of concordats. The outstanding event of this kind was, of course, the Lateran Treaty of 1929, which put a long-desired and satisfactory end to the Roman question.

Pius XI deeply appreciated the oneness of mankind. He ardently fostered mission activity and was eager to see native clergy, headed by native bishops, take over as many mission fields as possible. In what has been called the Magna Carta of the missions, Pius allowed certain customs which, once open to superstition, had become secularized with the centuries. He was keenly interested in the separated Eastern churches and yearned for reunion with them. His great heart was angered by base attacks on the Jews, and he bluntly told the world that to be antisemitic was to be un-Christian. It is characteristic of the man that one of his first acts was to continue feeding starving Russians in spite of Soviet ingratitude, and one of his last was to lash out at racist laws.

Pius had much sorrow. He grieved over the sufferings of his children in Mexico, Russia, Spain, and Germany. But he was not soured. Just before he died on February 10, 1939, Pius offered his life for the peace of the world.

Ury Müller. Collection of Cardinal Ferretti, Rome.

PIUS XII

1939-1958

MARCH 1939 WAS A TIME OF HIGH TENSION AS Hitler, unsatisfied with his Munich mouthful, was preparing to rend Europe. Faced with this situation the cardinals quickly elected Eugenio Pacelli, the late Pope's capable and experienced secretary of state.

Eugenio Pacelli was born at Rome on March 2, 1876, of a family devoted to the papal service. Eugenio, eager to become a priest, worked so hard at the Capranica Seminary that his health gave way and he was forced to leave the seminary. Leo XIII allowed young Pacelli to live at home while completing his courses and in this way Pacelli reached ordination in 1899.

Eugenio began his priestly career with a combination of parish work and professional study. He took a degree in Canon and Civil Law at the Apollinaris. Cardinal Rampolla, on the watch for talent, took Pacelli into his department of state. Pius X made him a monsignor and set him to work on the titanic task of re-codifying canon law. During the First World War Pacelli gained valuable experience helping Benedict XV and Cardinal Gaspari in their humane efforts.

In 1917 Benedict sent Pacelli as nuncio to Munich to forward the Pope's peace plans. Although Pacelli managed to secure an interview with the Kaiser, nothing came of it, and Germany went down in 1918. Red revolution swept Munich and Pacelli got a bitter taste of life under the hammer and sickle. Several times the Reds threatened him, but he managed to calm them down. Once an automobile in true gangster fashion roared by his house blasting it with machine-gun fire. When the Weimar Republic was established, Benedict created a nunciature at Berlin and sent Pacelli to be the first nuncio. He got along well with the Germans and left with regret in 1929 to be made a cardinal. The next year he succeeded the aged Gaspari as Secretary of State. Few popes have traveled as widely as Pius XII, and he is the first pope to have visited the United States.

In the gloomy days of the Second World War, Pius tried hard to keep a door open to peace. On December 24, 1939, he gave the world a sane five-point peace program. If he could not stop the war, at least he could and did relieve the sufferings of the miserable millions of refugees and war victims. Pius called on Catholics all over the world and especially in comparatively comfortable America to share with the needy. Pius also did much to save Rome from destruction; but he saved more than buildings. While Gestapo agents glared, Jews, refugees, and all manner of hunted folk found safety in the tiny Papal State.

After the war Pius continued to stress the need for a just peace. A realist, the Pope understood the thorny difficulties faced by the United Nations, but he approved of it and encouraged all good works tending to foster international understanding. As pastor of souls Pius keenly felt the need of modern man for spiritual sustenance. To make it easier for people to attend Mass and receive Holy Communion, Pius greatly relaxed the old rules governing the time of Mass and the fast necessary to receive Holy Communion. He also simplified the breviary.

Pius XII died on October 9, 1958. For suffering people of all faiths or no faith he had been a true father.

JOHN XXIII

1958-1963

ANGELO RONCALLI WAS BORN NOVEMBER 25, 1881, at Sotto il Monte near Bergamo in Northern Italy. His parents were small farmers, and in a large family Angelo learned the give and take which later made him so excellent a diplomat. After work in the fields, Angelo studied for the priesthood at the seminary in Bergamo. He won a scholarship to the Pontifical Seminary at Rome. Ordained in 1904, he said his first Mass in St. Peter's.

Young Father Roncalli returned to his diocese as secretary to Bishop Radini-Tedeschi and Professor of Church History and Apologetics at the Bergamo seminary. Somehow he found time to work for a diocesan organization of Catholic women and for a residence hall for students. World War I interrupted this busy life. Father Roncalli became Sergeant Roncalli of the medical corps and later Lieutenant Roncalli of the chaplains' corps.

When the guns fell silent, Roncalli returned to his old life, but not for long. Benedict XV called him to Rome to work for the important Congregation for the Propagation of the Faith. In 1925 Pius XI made him an archbishop and appointed him Apostolic Visitor to Bulgaria. Ten years later as Apostolic Delegate to Greece and Turkey, Roncalli moved on to Istanbul. There he spent most of World War II, and in that neutral city, so rife with suspicion and intrigue, Roncalli managed to get along with everybody. He did what he could to help the Greeks suffering from famine and occupation and to assure the Turks of his affection. These years in the Near East afforded him many contacts with members of the separated Eastern Churches, contacts which fanned the flame of his desire to heal the sad breach between so many Eastern Catholics and the See of Peter.

His success in Istanbul led Pius XII to send Roncalli as nuncio to France, a France seething with passions aroused by the disasters and heroisms of the war. Taking up his post in Paris early in 1945, Roncalli by delicate tact and warm sympathy managed to minimize difficulties between outraged Gaullists and nervous Vichyites, a task to appall the suavest of diplomats. He also displayed his grasp of the need for international understanding by his friendly attitude as unofficial observer at UNESCO. His ability to make friends and win respect for the Church was shown in a striking way in 1953 when Pius XII made him a cardinal. He received the red hat from his good friend President Auriol, a socialist.

Shortly after, Cardinal Roncalli was made Patriarch of Venice. He proved himself to be a people's patriarch, always accessible. Vigorous yet kindly, he led his flock in the path of Christian virtue.

Such was the man the cardinals elected Pope on October 28, 1958. John XXIII, as he chose to be called, soon showed himself to be an energetic man with far-reaching plans. On January 25, 1959, he announced plans for a general or ecumenical council which would be called the Second Vatican Council. He opened it on October 11, 1962. By then he knew of his own fatal illness. His death on June 3, 1963, followed a long agony. It evoked an astonishing wave of sympathy from all quarters which was a response to his exceptionally warm and outgoing personality.

Pope John XXIII, in the Papal Palace, Vatican City.
Wide World Photos.

[522]

PAUL VI

1963-1978

GIOVANNI BATTISTA MONTINI WAS BORN IN Brescia, Lombardy, on September 27, 1897. His father was a successful journalist and a member of the Italian Chamber of Deputies. As a young man the future pope had such poor health that he was allowed to attend the seminary as a day student. He was ordained at Brescia on May 29, 1920, and sent to Rome for further studies. Having entered the papal diplomatic service he was sent to Warsaw as secretary to the nuncio. His health failed and he returned to Rome, where he was assigned to the secretariat of state.

By 1937 he was under secretary, and by 1952 acting secretary, of state. During World War II he was in charge of the Vatican's work for refugees and prisoners of war. He was there all during the occupation of Rome when there was a real danger the Germans would take the Pope and his chief aides with them when they were driven north. On December 1, 1954, Pius XII made him Archbishop of Milan, the largest and, after Rome, the most important diocese in Italy.

Since Pius XII made no cardinals after 1953, the Archbishop of Milan was not a member of the conclave of 1958; but he was one of the first cardinals made by John XXIII in December of that year. He played a prominent role in the Council and since he was clearly the favorite of John XXIII, his election as his successor (June 21, 1963) was almost taken for granted.

The pontificate of Paul VI will always be linked with the Council. His was the task of bringing it to a successful conclusion (December 8, 1965) and of starting, though he knew he could not finish, the implementation of its decrees. One of its major themes was collegiality, or the collective responsibility of all the bishops, under the pope, for the general welfare of the Church. He wished to govern with and through the various national episcopal conferences. He was determined to hold firmly to basic Catholic teaching on faith and morals and to allow any other changes circumstances might suggest. Since conditions vary greatly from place to place and some people had unusual notions of the changes the Council had intended, there was some confusion about what could be done.

He will be remembered for his work toward the reunion of all Christians, his reaching out to the immense multitudes who belong to non-Christian religions or to none, his internationalizing the Roman Curia, and his untiring work for peace. He was deeply interested in the emerging nations of the Third World and supported every effort for their social advancement. He was the first pope to visit every continent, and the first since St. Peter to visit the Holy Land. The first papal visit to the Western Hemisphere was his visit to the United Nations Headquarters in New York on October 4, 1965. His attempt to establish better relations with communist governments had few results and aroused mixed feelings in various Catholic circles. His exceptional capacity for work lasted to the end, which came quite suddenly on August 6, 1978.

Pope Paul VI, December 22, 1965.
Wide World Photos.

[524]

JOHN PAUL I

1978

ALBINO LUCIANI WAS BORN ON OCTOBER 12, 1912, IN WHAT is now Canale d'Agordo, in the diocese of Belluno in the Dolomite Alps of Northern Italy. His father, a confirmed socialist who did not oppose his son's vocation to the priesthood, was a migrant worker and then a glassblower in Venice. The family, like those of Pius X and John XXIII, was always poor, and Albino knew from personal experience the hardships suffered by the modern urban proletariat. He was the first pope chosen from their ranks.

After studies in the local seminary and Rome, he was ordained on July 7, 1935. He was assigned at once to teach theology in the seminary, of which he was made vice-rector, and by 1947 he became vicar-general of Belluno. In December 1958 John XXIII made him Bishop of Vittorio Veneto, near Venice, and as a special mark of friendship consecrated him himself in St. Peter's in Rome. Paul VI made him Patriarch of Venice in December 1969, and Cardinal in March 1973.

In his years in Belluno, Vittorio Veneto, and Venice, Cardinal Luciani shunned the limelight so successfully that if he had died a week before his election as pope it would hardly have been noticed outside his home territory. He was helped by his unimpressive appearance and bearing, his lack of eloquence, and his absorption in the inner life of the Church. He kept out of the public controversies of the day unless, like communism and divorce, they affected the interests of religion. His field of special interest was catechetics, and he was a born teacher. He had a hobby that is rare among Italian ecclesiastics: English literature, with special attention to Mark Twain. He was not an accomplished linguist, and his first and last trip outside Italy was to Brazil in 1977. His health was always indifferent, but he compensated for it by careful use of his time.

The conclave of August 1978 was the largest ever, and one of the shortest. There were 114 eligible voters, including 27 Italians, but 111 were able to attend. The world was surprised by the conclave's duration — it ended on the third ballot on the first day of voting — and even more by its choice. In the worldwide speculation that preceded it, few thought of the Patriarch of Venice, though two of the six popes elected in this century came from that beautiful city. The new Pope, the first who ever used a double name, chose the names of his two immediate predecessors as a sign of continuity. He had never been in the diplomatic service of the Church, nor had he served in the central headquarters in Rome. The conclave sought and found a pastoral pope. The wisdom of its choice was proved by his instant rapport with people everywhere and by the sorrow caused by his sudden and wholly unexpected death on September 28, 1978. He had not had time even to outline the program of his pontificate.

Pope John Paul I, seated on his throne at the Vatican.
Wide World Photos.

JOHN PAUL II

1978-

KAROL WOJTYLA WAS BORN IN WADOWICE, near Cracow, Poland, on May 18, 1920. His father, a noncommissioned officer in the Polish Army, and all the other members of his immediate family died before his ordination. His university studies were interrupted by the German and Russian invasion of Poland in September 1939. Under the Nazi occupation he worked in a stone quarry and later in a chemical plant. When the Russians seized all of Poland he continued as a laborer while finishing his studies in an underground seminary in Cracow. He was ordained on November 1, 1946, and sent to Rome for further studies. There he began to show the flair for languages that was so evident later. He learned flawless Italian and also the French he used while working among the Polish workers in France and Belgium.

On his return to Poland he was assigned to parish work and then, in addition, to the university apostolate. Pius XII made him an auxiliary bishop of Cracow in July 1958; Paul VI made him Archbishop of Cracow in 1964, and Cardinal in June 1967. He was the second highest prelate in the Church in Poland; above him was Cardinal Wyszynski, Primate of Poland and the Archbishop of Warsaw, who was a prisoner from 1950-1953. These two worked in perfect harmony in spite of the efforts of the Communists to drive a wedge between them.

The difficult situation in which the Church finds herself in Poland is well known. Although about ninety percent of the people are practicing and even militant Catholics, the government is entirely in the hands of the local Communist Party backed up by the presence of Soviet troops. The government cannot get rid of the Church and the Church knows that any attempt to get rid of the government risks open intervention on a massive scale by the Soviets. While their basic principles are wholly incompatible, both sides are Polish and wish to avoid a greater Russian presence. In these circumstances Cardinal Wojtyla showed himself a courageous and adroit leader.

His election to the papacy astounded the world. He is not only the first non-Italian since 1523, but the first Pole or Slav ever chosen. He is also the first pope to have spent his entire priestly life under communist rule. He is a multilingual and many-faceted man whose numerous visits from Poland to Rome and to the Polish communities all over the world have given him an exceptional personal knowledge of the condition of the Church in many areas. Perhaps his outstanding gift is his capacity to communicate with ordinary people, which was shown so dramatically in his triumphal visits to Mexico and Poland in 1979 as well as his trips to Ireland and the United States.

Pope John Paul II, official portrait, October 1978.
Religious News Service.

INDEX

Edward I of England, 376, 378, 382
Edward III of England, 394
Edwin, King of Northumbria, 138
Egbert of York, 180
El Hakim, 286
El Kemil, 350
Election, of pope, 426
Eleutherius, 136, 138
Eleutherius, St., pope, 26
Elizabeth of England, 450, 454
Ember Days, 32
Encyclion, 94
Epistle to the Philippians, 8
Epistola tractoria, 82
Ervig, king, 162
Ethelberga, queen of Northumbria, 138
Ethelbert, king, 134
Ethelwulf, king, 208, 210
Eugene I, St., pope, 150
Eugene II, pope, 200, 202
Eugene III, Blessed, pope, 330, 334, 336, 338
Eugene IV, pope, 410, 418
Eulalius, 84
Eusebius, 18, 24, 26, 30, 40, 54
Eusebius, St., pope, 62
Eutyches, 90, 92
Eutychian, St., pope, 54
Evaristus, St., pope, 10
Exit qui seminat, 372
Exspurge Domine, 434

Fabian, St., pope, 36, 40
Fabius, bishop of Antioch, 42
Farnese, Cardinal, 462
Fausta, 64
Faustus of Riez, 108
Febronianism, 500
Febronius, 500
Felicissimus, 42
Felix, antipope, 72
Felix V, antipope, 410, 412
Felix of Ravenna, 176
Felix I, St., pope, 52
Felix II, St., pope, 96, 98
Felix III, St., pope, 108
Fermilian of Antioch, St., 46, 48
Festus, senator, 100, 102
First Council of Lyons, 356
Flavian, St., 90, 92, 94, 96
Flavian, bishop of Antioch, 76
Flodoard, 232, 236
"Flying Squadron," 474, 482
Formosus, pope, 214, 216, 218, 224, 228, 232 236
Four Articles of 1682, 480, 482, 484
Francis of Assisi, St., 348, 352, 372, 394
Francis I of France, 434, 438, 440
Francis Xavier, St., 440, 442, 468
Franciscans, 350, 352, 358, 372, 378, 388, 390, 420, 442
Frangipane family, 318, 322, 328, 330

Frederick, archbishop of Mainz, 254, 258
Frederick Barbarossa (I), 330, 332, 334, 336, 338, 340, 342, 344, 346
Frederick II, emperor, 348, 350, 352, 354, 356
Frederick III, emperor, 412, 416
Freemasonry, 492, 494
Friars Preachers, *see* Dominicans

Galenus, 58, 64
Galileo, 470
Gallienus, emperor, 50
Garabaldi, 510
Gelasius I, St., pope, 98
Gelasius II, pope, 318
Genseric, 90
George, patriarch of Constantinople, 158
George of the Aventine, 220
Gerbert, 274, 276, 278, 280
Germanus of Auxerre, 86
Gildas, 26
Gisulf, duke, 170
Gnosticism, 18, 20, 28
Godfrey, duke, 306, 308
Golden Bull, 394
Gordianus, emperor, 40
Goslin, abbot of Fleury, 284
"Great Refusal," 380
Great Western Schism, 402-408
Gregorian chant, 128
Gregorian University, 452
Gregory of Neo-Caesarea, 40
Gregory of Tours, 40
Gregory I (the Great), St., pope, 96, 126, 128, 130, 132, 134, 138, 212
Gregory II, St., pope, 178
Gregory III, St., pope, 180
Gregory IV, pope, 204
Gregory V, pope, 278
Gregory VI, pope, 292, 294, 310
Gregory VII, St., pope, 310, 312, 314, 316; *see also* Hildebrand
Gregory VIII, pope, 342, 344
Gregory IX, pope, 352, 354, 358, 388
Gregory X, Blessed, pope, 364, 374
Gregory XI, pope, 398
Gregory XII, pope, 406, 410
Gregory XIII, pope, 452
Gregory XIV, pope, 458
Gregory XV, pope, 468
Gregory XVI, pope, 508
Guelphs and Ghibellines, 360, 362
Guibert, antipope, 310, 312, 314
Guido, duke of Spoleto, 222, 224

Hadrian I, pope, 192, 198
Hadrian II, pope, 8, 14, 196, 214
Hadrian III, pope, 220
Hadrian IV, pope, 332, 334, 342, 346
Hadrian V, pope, 368
Hegesippus, 22
Henoticon, 94, 96, 98, 102, 104

Henry II, emperor, 284, 288
Henry III, emperor, 292, 294, 296, 298, 300, 302, 304
Henry IV, emperor, 302, 308, 310, 314, 316
Henry V, emperor, 316, 318, 320, 322
Henry VI, emperor, 338, 340, 344, 346
Henry II, king of England, 334, 336, 342, 344
Henry III, king of England, 350, 358, 362, 368
Henry VIII, king of England, 438
Henry IV of France, 454, 458, 460, 462, 464, 466, 468
Henry the Fowler, 254
Henry the Wrangler, 270
Heraclius, antipope, 62
Heraclius, emperor, 136, 138, 140, 142, 144
Heribert, 246
Hermas, 20
Hermes, 92
Hilary, St., pope, 92
Hildebrand, 294, 302, 304, 306, 308, 310; *see also* Gregory VII
Hildegarde, 330, 332
Himerius, bishop of Tarragona, 16
Hippolytus, St., antipope, 32, 36
Hitler, 520
Hohenstaufen-papacy fight, 334, 338, 360, 362
"Holy League," 432
Holy Name of Jesus, 418
Homilies (Gregory the Great), 128
Homilies (Origen), 78
Honorius II, antipope, 308
Honorius, emperor, 80, 84
Honorius I, pope, 140, 144
Honorius II, pope, 322, 326, 332
Honorius III, pope, 350, 376
Honorius IV, pope, 376
Hormisdas, St., pope, 104, 112, 116, 158
Hosius of Cordova, 68
Hospitallers, 320, 322, 386
Howel the Good, 242
Hroswitha, 260
Hugh, archbishop of Rheims, 246, 256, 260
Hugh Capet, 272, 276, 280
Hugh, duke of Francia, 256, 260
Hugh of Cluny, St., 310, 314
Hugh of Provence, 246, 252, 254, 256, 260
Hundred Years War, 390
Hunneric, 96
Hyginus, St., pope, 18

Ibas, 118
Iconoclasm, 178, 180, 192, 198
Ignatius Loyola, St., 440, 442, 468
Ignatius, St., patriarch, 212, 214
Immaculate Conception, 420, 468, 510

END PAPERS. Tapestry after Raphael.
"Christ Consigns the Keys to St. Peter."
The Vatican.